THE EXORCISM STORIES IN LUKE–ACTS

This is the first book in English to integrate detailed literary criticism of the exorcism stories in Luke–Acts with wide-ranging comparative study of ancient sources on demonology, spirit affliction and exorcistic healing. Methods from systemic functional linguistics and critical theory are explained and then applied to each story. Careful focus is placed on each narrative's linguistic functions and also on relevant aspects of its literary co-text and the wider context of culture. Implications of the analysis for the new perspective on Luke–Acts, especially the implied author's relationship with Judaism, are explored in relation to the Lucan stories' original context of reception. Largely neglected interfaces between Luke's narrative representation of exorcism and emerging academic discourse about religious experience, shamanism, health care in antiquity, ritual performance and ancient Jewish systems of impurity are probed in ways that shed fresh light on this supremely alien part of the Lucan writings.

TODD KLUTZ is a Lecturer in New Testament Studies, Department of Religions and Theology, University of Manchester.

SOCIETY FOR NEW TESTAMENT STUDIES
MONOGRAPH SERIES
General Editor: Richard Bauckham

129
THE EXORCISM STORIES IN LUKE–ACTS

Society for New Testament Studies
MONOGRAPH SERIES

Recent titles in the series

118	The Myth of a Gentile Galilee MARK A. CHANCEY 0 521 81487 1	
119	New Creation in Paul's Letters and Thought MOYER V. HUBBARD 0 521 81485 5	
120	Belly and Body in the Pauline Epistles KARL OLAV SANDNES 0 521 81535 5	
121	The First Christian Historian DANIEL MARGUERAT 0 521 81650 5	
122	An Aramaic Approach to Q MAURICE CASEY 0 521 81723 4	
123	Isaiah's Christ in Matthew's Gospel RICHARD BEATON 0 521 81888 5	
124	God and History in the Book of Revelation MICHAEL GILBERTSON 0 521 82466 4	
125	Jesus' Defeat of Death PETER G. BOLT 0 521 83036 2	
126	From Hope to Despair in Thessalonica COLIN R. NICHOLL 0 521 83142 3	
127	Trilogy of Parables WESLEY G. OLMSTEAD 0 521 83154 7	
128	The People of God in the Apocalypse STEPHEN PATTEMORE 0 521 83698 0	
129	The Exorcism Stories in Luke–Acts TODD KLUTZ 0 521 83804 5	

The Exorcism Stories in Luke–Acts

A Sociostylistic Reading

TODD KLUTZ
University of Manchester

PUBLISHED BY THE PRESS SYNDICATE OF THE UNIVERSITY OF CAMBRIDGE
The Pitt Building, Trumpington Street, Cambridge, United Kingdom

CAMBRIDGE UNIVERSITY PRESS
The Edinburgh Building, Cambridge CB2 2RU, UK
40 West 20th Street, New York, NY 10011-4211, USA
477 Williamstown Road, Port Melbourne, VIC 3207, Australia
Ruiz de Alarcón 13, 28014 Madrid, Spain
Dock House, The Waterfront, Cape Town 8001, South Africa

http://www.cambridge.org

© Todd Klutz 2004

This book is in copyright. Subject to statutory exception
and to the provisions of relevant collective licensing agreements,
no reproduction of any part may take place without
the written permission of Cambridge University Press.

First published 2004

Printed in the United Kingdom at the University Press, Cambridge

Typeface Times 10/12 pt   *System* LATEX 2_ε [TB]

A catalogue record for this book is available from the British Library

Library of Congress Cataloguing in Publication data

Klutz, Todd.
The Exorcism stories in Luke–Acts : a sociostylistic reading / Todd Klutz.
    p. cm. – (Society for New Testament studies monograph series ; 129)
Includes bibliographical references and index.
ISBN 0-521-83804-5
1. Exorcism in the Bible.   2. Bible. N.T. Luke – Socio-rhetorical criticism.
3. Bible. N.T. Acts – Socio-rhetorical criticism.   I. Title.   II. Monograph series (Society
for New Testament Studies) ; 129.
BS2589.6.D5K57   2004
226.4'06 – dc22   2003065417

ISBN 0 521 83804 5 hardback

CONTENTS

Acknowledgements	page x
List of abbreviations	xi

	Introduction	**1**
1	**Sociostylistics and the exorcism in Luke 4.33–37**	**15**
	Sociostylistic theory	15
	Sociostylistics and literary theory	17
	Sociostylistics and linguistic theory	22
	Formalism versus functionalism	22
	Systemic-functional linguistics: an overview	26
	A sociostylistic reading of Luke 4.33–37	29
	Cohesion	29
	Story structure	31
	Repetition	33
	Iconicity	35
	Thematic organisation and information structure	36
	Transitivity	39
	Vocabulary	43
	Verbal aspect	49
	Presupposition	50
	Implicature	52
	Intertextuality	55
	Co-text	57
	Context of culture	61
	Conclusion	80
2	**Purity and the exorcism in Luke 8.26–39**	**82**
	Cohesion and boundaries	84
	Story structure	85
	Repetition	89
	Word order and information structure	95

Lexis: collocations and connotations	96
Transitivity	102
Verbal aspect	107
Intertextuality	109
Presuppositions, implicatures and entailments	113
Co-text	115
Context of culture	121
Apollonius the exorcist	121
Unclean spirits and systems of impurity	125
Key features on the demonology–impurity interface	133
Possession, unconventionality and socioreligious change	137
Ritual of relocation and 'anti-rite' in Jesus' performance of exorcism	144
Master of the storm demon	148
Conclusion	150
3 Discipleship and the exorcism in Luke 9.37–43a	**152**
Boundaries and cohesion	153
Story structure	155
Repetition	159
Iconicity	160
Thematic organisation and information structure	161
Lexis	162
συναντάω	162
σπαράσσω, ἐκπλήσσω and μεγαλειότης	165
ἐκβάλλω	167
Transitivity	168
Verbal aspect	171
Intertextuality	173
Presuppositions and implicatures	176
Co-text	178
Cultural context	186
Success and failure in the context of exorcistic culture	188
The grammar of exorcistic rebuke in *1QGenesis Apocryphon*	192
Shamanic ecstasy, exorcistic ritual and narrative transformation	194
Fasting, shamanic healing, and the text of Mark 9.29	199
Conclusion	205

4 Paul, Jewish identity, and the exorcism in Acts 16.16–18 — **207**

Cohesion, boundaries and story structure — 208
Repetition and paronomasia — 210
Lexis — 212
Transitivity — 219
Verbal aspect — 222
Presuppositions and implicatures — 223
Intertextuality — 224
Immediate co-text — 226
Macrostructural co-text and implied situation — 228
   Expanding the co-textual frame — 228
   Jesus' affirmation of Paul — 229
   Paul among the greedy and the Judeophobic — 231
   Paul: ally of Jesus and foe of magicians — 233
   Paul and Jesus in the architecture of Luke–Acts — 236
   Prominence, relevance and situation — 239
Context of culture — 242
   Prophecy, polyphony and the social construction of demon-possession — 243
   Manumission, damaged property and the politics of Jewish identity — 247
   The name of the exorcist — 251
   Of genre and gender: why Luke is silent about the fate of the slave-girl — 260
Conclusion — 262

Conclusion — **265**

Bibliography — 270
Index of sources discussed — 289
Index of names and subjects — 297

ACKNOWLEDGEMENTS

The main argument and most of the ideas in this book were presented in the form of a thesis which was awarded a PhD at the University of Sheffield in May 1996. Various parts of the work have been presented at one stage of development or another to the University of Sheffield's Department of Biblical Studies seminar (1991–2), the University of Manchester's Ehrhardt Seminar (1996–7), the British New Testament Conference (Sheffield 1991, Leeds 1997), and the Biblical Greek Language and Linguistics Section of the Society of Biblical Literature (Boston 1999). In revising the thesis for publication, I have benefited immensely from suggestions made by Professor Richard Bauckham, Dr Margaret Davies, and Dr Max Turner.

The Revd Professor Loveday Alexander, as supervisor and mentor, has my warmest thanks for exemplifying high ideals of interdisciplinarity, encouraging me to experiment with stylistic methods, and giving useful criticism at every stage in my research. For his editorial advice and good-humoured patience up to the last moment of his editorship, I am deeply indebted to Professor Richard Bauckham. The book is dedicated to my wife Liz and to our three sons – Austin, Eliot, and Nathaniel – who worked hard (and usually with success) to protect me against the demon of madness throughout the process of revision.

ABBREVIATIONS

Abbreviations for biblical writings are those customarily used in the Society for New Testament Studies Monograph Series. Apart from the items listed below, other abbreviations follow the recommendations for contributors to the *Journal of Biblical Literature*.

ACNT	Augsburg Commentary on the New Testament
AEMT	J. F. Borghouts (ed.), *Ancient Egyptian Magical Texts*
AMB	J. Naveh and S. Shaked (eds), *Amulets and Magic Bowls: Aramaic Incantations of Late Antiquity*, vol. I
ANESTP	J. B. Pritchard (ed.), *Ancient Near Eastern Supplementary Texts and Pictures*
CAIB	C. D. Isbell (ed.), *Corpus of the Aramaic Incantation Bowls*
CTBS	J. G. Gager (ed.), *Curse Tablets and Binding Spells from the Ancient World*
DDD	K. van der Torn, B. Becking and P. W. van der Horst (eds), *Dictionary of Deities and Demons in the Bible*
DESB	R. C. Thompson (ed.), *The Devils and Evil Spirits of Babylonia*
DS	K. Wales (ed.), *A Dictionary of Stylistics*
DSD	*Dead Sea Discoveries*
DT	A. Audollent (ed.), *Defixionum Tabellae*
EpR	*Epworth Review*
ExAud	*Ex Auditu: An International Journal of Theological Interpretation of Scripture*
FTS	*Frankfurter Theologische Studien*
FUH	M. J. Geller (ed.), *Forerunners to Udug-hul: Sumerian Exorcistic Incantations*
GMPT	H. D. Betz (ed.), *The Greek Magical Papyri in Translation Including the Demotic Spells*
JSPSup	Journal for the Study of the Pseudepigrapha Supplement Series
KTU	M. Dietrich, O. Loretz and J. Sanmartin (eds), *Keilalphabetischen Texte aus Ugarit*, vol. I
L.A.B.	*Liber Antiquitatum Biblicarum* (Pseudo-Philo)
LumVie	*Lumière et Vie*

NERTOT	W. Beyerlin (ed.), *Near Eastern Religious Texts Relating to the Old Testament*
NIDNTT	C. Brown (ed.), *The New International Dictionary of New Testament Theology*
PLu	*Positions Luthériennes*
SNTU	Studien zum Neuen Testament und seiner Umwelt
TLG	*Thesaurus Linguae Graecae*
TNTC	Tyndale New Testament Commentaries
TPINTC	Trinity Press International New Testament Commentary Series
T. Sol.	*Testament of Solomon*
Y.	*Yasna*

INTRODUCTION

A wide selection of critical commentaries on the Gospel of Luke has been available for several decades;[1] and although the Lucan Gospel's companion volume, the Acts of the Apostles, is not covered by a comparable range and depth of exegetical comment, it cannot seriously claim to be a victim of neglect.[2] As the attention these commentaries give in particular to the Lucan exorcism stories differs in no obvious way from the care they bestow on other kinds of materials in Luke's writings, potential readers of the present study may wonder what could possibly be provided here that is not already available in the best commentaries. This question deserves a considered reply. It also leads very naturally into other matters – the precise topic and aims of the present study, for instance, and how it is similar to and different from other works of scholarship on related subjects – which likewise ought to be addressed in an introduction to this sort of work.

Like modern critical commentaries on other writings of the New Testament, those devoted to the Gospel of Luke and the Acts of the Apostles prove on close inspection to be richly interdiscursive events; for they not only tend to fulfil their obligation to engage with the ancient text in its original language but also either assume or explicitly interact with an impressive range of other discourses, for the most part modern scholarly ones, including but not limited to other commentaries on the same text. Indeed, as a set of hermeneutical gestures ranging from cool self-awareness to conspicuous self-unmasking increasingly finds expression in the writing of textual scholars in various disciplines,[3] most of the

---

[1] See the commentary section of the bibliography in J. B. Green, *The Gospel of Luke*, NICNT (Grand Rapids, 1997), pp. xxvi–ii.

[2] Historical-critical coverage of the Acts of the Apostles has been improved considerably by the recent publication of C. K. Barrett, *A Critical and Exegetical Commentary on the Acts of the Apostles*, ICC, 2 vols (Edinburgh, 1994, 1998); and J. A. Fitzmyer, *The Acts of the Apostles: A New Translation with Introduction and Commentary*, AB 31 (New York, 1998).

[3] On the prominence of these gestures in one influential school of contemporary critical theory, see H. A. Veeser, 'The New Historicism', in *The New Historicism Reader* (London,

1

present generation's commentators on Luke and Acts would probably acknowledge that their own exegetical judgements are powerfully conditioned by other works of scholarship.[4] And prominent amongst those other works are monographs such as those in the present series.

For purposes of the present study, the most significant aspect of this commentary–monograph dialectic is the relationship between recent exegetical commentaries on Luke and Acts on the one hand, and monographs and related studies (e.g., articles in journals and edited collections of essays) devoted specifically to exorcism in these writings on the other. More particularly, and as the scholarly references and bibliographies in recent commentaries on Luke and Acts well illustrate, neither monographs nor published articles on the Lucan exorcism stories occupy a conspicuous position in the analytical discourses presupposed in the commentary literature. For instance, in the second volume of John Nolland's outstanding commentary on the Gospel of Luke, the thirteen items in the bibliography for Luke 9.37–43a – the Lucan Gospel's third exorcism narrative – consist of five studies dealing with one topically related aspect or another of the Gospel of *Mark*, four that deal with the interrelations of all three Synoptic accounts of the same event, two that treat the broader subject of Jesus' miracles, one that belongs to the more general field of Gospel scholarship, and most important of all only one devoted to the specifically Lucan perspective on exorcism.[5] Similar observations could be made regarding the scholarly references and bibliographies provided in other commentators' treatments of any of the four stories analysed in the present study.[6]

The point of these remarks is, of course, not that Nolland or any other modern commentator on Luke's writings is at fault for this state of affairs, but rather that up to recent times – indeed, up to the very present – the distinctively Lucan rendition of the exorcism stories has attracted relatively little interest from scholars in New Testament studies and related disciplines. As the probable causes of this neglect are undoubtedly

---

1994), pp. 6–7, 15–16; on their role in recent anthropological theory, see C. Geertz, *Available Light: Anthropological Reflections on Philosophical Topics* (Princeton, 2000), pp. 95–107.

[4] See e.g. L. C. A. Alexander, review of *A Critical and Exegetical Commentary on the Acts of the Apostles*, by C. K. Barrett; and of *The Acts of the Apostles: A Socio-Rhetorical Commentary*, by B. Witherington, III, *JTS* 52/2 (2001), 691–3.

[5] J. Nolland, *Luke*, WBC 35 (Dallas, 1993), II, p. 505.

[6] E.g. the sole work cited by Nolland on exorcism in Luke–Acts (i.e., W. Kirschläger, *Jesu exorzistisches Wirken aus der Sicht des Lukas: Ein Beitrag zur lukanischen Redaktion*, ÖBS 3 (Klosterneuburg, 1981)) is absent from the bibliographical references and notes in both F. Bovon, *L'Evangile selon saint Luc (1,1–9, 50)*, CNT 3A (Geneva, 1991), pp. 9–18, 211–12; and Fitzmyer, *Acts*, pp. 175–87, 590–1, neither of which cites a work of comparable focus and depth on the same topic.

Introduction

numerous and complex, I have no intention of surveying them all here; among them, however, is one that I do very much intend to challenge in the present study, namely the abiding scholarly tendency to read the exorcism stories in Luke's Gospel chiefly as units of Synoptic tradition rather than as integral parts of the two-volume narrative Luke–Acts.[7] Although interpreters who lean in this direction by no means ignore the exorcism materials in Acts altogether, they exemplify in numerous ways the conviction that Luke's view of exorcism is seen most clearly in the changes he made in the relevant traditions of his assumed sources (normally taken to be Mark and 'Q').[8] As suggested at the end of this Introduction and implied repeatedly in the analysis that follows, this type of approach seriously underestimates the co-textual[9] and structural impact of Luke's second volume on the significance of everything in his first, not least the exorcism stories.

For purposes of the immediate discussion, however, the various causes of scholarly lack of interest are less significant than the mere fact of it. The only comprehensive and detailed study of the topic is Walter Kirschläger's 1981 work *Jesu exorzistisches Wirken aus der Sicht des Lukas: Ein Beitrag zur lukanischen Redaktion*.[10] As noted in an appropriately brief *Forschungsgeschichte* in that work, no work of monographic proportions had been devoted to the matter prior to the writing of Kirschläger's volume.[11] To be sure, both prior to Kirschläger's work and in the last couple of decades, numerous books and articles have been published that have one topical interface or another with the matters explored here;[12] but an accurate observation made by Kirschläger about his

---

[7] The tendency is apparent, e.g., both in Kirschläger, *Jesu exorzistisches Wirken*, which devotes far more attention to Luke's assumed redaction of Mark (e.g. pp. 55–8, 93–101) than to the intratextual relations between the material in the Gospel and that in Acts (noted in passing but not developed on pp. 259, 273); and in G. H. Twelftree, *Jesus the Miracle Worker: A Historical and Theological Study* (Downers Grove, IL, 1999), pp. 175–8, whose brief treatment of the exorcisms in Acts interprets them not as part of a strong gesture of re-framing but rather as a confirmation of what is already communicated in the Gospel.

[8] Twelftree (*Jesus the Miracle Worker*, pp. 167–88), e.g., in rating the differences between the Lucan and Marcan presentations as among the most important issues for understanding the miracles of Jesus in Luke, addresses these at length (pp. 173–9) but leaves questions about the unity of Luke–Acts and their potential relevance to understanding the Lucan perspective outside the discussion.

[9] As discussed under 'Co-text' in the next chapter, this term is increasingly used in discourse analysis to refer to the specifically linguistic structures that surround a given segment of text and constrain its potential meaning.

[10] For details see n. 6 above.

[11] Kirschläger, *Jesu exorzistisches Wirken*, p. 10.

[12] See, e.g., S. R. Garrett, *The Demise of the Devil: Magic and the Demonic in Luke's Writings* (Minneapolis, 1989); H.-J. Klauck, *Magie und Heidentum in der Apostelgeschichte*

scholarly precursors in 1981 also holds true for more recent contributions on related topics: namely, in each case exorcism in Luke–Acts is handled only in a cursory way.[13]

Accordingly, both for its potential utility in setting the stage for my own analysis and for its unique position in scholarship on my chosen topic, Kirschläger's study deserves special consideration here. Particularly in regard to topical boundaries, the first point worth noting about Kirschläger's work is that although it stands far closer to the present study than does any other previous contribution to scholarship, the limits which it sets for itself within the Lucan materials are considerably more encompassing than those I choose to work within here. More specifically, in contrast to Kirschläger's study, which covers every unit that contributes to exorcism as a theme,[14] the focus of the present work falls solely on narrative episodes whose climax includes the expulsion of one demonic being or more from a human victim of possession.

This particular difference in conceptualisation, moreover, has a couple of consequences that are worth making explicit. On the one hand, as the present study is not designed to cover all the Lucan materials of whatever genre pertaining to exorcism *as a theme*, it need not be read as an attempt to overcome Kirschläger or beat him at his own topical game. Despite their similarities, the two works are sufficiently different in topic to allow this kind of exegetical one-upmanship to be avoided; and whatever positive results my own study may achieve, Kirschläger's work will remain after the publication of this one the only comprehensive treatment of exorcism in Luke–Acts as a thematic phenomenon. On the other hand – and here, I fear, at least the appearance of one-upmanship is impossible to avoid – having

---

des Lukas, SBS 167 (Stuttgart, 1996); P. J. Achtemeier, 'The Lukan Perspective on the Miracles of Jesus: A Preliminary Sketch', in C. H. Talbert (ed.), *Perspectives on Luke–Acts* (Edinburgh, 1978), pp. 153–67; U. Busse, *Die Wunder des Propheten Jesus: Die Rezeption, Komposition und Interpretation der Wundertradition im Evangelium des Lukas*, FB 24 (Stuttgart, 1979); J. D. G. Dunn and G. H. Twelftree, 'Demon-Possession and Exorcism in the New Testament', *Churchman* 94/3 (1980), 210–25; H. C. Kee, *Medicine, Miracle, and Magic in New Testament Times*, SNTSMS 55 (Cambridge, 1986); G. Theissen, *Urchristliche Wundergeschichte: Ein Beitrag zur formgeschichtlichen Erforschung der synoptischen Evangelien*, SNT 8 (Gütersloh, 1974); J. A. Fitzmyer, 'Satan and Demons in Luke–Acts', in *Luke the Theologian: Aspects of His Teaching* (London, 1989), pp. 146–74; G. H. Twelftree, *Jesus the Exorcist: A Contribution to the Study of the Historical Jesus*, WUNT 54 (Tübingen, 1993); J. M. Hull, *Hellenistic Magic and the Synoptic Tradition*, SBT 2/28 (London, 1974).

[13] See Kirschläger, *Jesu exorzistisches Wirken*, pp. 11–14, commenting on earlier works by T. Schramm, M. Limbeck, U. Busse, H. M. Miller and P. J. Achtemeier.

[14] I.e., Luke 4.31–37, 38–39, 40–41, 42–44; 6.12–16, 17–19; 7.21, 33; 8.1–3, 22–25, 26–39; 9.1–6, 37–43a, 49–50; 10.17–20; 11.14–23, 24–26; 13.10–17, 32; Acts 5.16; 8.7; 16.16–18; 19.11–16.

Introduction 5

chosen as I have to interpret a much smaller corpus of generically similar passages, I have given myself much greater space than Kirschläger gives himself for contextualizing the exorcism stories in relation to their ancient cultural milieu. As the interpreter's understanding of the Lucan stories' original context of culture pervasively influences the meanings they assign to these texts, Kirschläger's treatment of this level of the stories' environment invites closer scrutiny.

First of all, and precisely in view of how decisive both real and imagined (i.e., historically reconstructed) contexts of reading are for every act of interpretation,[15] a simple but potentially significant observation should be made about the size and proportion of Kirschläger's discussion of these matters vis-à-vis the more strictly textual aspects of his analysis. To be precise, by attempting to cover the exorcism theme's cultural context in an excursus only ten pages long, Kirschläger devotes less than five per cent of his entire study to the analysis of ancient comparative materials and their potential significance for contextualising the Lucan passages.[16] Consequently, although Kirschläger is admirably able in that space to demonstrate the inadequacy of Jewish Scripture as an explanatory resource for the demonological and exorcistic assumptions of Luke–Acts,[17] he neither formulates the hermeneutically critical questions which that insight inspires – for instance, where then do Luke's assumptions in these areas come from? What kinds of ancient sources can be used properly to illuminate them? And how do these assumptions relate to beliefs and practices attested in the numerous corpora of apotropaic and exorcistic incantations that have survived from a wide range of ancient Near Eastern and Late Antique contexts?[18] – nor therefore can he contextualise the Lucan materials with an appropriate measure of complexity. By contrast, the chapters below address each of these questions at one or more points in my cultural analyses, in ways that allow the Lucan narratives to be embedded in a web of frequently overlooked but significant intertextual relationships.

---

[15] See, e.g., B. K. Blount, *Cultural Interpretation: Reorienting New Testament Criticism* (Minneapolis, 1995), pp. 12–16.
[16] Kirschläger, *Jesu exorzistisches Wirken*, pp. 45–54.
[17] Ibid., pp. 46–7.
[18] Perhaps because Kirschläger's study allows such little space for comparative analysis of extrabiblical sources, it can only deal briefly (p. 46) and in very general terms with the ancient Near Eastern and Late Antique incantatory traditions, leaving two of the most topically relevant corpora of these – R. C. Thompson (ed.), *The Devils and Evil Spirits of Babylonia*, Luzac's Semitic Texts and Translation Series 14 (London, 1903–4); and C. D. Isbell (ed.), *Corpus of the Aramaic Incantation Bowls*, SBLDS 17 (Missoula, 1975) – completely unmentioned.

One further aspect of Kirschläger's treatment of the Lucan materials' *Umwelt* invites comment. In addressing an important difficulty that I likewise must discuss, namely, why Jewish and pagan literary sources from earlier than the second century CE say so very little about exorcism, Kirschläger makes the following observation (pp. 53–4):

> Es neben der 'offiziellen' religiösen Strömung auch eine breite Tradition des Volksglaubens gab, der bisweilen bis in das Grenzgebiet des *Aberglaubens* reichte. Freilich fehlen hier die Textbelege, weil diese Überlieferungen mündlich weitergegeben und nicht aufgezeichnet wurden (italics mine).
>
> Alongside the official religious current there was also a broad tradition of popular belief, which from time to time extended into the border area of *superstition*. Admittedly the textual evidence is missing here, for these traditions were transmitted orally and not recorded.

On a strictly denotative level and in the context of Kirschläger's work, these two sentences contribute to the formulation of a valid argument: as Morton Smith and others have also observed, the paucity of literary evidence outside the New Testament regarding exorcism prior to the second century CE almost certainly says less about how familiar exorcistic practices were to the masses of the Mediterranean world in the immediately preceding centuries than about the elitism of the surviving literature from this period. However, on the level of evaluative connotations and ideological effects, these sentences also exemplify a widespread and regrettable scholarly habit which, although it is now increasingly being undermined by new approaches to studying the religions of others, has proved its tenacity and persists to the present time. The habit I have in mind here is the tendency to use a particular set of abstract categories of classification – ideas such as 'superstition', 'magic', and 'primitive mentality' – which, though employed in a spirit of scholarly analysis, carry a heavy load of ideological baggage that puts the interpreter in a position inimical to interpretative clarity:[19] namely, either high above the

---

[19] For further discussion of the difficulty, see esp. N. Janowitz, *Magic in the Roman World: Pagans, Jews and Christians*, Religion in the First Christian Centuries (London, 2001), pp. 1–8, 16–20; W. J. Lyons and A. M. Reimer, 'The Demonic Virus and Qumran Studies: Some Preventative Measures', *DSD* 5/1 (1998), 16–32; G. Poupon, 'L'accusation de magie dans les Actes apocryphes', in F. Bovon (ed.), *Les actes apocryphes des apôtres* (Geneva, 1981), pp. 71–85; A. F. Segal, 'Hellenistic Magic: Some Questions of Definition', in R. van den Broek and M. J. Vermaseren (eds), *Studies in Gnosticism and Hellenistic*

whole scramble of ancient magico-religious discourses and the historically particular conditions of their production, which of course cannot be imagined vividly from afar; or under the spell of the deviance-labelling rhetoric used by the ancient antagonists themselves, whose vocabulary (γόης, μάγος, δεισιδαιμονία, etc.) was designed less for facilitating historical understanding than for winning ideological contests.

But more importantly, although less problematic ways of talking about folk illness and religious healing *were* available when Kirschläger wrote these lines,[20] my chief aim at this juncture is not so much to criticise his choice of words as to highlight a contrasting feature of my own discussion in the ensuing chapters. Precisely because terms such as 'magic' and 'superstition' often serve as translation equivalents for the highly pejorative lexis used by ancient antagonists in the heat of religious conflict,[21] they are not used in the chapters below except where no better term can be found for representing the meanings conveyed in the deviance-labelling rhetoric of the ancient sources. Thereby, in my various discussions of the Lucan stories' cultural context, I am able to avoid the pitfalls of implying either that all ancient demonological belief and exorcistic practice – Jesus' and Paul's included – were based on 'protological thinking';[22] or that while this judgement largely holds true for the inherited conglomerate of ancient Jewish and pagan assumptions, Jesus and his followers somehow lifted their inheritance above all this, say, by giving it eschatological meaning that it previously lacked.[23]

Religions, EPRO 91 (Leiden, 1981), pp. 349–75; J. Z. Smith, 'Trading Places', in M. Meyer and P. Mirecki (eds), *Ancient Magic and Ritual Power*, Religions in the Graeco-Roman World 129 (Leiden, 1995), pp. 13–27; D. Aune, 'Magic in Early Christianity', *ANRW* II.23.2, pp. 1507–57; Garrett, *Demise of the Devil*, pp. 2–5, 11–36; F. Graf, *La magie dans l'antiquité gréco-romaine: Idéologie et pratique* (Paris, 1994), pp. 17–29; J. G. Gager, 'Introduction', in *Curse Tablets and Binding Spells from the Ancient World* (Oxford, 1992), pp. 22–5.

[20] See, e.g., F. Boas, *The Mind of Primitive Man*, rev. edn (New York, 1938; repr., 1965), pp. 128–9, 135–6; and E. R. Goodenough, *Jewish Symbols in the Greco-Roman Period*, II, *The Archaeological Evidence from the Diaspora* (New York, 1953), p. 156.

[21] See e.g. Acts 8.9, 11; 13.6, 8; *Acts of Peter* 6.17; 9.31; *Acts of Andrew* A.10.11–30 (in *NTAp*, II, pp. 404–5); *Acts of John* 43; and *Pseudo-Clementine Homilies* 4.4; 7.3. As noted by Poupon, 'L'accusation de magie', p. 71, in the apocryphal Acts Christians and their opponents accuse one another so frequently of practising magic (and thus of relying on demonic power) that such allegations constitute a major theme in this literature. On the terminology's negative connotations in other contexts, see Graf, *La magie dans l'antiquité gréco-romaine*, pp. 46–73.

[22] The phrase is used e.g. in J. A. Fitzmyer, *The Gospel according to Luke (I–IX): Introduction, Translation, and Notes*, AB 28 (New York, 1981), p. 545, where it is defined as an inability 'to ascribe physical or psychic disorders to proper secondary causes'; people who think this way therefore attribute these disorders 'to beings of an intermediate spirit-world'.

[23] The latter view is that articulated in Kee, *Medicine, Miracle and Magic*, pp. 127–30.

8   *Introduction*

As Kirschläger's work is the uncontested authority on exorcism in Luke–Acts, it has had unique opportunity to influence the views of commentators and other exegetes who have had to wrestle with the Lucan exorcism stories. Not surprisingly, therefore, the same tendencies noted above in regard to Kirschläger's treatment of the exorcism theme's cultural context can be observed in the major commentaries published in more recent years. Comparative texts are of course frequently mentioned in these studies but rarely analysed in detail or compared with the Lucan passages in a way that produces a meaningful set of similarities and differences; and terms such as 'magic', 'superstition', and 'protological thinking' continue to be used in ways that both ignore the serious theoretical objections long voiced against these categories and bring more confusion than light to the business of interpretation. Thus, in relation to Kirschläger and the numerous commentators his work has influenced, the present study constitutes a significant shift in regard to how the Lucan materials' cultural context is handled.

As discussed in the next chapter, context is treated in the present study as consisting not only of the text's cultural environment – that is, the system of meaning potential and semantic-behavioural conventions to which an individual language user has access – but also of the text's situation, which consists of the more immediate constraints that influence the user's linguistic choices and determine what kinds of selections might be considered relevant or rhetorically effective. Although ideas of context in general have not been conceptualised in precisely this way by most New Testament scholars, broadly analogous concepts have been around for some time; and here, at least partly in order to position my own analysis in relation both to Kirschläger's and to more recent developments in Lucan studies, I want to offer some observations on the way his study in particular understands the relationship between the exorcism theme and the Lucan writings' context of situation.

The aspects of the Lucan situation that hold greatest interest for Kirschläger are the date of the writings' composition and the ethnic background of the author and audience. In brief, Kirschläger understands the author of Luke–Acts to have been an educated Gentile who came to Christ straight from a pagan background and, some time between 70 and 90 CE, composed his two volumes for a community of Gentile Christians.[24] Kirschläger's interpretation of the Lucan situation as marked by an essentially Gentile, non-Jewish tenor required no rigorous defence in 1981; for at that time it was the view most widely accepted in the standard

---

[24] Kirschläger, *Jesu exorzistisches Wirken*, pp. 9–10 n. 4.

Introduction

commentaries on Luke and Acts and in the major works of New Testament introduction.[25] Since that time, however, confidence in the adequacy of this scenario has been gradually eroded by a stream of monographs, new commentaries, and scholarly essays which, though by no means uniform in outlook, have tended to see the main participants in the Lucan discourse as either Jews, Gentiles who had attached themselves to Jewish synagogues before joining the Christ cult, or some combination of these two.[26] Consequently, although little can be said against Kirschläger for merely inhaling the scholarly air that in 1981 surrounded him on almost every side, the more recent scholarship on the Lucan writings' relationship with the Judaisms of the first century CE has created a discursive space in which it is now appropriate to ask what light the exorcism theme (or more specifically the exorcism stories) in particular sheds on these matters; accordingly, once all four exorcism stories have been analysed below in their immediate co-texts, this question is given focused attention, being treated in my final chapter under the heading of 'Macrostructural co-text and implied situation'.

The need for a fresh analysis of Luke's exorcism stories is heightened by several other developments that have significantly changed the character of New Testament studies since Kirschläger published his work. For instance, in contrast to Kirschläger himself, who assumed the validity of the two-source hypothesis and took a primarily redaction-critical approach to the exorcism passages,[27] a growing number of scholarly works on the Gospels and Acts are experimenting with methods adapted from literary criticism and the social sciences, with questions about the ancient

---

[25] See, e.g., W. Schmithals, *Die Apostelgeschichte des Lukas*, Zürcher Bibelkommentare (Zurich, 1982), p. 17; F. F. Bruce, *The Book of the Acts*, NICNT, rev. edn (Grand Rapids, 1988), p. 314. For a survey of the scholarly positions up to the late 1980s, see W. W. Gasque, *A History of the Interpretation of the Acts of the Apostles*, 2nd edn (Peabody, 1989), p. 347.

[26] See, e.g., D. P. Moessner and D. L. Tiede, 'Conclusion: "And some were persuaded...."', in D. P. Moessner (ed.), *Jesus and the Heritage of Israel: Luke's Narrative Claim upon Israel's Legacy* (Harrisburg, 1999), pp. 362–3; J. Jervell, *Luke and the People of God: A New Look at Luke–Acts* (Minneapolis, 1972), pp. 163–5, 173–5; R. L. Brawley, *Luke–Acts and the Jews: Conflict, Apology, and Conciliation*, SBLMS 33 (Atlanta, 1987), p. 157; P. F. Esler, *Community and Gospel in Luke–Acts: The Social and Political Motivations of Lucan Theology*, SNTSMS 57 (Cambridge, 1987), pp. 36–45; J. B. Tyson, *Images of Judaism in Luke–Acts* (Columbia, 1992), pp. 33–6; W. Radl, *Das Lukas-Evangelium*, ErFor 261 (Darmstadt, 1988), pp. 23–4; D. L. Tiede, *Prophecy and History in Luke–Acts* (Philadelphia, 1980), pp. 7–8, 107–11; J. G. Gager, 'Jews, Gentiles, and Synagogues in the Book of Acts', *HTR* 79/1–3 (1986), pp. 97–9; M. Salmon, 'Insider or Outsider? Luke's Relationship with Judaism', in J. B. Tyson (ed.), *Luke–Acts and the Jewish People: Eight Critical Perspectives* (Minneapolis, 1988), pp. 76–81; Bovon, *Luc (1,1–9,50)*, p. 27; J. Wenham, 'The Identification of Luke', *EvQ* 63/1 (1991), pp. 7–8.

[27] Kirschläger, *Jesu exorzistisches Wirken*, pp. 18–22.

author's Christian sources often being either backgrounded or completely bracketed.[28] Many of these studies, moreover, are utilising methods that allow the literary-critical and social-scientific tools to be integrated, creating opportunities for texts and contexts to be brought into mutually illuminating dialogues that earlier methods did not consistently facilitate.[29] Clearly, all these methods and the influence they are exerting on the discipline cannot be discussed in detail here; instead, it is sufficient to point out that by focusing more analytical energy on how the Lucan exorcism stories relate to their immediate and schematic co-texts within Luke–Acts than on how their author modified the Gospel of Mark and his other assumed sources, the methods used in the present study produce a significantly different set of meanings and contextual scenarios than those normally produced by redaction criticism.

Although the type of discourse analysis I have chosen to apply to the Lucan narratives is fully explained in the next chapter, it has two features in particular which, as they belong to the ongoing process of methodological ferment noted above and facilitate several fresh findings below, deserve at least brief mention here. The features in question revolve around the analysis of intertextuality and verbal aspect,[30] whose contributions to the Lucan narratives' relevance and force are estimated in the chapters below to be greater than the existing commentary literature and other studies have suggested. By contributing both meaning and salience to some of the Lucan stories' most prominent themes, these same findings also impinge on the contextual questions noted above; for the richest source of clues to the ancient text's original situation remains the particular configuration of prominent themes in the text itself.

Three other recent developments in New Testament studies and related disciplines contribute to the need for a study such as the one undertaken in the present work. First, Graham Twelftree's *Jesus the Exorcist: A Contribution to the Study of the Historical Jesus* (1993), though marred by an underestimation of the importance of the interface between demonology

---

[28] See e.g. J. B. Tyson, *The Death of Jesus in Luke–Acts* (Columbia, 1986), pp. 6–9. For more recent examples see (on literary approaches) E. A. Castelli et al. (eds), *The Postmodern Bible* (New Haven, 1995); and (on social-scientific analyses) P. F. Esler (ed.), *Modelling Early Christianity: Social-Scientific Studies of the New Testament in Its Context* (London, 1995).

[29] Desire to integrate social-scientific and textualist methods has played a key role in the development of socio-rhetorical criticism, on which see esp. V. K. Robbins, 'Social-Scientific Criticism and Literary Studies: Prospects for Cooperation in Biblical Interpretation', in Esler (ed.), *Modelling Early Christianity*, pp. 274–89; and *Exploring the Texture of Texts: A Guide to Socio-Rhetorical Interpretation* (Valley Forge, 1996), pp. 1–2.

[30] Definitions and recent scholarly literature are provided in the next chapter under 'Verbal aspect' and 'Intertextuality'.

and impurity for understanding Jesus' exorcisms,[31] has none the less established with unparalleled rigour both that exorcism was a prominent feature in the activities of the historical Jesus and that Jesus himself understood this aspect of his work in a strongly eschatological way.[32] By improving our understanding of this facet of Jesus' activities, Twelftree has increased our chances of making meaningful observations about the continuities and discontinuities between exorcism in the historical Jesus' context and the narrative representation of exorcism in the NT Gospels and Acts.

Second, although neither Twelftree nor Kirschläger undertook to compare the NT accounts of exorcism with the wealth of historical and ethnographic data concerning shamanism and shamanistic healing, more recent scholarship has begun to press the case for comparative work in this area to be given much higher priority. In a monograph published in 1996, for instance, Bernd Kollmann argues that virtually no authentic material in the Jesus tradition supports the notion that Jesus was a shaman;[33] however, as Kollmann derives his concept of '*Schamanismus*' almost entirely from early research in this field by a single comparativist (i.e., M. Eliade[34]) and furthermore associates '*Schamane*' with '*Magier*' in a way that severely limits the former category's analytical utility,[35] his argument is weakened by undertheorized categories and terminological ambiguities. Moreover, in John Ashton's *The Religion of Paul the Apostle* (2000), which offers a more thorough critique of Kollmann's book than I can provide here,[36] a compelling case is made for understanding the religious experience of both Jesus and Paul along shamanic lines.[37] Convinced as I therefore am

---

[31] As the demon–impurity nexus is presupposed in multiple layers and forms of the Synoptic tradition, it calls for more attention than the brief notice it receives in Twelftree, *Jesus the Exorcist*, p. 144.

[32] Twelftree, *Jesus the Exorcist*, pp. 136–42, 217–24.

[33] B. Kollmann, *Jesus und die Christen als Wundertäter: Studien zu Magie, Medizin und Schamanismus in Antike und Christentum*, FRLANT 170 (Göttingen, 1996), pp. 272–4, 286, 314–15.

[34] Ibid., pp. 91 n. 6, 100 n. 35, 194 n. 88, citing M. Eliade, *Shamanism: Archaic Techniques of Ecstasy*, trans. W. R. Trask (Princeton, 1964), the French original of which was published in 1951. Although Eliade's work remains immensely valuable, the bibliography on shamanism has grown enormously in the last fifty years, with competing definitions and typological constructs being at the centre of scholarly debates; see, e.g., the terminological discussion in R. N. Walsh, *The Spirit of Shamanism* (New York, 1990), pp. 8–17; and the bibliography in M. Winkelman, *Shamanism: The Neural Ecology of Consciousness and Healing* (Westport, 2000), pp. 277–306.

[35] Kollmann, *Jesus und die Christen*, pp. 89, 100–1, 172, 271–5, 286. At least in part the difficulty is that of confusing an etic category (i.e., *Schamane*) with an emic one (i.e., *Magier*).

[36] J. Ashton, *The Religion of Paul the Apostle* (New Haven, 2000), pp. 63–9.

[37] Ibid., pp. 62–72.

of the general validity of Ashton's thesis, and availing myself of a handful of recently published anthropological studies of shamanism not used in previous New Testament research,[38] I employ a typological construct of shamanism below – especially in the analysis of Luke 9.37–43a – in order to sketch a few significant continuities and discontinuities between the historical Jesus as shamanic healer and the demon-vanquishing god of Luke's narrative.

And finally, early Christian and other ancient Mediterranean modes of healing have recently been re-examined by John Pilch and Hector Avalos from perspectives informed by medical anthropology and comparative studies of health care.[39] Pilch for instance has issued a much-needed warning about the dangers of 'medicocentrism' in contemporary western interpretation of ancient accounts of religious healing.[40] As the type of problem against which he warns is well illustrated every time commentators on Luke 9.37–43a refer to the possessed boy in that context as an 'epileptic',[41] Pilch's work is especially valuable for helping us to view the condition in that context not as an ancient illustration of a precise diagnostic category but rather as an instance of folk illness. Avalos, on the other hand, has made several very stimulating comments both on the interface between spirit-affliction and impurity in first-century Judaism, and on the likelihood that Jesus' practice of healing consisted in part of a critique of existing Levitical approaches to illness and health care.[42] This perspective has special relevance to my cultural analysis of the story in Luke 8.26–39, where the demon–impurity nexus is particularly conspicuous; but it

---

[38] The most theoretically rigorous and useful are those by Winkelman and Walsh mentioned above in n. 34; but also valuable is Walsh's more recent article, 'The Psychological Health of Shamans: A Reevaluation', *JAAR* 65/1 (1997), 101–24.

[39] See J. J. Pilch, 'Sickness and Healing in Luke–Acts', in J. H. Neyrey (ed.), *The Social World of Luke–Acts: Models for Interpretation* (Peabody, 1991), pp. 181–210, reprinted with minor revisions in J. J. Pilch, *Healing in the New Testament: Insights from Medical and Mediterranean Anthropology* (Minneapolis, 2000), pp. 89–118; H. Avalos, *Health Care and the Rise of Christianity* (Peabody, 1999); and *Illness and Health Care in the Ancient Near East: The Role of the Temple in Greece, Mesopotamia, and Israel*, HSM 54 (Atlanta, 1995).

[40] Pilch, 'Sickness and Healing', pp. 182–3.

[41] J. Wilkinson, *The Bible and Healing: A Medical and Theological Commentary* (Grand Rapids, 1998), pp. 121–30 offers several lines of evidence for understanding the boy in this story as epileptic but ultimately underestimates the dangers of basing a diagnosis on a religious narrative written at least three decades after the therapeutic event. Regarding the difficulties of diagnosing epilepsy on the basis of evidence like that provided in Luke 9.37–43a and its parallels, see J. K. Howard, *Disease and Healing in the New Testament: An Analysis and Interpretation* (Lanham, MD, 2001), pp. 112–15; and Walsh, *Spirit of Shamanism*, pp. 76–9.

[42] Avalos, *Illness and Health Care*, pp. 375–7, 391–4; Avalos, *Health Care and the Rise of Christianity*, pp. 66–71.

also has implications for our understanding of all the other references in Luke–Acts to 'impure spirit(s)' as well.[43] However, as neither Avalos nor Pilch has focused in depth as I do here on the exorcism stories of a single New Testament evangelist, the present study does not substantially overlap either of theirs but rather seeks to integrate their insights into areas of research which they have addressed only briefly.

Are the exorcism stories in Luke–Acts really worth all this fuss? After all, while many societies in today's world continue to believe in spirit-affliction and possession, most of this study's readers (including Christian ones) probably have little or no room for such beliefs within their own *Weltanschauung*; and in addition to the many modern exegetes who are apparently content with my topic's neglect, some New Testament scholars have supported this lack of interest more actively by explicitly relegating exorcism to the outer margins of New Testament theology.[44] Although the present study has no interest in the ontological questions surrounding spirit beings and demon-possession, its main argument does address *inter alia* whether exorcism can rightly be assigned peripheral importance in the largest block of writings in the NT. More specifically, although my treatments of Luke 9.37–43a and Acts 16.16–18 show that exorcism does not occupy the centre of the Lucan writings' rhetorical thrust, they also demonstrate that it can by no means be relegated to the periphery; on the contrary, partly by virtue of its prominent position in the chiastic structure of Luke 9.1–50 and partly through its frequently unnoticed contribution to the Jesus–Paul parallels realised by Acts 16.16–18 and 19.11–20, exorcism stands somewhere between the background and the frontground in Luke's writings, between periphery and centre, enjoying an intermediate level of prominence that might best be characterised as the narrative's foreground.

But equally significant, by contributing as just noted to the Jesus–Paul parallels completed in the book of Acts, the exorcism stories play an integral role in the implied author's response to one of the most pressing concerns behind the composition of Luke–Acts as a whole, namely the debates that were taking place in several first-century churches over Paul's relation to Jesus and over both men's status vis-à-vis the heritage of Israel, to which both their followers and many of their critics were making hotly contested claims. This interpretation, moreover, entails that Luke's audacious move of conjoining a βίος about Jesus and a volume whose dominant concern is the reputation of Paul has far more dramatic

---

[43] E.g., Luke 4.33, 36; 9.42.
[44] See, e.g., K. Grayston, 'Exorcism in the New Testament', *EpR* 2 (1975), 90–4.

implications for understanding the exorcism stories in these writings than previous readings have suggested.[45] How I arrive at this judgement has much to do with the theory and methods that inform my analysis, and which are explained and applied to Luke 4.33–37 in the next chapter.

[45] See e.g. Kirschläger, *Jesu exorzistisches Wirken*, pp. 255–6, whose analysis of the story in Acts 16.16–18 overlooks the most macrostructurally significant feature of the episode, namely its correspondence to the exorcism story in Luke 8.26–39 (and thus its realisation of a Jesus–Paul parallel).

1

SOCIOSTYLISTICS AND THE EXORCISM IN LUKE 4.33–37

Recent efforts by linguists and literary theorists to build an interface between their respective disciplines have produced analytical methods that have much to offer anyone interested in the relations between texts and their extratextual contexts of production. As these methods not only contribute to the type of discourse analysis used in the present study but also differ in various ways from most other forms of critical practice in biblical studies, their distinctive vocabulary and position in contemporary theoretical discussion ought to be clarified at the outset. However, in order to keep this part of the work close to my primary interest (i.e., to apply the methods to the exorcism stories of Luke–Acts), the illustration of critical concepts in the present chapter focuses as much as possible on the exorcism in Luke 4.33–37; thus, while a few essential matters of terminology and theory are treated on their own in the immediately ensuing sections, the method and its application are tightly integrated throughout the rest of the chapter.

Sociostylistic theory

Like most varieties of stylistics, the critical practice of sociostylistics consists primarily of the analysis of linguistic style. However, as the phrase 'linguistic style' can convey several different meanings,[1] it too needs to be defined if the method and object of the present study are to be understood clearly. In this connection, the definition offered by the Finnish linguist N. Enkvist is particularly helpful. In Enkvist's view, linguistic style is situationally conditioned choice.[2]

---

[1] E.g., (1) the everyday language habits of an individual person, (2) the characteristic language habits of an entire group of people, (3) the appropriateness of a particular expression, (4) the quality of exclusively written or literary expression, and (5) the connotative aspects of language use. D. Crystal and D. Davy, *Investigating English Style*, English Language Series 1 (Essex, 1969), pp. 9–10; G. W. Turner, *Stylistics* (Harmondsworth, 1973), p. 27.

[2] N. Enkvist, 'What Ever Happened to Stylistics?', in U. Fries (ed.), *The Structure of Texts*, Swiss Papers in Language and Literature 3 (Tübingen, 1987), p. 15; cf. Z. Szabó, 'Text

A key presupposition of this definition is that the formal and semantic properties of texts are powerfully conditioned by situational and other extralinguistic factors in the environment(s) of textual production and reception.[3] According to this assumption, stylistic analysis of any given text gives careful attention not only to the linguistic structures of the text itself but also to the various kinds of extratextual forces that constrained and shaped the text's production in the first place; thus any self-conscious effort to understand a text by systematically relating its linguistic features to various levels of its sociocultural environment might be thought of as an exercise in sociostylistics.

The main point of adding the prefix 'socio-' to 'stylistics', therefore, is not to distinguish sharply the designated type of analysis from all other forms of stylistics but rather to highlight its strongly contextualist approach to understanding texts. At the same time, though, as the simpler term 'stylistics' has unfortunately been misused by certain critics as if it were synonymous with 'stylometrics' (i.e., a quantitative method that forms only part of the larger field of stylistics),[4] my use of the prefixed term is also motivated by a desire to save the present study from being misunderstood as a primarily quantitative exercise.

Like rhetorical criticism, moreover, this type of stylistics assumes that the communicative force of a text's style usually has something to do with the goals of the text's producer, whose conformity to expectations of relevance normally entails that the assumed audience and situation are implied in the text itself.[5] Yet, in order to infer the situation responsibly and interpret it in relation to the decisive continuities and discontinuities between the world of the text's production and that of its reception, the stylistician must be ready to learn from any field of inquiry – history, anthropology, psychology, sociology – that might illuminate why certain types of texts are produced in certain types of contexts.[6] Since sociostylistics therefore seeks to historicise and situate texts in their contingency as singular instances of social discourse, its location on the map

and Style: An Outline of the Methodological Bases of Stylistic Analysis', *Revue Romaine des Linguistiques* 30 (1985), p. 485, who defines style as 'contextually conditioned variation' in language performance.

[3] Enkvist, 'What Ever Happened to Stylistics?', pp. 12–15.

[4] On the need for a term such as 'sociostylistics' to denote a specific theoretical development within the broader field of stylistics, see ibid., p. 25; and *DS*, s.v. 'Stylistics'.

[5] G. Kress, 'Textual Matters: The Social Effectiveness of Style', in D. Birch and L. M. O'Toole (eds), *Functions of Style* (London, 1988), p. 127. On textual communication as 'goal-directed', see G. N. Leech, *The Principles of Pragmatics*, Longman Linguistics Library (London, 1983), pp. 13–14.

[6] Cf. Szabò, 'Text and Style', p. 486; and R. Fowler, *Linguistic Criticism* (Oxford, 1986), pp. 172–3, 176–9.

of contemporary theory and method stands far closer to some forms of critical practice – for instance, the New Historicism and socio-rhetorical criticism – than to others (e.g. reader response criticism). Locating sociostylistics in relation to a few other key spots on the map is my chief interest in the next two sections below.

Sociostylistics and literary theory

According to Stanley Fish, stylistics is essentially a specimen of formalism which, much like Russian formalism in particular and the American New Criticism, tends to be so preoccupied with matters of aesthetic form that it has almost no time for questions of rhetorical effect.[7] *Contra* Fish, however, while most varieties of stylistics do have a strong interest in the aesthetic properties of texts qua texts, none of them can be accurately identified as a mere extension or specimen of either formalism or New Criticism, both of which put primary emphasis on literature's aesthetic properties and minimise the interpretative significance of authorial ideology and socio-economic interest.[8] By contrast, sociostylistics and related linguistic methods pay just as much attention to the extratextual conditions, causes, motives and effects of texts as they do to the aesthetic qualities of the texts themselves; indeed, one of the main reasons these techniques have been chosen for use in the present study is that they offer a particularly helpful framework for interpreting texts in relation to their cultural, situational and social contexts.

The sociocultural facet of stylistics has been developed in several books by the British linguist Roger Fowler, whose techniques of 'linguistic criticism' have contributed much to the methods used in the ensuing pages. In his *Literature as Social Discourse: The Practice of Linguistic Criticism* (1981), Fowler offers a powerful critique of formalism, New Criticism and more recent methodologies that share their dehistoricising tendencies. In this connection he devotes special attention to the assumption that 'literary language' can be distinguished from 'ordinary language' with the aid of criteria relatively free of ideological self-interest.[9] According

---

[7] S. Fish, *Is There a Text in This Class? The Authority of Interpretative Communities* (Cambridge, MA, 1980), pp. 69–71. On the common emphasis in formalism and New Criticism that literary analysis should focus on the intrinsic qualities of texts themselves, rather than on extrinsic considerations such as the background of the author, the historical context, and the text's origins and effects, see T. Eagleton, *Literary Theory: An Introduction* (Oxford, 1983), p. 92; and *DS*, s.v. 'Formalism'.

[8] J. Culler, *Framing the Sign: Criticism and Its Institutions* (Oxford, 1988), pp. 79–80.

[9] R. Fowler, *Literature as Social Discourse: The Practice of Linguistic Criticism* (London, 1981), pp. 20, 80–5.

to this assumption, literary language, because it is an art form, lacks the utilitarian, pragmatic features of ordinary language; to put this another way, ordinary language is language that *does*, whereas literary language is language that *is*.[10]

Although respected academics often take this distinction for granted, Fowler argues that, from a linguist's standpoint, it is both impressionistic and naïve.[11] To be sure, what is normally called 'literature' does often foreground artful language with an intensity that is not commonly found in ordinary discourse; but so-called 'literary' and everyday occurrences of language overlap far more than most literary critics have been willing to admit.[12] Indeed, the varieties of language that constitute what formalists call 'literary texts' are essentially the same as those that comprise non-literary texts.[13] What critics designate as 'literary' depends more on the culturally contingent biases of academic elites in English and other humanities departments than on some universally recognisable distinctive of 'literary' texts themselves.[14]

Furthermore, in Fowler's view the efforts by some theorists to downplay the continuity between 'literary' and ordinary language ought to be seen as serving the theorists' own professional and ideological self-interests. More specifically, both the literary/ordinary distinction and the marginalisation of ideological context serve (1) to protect society (and so also the critic) against the potentially subversive power of literature by denying literature a social function; (2) to strengthen the fragile prestige of literature and criticism vis-à-vis the natural sciences by establishing a special set of 'literary competencies' as the intellectual prerequisite of legitimate interpretative activity; and (3) to immunise the academic profession of literary studies against infection from other academic disciplines by tacitly minimising the relevance of these fields – especially history and the social sciences – to the analysis of texts.[15] But just as

---

[10] P. K. W. Tan, 'Falling from Grice: the Ideological Trap of Pragmatic Stylistics', *Edinburgh Working Papers in Applied Linguistics* 1/1 (1990), 1, 4–5.
[11] Fowler, *Literature as Social Discourse*, p. 21.   [12] Ibid., pp. 20–1.
[13] Ibid., p. 21.
[14] Ibid., p. 85. For further discussion of the difficulties in distinguishing literary from non-literary texts, see A. Durant and N. Fabb, 'Introduction', in D. Attridge et al. (eds), *The Linguistics of Writing: Arguments Between Language and Literature* (Manchester, 1987), p. 6; and G. Wienold, 'Textlinguistic Approaches to Written Works of Art', in W. Dressler (ed.), *Current Trends in Textlinguistics*, Research in Text Theory (Berlin, 1978), pp. 136–7.
[15] Fowler, *Literature as Social Discourse*, p. 85. Also see Eagleton, *Literary Theory*, pp. 47–53, 200–7; T. Eagleton, *The Ideology of the Aesthetic* (Oxford, 1990), pp. 367–8; and R. Carter, 'Introduction', in J. Sinclair (ed.), *Language and Literature: An Introductory*

important, since these sorts of criticisms can be found in many recent contributions to stylistic theory,[16] formalism is neither what most contemporary stylisticians understand *themselves* to be practising nor, unless they are all uncommonly oblivious to the character of their own critical activities, what they are practising in fact.

As stylistics and formalism are therefore found on very different parts of the map, it may prove helpful to explore areas that lie closer to the former. Similar for instance to the Marxist perspectives of T. Eagleton, F. Jameson and others, most contextualist varieties of stylistics view texts in general, including the most aesthetically rich 'literature', as vehicles of social and ideological power. Regarding narrative genres of text in particular, the stylistician M. Toolan asserts:

> Because any narrative inevitably has some effect on its addressees and consequences in the real world (whether or not these effects and consequences are overt or hidden), we have to recognize that narratives are, among other things, a kind of political action. Narratives, in short, carry political and ideological freight.[17]

Toolan's conception of narrative as a form of political action coincides with what a large number of stylisticians, linguists and New Historicists have been saying in recent years. Furthermore, many of these theorists have argued strongly that the varieties of language used in literary and canonical texts cannot be sharply distinguished from those used in everyday social discourse; that a dialectical relationship can normally be demonstrated to exist between language events (including so-called 'literary' ones) and their social contexts;[18] and that every text realises a culturally contingent world-view and ideological context. The critical promise of sociostylistics, therefore, resides to a great degree in its potential for redescribing the supposedly 'timeless' classic as an instantiation of

---

Reader in Stylistics, Aspects of English (London, 1982), pp. 1–5. The perspectives criticised above have achieved much of their influence through their formulation in W. K. Wimsatt and M. Beardsley, *The Verbal Icon* (Lexington, 1954), who argue that inquiry into the extratextual causes and effects of a text typically results in an impressionistic style of criticism that loses sight of the text itself (p. 21).

[16] See, e.g., Crystal and Davy, *Investigating English Style*, pp. 78–81; G. N. Leech and M. H. Short, *Style in Fiction: A Linguistic Introduction to English Fictional Prose*, English Language Series 13 (London, 1981), pp. 25–38.

[17] M. Toolan, *Narrative: A Critical Linguistic Introduction* (London, 1988), p. 227.

[18] Fowler, *Literature as Social Discourse*, p. 21.

culture-specific meanings whose true relevance is limited to a historically particular type of situation.[19]

The continuity that stylisticians find between 'literary' and ordinary varieties of language, however, scarcely entails that written text can be contextualised in exactly the same way spoken text can be. On the contrary, and as several linguists of functionalist outlook have urged, it is useful to think of written and spoken texts as representing different *modes* of language, with a continuum of 'mixed modes' lying between the extremes.[20] Furthermore, written texts have far greater potential to be decontextualised – and thus reinterpreted and assigned new meanings – than spoken ones normally have.[21] For instance, the written text of the present paragraph might be read a decade from now by a seminarian in South Korea and used for purposes unforeseen by me, whereas the unrecorded utterances produced by my two-year-old son at lunch-time today are exceedingly unlikely to be either reiterated in another context or used for purposes different from those he intended.

On the other hand, the difference between written and spoken texts in this regard is easy to exaggerate. The divergence is only a matter of degree, for instance, in regard to the kinds of background knowledge which producers presuppose of their audience;[22] for written texts, like spoken ones, invariably contain traces of their contexts of production, providing clues to the cultural and situational frames shared by the communication's participants.[23] Consequently, while written texts can often be read in contexts that differ significantly from those in which they were produced, they can also be interpreted in ways that allow their original contexts of production to be partly reconstructed.[24] Indeed, extended pieces of written narrative such as Luke–Acts usually contain far more clues to their original context than short spoken texts do.

[19] Ibid., p. 22. Similar are the critical goals advanced by Eagleton, *Literary Theory*, pp. 205–11; and Veeser, 'The New Historicism', p. 2.

[20] E.g., the written representation of oral dialogue (real or fictitious), and the oral 'performance' of written text. On the combination of oral and written modes, see M. A. K. Halliday, *Language as Social Semiotic: The Social Interpretation of Language and Meaning* (London, 1978), pp. 144, 224; and M. Gregory and S. Carroll, *Language and Situation*, Language and Society Series (London, 1978), p. 47.

[21] Toolan, *Narrative*, pp. 226–7.

[22] What pragmaticians call 'presupposition' (i.e., knowledge which a text assumes rather than asserts) is so important to *literary* discourse, in fact, that some stylisticians consider it an integral feature of style and thus a key object of stylistic analysis. See, e.g., N. Enkvist, 'Stylistics and Textlinguistics', in Dressler (ed.), *Current Trends in Textlinguistics*, p. 178.

[23] Toolan, *Narrative*, pp. 226–7; and S. Eggins, *An Introduction to Systemic Functional Linguistics* (London, 1994), p. 49.

[24] See, e.g., S. C. Levinson, *Pragmatics*, Cambridge Textbooks in Linguistics (Cambridge, 1983), pp. 47–53.

Sociostylistics, then, with its contextualist notions of linguistic choice and textual production, views all forms of verbal communication as social discourse. Much like its better-known theoretical cousin, sociolinguistics, it takes a strong interest in how variation in linguistic form and meaning is related to variation in social and cultural context.[25] Using this type of theory to interpret the exorcism narratives of Luke–Acts therefore requires that ample attention be given to the social and cultural milieus in which these stories were originally composed; accordingly, in the present study matters of context are treated at length near the end of each analysis.

To scholars and students of the New Testament, the hermeneutical stance just sketched may sound at least faintly familiar; for in certain respects it resembles the form-critical methods which K. L. Schmidt, M. Dibelius, and R. Bultmann used so influentially in their studies of the Synoptic tradition.[26] Yet there are also important differences. For instance, like most methods informed by modern literary theory, sociostylistics focuses on the final form of the extant text in its literary co-text rather than on pre-literary units of tradition isolated from their editorial framework. Furthermore, in line with neopragmatist theories of human language and historical contingency, sociostylistics recognises that its own contextual reconstructions are conditioned by its own historically particular vocabularies and are at best knowledgeable attempts to redescribe the past for the purposes of those who must face the present.[27] And finally, sociostylistics is strongly rooted in linguistic theories that show only a vague resemblance to their early and mid-twentieth-century precursors.[28] This third distinctive, moreover, exerts so much influence on the present study's approach to the Lucan writings that it warrants further elaboration before the analysis proper is actually undertaken.

[25] See, e.g., D. Crystal, *Linguistics*, 2nd edn. (London, 1985), pp. 260–1; P. Trudgill, *Sociolinguistics: An Introduction to Language and Society*, rev. edn (London, 1983), pp. 121–6; A. Cluysenaar, *Introduction to Literary Stylistics: A Discussion of the Dominant Structures in Verse and Prose* (London, 1976), p. 11; Toolan, *Narrative*, pp. 146–75; and Fowler, *Linguistic Criticism*, pp. 85–101.
[26] See K. L. Schmidt, *Der Rahmen der Geschichte Jesu: Literarkritische Untersuchungen zur ältesten Jesusüberlieferung* (Berlin, 1919); M. Dibelius, *Die Formgeschichte des Evangeliums* (Tübingen, 1919); R. Bultmann, *Die Geschichte der synoptischen Tradition* (Göttingen, 1921).
[27] Cf. N. Fairclough, *Critical Discourse Analysis: The Critical Study of Language*, Language in Social Life Series (London, 1995), pp. 227–32.
[28] Although the present study does not rely directly at many points on the published work of Noam Chomsky, it recognises Chomsky's revolutionary influence on the study of language since the late 1950s – on which see, e.g., S. Pinker, *The Language Instinct: The New Science of Language and Mind* (London, 1995), pp. 21–4; J. Lyons, *Chomsky*, Modern Masters (London, 1970), pp. 9–15.

Sociostylistics and linguistic theory

As one of several subdisciplines within the field of linguistics, stylistics is almost constantly influenced by debates and developments in the field of linguistic theory.[29] Tensions between the psycholinguistic focus of generative grammar (e.g., Chomsky) and the sociolinguistic orientation of the systemic-functionalists (e.g., M. A. K. Halliday), for example, have contributed to the formation of two different approaches to stylistic analysis, one concentrating largely on matters of grammatical form and propositional sense, the other giving more attention to phenomena such as illocutionary force and context. Doubts concerning the adequacy of grammar on its own – understood as the study of semantic, syntactical and phonological matters – to give a satisfactory account of flesh-and-blood instances of language use are also significant for stylistics; for as several prominent linguists and philosophers of language have recently argued, grammar needs to be supplemented by pragmatics wherever the interpretative task involves questions of interpersonal meaning or social discourse.[30] Accordingly, within a broadly functionalist framework that gives ample scope for the concerns of grammar, pragmaticist notions such as 'implicature' and 'entailment' and 'relevance' have a prominent place in the present study. Both the functionalist framework and the character of the concepts just mentioned are described below in greater detail.

Formalism versus functionalism

Of the numerous issues debated in modern linguistic theory, the most far-reaching is probably that concerning whether language ought to be conceptualised primarily as a cognitive and psychological phenomenon, or as a social and interactive one. Up to the late 1980s, this question represented the major conceptual dilemma facing systemic linguistics over the previous ten-year period;[31] and efforts to answer it, reconfigure it, or dissolve it have contributed to some of the most interesting developments in linguistic theory in the last twenty years.[32]

---

[29] Crystal, *Linguistics*, pp. 260–1.
[30] J. Lyons, *Language, Meaning and Context*, Fontana Linguistics (London, 1981), pp. 30–5; Crystal, *Linguistics*, pp. 243–7; F. R. Palmer, *Semantics*, 2nd edn (Cambridge, 1981), p. 8; Leech, *Pragmatics*, pp. 19–35; and U. Eco, *Semiotics and the Philosophy of Language* (London, 1984), pp. 68–9, 78.
[31] E. H. Steiner and R. Veltman, 'Introduction', in *Pragmatics, Discourse, and Text: Some Systemically-Inspired Approaches* (London, 1988), p. 9.
[32] See, e.g., Pinker, *The Language Instinct*, pp. 227–30; D. Sperber and D. Wilson, *Relevance: Communication and Cognition*, 2nd edn (Oxford, 1995), pp. 9–15.

As much of the debate is technical and subtle, only its most important contours can be treated here.[33] The two main orientations, representing as they do very different perspectives on the nature of language, have sometimes appeared to be irreconcilably opposed to one another. Linguistic formalists such as Noam Chomsky, for instance, treat language primarily as a mental phenomenon, whereas linguistic functionalists such as M. A. K. Halliday treat it largely as a social phenomenon.[34] Similarly, formalists see language as an innate and remarkable ability of individual human beings, whereas functionalists see it as a sociocultural system of shared meanings and knowledge. And finally, while formalists are disposed to explain language universals as stemming from human genetic inheritance, functionalists are inclined to explain them as resulting from the evolution of culturally conditioned uses of language in society.

Although these differences are weighty, and although each orientation has had its avid supporters, an increasing number of linguists are rightly viewing this contrast as more perspectival than substantive.[35] Halliday for example has suggested that the two approaches are complementary and that the future health of linguistics as a discipline will depend at least partly on the degree to which the two can be successfully integrated.[36] Similarly, in treating the relationship between structuralist varieties of linguistic theory and literary studies, Jonathan Culler has argued that criticism needs to deal not only with the sociolinguistic conventions that texts everywhere presuppose but also with the equally abundant (yet oft-neglected) indications of the individual language user's creative agency,[37] an emphasis fully consistent with one of the major themes in Chomskyan writing.[38] According to theorists such as these, any comprehensive explanation of actual language use has to deal both with cognition and with interaction because both are involved in every linguistic event.[39] Whenever people think about what they should say or write in particular

---

[33] This summary of the debate is adapted from Leech, *Pragmatics*, pp. 46–7.

[34] Compare, e.g., N. Chomsky, *Language and Mind* (New York, 1972), pp. vii–x, with Halliday, *Language as Social Semiotic*, pp. 1–5.

[35] See, e.g., J. Fine, 'Cognitive Processes in Context: A Systemic Approach to Problems in Oral Language Use', in Steiner and Veltman (eds), *Pragmatics, Discourse and Text*, pp. 171–2; Pinker, *The Language Instinct*, pp. 226–30; Steiner and Veltman, 'Introduction', p. 9; Halliday, *Language as Social Semiotic*, pp. 56–7; Leech, *Pragmatics*, p. 46.

[36] Halliday, *Language as Social Semiotic*, pp. 56–7.

[37] J. Culler, *Structuralist Poetics: Structuralism, Linguistics, and the Study of Literature* (London, 1975), p. 30.

[38] See, e.g., Pinker, *The Language Instinct*, p. 22.

[39] See, e.g., Fine, 'Cognitive Processes', pp. 171–2; Sperber and Wilson, *Relevance*, p. 279.

situations, their cognitive processes are at least weakly constrained by the limitations of the linguistic system which their sociocultural environment gives them access to.[40] Furthermore, since nothing more than a tiny portion of the system's total potential for making meanings ever needs to be utilised in a single situation of discourse, the production of meaning always involves choice, the selection of one combination of signs and meanings instead of others. And just as these choices emerge from an interplay of social context and individual cognition, so they set in motion both cognitive and social effects.[41]

In regard to the theoretical discussion, therefore, formalism and functionalism ought to be seen chiefly as complementary perspectives on the same complex phenomenon. To be sure, the cognitive and social facets of language are distinguishable, and they undoubtedly should be distinguished in many exercises in discourse analysis; but in actual events of human communication, they occur together.[42]

Seeing the cognitive and social aspects of communication as two sides of the same coin, however, does not entail that the formalist and functionalist theories of language are of equal utility for the analytical task pursued below. For at least three reasons, in fact, the functionalist perspective is adopted in the present study as the more comprehensive and useful framework for discourse analysis. First, as discussed more fully below, M. A. K. Halliday's systemic-functional theory includes not only an interpersonal (i.e., social) metafunction but also an ideational (i.e., cognitive) one, the latter consisting largely of a system of 'transitivity' options that can be fruitfully analysed in terms of participants and processes and circumstances. By contrast, because formalist grammar focuses primarily on how the mind transforms deep cognitive structures into surface linguistic patterns according to generative rules, it offers little help towards explaining either the relationship between the mind's transformational activity and its sociolinguistic environment or the connection between linguistic form and the situations in which forms are chosen for use. Thus, although formalism has exerted enormous influence on modern linguistics through the rise of generative grammar,[43] the more comprehensive and

---

[40] Saying that linguistic resources *constrain* thought is not the same as saying, with Wittgenstein and many others, that they *determine* thought; rather, it is to agree with D. Davidson, 'Thought and Talk', in *Inquiries into Truth and Interpretation* (Oxford, 1984), pp. 155-70, that language and thought closely interact with, parallel, and limit one another in a variety of ways. For an impressive survey of recent research in cognitive science and psycholinguistics contravening linguistic determinism see Pinker, *The Language Instinct*, pp. 55-82.

[41] Fine, 'Cognitive Processes', p. 181.   [42] Steiner and Veltman, 'Introduction', p. 9.

[43] D. Crystal, *The Cambridge Encyclopedia of Language* (Cambridge, 1987), p. 409.

useful set of tools for purposes of discourse analysis is provided by the systemic-functionalist perspective.

Second, functionalism is better suited for analysis of texts longer than a single sentence. Halliday's concept of the 'textual function', for example, about which more will be said below, encompasses not only intra-clausal concerns such as information structure (i.e., the order of constituents in the clause) but also patterns of cohesion between sentences.[44] By contrast, as transformational-generative grammar is chiefly interested in the mental competencies by which normal human beings produce and understand the astonishing range of sentences they use and interpret, it tends to focus on linguistic units no higher in rank than the sentence, putting suprasentential stretches of text outside the margins of its inquiries. The limitations of sentence grammars, it is true, have been creatively addressed from inside the generative grammar camp through the development of 'text grammars';[45] but a few limitations of the latter ought to be noted. One is that, in addition to being enormously complicated and difficult to use, the text grammars that stay theoretically close to their generativist roots focus more attention on how the linguistic system generates texts than on the texts themselves.[46] But just as importantly, the text grammars that have managed to prove themselves useful for purposes of interpretation have tended to stray far from their generativist foundation by incorporating insights from pragmatics and speech act theory, which due to their interest in language performance and context sit rather uneasily beside the abstractions of generative grammar.[47]

Finally, whereas formalist theory tends to be uninterested in the relationship between linguistic choice and the context of selection, functionalism devotes ample attention to such matters.[48] Halliday and several other systemicists, for instance, have developed useful models of register that correlate the different metafunctions of language with different aspects of situational context.[49] Unfortunately, only a tiny fraction of recent theorising about register and situation can be used in the present study;

---

[44] M. A. K. Halliday and R. Hasan, *Language, Context, and Text: Aspects of Language in a Social-Semiotic Perspective*, 2nd edn, Language Education (Oxford, 1989), pp. 12, 25; and Halliday, *Language as Social Semiotic*, p. 144.

[45] See, e.g., M. L. Pratt and E. C. Traugott, *Linguistics for Students of Literature* (New York, 1980), pp. 24–9; and T. A. van Dijk, *Text and Context: Explorations in the Semantics and Pragmatics of Discourse*, Longman Linguistics Library 21 (London, 1977), pp. 1–8.

[46] D. Birch, *Language, Literature, and Critical Practice*, Interface Series (London, 1989), pp. 145–7. For other criticisms of generative text grammars, see Wienold, 'Textlinguistic Approaches', pp. 141–2.

[47] Birch, *Language, Literature, and Critical Practice*, pp. 148–9.

[48] Durant and Fabb, 'Introduction', p. 10.

[49] See, e.g., Eggins, *Systemic Functional Linguistics*, pp. 49–68.

but if the little of it that is used serves to prevent my efforts at contextualisation from treating 'culture' as the only layer of context worthy of discussion, it will have served my analysis very well.

Functionalism's contribution to the development of these kinds of tools helps to explain why most exercises in stylistic analysis operate on the basis of a functionalist theory of language.[50] For in addition to being interested in language's grammatical and ideational aspects, most stylisticians work with texts longer than a single sentence and view the meanings of these texts as having at least a vaguely specifiable connection to the interests, values, beliefs and goals of their senders and receivers. As the present study has a strong interest in the multi-level relationship between the Lucan stories of exorcism and their original context of production, its theoretical framework is adapted very self-consciously from systemic-functional linguistics. Here, though, before the theory's application to Luke 4.33–37 is explored below, further clarification of what this framework involves may prove helpful.

Systemic-functional linguistics: an overview

According to Halliday and several theorists associated with him, human language is best conceptualised as consisting of three different metafunctional levels of meaning potential.[51] These three levels are most commonly called the textual, ideational, and interpersonal functions. The textual function involves the use of language to produce palpable sequences of signs and meanings, either spoken or written, which exemplify qualities of cohesion and coherence.[52] The ideational function consists of the use of language to categorise, simplify, interpret, and convey experience of the world.[53] And the interpersonal function involves the use of language to influence the experience (i.e., beliefs and behaviour) of others.[54] Although the relative prominence of each function varies from text to text according to situation, the three are instantiated simultaneously and fused together in the production of all discourse. All three levels, therefore, will be treated below in each of my analyses of the Lucan stories of exorcism.

---

[50] G. N. Leech, 'Stylistics and Functionalism', in Attridge (ed.), *The Linguistics of Writing*, p. 87.

[51] See, e.g., Halliday, *Language as Social Semiotic*, pp. 46–7; and Eggins, *Systemic Functional Linguistics*, pp. 2–3.

[52] See Halliday, *Language as Social Semiotic*, p. 48; Leech, *Pragmatics*, p. 56; and *DS*, s.v. 'Text'.

[53] Leech, *Pragmatics*, p. 56; Fowler, *Linguistic Criticism*, pp. 16–22, 147; Halliday, *Language as Social Semiotic*, pp. 46–50.

[54] Leech, *Pragmatics*, p. 56; and M. A. K. Halliday, *An Introduction to Functional Grammar* (London, 1985), p. xiii.

As implied earlier in this chapter, instantiations of these functions in the form of texts are viewed by functionalist stylistics not as aesthetic objects free of socio-ideological utility but rather as products of particular contexts, conflicts and values. According to this perspective every text realises information about the sociocultural system of which it is a product, while simultaneously effecting both constancy and change in the same system.[55] As texts not only constitute but also are constituted by their contexts of production, they inevitably contain traces of those contexts within their own linguistic structures.[56] Thus, any attempt such as that undertaken in the present study to interpret a group of ancient texts in relation to their original context of production will not progress far without prior reflection on what context is and how it gets into text.

Although terminologies concerning context differ from one linguist to the next,[57] at least two useful concepts are found in most linguistic discussions of this topic: a general context of culture, and a more specific context of situation. Context of culture consists of the entire system of knowledge, beliefs and meanings which both enable and constrain every act of textual production.[58] However, in order to be usable as a semantic resource, the cultural system cannot be a shapeless mass of undifferentiated semiosis; rather, it has to be organised in a way that facilitates efficient selection of particular types of text (e.g., stories, poems, interviews, conversations) for the achievement of particular types of communicative goals. In systemic terms, the diverse types of textual patterning correspond to different 'genres', with the whole network of textual options in a given culture constituting that particular culture's 'genre potential'.[59] Of course, the total genre potential of the Lucan writings' cultural context is far too big and complex a topic for satisfactory treatment in the present study; but much of the ensuing discussion of cultural context does involve, either implicitly or explicitly, analysis of genre, a task pursued in this context by comparing the Lucan stories with various ancient Near Eastern and Graeco-Roman texts on the same field of discourse (e.g., demons, exorcism, illness).

---

[55] Halliday, *Language as Social Semiotic*, p. 141.
[56] Eggins, *Systemic Functional Linguistics*, pp. 7–9, 49–52.
[57] Note, e.g., the differences between Fowler, *Linguistic Criticism*, pp. 85–90; Halliday and Hasan, *Language, Context, and Text*, pp. 5–12, 25; Leech, *Pragmatics*, pp. 13–15; and T. A. van Dijk, *Studies in the Pragmatics of Discourse*, Janua Linguarum, Series Maior 101 (The Hague, 1981), pp. 222–9.
[58] Halliday, *Language as Social Semiotic*, pp. 122–3; and M. Saville-Troike, *The Ethnography of Communication: An Introduction*, 2nd edn, Language in Society 3 (Oxford, 1989), p. 22.
[59] Eggins, *Systemic Functional Linguistics*, pp. 34–5.

Context of culture, moreover, not only provides the language user with their potential to mean but also serves as the source of all specific contexts of situation,[60] each of which is constituted by a set of constraints influencing choices of genre and the individual shapes into which the chosen genres are bent. In recent linguistic theory these constraints have been conceptualised in ways which a comprehensive study of the Lucan writings' situation could use to very good effect.[61] For the purposes of the more limited inquiry undertaken here, however, a simplified version of these conceptualisations ought to suffice, with context of situation being constituted by 'co-text'[62] (i.e., the particular story's verbal surroundings) and 'implied situation' (i.e., the type of social context in which the combined emphases of the stories would have been optimally relevant). As matters of co-text directly impact the meanings and force of each story, they receive attention in all four of the analyses below. My treatment of implied situation, on the other hand, is suspended until the story in Acts 16.16–18 has been carefully analysed; for by realising several prominent correspondences between the exorcistic ministry of Jesus and that of Paul, the story in Acts powerfully affects the interpretation of the Gospel narratives and therefore impinges on how the latter ought to be contextualised.

In the task of contextualisation, there is no substitute for detailed analysis, knowledge and description of the text, which, though hardly an unproblematic concept in the wake of postmodern theory and deconstruction, at least has the merit of being less ethereal than most notions of 'context'. Below and in the chapters that follow, the broad framework for this level of analysis (i.e., of text) is provided by Halliday's three linguistic metafunctions (i.e., the textual, ideational and interpersonal functions); but in order to transform this framework into a useful set of heuristic tools, each of the metafunctions needs to be broken down into the less abstract types of phenomena that realise its particular kind of potential. The textual function, for instance, can be broken down into phenomena such as cohesion, story structure, repetition, iconicity, thematic organisation and information structure.[63] The ideational function, on the other hand, is realised through features such as lexis, transitivity and verbal aspect.

---

[60] Halliday, *Language as Social Semiotic*, p. 68.
[61] See, e.g., G. Brown and G. Yule, *Discourse Analysis*, Cambridge Textbooks in Linguistics (Cambridge, 1983), pp. 38–9; Saville-Troike, *Ethnography*, pp. 138–57; Eggins, *Systemic Functional Linguistics*, pp. 49–80; van Dijk, *Pragmatics of Discourse*, pp. 224–8.
[62] For further discussion of co-text and its importance in discourse analysis, see, e.g., Brown and Yule, *Discourse Analysis*, pp. 46–50; Lyons, *Language, Meaning and Context*, p. 206; Halliday, *Language as Social Semiotic*, p. 133.
[63] On the types of linguistic features that belong to each of the three components, see Halliday, *Language as Social Semiotic*, p. 64.

And the interpersonal function is instantiated through features such as presupposition, implicature and intertextuality. Of course, which types of phenomena we map onto which metafunctions matters very little for purposes of linguistic analysis. What counts is that none of these phenomena get overlooked in the process of the analysis.

The categories just specified, therefore, are used in the present study as a linguistic-critical checklist. Each category is discussed further in the appropriate section below before being used in the analysis of Luke 4.33–37; but familiarity with them all will be assumed in the ensuing chapters.

A sociostylistic reading of Luke 4.33–37

The Greek text of the first exorcism story in Luke's Gospel reads as follows:

33 Καὶ ἐν τῇ συναγωγῇ ἦν ἄνθρωπος ἔχων πνεῦμα δαιμονίου ἀκαθάρτου καὶ ἀνέκραξεν φωνῇ μεγάλῃ· 34 Ἔα, τί ἡμῖν καὶ σοί, Ἰησοῦ Ναζαρηνέ; ἦλθες ἀπολέσαι ἡμᾶς; οἶδά σε τίς εἶ, ὁ ἅγιος τοῦ θεοῦ. 35 καὶ ἐπετίμησεν αὐτῷ ὁ Ἰησοῦς λέγων· φιμώθητι καὶ ἔξελθε ἀπ' αὐτοῦ. Καὶ ῥῖψαν αὐτὸν τὸ δαιμόνιον εἰς τὸ μέσον ἐξῆλθεν ἀπ' αὐτοῦ μηδὲν βλάψαν αὐτόν. 36 Καὶ ἐγένετο θάμβος ἐπὶ πάντας καὶ συνελάλουν πρὸς ἀλλήλους λέγοντες· τίς ὁ λόγος οὗτος ὅτι ἐν ἐξουσίᾳ καὶ δυνάμει ἐπιτάσσει τοῖς ἀκαθάρτοις πνεύμασιν καὶ ἐξέρχονται; 37 καὶ ἐξεπορεύετο ἦχος περὶ αὐτοῦ εἰς πάντα τόπον τῆς περιχώρου.

By locating the story's opening boundary at the beginning of 4.33, the interpretation offered in the present chapter already deviates from the majority of critical opinion. Most of my reasons for this divergence involve matters of cohesion and story structure, in which connection the boundaries are discussed further below; but the consequences of this judgement can be felt, in one way or another, on every level of the text's interpretation.

Cohesion

One of the main differences between word salad, or a nonsensical jumble of randomly combined verbal signs, and a bona fide text is that the constituents of the latter, unlike those of the former, evince a network of conventional and socially recognisable interconnections with each other. Indeed, in order to constitute a text, the individual words and larger elements of a verbal sequence have to be tied together by features other than mere spatio-temporal concurrence; collectively, they must manifest a quality that many linguists call 'cohesion',[64] which is created by several different types of linguistic phenomena. The most important of these are co-reference, ellipsis, lexical cohesion (e.g., repetition and collocation), and conjunction.[65]

An analysis of these devices in Luke 4.33–37 accomplishes at least two worthwhile purposes. First of all, it makes explicit the particular linguistic mechanisms that cause virtually all readers of this text to see its individual constituents as sticking together to form a larger unit. For example, the second καί in verse 33, directly preceding ἀνέκραξεν, ties together two complex constructions into a single sentence that does not conclude until the end of the demoniac's speech (4.34). In verse 35, moreover, the dative pronoun αὐτῷ, which functions as the direct object of ἐπετίμησεν, connects the story's second complex of clauses (4.35) to the first (4.33–34) by implicitly pointing back to the unclean demon of verses 33–34; and the link between these same two complexes is strengthened by an instance of lexical repetition, with ὁ Ἰησοῦς in 4.35 having the same referent as Ἰησοῦ Ναζαρηνέ back in 4.34.

Several other instances of lexical repetition – δαιμόνιον in verses 33 and 35, πνεῦμα and ἀκάθαρτον in verses 33 and 36, and ἐξέρχομαι in verses 35 and 36 – serve either to reinforce this linkage between the story's first two clause complexes, or to create a bond between those two and the third in 4.36, which consists of the bystanders' response to the exorcism. This latter relation is also tightened by the bystanders' use of ὁ λόγος οὗτος (4.36), where the demonstrative pronoun forges a link between this phrase and Jesus' command back in the preceding sentence (4.35). And finally, the story's last clause (καὶ ἐξεπορεύετο ἦχος περὶ αὐτοῦ εἰς πάντα τόπον τῆς περιχώρου) is tied to what precedes it not only by the additive καί but also by two anaphoric expressions: the pronoun αὐτοῦ, whose referent (i.e., Jesus) can be recovered only from the immediately preceding clauses, and the article τῆς qualifying περιχώρου, whose sense is entirely dependent on the earlier spatial references to the synagogue of Capernaum (4.31, 33).

In addition to explaining why the cohesion of these clauses is sensed almost intuitively by the non-exegete, this sort of analysis often produces insights that transcend those available to unaided intuition. For instance, although all of Luke 4.31–37, and not just 4.33–37, is related in one way

---

[64] See, e.g., Fowler, *Linguistic Criticism*, p. 61; *DS*, s.v. 'Coherence, Cohesion'.
[65] Fowler, *Linguistic Criticism*, pp. 61–8.

or another to the parallel material in Mark 1.21–28, differences between the two accounts' patterns of cohesion suggest that Luke 4.31–32 (unlike Mark 1.21–22) should be read as part of the exorcism story's co-text rather than as part of the story itself. To be more precise, in contrast to the direct speech of the bystanders in the Marcan account, whose reference to Jesus' exorcistic rebuke as a new διδαχή builds a strong cohesive tie back to the emphasis on Jesus' 'teaching' in Mark 1.21–22, the speech of the Lucan narrative's bystanders has no mention whatsoever of teaching; instead, as noted above, it refers to 'this word' (ὁ λόγος οὗτος), which is explicitly identified as Jesus' word of exorcism (ὅτι ἐν ἐξουσίᾳ καὶ δυνάμει ἐπιτάσσει τοῖς ἀκαθάρτοις πνεύμασιν) and implicitly distinguished from the word of teaching mentioned back in 4.32 (τῇ διδαχῇ αὐτοῦ... ὁ λόγος αὐτοῦ).

In other words, through careful analysis of the patterns of cohesion in the Lucan story and its Marcan parallel, a noteworthy contrast can be detected between Luke's and Mark's interpretation of the same material: everything that Jesus does in Mark 1.21–28 can be classified as 'teaching', whereas in Luke 4.31–37 the 'word' of Jesus' teaching (4.31–32) is tacitly distinguished from the 'word' of his exorcistic commands (4.35–36). Consequently, while Luke 4.31–37 is interpreted by most exegetes as a single unit, it should probably be read as two. Further support for this stance is offered below on the basis of other kinds of linguistic phenomena.

Story structure

Expanding on research published in 1972 by the sociolinguist W. Labov,[66] the stylistician M. Toolan has recently demonstrated that ordinary oral stories are made of the same structural and functional components that 'literary' narratives are made of.[67] In brief, those components are an *abstract*, which introduces the story proper by outlining it in a very abbreviated form;[68] an *orientation*, specifying what participants and circumstances are central to the world depicted in the narrative (i.e., the context of reference); *complicating action*, consisting of temporally ordered independent clauses that lead up to but do not include the climax of the story; *evaluation*, involving all the means used by the storyteller to establish the contextual value and significance of the story; a *resolution*, which is the most intense point in the sequence of narrated actions;

[66] See W. Labov, *Language in the Inner City* (Philadelphia, 1972).
[67] Toolan, *Narrative*, pp. 146–53.
[68] The definitions above are based on ibid., pp. 152–64.

and a *coda*, signalling that the end of the story has been reached. As Toolan observes, both the coda and the abstract can be thought of as a narrative's 'optional margins';[69] that is, unlike the other components just mentioned, the coda and abstract are not indispensable elements of story structure. In the analyses below this understanding of narrative structure will prove particularly valuable as an aid to establishing the boundaries of each narrative and clarifying the various functions of its parts.

As hinted above, while some interpreters have observed that the relationship between Luke 4.33–37 and the two verses that immediately precede it is quite ambiguous,[70] the two segments are usually treated not as two distinct units but rather as two components of one unified exorcism story.[71] If this approach were valid, 4.31–32 in particular ought to fulfil the narrative function of 'orientation'; that is, these verses should serve chiefly to specify the participants and circumstances of the ensuing account of exorcism. However, this understanding has some notable liabilities that most commentaries on Luke's Gospel do not mention. For one thing, although 4.31–32 does contain features that are best described as 'orientation' (e.g., 'he went down to Capernaum, a city of Galilee', 4.31), these verses also contain so many other features of narrative structure that, taken together, they resemble an embryonic story more than they resemble a mere orientation for what follows them.[72]

Furthermore, the last clause of 4.32 (ὅτι ἐν ἐξουσίᾳ ἦν ὁ λόγος αὐτοῦ), when read in the light of its ensuing co-text, can easily be read as a topical preview not just of 4.33–37 but of 4.33–44 as a whole.[73] For the motif of Jesus' authoritative word runs through all four of the units that constitute this section (4.33–37, 38–39, 40–41, 42–44).[74] Thus, to the degree that

---

[69] Ibid., p. 153.

[70] See, e.g., Fitzmyer, *Luke I–IX*, p. 542; and I. H. Marshall, *The Gospel of Luke: A Commentary on the Greek Text*, NIGTC (Grand Rapids, 1978), p. 191.

[71] See, e.g., Kirschläger, *Jesu exorzistisches Wirken*, p. 28. Marshall, *Gospel of Luke*, pp. 190–2, and L. Sabourin, *L'Evangile de Luc: Introduction et commentaire* (Rome, 1985), pp. 137–8, are exceptions.

[72] Verse 31b (καὶ ἦν διδάσκων αὐτοὺς ἐν τοῖς σάββασιν), e.g., includes not only 'orientation' but also 'complicating action', while 4.32 (καὶ ἐξεπλήσσοντο ἐπὶ τῇ διδαχῇ αὐτοῦ, ὅτι ἐν ἐξουσίᾳ ἦν ὁ λόγος αὐτοῦ) is a combination of 'resolution' and 'evaluation'.

[73] Cf. Marshall, *Gospel of Luke*, p. 190. Kirschläger, *Jesu exorzistisches Wirken*, pp. 28–32, which treats 4.31–37 as a single unit, emphasises the links between 4.31–32 and 4.33–37 but says nothing about the connections between 4.31–32 and 4.38–44.

[74] In 4.33–37 there is, e.g., Jesus' exorcistic rebuke (4.35) and the witnesses' attribution of authority and power to Jesus' word (4.36); in 4.38–39 is Jesus' rebuke of the fever (4.39); in 4.40–41 Jesus expels more demons, refusing them permission to speak of his messianic identity (4.41); and in 4.42–44 Jesus does not allow the Caperneans to keep him in their city but draws attention to the divine necessity that he preach the kingdom of God in other

4.31–32 functions as an orientation at all, it orientates the reader to the next four pericopes of the narrative rather than merely to 4.33–37;[75] the two verses are best understood, therefore, not as an integral element of the Gospel's first exorcism narrative but rather as part of that story's co-text.

This interpretation of the relationship between 4.31–32 and 4.33–37 is confirmed, moreover, by an examination of the latter unit's own internal structure. For 4.33–37 contains all the essential elements of a fully formed narrative. There is (1) an orientation, specifying the participants of the action (e.g., a possessed man and an unclean demon) and the circumstances in which it occurred ('in the synagogue'); (2) complicating action, consisting of the demon's recognition of Jesus and Jesus' words of rebuke; (3) a resolution, constituted by the demon's submissive and non-injurious departure from the man; and (4) an evaluation, establishing the story's relevance by disclosing the amazement and reports which the exorcism produced. To be sure, 4.33–37 does not include either an abstract or a coda; but as already noted above, these two elements are not essential to the structure of a complete narrative.

Repetition

In addition to aiding cohesion, the reiteration of a particular lexical item or grammatical structure can create a layer of meaning that goes beyond the propositional sense of the text. It can contribute, more precisely, to a phenomenon that many linguists and literary theorists call 'foregrounding', which is the highlighting of particular linguistic features against the unmarked background of the rest of the text.[76] As Fowler notes, general guidelines as to what degree of repetition is necessary to produce an instance of foregrounding are extremely difficult to devise;[77] but a useful rule of thumb is that if a particular instance of repetition is not essential

---

cities too. For additional evidence of the unity of 4.31–44, see M. D. Goulder, *Luke: A New Paradigm*, JSNTSup 20 (Sheffield, 1989), I, pp. 312, 315–16; Busse, *Die Wunder des Propheten Jesus*, I, pp. 67–9; and H. Schürmann, *Das Lukasevangelium: Erster Teil: Kommentar zu Kap. 1,1–9,50*, HKNT 3/1 (Freiburg, 1969), I, pp. 244–5, each of whom understands 4.31–32 and 4.42–44 as providing a frame for 4.31–44 as a whole.

[75] The place (Capernaum) and time (on the sabbath) mentioned in 4.31 are the place and time in which all the activities of 4.33–43 occur, as the references to time and place in verses 40, 42 and 43 suggest. Moreover, the inclusio created by the occurrence of πόλις in verses 31 and 43 reinforces the impression that 4.31–32 serves as an introduction for all of 4.33–43, not just for 4.33–37; on this latter point, cf. F. O. Fearghail, *The Introduction to Luke–Acts: A Study of the Role of Luke 1,1–4,44 in the Composition of Luke's Two Volume Work*, AnBib 126 (Rome, 1991), p. 25.

[76] Fowler, *Linguistic Criticism*, p. 73.   [77] Ibid.

for sense or clarity and exceeds the frequency of occurrence the repeated item might be expected to have in similar types of text, then the feature in question may well possess foregrounded status.[78]

For instance, although the noun συναγωγή occurs only once in 4.33–37, its repeated occurrence in the immediately preceding co-text (4.15, 16, 20, 28) raises the possibility that it may have special prominence in this context. This begins to look likely, moreover, when we recognise that the same instance of repetition gives rise to both a startling contrast and a case of dramatic irony. As for the contrast, whereas the synagogue of Nazareth emerges by Luke 4.28 as a place where 'everyone' (πάντες) feels great 'wrath' (θυμός) toward Jesus, the synagogue of Capernaum develops by Luke 4.36 into a place where 'everyone' (πάντας) is overwhelmed with 'amazement' (θάμβος).[79] The foregrounding of συναγωγή therefore draws attention to the conflicting responses which Jesus evokes in the synagogues. As for the irony, whereas the συναγωγή of Nazareth virtually demonises Jesus, treating him as a danger that ought to be cast outside the city (4.29), the συναγωγή of Capernaum is itself demonised, having to rely on Jesus to cast an unclean spirit from its midst.

Foregrounding also arises from the repetition of ἐξέρχομαι, which occurs three times in 4.35–36 (cf. Mark 1.25–26). In 4.35a Jesus commands the demon, ἔξελθε ἀπ' αὐτοῦ; in 4.35b the demon's departure is represented in ἐξῆλθεν ἀπ' αὐτοῦ; and in 4.36 the bystanders marvel that when Jesus issues his exorcistic injunctions, the unclean spirits ἐξέρχονται. The repetition in this instance foregrounds the correspondence between Jesus' command, the demon's response, and the bystanders' observation;[80] and since the constructions that represent Jesus' command and the demon's departure are particularly close to one another both in form and in the

---

[78] Cf. S. Bar-Efrat, *Narrative Art in the Bible*, trans. D. Shefer-Vanson, JSOTSup 70 (Sheffield, 1989), p. 212.

[79] The narrator's descriptions of the responses in verses 28 and 36 as θυμός and θάμβος may represent a deliberate paronomasia, for θάμβος, which occurs only three times in the NT, is relatively uncommon. The wordplay would make the contrast between the two responses even more noteworthy. θάμβος also occurs in a second-century BCE inscription in which a young priest of Serapis is described as having been astonished by a nocturnal epiphany of the deity; and just as Luke must show Jesus' identification with ancestral custom (i.e., Elijah and Isaianic prophecy), so the narrator of this inscription must accentuate his own connection with a long line of priests, one of the most recent being described as having 'performed his service in accordance with the ancestral custom'. For the inscription see F. W. Danker, *Benefactor: Epigraphic Study of a Graeco-Roman and New Testament Semantic Field* (St. Louis, 1982), pp. 186–90 (no. 27).

[80] The correspondence noted here is more intense in Luke than in Mark, for the Marcan parallel to Luke's third ἐξέρχομαι is the lexically unrelated ὑπακούουσιν (Mark 1.27).

text's sequencing, the authority and power of Jesus' word are almost impossible to overlook in this context. The same emphasis, moreover, is reinforced by other features noted below.

Iconicity

Although the vast majority of individual linguistic signs are related to their meanings in an entirely conventional way, a few are widely understood to function in a less arbitrary fashion, to mimic or imitate somehow the objects they signify.[81] This latter phenomenon, often referred to as 'iconicity', has been limited by many theorists to instances of onomatopoeia, which involves the use of words that actually sound like the phenomena they refer to (e.g., cuckoo, zoom, pop);[82] but some linguists have recently suggested that, especially once analysis moves beyond individual words to larger linguistic structures, the impression that certain aspects of language are being used to imitate certain aspects of reality is commonplace even in everyday usage.[83] For instance, chronological sequencing in a narrative creates the impression that real time in the context of reference is being imitated by textual time in the linear sequencing of the story; a similar impression is conveyed when effects are narrated after their assumed causes, particularly since this sequence corresponds to that of so much experience in real time.[84]

Narrative sequencing of this latter variety constitutes the most noteworthy instance of iconicity in the present story. As noted above in regard to repetition, the recurrence of the verb ἐξέρχομαι with ἀπ' αὐτοῦ in 4.35 foregrounds the correspondence between Jesus' command and the demon's response. What is easily overlooked, however, is that the cause–effect relationship between Jesus' command and the demon's departure is never asserted explicitly in the text; rather, it is merely implied by means of the sequencing and juxtaposition of the two processes. And since one of this strategy's primary consequences is to reinforce the instance of repetition just noted, it causes the motif of Jesus' ability to influence the impure spirits to stand out very prominently in this context.

If by the end of 4.35 Jesus' power and authority do not already enjoy a frontgrounded status, they surely do so by the end of 4.36, where, in the bystanders' speech and by means of the same iconic type of strategy

---

[81] *DS*, s.v. 'Icon, Iconicity'; Leech and Short, *Style in Fiction*, pp. 233–5.
[82] *DS*, s.v. 'Onomatopoeia'. [83] Leech and Short, *Style in Fiction*, p. 234.
[84] Ibid., pp. 234–5.

just observed, the authority-and-power motif is accentuated yet again. More specifically, when the bystanders observe that Jesus ἐπιτάσσει τοῖς ἀκαθάρτοις πνεύμασιν καὶ ἐξέρχονται, the causal link between command and response is conveyed neither by the propositional sense of the assertions themselves nor by the logic of their interconnection but rather, as in 4.35, by means of juxtaposition and sequencing.

Thematic organisation and information structure

Because texts are composed only one constituent (i.e., word, phrase, clause, etc.) at a time, all language users are confronted – whether they realise it or not – by what discourse analysts call the 'linearisation problem'.[85] That is, the language user has to choose a point of departure, to decide which constituents of the text shall be placed first and which later; and since what comes first constitutes the initial co-text for what comes afterward, the linear sequencing of words and groups constrains how any particular word or group can be interpreted.[86]

Unfortunately, any serious attempt to analyse linearisation in the Lucan exorcism stories must face at the outset a couple of difficulties. In the first place, among modern linguists there is nothing approaching unanimity regarding how this kind of analysis ought to be carried out; and just as importantly, much of the conventional wisdom concerning word order in Hellenistic Greek – a topic that bears very directly on the study of linearisation in the Greek New Testament – is being increasingly recognised as linguistically naïve and empirically unrefined.[87] Nevertheless, the possibility of gaining interpretative insight into this aspect of the Lucan stories should by no means be dismissed; for the difficulties just noted have been made less obstructive by recent developments in the study of Hellenistic Greek and the functionalist approach to grammar.

A promising method of analysing linearisation within individual clauses, for instance, has been adapted by Halliday from the post-war Prague School's concept of Functional Sentence Perspective, and developed so as to view the clause's internal order from two different angles. On the one hand, a clause can be seen as consisting of a theme (i.e., a topic or beginning) and a rheme (i.e., a comment, or the part in which the theme is developed), the theme being what the sender chooses as the clause's linear point of departure.[88] On the other hand, a clause can also

---

[85] Brown and Yule, *Discourse Analysis*, p. 125.   [86] Ibid., pp. 125–6.
[87] See, e.g., S. E. Porter, *Idioms of the Greek New Testament*, Biblical Languages: Greek 2 (Sheffield, 1992), pp. 293, 295.
[88] Halliday, *Functional Grammar*, pp. 38–9, 278.

be understood as an interplay of information that is 'given' (i.e., easily known or predictable by the receiver on the basis of preceding co-text or situation) and information that is 'new', with some clauses consisting entirely of the new.[89] Moreover, when information of the given variety occupies the position of theme, and new occupies that of rheme, the linearisation of the clause can be characterised as unmarked; that is, the way the information and thematic structures have been mapped onto one another is semantically unremarkable.[90] But quite often what is informationally new can be found either in a clause's thematic element, or with one foot in the theme and the other foot in the rheme;[91] and when this occurs, the receiver is presented with an interpretative possibility. Does the departure from standard order reflect an effort by the sender to place special emphasis on the new information? Or does it serve some other purpose — for instance, to indicate a change of grammatical subject so that the receiver might not be baffled by the ensuing main verb?[92]

As Halliday and others have pointed out, these sorts of questions can be answered responsibly only if the interpreter considers the 'local conditions' (especially the immediately preceding co-text) of the clause in question.[93] But another factor that has to be taken into account is the distinctiveness of Greek word order. While further study in this area is sorely needed, a modest but growing body of research is suggesting that what constitutes marked and unmarked sequences in Greek depends a great deal on what elements (verb, subject, object, etc.) are actually expressed in the clause being analysed.[94] Many clauses in the Greek NT, for instance, have a predicate (i.e., a verb or verb phrase) but neither an expressed subject nor a complement (i.e., a direct or indirect object).[95] Many others, moreover, have both a predicate and a complement but no expressed subject, the predicate–complement order and the complement–predicate sequence being almost equal in frequency. And when the subject of a clause *is* expressed, it usually precedes both the predicate and the complement.[96] Consequently, when we look for potential departures

---

[89] Ibid., pp. 274–5.   [90] Ibid., pp. 276–7.   [91] Ibid., pp. 274–6.
[92] For further discussion of this dilemma and its relevance to the Greek NT, see S. Levinsohn, *Textual Connections in Acts*, SBLMS 31 (Atlanta, 1987), pp. xv, 1, 6; and Porter, *Idioms*, pp. 295–6.
[93] Halliday, *Functional Grammar*, pp. 278–9; Brown and Yule, *Discourse Analysis*, p. 180.
[94] See Porter, *Idioms*, pp. 293–6.
[95] For examples of this and the other types of clauses mentioned here, see ibid., pp. 294–5.
[96] Ibid., p. 295.

from 'normal' (i.e., unmarked) structures of thematisation and information in the Lucan narratives, our assumptions about what would be normal for a particular clause need to be informed by the complications just mentioned.

In Luke 4.33–37 two instances of unusual sequencing invite comment. First, in contrast both to the parallel in Mark 1.23 and to Luke's own normal word order, the first clause of our story has a prepositional phrase – ἐν τῇ συναγωγῇ – in front of the verb to which it is linked (ἦν).[97] Although most commentators give no attention to this feature,[98] it definitely deviates from the usual sequencing and calls for explanation. Since συναγωγή is used four times as an object of preposition in the immediately preceding co-text (4.15, 16, 20, 28), we might be tempted to view ἐν τῇ συναγωγῇ in 4.33 as 'given' rather than 'new', the unusual sequencing therefore being due to the phrase's allegedly low information value rather than to a desire to stress it. Against this explanation, however, are (a) the newness of the referent envisaged by συναγωγή in 4.33 – the synagogue in the first exorcism story is *not* the one envisaged back in 4.15–30 – and (b) the unmarked location of εἰς τὴν συναγωγήν in 4.16, which, by echoing the normal order of the immediately preceding verse (ἐδίδασκεν ἐν ταῖς συναγωγαῖς αὐτῶν, 4.15), indicates that even a prepositional phrase that is informationally 'given' is likely to occur *after* the verb to which it is linked.

Consequently, the sequencing of 4.33 is best understood as foregrounding ἐν τῇ συναγωγῇ; and, in light of the repetition of συναγωγή in the antecedent co-text (4.15, 16, 20, 28), where Jesus' impolite interpretation of Scripture almost gets him killed by people from the synagogue (4.23–30), the phrase's prominence has a couple of noteworthy effects: paradoxically, while it reinforces the image of Jesus as a good Jew who routinely participates in Jewish assemblies, it also represents these assemblies as places of unholy influence – unclean demons (4.33, 36), for instance, and people with murderous inclinations (4.28–29) – which have nothing in common with the holy God of Jewish Scripture.[99] This

---

[97] Of ninety-nine prepositional phrases with expressed verbs in Luke 1.1–38 and 4.1–30, only twelve occur before the verb; we therefore might assume, at least tentatively, that the typical location of prepositional phrases in Luke is after the verbs to which they are connected.

[98] See, e.g., Bovon, *Luc (1,1–9,50)*, p. 216; Kirschläger, *Jesu exorzistisches Wirken*, p. 35; Fitzmyer, *Luke I–IX*, pp. 542–4.

[99] A similar strategy is probably operative in Acts 3.1–10, where, in the space of ten verses, Luke reminds the reader six times that Peter's healing of the lame man took place at the ἱερός, the heart of the Jewish cult.

combination of emphases would have had much relevance in a context of intra-Jewish social conflict, a scenario explored in further detail below in my treatment of the Lucan stories' implied situation.

The second instance of marked sequencing occurs on the lips of the witnesses (4.36). After asking in amazement τίς ὁ λόγος οὗτος, they proceed to marvel, ὅτι ἐν ἐξουσίᾳ καὶ δυνάμει ἐπιτάσσει τοῖς ἀκαθάρτοις πνεύμασιν καὶ ἐξέρχονται. Once again, the construction in marked position is a prepositional phrase – in this instance, ἐν ἐξουσίᾳ καὶ δυνάμει – whose prominence is signalled, like that of ἐν τῇ συναγωγῇ in 4.33, by its pre-verbal position in the clause; and, since the immediate effect of this sequencing is to highlight the authority and power of Jesus' exorcistic 'word', it ultimately reinforces an idea already foregrounded by several of the features noted above (e.g., the repetition of ἐξέρχομαι). Furthermore, as the 'word' (λόγος) in Luke's writings can denote not only Jesus' therapeutic utterance but also his teaching (4.32) and that of his earliest followers,[100] its occurrence here in 4.36 could have heightened the relevance of this story for the audience of converts to which Luke–Acts was probably first addressed.[101]

Transitivity

In the prescriptive tradition of grammar taught in English composition and many foreign language courses, discussion of transitivity normally involves whether a given verb needs a direct object in order to complete its meaning.[102] In the vocabulary of functional grammar, however, transitivity involves the entire intra-clausal structure of relations between processes (represented by verb phrases), participants (noun phrases), and circumstances (adverbial phrases).[103] By analysing a text's transitivity in this latter sense, and thus in terms of the choices it reflects in the three

---

[100] See, e.g., Acts 2.41; 4.4; 10.44; 15.32; 20.2; cf. Schürmann, *Das Lukasevangelium*, I, p. 245.

[101] The parallel in Mark 1.27, which has an anaphoric τοῦτο without λόγος, does less to establish the story's relevance. The Christian character of Luke's intended audience is discussed further in ch. 4, pp. 241–2; but see also M. P. Bonz, *The Past as Legacy: Luke–Acts and Ancient Epic* (Minneapolis, 2000), pp. 25–9; J. Jervell, 'The Church of Jews and Godfearers', in Tyson (ed.), *Luke–Acts and the Jewish People*, pp. 11–20; L. C. A. Alexander, *The Preface to Luke's Gospel: Literary Convention and Social Context in Luke 1.1–4 and Acts 1.1*, SNTSMS 78 (Cambridge, 1993), p. 112; Esler, *Community and Gospel*, pp. 24–6.

[102] J. C. Hodges and M. E. Whitten, *Harbrace College Handbook*, 7th edn (New York, 1972), p. 490.

[103] Toolan, *Narrative*, pp. 112, 238–9; *DS*, s.v. 'Transitive Verb, Transitivity'.

areas just noted and the way these choices are combined to make clauses, we can learn a great deal about the world-view of the text's producer. In order therefore to understand the world-view(s) represented in Luke's exorcism stories, the present study gives ample attention both to the transitivity of select clauses in each story and to any interesting patterns that emerge from the sequencing and distribution of different clause types across the story as a whole.

One of the most useful contributions of functional grammar to linguistic criticism is its observation that, for purposes of grammatical analysis, differences between verbs are just as important as their similarities. Most notably, verbs differ in regard to the character of the processes they can signify; and according to Halliday and several other functionalists, these differences are best conceptualised as a system of six alternative process types, namely (1) the material (i.e., processes of doing), (2) the mental (i.e., processes of thinking and knowing), (3) the relational (i.e., processes of being), (4) the behavioural (physiological and psychological behaviour, typically involving only one participant), (5) the verbal (i.e., saying), and (6) the existential.[104] While all these types of processes can appear in a single brief text, in many instances one kind of process will be more prominent than the others; or, just as significantly, a particular character in the text might be frequently associated with one or two types of processes, whereas other characters might be repeatedly associated with other types.

Choices of verb, therefore, can powerfully influence the way a text's various participants are characterised. Indeed, one of the greatest strengths of the functionalist approach is that, unlike prescriptive grammar, it provides a terminology for distinguishing the types of participants associated with one kind of process from those associated with another. For instance, whereas traditional grammar would refer to 'I' as the *subject* in both 'I am sick' and 'I hit the ball', Hallidayan functionalism would refer to 'I' as a 'token' (or 'carrier') in the first clause but call the 'I' in the second clause an 'actor' (or 'agent'), the basis of the distinction being that the difference between a material process like 'hit' and a relational one like 'am' necessarily creates a significant functional difference between the two grammatical subjects – even if, as here, the subject is formally the same word in both cases. By reminding the interpreter that not all 'subjects' are created equal,[105] this type of analysis can powerfully refine

---

[104] Halliday, *Functional Grammar*, pp. 102–31; Toolan, *Narrative*, pp. 113–15.
[105] What I am saying here about subjects is equally true of direct objects, indirect objects, and other types of nominal groups.

exegesis. The following table summarises the participant roles related to each of the six process types.

Process	Participant(s)
material	– actor (or agent), goal
behavioural	– behaver
mental	– senser, phenomenon
verbal	– sayer, target, verbiage, receiver
relational	– token (i.e., carrier or identified) and value (i.e. attribute or identifier)
existential	– existent[106]

Finally, in addition to including processes and participants, many clauses contain circumstantial elements, which can function in all the ways known to traditional syntax. Adverbials carry a variety of semantic nuances – modal, instrumental, agentive, temporal, causal, conditional and concessional being probably the most common. However, as M. Toolan observes, circumstantial elements often convey evaluative overtones that transcend their overt sense.[107] For instance, in the clause 'Brian lost his mind in the Department of Economics', the overt function of the circumstantial element 'in the Department of Economics' is merely to indicate the environment in which Brian lost his mind; but in certain types of context, the same construction could easily realise an incriminating, causal meaning – to be precise, 'Brian lost his mind *because* of the Department of Economics'.

When the approach to transitivity just outlined is applied to Luke 4.33–37, some significant patterns become evident in the relations between process types and the characters associated with them in the story. First of all, consider the possessed man. In 4.33 the narrator says that the man 'was' in the synagogue, that he 'had' a demon, and that he 'cried out with a great voice'. None of the verbs in these clauses signifies a material process; two of them represent relational processes ('was' and 'had'); and the third denotes a verbal (or symbolic) one. But perhaps most importantly, none of these verbs involves the man in a process that affects the state of another participant.

Subsequently, in 4.35, the same man is directly involved in two material processes – those represented by καὶ ῥῖψαν αὐτὸν τὸ δαιμόνιον εἰς τὸ μέσον and μηδὲν βλάψαν αὐτόν – but in both cases he is the 'goal' (i.e.,

---

[106] This summary is based on Halliday, *Functional Grammar*, p. 131. In the next four chapters, every reference made to a participant (e.g., 'actor', 'existent') will be placed between quotation marks in order to indicate that the term is being used in a special sense.

[107] Toolan, *Narrative*, p. 239.

the affected participant) rather than the 'actor'. After the second of these processes, moreover, he is not mentioned again. Not once, therefore, is this man portrayed as an agent of a material action.

Consider next the demon. If understood as inspiring the speech of his unfortunate host (4.34), he can be seen as the 'sayer' in the verbal process signified by ἀνέκραξεν (4.33). Afterwards, he is the 'senser' in the mental process represented by οἶδα (4.34), and the 'behaver' in the behavioural process denoted by ἐξῆλθεν (4.35). In both ἔα ('Leave us alone') and ἦλθες ἀπολέσαι ἡμᾶς (4.34), moreover, the demon characterises himself as a potential 'goal' in material actions he fears Jesus might perform. Consequently, apart from his inspiration of the man's loud cry, the demon's only action that affects anyone other than himself is his propulsion of the man into the middle of the synagogue (ῥῖψαν αὐτὸν... τὸ μέσον, 4.35). After this, he is distinguished more by what he fails to do than by what he does: at his departure, he is unable to harm the man (μηδὲν βλάψαν αὐτόν, 4.35). Thus, while the demon is more dynamic in this story's processes than his human victim is, he nevertheless appears to be severely inhibited by the presence of Jesus.

The exorcism's witnesses, who are not mentioned until 4.36, are comparable to the demon and his victim in regard to how little they affect their environment; but from the standpoint of transitivity and its contribution to characterisation, they are potentially more interesting. Most significantly, although the witnesses function collectively as the 'sayer' in the verbal processes signified by συνελάλουν πρὸς ἀλλήλους λέγοντες, they are backgrounded elsewhere in the story by virtue of two noteworthy instances of nominalisation.[108] One of these finds expression in καὶ ἐγένετο θάμβος ἐπὶ πάντας, where use of the deverbal noun θάμβος as the clause's subject tacitly portrays 'amazement' as an abstract force impacting the witnesses from without, who therefore fill a passive role in the action's circumstances.[109] The second occurs in the note about the consequent

---

[108] Nominalisation, which is rarely explained or commented on in conventional commentaries and exegetical tools, is that process of word-formation whereby nouns (e.g. θάμβος) are derived from verbs (e.g., θαμβέω) so that processes can be represented as abstract participants in yet other processes (e.g., '*amazement* came upon them'); *DS*, s.v. 'Nominal group; noun phrase (NP); nominalization'.

[109] On ἐγένετο θάμβος as a circumlocution for ἐθαμβήθησαν, see E. Klostermann, *Das Lukasevangelium*, 3rd edn, HNT 5 (Tübingen, 1975), p. 429. As ἐγένετο is introduced by καί in this instance, Bovon, *Luc (1,1–9,50)*, p. 213, suggests this might be an occurrence of the septuagintism that corresponds to discourse-initial ויהי in biblical narrative; but since the latter usage is typically followed by either a finite verb or an infinitive (e.g., Luke 1.8, 23, 41, 59; 2.1, 6, 15, 46; 3.21; 5.1 et al.), neither of which is present here, it is unlikely in this context.

report's dissemination into the surrounding region (καὶ ἐξεπορεύετο ἦχος περὶ αὐτοῦ εἰς πάντα τόπον τῆς περιχώρου, 4.37), in which the absence of human agents in the participant slot combines with the abstract noun ἦχος ('report') to represent a thoroughly human process as if it had occurred without human instrumentality. As a result, the witnesses do not directly affect any other participant in the narrative but rather are affected by what transpires around them.

And finally, there is the participant profile of Jesus. As noted above, the first word uttered by the demon (ἔα, 'leave us alone') implicitly characterises Jesus as a potential agent of material action that would directly impact the collective speaker. Then, in the demon's claim οἶδά σε τίς εἶ (4.35), Jesus functions as the 'identified' participant in a relational process. And finally, in both ἐπετίμησεν αὐτῷ ὁ 'Ιησοῦς (4.35) and ἐπιτάσσει τοῖς ἀκαθάρτοις πνεύμασιν (4.36), Jesus is portrayed as the powerful 'sayer' in processes which, though overtly verbal, have material effects on the spirit(s) and consequences for everyone in the synagogue. Jesus, therefore, stands out as an agent of highly influential action in a context where, by contrast, every other participant is defined chiefly by how much they are affected by what goes on around them.

Vocabulary

While linguists and philosophers of language have by no means ceased arguing about how the relationship between language and thought may best be characterised, few would deny that one of the most important resources for creating ideational meaning is the lexicon – the vocabulary or stock of words – to which the language user has access. The study of individual lexemes in their respective contexts therefore plays a significant part in the analyses below.

Fortunately, in the last forty years the field of lexical semantics has contributed so much to biblical studies that explanation of concepts can be kept to a minimum here.[110] The only explanation necessary, in fact, concerns the difference between denotative and connotative levels of lexical meaning. The former, which some stylisticians prefer to designate 'sense', corresponds to the basic conceptual or paraphrasable layer of meaning normally indicated by dictionaries.[111] Connotations, on the other hand, consist of the various emotive, evaluative and associative

---

[110] On key works that have mediated the contribution, see J. P. Louw and E. A. Nida, *Lexical Semantics of the Greek New Testament*, SBLRBS 25 (Atlanta, 1992), pp. 120–1.

[111] Leech and Short, *Style in Fiction*, pp. 23, 31.

overtones that often get added to a word or phrase by virtue of its context.[112] Although both types of phenomena need to be considered by the interpreter, the connotative level often suffers neglect in biblical exegesis and commentary, perhaps because much of the original context of usage is unrecoverable. Nevertheless, by consciously probing for connotations in the light of each story's immediate co-text and patterns of lexical collocation, the present study raises a number of interpretative possibilities that tend to be overlooked in the normal denotative approach to exegesis.

In Luke 4.33–37 several items of vocabulary merit special attention, some due to their ambiguity and others due to their importance to Luke's message. The first lexical difficulty in this passage is found in the phrase πνεῦμα δαιμονίου ἀκαθάρτου (4.33), which occurs nowhere else in the NT[113] and where either δαιμόνιον by itself, πνεῦμα ἀκαθάρτον, or πνεῦμα πονηρόν might have been expected. Although the basic sense of the words is clarified by their syntax – δαιμονίου ἀκαθάρτου is best read as appositional to πνεῦμα ('a spirit, that is, an unclean demon')[114] – we still might wish to learn why this unusual construction was used rather than one of the more common expressions just mentioned. Consideration of the preceding co-text affords a most useful clue: unlike Mark, who employs πνεῦμα only three times prior to his parallel in 1.23, Luke has by this point in his narrative already established a pattern of usage that strongly associates πνεῦμα with the Holy Spirit. Having used πνεῦμα in this latter connection no less than fourteen times in Luke 1.1–4.32,[115] Luke may have sensed a need, especially after beginning the key phrase in 4.33 with πνεῦμα, to underscore the difference between the referent of all his previous uses of this term and that envisaged here.[116] δαιμονίου ἀκαθάρτου, precisely because it is unusual, achieves this effect very well.

Despite the peculiarity of this particular combination, however, the occurrence of δαιμόνιον in 4.33 marks the beginning of what eventually becomes a pattern in Luke's usage: with twenty-two occurrences of δαιμόνιον in his Gospel, Luke is by far the NT's most enthusiastic user of the term. Furthermore, as δαιμόνιον in the LXX usually has

---

[112] Turner, *Stylistics*, pp. 27–8.
[113] The parallel in Mark 1.23, e.g., reads πνεύματι ἀκαθάρτῳ.
[114] Cf. J. Schmid, *Das Evangelium nach Lukas*, 4th edn, RNT 3 (Regensburg, 1960), p. 117; Klostermann, *Das Lukasevangelium*, p. 429; BAGD, s.v. 'πνεῦμα'. For an unusual and unconvincing alternative, see H. Hendrickx, *The Miracle Stories of the Synoptic Gospels* (San Francisco, 1987), p. 58, who views the man's spirit as being 'caused' by the unclean demon.
[115] E.g., Luke 1.15, 35; 2.25–26; 3.22; 4.1.   [116] Cf. Green, *Gospel of Luke*, p. 222.

associations with foreign deities and idolatry,[117] its employment in this context evokes an analogy between Jesus' battle against the demons and the Israelite prophets' warfare against pagan idols.[118] The analogy is reinforced, moreover, by the demon's words τί ἡμῖν καὶ σοί (Luke 4.34), which as discussed below echo the context of Elijah's fight against Israelite idolatry.[119]

The attributive adjective ἀκάθαρτος also deserves attention. As nothing in this episode itself compels us to see ritual impurity here, it is tempting to assume that the uncleanness in question is of a strictly moral variety;[120] but this sort of assumption undoubtedly oversimplifies the matter. In the first place, although the setting in which this impurity is found – the συναγωγή – is best understood as an assembly whose functions were not limited to strictly religious matters, it none the less would have been associated in the minds of many readers with Jewish identity, community cohesion and religious celebrations,[121] all of which could be profoundly affected by instances of ritual impurity. But more significantly, since the use of καθαρίζω in the immediately preceding co-text (4.27) denotes the removal of a specifically ritual type of impurity (i.e., Naaman's skin disorder), the use of ἀκάθαρτος in this context has excellent potential for connoting a condition of ritual impurity, whose cause is understood to be demonic in nature.[122] As discussed below however in my treatment of Luke 8.26–39, the moral and ritual aspects of impurity in Luke's context of culture could in some instances become so tightly intertwined that separating them is impossible.

Particularly in view of the eschatological reverberations that permeate the preceding co-text of this passage (cf. 4.18), this same occurrence of ἀκάθαρτος may furthermore serve to evoke an additional, connotative layer of meaning; for in LXX Zechariah 13.2 the Lord says that the eschatological renewal will be distinguished by the removal not only

---

[117] See, e.g., Deut. 32.17; LXX Pss. 95.5; 105.37; Isa. 13.21; 34.14; 65.11; Bar. 4.7, 35; cf. BAGD, s.v. 'δαιμόνιον'.

[118] Cf. G. Theissen, *The Miracle Stories of the Early Christian Tradition*, trans. F. McDonagh (Edinburgh, 1983), p. 256.

[119] Ibid., pp. 255–6.

[120] Cf. BAGD, s.v. 'ἀκάθαρτος'.

[121] On the diverse functions of Galilean synagogues in this milieu, see R. A. Horsley, *Archaeology, History, and Society in Galilee: The Social Context of Jesus and the Rabbis* (Valley Forge, 1996), pp. 150–1. On the wide and abiding influence of Levitical concepts of impurity and illness in late Second Temple Judaism, see Avalos, *Health Care and the Rise of Christianity*, pp. 67–71.

[122] On the cultic connotations of πνεύματα ἀκάθαρτα, see R. Leivestad, *Christ the Conqueror: Ideas of Conflict and Victory in the New Testament* (London, 1954), p. 42.

of the ψευδοπροφήτας[123] but also of 'the unclean spirit' (τὸ πνεῦμα τὸ ἀκάθαρτον). Now as the removal of an unclean spirit is precisely what the Lucan story represents at its climax (4.35), the co-occurrence of ἀκάθαρτον with πνεῦμα in verses 33 and 36 can easily be interpreted as part of an intertextual strategy designed to portray the exorcistic work of Jesus as a fulfilment of Zechariah's prophecy.

This eschatological flavour of the passage becomes even stronger when Luke uses ἐπιτιμάω in 4.35 to denote Jesus' mighty rebuke of the demon. As H. C. Kee has observed, both ἐπιτιμάω in the LXX and its Hebrew equivalent גער frequently refer to the sovereign word of command by which the Lord asserts his rule and brings the forces of chaos into subjection.[124] Jesus' rebuke of unclean spirits (here and 9.42), fever demons (4.39), and powers of the wind and sea (8.24) strongly resemble the processes denoted by the same term in the LXX, so that the authoritative word of Jesus in these contexts becomes closely associated with the cosmic rule of Israel's God. The eschatological dimension of this theme furthermore coheres well with the strategic logion of Jesus in Luke 11.20: 'If it is by the finger of God that I cast out demons, then the kingdom of God has come upon you.'

The words quoted in 4.35, φιμώθητι καὶ ἔξελθε ἀπ' αὐτοῦ, give additional insight into the meaning of ἐπετίμησεν in this context. Most notably, the rebuke consists of a couple of highly direct injunctions,[125] which not only express Jesus' desire to stifle and relocate the demon but also imply that he had confidence in his own ability to achieve these ends. Both the reality and the validity of this confidence, moreover, are accentuated in the ensuing observation by the exorcism's witnesses, ἐν ἐξουσίᾳ καὶ δυνάμει ἐπιτάσσει τοῖς ἀκαθάρτοις πνεύμασιν καὶ ἐξέρχονται (4.36).

Several other key words warrant at least brief attention. In the demon's rhetorical question in 4.34, ἦλθες ἀπολέσαι ἡμᾶς, the verb ἀπόλλυμι has the relatively straightforward sense of 'destroy'; but in view of this term's frequent use in the LXX to signify the destruction of Israel's enemies (e.g., the Egyptians in Exod. 10.7; the Canaanites and foreign idols in Num.

---

[123] Cf. the MT, which reads simply הנבים ('the prophets').

[124] E.g., Pss. 9.5; 67(68).30; 105(106).9; 118(119).21; Zech. 3.3(2). H. C. Kee, 'The Terminology of Mark's Exorcism Stories', *NTS* 14 (1967–8), pp. 233–8, 245; cf. J. Wojcik, *The Road to Emmaus: Reading Luke's Gospel* (West Lafayette, 1989), p. 118.

[125] As noted by O. Böcher, *Das Neue Testament und die dämonischen Mächte*, SBS 58 (Stuttgart, 1972), pp. 34–5, φιμόω and ἐξέρχομαι are used in Late Antique formulas (e.g. *DT* 15.24; 22.42; and *PGM* 4.1243; 36.164) with meanings similar to those found here. Although determining how widespread this usage was around the end of the first century CE is impossible, the conservatism of incantatory and similar formulas in general would suggest it was not uncommon.

33.52–55), it has potential in its Lucan context to compare the exorcisms of Jesus to the holy wars of Israel in the OT.[126] The mood of conflict engendered by such connotations is intensified by the sharp antithesis between ἀκάθαρτος (in δαιμονίου ἀκαθάρτου mentioned earlier, 4.33) and ὁ ἅγιος τοῦ θεοῦ.[127]

Its only Synoptic occurrences being here and in Mark's parallel, ὁ ἅγιος τοῦ θεοῦ should probably be understood in light of substantival ἅγιον in Luke 1.35, where the word signifies one begotten of God and uniquely close to him.[128] Furthermore, as the phrase in 4.34 is part of the demon's utterance, it has been construed by some interpreters as part of an effort by the demon to defend itself by means of 'magic',[129] which in this instance would consist chiefly of an apotropaic use of supernatural knowledge. On the level of dialogue between Jesus and the demon, this suggestion is not implausible, particularly since demons are sometimes associated with 'magic' in the negative sense elsewhere in Luke–Acts (e.g., Acts 13.6, 10); however, on the level of discourse between narrator and narratee, any hint of this meaning is surely eclipsed by the narrator's desire to use the demon as a witness to Jesus' lofty identity.[130] This same testimony, moreover, can also be read as highlighting Jesus' antagonism toward the demonic realm: the opposition between 'the Holy One of God' and the 'unclean demon' is recognised not only by the narrator but also by the demons themselves,[131] whose announcements about Jesus' character

---

[126] Cf. Theissen, *Miracle Stories*, p. 255.

[127] Cf. Schürmann, *Das Lukasevangelium*, I, p. 248.

[128] Cf. Fitzmyer, *Luke I–IX*, p. 546; Nolland, *Luke*, I, p. 207; and S. V. McCasland, *By the Finger of God: Demon Possession and Exorcism in Early Christianity in the Light of Modern Views of Mental Illness* (New York, 1951), pp. 91–2. As the phrase 'Holy One of God' is not attested in ancient Jewish sources as a messianic title, the effort by J.-M. Fenasse, 'Le Christ "Saint de Dieu"', *MScRel* 22 (1965), pp. 30–2 to find specifically messianic overtones in 4.34 is unpersuasive.

[129] See, e.g., A. Fridrichsen, 'Jesu Kampf gegen die unreinen Geister', in A. Suhl (ed.), *Der Wunderbegriff im Neuen Testament*, trans. D. Fehling (Darmstadt, 1980), p. 252; O. Bauernfeind, *Die Worte der Dämonen im Markusevangelium* (Stuttgart, 1927), pp. 12–18; McCasland, *By the Finger of God*, pp. 90–2; Schmithals, *Apostelgeschichte*, p. 176; H. Van der Loos, *The Miracles of Jesus*, NovTSup 9 (Leiden, 1965), pp. 379–80. Several passages in the Greek magical papyri (e.g., 4.2251–4, 2285–9, 2343–4), which preserve numerous formulas and concepts contemporaneous with the NT, exemplify the belief that supramundane knowledge (and knowledge of powerful names in particular) can be used for protection against demonic assault.

[130] *Contra* G. H. Twelftree, *Christ Triumphant: Exorcism Then and Now* (London, 1985), pp. 61–3, who, by treating the embedded dialogue between Jesus and the demon as the sole locus of meaning, ignores the equally important discourse between narrator and narratee.

[131] Cf. H. Eberlein, 'Zur Frage der Dämonischen im Neuen Testament', *NKZ* 42 (1931), p. 506; G. Schneider, *Das Evangelium nach Lukas*, ÖTKNT 3, 2 vols (Gütersloh, 1977), I, p. 114.

both anticipate and rebut the subsequent accusation that Jesus is allied with Satan (Luke 11.15).[132]

Another lexical problem in the demon's speech is the identity of his very first word, ἔα, which corresponds in form both to the classical particle of exclamation ('Ah!' or 'Ha!') and to the second person singular imperative of ἐάω (meaning in this context something like 'Leave us alone').[133] The latter option has support both from considerations of authorial usage and from the immediate co-text: unlike the particle, which is not found elsewhere in Luke–Acts, the verb ἐάω is used in nine other Lucan passages;[134] and, if the word is read verbally and thus construed as a request by the demon to be left alone, it would cohere with other features in the narrative that represent Jesus as antagonistic to and stronger than the unclean spirits.[135]

And finally, something ought to be said about the relationship between ἐξουσία and δύναμις, which are closely conjoined in the bystanders' response to Jesus' exorcism (4.36). As suggested by the Bauer lexicon's translation of ἐξουσία in this context as 'power'[136] the two nouns overlap one another in semantic range; yet here in 4.36 a subtle difference between the two should be observed. The distinction can be seen most clearly in Luke 10.19, where Jesus tells the disciples that they have received τὴν ἐξουσίαν... ἐπὶ πᾶσαν τὴν δύναμιν τοῦ ἐχθροῦ. As indicated in this context by the preposition ἐπί, possession of authority entails having a position over others in a hierarchy; and having a position over others in a hierarchy involves having the prerogative to give them orders and commands.[137] The authority of Jesus, therefore, is evident in his prerogative

---

[132] Cf. A. Fridrichsen, *The Problem of Miracle in Primitive Christianity*, trans. R. A. Harrisville and J. S. Hanson (Minneapolis, 1972), p. 113.

[133] In favour of the former: Bovon, *Luc (1,1–9,50)*, p. 217; Kirschläger, *Jesu exorzistisches Wirken*, p. 37; Fitzmyer, *Luke I–IX*, p. 545; Busse, *Die Wunder des Propheten Jesus*, p. 81; and W. Grundmann, *Das Evangelium nach Lukas*, 2nd edn, THKNT 3 (Berlin, 1961), p. 125. In defence of the latter: Schürmann, *Das Lukasevangelium*, pp. 245, 247–8 n. 194; Green, *Gospel of Luke*, p. 223; A. Loisy, *L'Evangile selon Luc* (Paris, 1924), p. 165; Goulder, *Luke*, pp. 312, 314.

[134] Luke 4.41; 22.51; Acts 14.16; 16.7; 19.30; 23.32; 27.32, 40; 28.4.

[135] E.g., the contrast between πνεῦμα δαιμονίου ἀκαθάρτου and ὁ ἅγιος τοῦ θεοῦ. *Contra* Kirschläger, *Jesu exorzistisches Wirken*, p. 37, the attribution of an imperative to the demon is not precluded by the demon's fear of and humility before Jesus, for the imperatival form can (and in this case, would) function as a request; on the use of the imperative in requests, see BDF, p. 195.

[136] BAGD, s.v. 'ἐξουσία'.

[137] See esp. Luke 7.6–8, where the centurion who asks Jesus to heal his slave defines his own authority as consisting of his right to issue binding orders to the soldiers and slaves who are beneath him in the social hierarchy. The word often has associations with social or political hierarchy, as, e.g., in Luke 20.2, 8 (par. Matt. 21.23, 27); 20.20; 23.7; Acts 9.14;

to issue commands to the unclean spirits (ἐπιτάσσει τοῖς ἀκαθάρτοις πνεύμασιν), while his power is evident in the spirits' obedience to these commands (καὶ ἐξέρχονται).[138]

Verbal aspect

As a handful of exegetes have recently emphasised, the tense forms in Hellenistic Greek normally disclose less about the time or perceived nature of the action in question than about the perspective from which it is seen (e.g., internal versus external) and its relative discursive prominence (e.g., background versus foreground).[139] In Luke 4.36b, for instance, the bystanders deduce from the single exorcism they have just witnessed a general principle concerning Jesus' ability to exorcise: ἐν ἐξουσίᾳ καὶ δυνάμει ἐπιτάσσει τοῖς ἀκαθάρτοις πνεύμασιν καὶ ἐξέρχονται. The present tense verbs ἐπιτάσσει and ἐξέρχονται probably possess an iterative sense, which the shift from singular πνεῦμα (4.33) to plural πνεύμασιν reinforces. But just as important, the use of the present forms instead of the aorist serves to foreground the processes of commanding and departing.[140] From the perspective of the bystanders at least, exorcisms like that performed in the assembly were by no means peripheral to Jesus' activities but rather constituted a prominent part of his ministry.[141]

26.10, 12; Josephus *J. W.* 2.140; 1 Esd. 4.28; 8.22; Sir. 17.2; 33.19; 1 Macc. 1.13; 10.6, 8, 32, 35; 11.58; 2 Macc. 3.6; 4.9; 7.16; LXX Dan. 5.7, 16, 29. Cf. Garrett, *Demise of the Devil*, p. 39.

[138] In view of the implicit links between the citation of Isa. 61.1–3 in Luke 4.18 and the deeds narrated in 4.33–44 (discussed below under 'Co-text'), the power and authority mentioned in 4.36 was probably understood by Luke himself as arising out of Jesus' unique relationship with the Spirit of the Lord. Thus, *contra* R. P. Menzies, *The Development of Early Christian Pneumatology with Special Reference to Luke–Acts*, JSNTSup 54 (Sheffield, 1991), pp. 124–6; W. Grundmann, *Der Begriff der Kraft in der neutestamentlichen Gedankenwelt* (Stuttgart, 1932), pp. 61–3, 98; and Hull, *Hellenistic Magic*, pp. 105–6, Luke conceptualises 'power' in this context neither as an entity that stands between the Spirit and miracles nor as an impersonal substance, but rather as an extraordinary ability which Jesus possesses due to his unique relationship with the Spirit of the Lord (as, e.g., in Luke 1.17, 35; 4.14; Acts 1.8; 10.38). Cf. M. Turner, 'The Spirit and the Power of Jesus' Miracles in the Lucan Conception', *NovT* 33 (2, 1991), pp. 132–46; O. Betz, 'δύναμις', *NIDNTT* II, p. 603; W. Grundmann, 'δύναμαι', *TDNT* II, p. 301; and Schürmann, *Das Lukasevangelium*, p. 245.

[139] See esp. B. M. Fanning, *Verbal Aspect in New Testament Greek*, Oxford Theological Monographs (Oxford, 1990), pp. 84–5; S. E. Porter, *Verbal Aspect in the Greek of the New Testament, with Reference to Tense and Mood*, Studies in Biblical Greek 1 (New York, 1989), pp. 83–97; Porter, *Idioms*, pp. 22–3.

[140] On the present as a potentially foreground aspect, see Porter, *Idioms*, pp. 22–3.

[141] Cf. Kirschläger, *Jesu exorzistisches Wirken*, p. 40.

The complex of clauses in which these same verbs occur, moreover, has already been shown above to possess special salience by virtue of several other stylistic devices (e.g., iconic juxtaposition and sequencing, lexical repetition, and marked word order). The layer of prominence which ἐπιτάσσει and ἐξέρχονται therefore add to this already foregrounded complex gives the motif of Jesus' authority and power a frontgrounded quality in this context. As this whole instance of multi-level foregrounding is furthermore embedded in what was identified above as one of the story's evaluative elements, whose function is to help the reader grasp the story's relevance, it tells us much about how Luke wanted this episode to be received: namely, not merely as an account of Jesus' expulsion of a demon from a possessed man in the Jewish assembly but rather as a demonstration of the cosmic authority and power which Jesus embodies over the whole demonic realm and its impure schemes.

Presupposition

Only in the last twenty-five years has stylistic theory begun to include presupposition and implicature among the elements of linguistic style.[142] The works by Crystal and Davy (1969), G. W. Turner (1973), and Anne Cluysenaar (1976), for instance, omit presupposition and implicature from their lists of stylistic categories; but due chiefly to the widening influence of pragmatics, which has begun to impact everything from language therapy to systemic linguistics,[143] the two concepts are becoming increasingly important in stylistic theory and analysis.

As in informal usage, presuppositions are what participants in discourse treat as uncontroversial facts or common-sense knowledge of the world – 'the necessary preconditions or assumptions they make in speaking or writing'[144] – in contrast to what they straightforwardly assert.[145] When for instance Luke says of Zechariah and Elizabeth that 'they were both righteous before God' (Luke 1.6, RSV), he is presupposing rather

---

[142] One of the earliest recommendations in print that stylistic criticism should give attention to presupposition and implicature came from N. Enkvist in 1978, in his 'Stylistics and Textlinguistics' (p. 178). For more recent discussion of the relevance of these concepts to biblical exegesis in particular, see P. Cotterell and M. Turner, *Linguistics and Biblical Interpretation* (Downers Grove, IL, 1989), pp. 90–7.

[143] On the contribution of pragmatics to systemic linguistics and other language disciplines, see, e.g., C. S. Butler, 'Systemic Linguistics, Semantics, and Pragmatics', in Steiner and Veltman (eds), *Pragmatics, Discourse and Text*, pp. 18–21, 25; and Pinker, *The Language Instinct*, pp. 228–30.

[144] *DS*, s.v. 'Presupposition'.

[145] Butler, 'Systemic Linguistics', p. 21; Lyons, *Language, Meaning and Context*, p. 201.

than asserting the existence of God; for Zechariah and Elizabeth can be neither righteous nor unrighteous before God unless God actually exists. This same example, moreover, illustrates an easy way to test for the presence of a genuine presupposition: if we reverse the polarity of the main assertion (i.e., from positive to negative or vice versa) and find that the presupposition remains intact, then a genuine presupposition exists.[146] Thus, by transforming the example above into 'they were *not* both righteous before God', the sentence still presupposes the existence of God because the transformation in polarity only impacts the explicit assertion, not its preconditions. Presuppositions such as this one constitute an important but seldom analysed level of meaning in all kinds of texts, including biblical ones; for they usually indicate what producers of texts both take for granted themselves and expect their audiences to know or believe.

Like most multi-clausal texts, Luke 4.33–37 contains numerous presuppositions, most of which are so ordinary that they do not merit comment. In 4.33, however, the narrator makes two assumptions which shed potentially interesting light on the cultural context of the implied author and reader(s). As in the immediately preceding co-text (4.15, 16, 20, 28) so also here, in the construction Καὶ ἐν τῇ συναγωγῇ ἦν ἄνθρωπος, the social phenomenon of the synagogue is neither defined nor explained but simply assumed to be understood by the reader. Although by itself this assumed understanding does not distinguish Luke from the other Synoptists – the first references to synagogues in Matthew and Mark (see Matt. 4.23; Mark 1.21) are comparably compact – it coheres notably with assumptions made earlier in the Gospel, where for instance Aaron (1.5) and the temple (1.9) and the hour of incense (1.10) and the commandments of the Lord (1.6) are all mentioned in a way that implies the reader is expected to know about them. But more importantly, all these assumptions belong to a particular construct of meanings and values that were used to distinguish certain social groups in the ancient Mediterranean world from others. That construct, of course, is the symbolic world of Jewish society and culture, about which the implied audience of the present story and its antecedent co-text is expected to possess more than superficial knowledge.

The other noteworthy assumption in this story is embedded in the construction, ἄνθρωπος ἔχων πνεῦμα δαιμονίου ἀκαθάρτου (4.33). What is being taken for granted in this context is that someone can have, or be possessed by, the spirit of an 'unclean demon'. Since neither the existence

---

[146] Pratt and Traugott, *Linguistics for Students of Literature*, p. 239.

of spirits nor the phenomenon of 'having' them is either explained or defended by the narrator, we might infer – even prior to the cultural and comparative analysis offered at the end of each chapter in this study – that belief in the existence of demons and in the phenomenon of possession was part of the cultural system shared by the author and reader. Furthermore and once again, an assumption in Luke's first exorcism story coheres perfectly with knowledge that is presupposed and progressively built up from the outset of the antecedent co-text. As the realities of God, the Holy Spirit, angels and prophecy are all taken for granted rather than asserted in earlier portions of the Gospel,[147] the assumptions that unclean spirits exist and that they can take control of human beings is scarcely surprising.

Implicature

Unlike presuppositions, which often consist of thoughts so ingrained we are hardly aware of them, implicatures are related very directly to the goals and meanings which a speaker or writer has in mind when they communicate. The word 'implicature' has been defined, in fact, as an instance in which a writer or speaker consciously *means* more than they say;[148] so in contrast to an utterance's basic semantic sense, which is concerned with the question 'what is the meaning of utterance x?', implicature is concerned with the question 'what does S (i.e. sender) mean by utterance x?'[149]

The difference between sense and implicature can be illustrated by the dinner-table utterance 'Can you pass me the salt, please?' The sense of this sentence can be represented in an untechnical but immediately useful way by offering a paraphrase of it – for instance, 'What I am politely requesting of you is that you manually transfer the salt shaker to me'. To be sure, other paraphrases could be provided which might have advantages over this one, and more analytical approaches could be taken to representing the sense of a sentence; but the paraphrase offered here adequately demonstrates that interpreting a sentence's sense is essentially a matter of expressing the same proposition(s) in another way.[150]

---

[147] On God, see, e.g., Luke 1.6, 8, 16; on the Holy Spirit, see, e.g., Luke 1.15, 35, 41; on angels, see Luke 1.11, 13, 19, 26; and on prophecy, see, e.g., Luke 1.67; 2.27–32.
[148] *DS*, s.v. 'Conversational Maxims'; G. Prince, *Narratology: The Form and Function of Narrative*, Janua Linguarum, Series Maior 108 (The Hague and Berlin, 1982), pp. 37–8.
[149] Leech, *Pragmatics*, pp. 5–6.
[150] On the value of careful paraphrase in representing the sense of sentences, see G. N. Leech, *Semantics* (Harmondsworth, 1974), p. 153; and Cotterell and Turner, *Linguistics and Biblical Interpretation*, pp. 78–9.

When our interest shifts from sense to implicature, however, and thus to what a particular speaker might mean by this utterance in a given context, we might infer from it additional meanings which do not correspond in any simple or direct way to its propositional sense. Depending on the utterance's context, for instance, we might infer either (1) that the speaker is justifiably wanting to put a little salt on their incontrovertibly flavourless vegetables; (2) that the speaker is wanting to criticise the addressee for once again using too little seasoning in their cooking; or (3) that the speaker is wanting to put the salt out of the addressee's reach so that the latter might not be able to put too much of it on their own food. All three of these additional meanings would be examples of implicature, which in one form or other is present in nearly all acts of communication and must be inferred from the utterance on the basis of its context.

In this same example, moreover, what pragmaticists call an utterance's 'illocutionary goal' would be the actual transference of the salt from the speaker to the addressee. More generally, the illocutionary goal of any utterance can be defined as the extralinguistic effect which the sender wishes to have upon the receiver as a result of a given utterance, from which the receiver is expected to infer what the sender is trying to achieve. As implicatures are part of this latter process of inferencing, they might be helpfully conceptualised as the interpretative steps that lead from an utterance's propositional sense to its illocutionary goal and force.

Underlying this notion of implicature are two important presuppositions concerning the use of language in general. The first, sometimes called the 'communicative presumption', maintains that whenever someone utters something to someone else, they do so with an illocutionary goal in mind (e.g., getting a job interview, maintaining goodwill in a personal relationship, or simply getting some salt to put on their tasteless food). The other key assumption holds that, in order to achieve their illocutionary goals, people almost always employ indirectness to one degree or other,[151] which determines the distance between the sense of what they say and its force. Normally, therefore, utterances can be expected to possess both a sense and a force, the latter being derivable from the former in given contexts of utterance.[152]

Since narrative genres of text convey much of their force indirectly, they require their interpreters to be alert to implicature. The story in Luke 4.33–37 is no exception. In the discourse of the demon, for instance, the words τί ἡμῖν καὶ σοί, ᾽Ιησοῦ Ναζαρηνέ (4.34) are best understood not as a bona fide question – say, 'What do you and we have in common,

---

[151] Leech, *Pragmatics*, pp. 17, 33, 80, 180.   [152] Ibid., p. 17.

Jesus of Nazareth?', which is a fair representation of the construction's propositional sense – but rather as an indirect assertion, namely 'We demons have nothing in common with you'.[153] Significantly, although this force is at least vaguely captured by some commentators without mention being made of implicature, it is completely overlooked by others.[154] But just as important, in addition to the force this question has in the dialogue between the demon and Jesus, it has a related but different function in the discourse between the implied author and reader. More specifically, and precisely by embedding the demon's speech in his own narrative discourse with the implied reader, the implied author is communicating via implicature that Jesus has nothing in common with the unclean spirits. While the relevance of this message would of course be low in a context where no one views Jesus as being in league with Satan, it would have been highly relevant in agonistic contexts where Jesus' followers were labelled as impure devotees of a demon-inspired deviant.[155]

Of the many other indirect meanings that can be inferred from this story, only two are sufficiently interesting to merit comment here. First, when the narrator mentions in 4.35 that the demon departed 'without harming' the man, the reader is not explicitly told that exorcism in this milieu was often a violent business; yet the pragmatic maxim of relation, which constrains the production and interpretation of all utterances so as to make them relevant to the interests of those taking part,[156] would require that unless this comment was utterly irrelevant to its original context, exorcism in general must have been perceived as a potentially injurious process. The validity of this inference is confirmed below, in my treatment of the cultural context of the story in Luke 9.37–43a. And finally, in the very next clause, where the narrator notes that amazement came upon everyone in the assembly (4.36), the reader is nowhere told in a straightforward manner that exorcism by means of the healer's own direct rebuke was an unusual or remarkable achievement; yet once again the maxim of relation exerts a powerful influence, suggesting in this instance that in

---

[153] As noted by R. Pesch, 'Ein Tag vollmächtigen Wirkens Jesu in Kapharnaum (Mk 1:21–34.35–39)', *BibLeb* 9/2 (1968), p. 117, the demon's use of the plural pronouns ἡμῖν and ἡμᾶς implies the existence of an entire demonic alliance, so that a single exorcism can be seen as a victory against the whole realm of evil and thus as a spiritual triumph of cosmic proportions. The demonology implicit in these plural pronouns therefore prepares the reader for the eschatological significance which Jesus ascribes to his exorcistic ministry in Luke 11.20.

[154] Green, *Gospel of Luke*, p. 223, e.g., is aware of it, whereas Bovon, *Luc (1,1–9,50)*, pp. 216–17, is not.

[155] See, e.g., Luke 11.14–23 (par. Matt. 12.22–30); cf. Mark 3.22, 30; John 7.20; 8.48–49; 10.20–21.

[156] Cf. Leech, *Pragmatics*, p. 42.

order to make the bystanders' amazement intelligible, a non-propositional meaning has to be inferred by the reader on the basis of context. As argued below in the chapter on Luke 9.37–43a, what would have struck the bystanders as amazing in this context was neither the general phenomenon of exorcism in itself nor even its successful outcome – after all, several other figures from this era were famous for their abilities in this area – but rather the way Jesus accomplished it, namely by uttering the rebuke himself rather than relying on God to pronounce it (4.35).[157]

Intertextuality

As M. Halliday and R. Hasan have observed, 'part of the environment for any text is a set of previous texts, texts that are taken for granted as shared among those taking part' in the communicative event.[158] Indeed, in company with a growing number of theorists, we could speak more boldly than this and say that every text actually *consists* of other texts – or at least scraps and fragments of texts which the speaker/writer has been able to recall and recombine from previous discursive experience.[159] An immediate example of this phenomenon is the present study, which not only follows general conventions of writing established by earlier monographs in the field of biblical studies but also consists of words and phrases whose semantic potential is a product of their multiple occurrences in previous discourse.

This idea of texts being inseparably linked, both formally and semantically, to other texts is what most critics mean by 'intertextuality'.[160] In this broad sense, moreover, intertextuality can be approached either

---

[157] Cf. T. E. Klutz, 'The Grammar of Exorcism in the Ancient Mediterranean World: Some Cosmological, Semantic, and Pragmatic Reflections on How Exorcistic Prowess Contributed to the Worship of Jesus', in C. C. Newman, J. R. Davila and G. S. Lewis (eds), *The Jewish Roots of Christological Monotheism: Papers from the St. Andrews Conference on the Historical Origins of the Worship of Jesus* (Leiden, 1999), pp. 157–8; Twelftree, *Jesus the Exorcist*, pp. 69–71, 95–7.

[158] Halliday and Hasan, *Language, Context, and Text*, p. 47; cf. J. L. Lemke, 'Text Structure and Text Semantics', in Steiner and Veltman (eds), *Pragmatics, Discourse, and Text*, p. 165.

[159] R. Fowler, *Linguistics and the Novel*, New Accents (London, 1977), p. 124.

[160] Published material on 'intertextuality' is now so voluminous that neither a survey nor a bibliography of the topic can be offered here. However, two particularly valuable integrations of intertextual theory and exegetical practice in New Testament studies are R. L. Brawley, *Text to Text Pours Forth Speech: Voices of Scripture in Luke–Acts*, Indiana Studies in Biblical Literature (Bloomington, 1995), pp. 1–14; and R. B. Hays, *Echoes of Scripture in the Letters of Paul* (New Haven, 1989), pp. 14–33. The sections on intertextuality in the present study have benefited especially from Hays' criteria for identifying intertextual echoes.

from the standpoint of the text's production or from that of its reception. In the latter case, for instance, one could ask what meanings Luke 4.33–37 might yield when it is read in conversation with William Peter Blatty's best-selling novel *The Exorcist* (1971), or how knowledge of any other text a reader may have experienced – regardless of the text's topic or date of composition – might affect their reading of the Lucan story. However, in keeping with the historical focus of my topic, the analysis of intertextuality in the present study approaches the phenomenon as much as possible from the standpoint of textual production; consequently, although my own reading of the Lucan stories is overtly influenced by hundreds of texts which the author of Luke–Acts could not have known (e.g., biblical commentaries and linguistics monographs), the treatment of intertextuality below and in the ensuing chapters focuses on how texts known by the ancient author of Luke–Acts may have contributed to the exorcism stories' original meaning and force.

As hinted above in my treatment of implicature, the rhetorical question τί ἡμῖν καὶ σοί, uttered by the demon in 4.34, should probably be understood as an allusion to the words spoken by the widow of Zarephath to the prophet Elijah in LXX 1 Kings 17.18. However, as the very similar construction τί ἐμοὶ καὶ σοί occurs in several passages elsewhere in the LXX,[161] the question deserves to be asked why 1 Kings 17.18 rather than one of these comparable passages should be taken as the intertext in this setting.[162]

In order to address this question appropriately, the immediate co-text of Luke 4.34 needs to be compared with the co-text of each of the septuagintal texts cited above. In each of the septuagintal passages, for instance, as in the Lucan story, the envisaged situation in which the key construction is uttered involves interpersonal conflict between the speaker and the addressee. However, once significant correspondences other than this are sought, only one of the potential intertexts is found to have any; and that is the story of Elijah and the widow. Like both the Lucan story and its Marcan parallel, for instance, the septuagintal version of the Elijah narrative collocates the words πνεῦμα, τοῦ θεοῦ, and -ερχομαι (Luke 4.33–36; 1 Kgs 17.17–18). Furthermore, the two stories have almost identical structures: (1) the presentation of a health problem (1 Kgs 17.17; Luke 4.33), (2) a hostile challenge to the prophet of the Lord (1 Kgs 17.18; Luke 4.34), (3) a miraculous cure (1 Kgs 17.19–22; Luke 4.35), and (4) a response

---

[161] E.g., Judg. 11.12; 2 Sam. 16.10; 2 Kgs 3.13.

[162] Some interpreters, after all, do not entertain even the possibility of this connection – see, e.g., Busse, *Die Wunder des Propheten Jesus*, pp. 66–90; and Kirschläger, *Jesu exorzistisches Wirken*, pp. 27–44.

focusing on the efficacious word of the wonder-working prophet (1 Kgs 17.24; Luke 4.36). And finally, in the immediately preceding co-text of the exorcism story (Luke 4.25–26), the Lucan Jesus alludes to the immediate co-text of the Elijah narrative (1 Kgs 17.1, 9), using it to illustrate the proverb that 'no prophet is accepted in his own country' (4.24).

As this latter allusion to 1 Kings 17.1, 9 is absent from both the Matthaean and the Marcan parallels (Matt. 13.53–58; Mark 6.1–6a), the likelihood that Luke himself produced the link and was therefore conscious of the subsequent echo in 4.34 ought to be rated very high.[163] To the Lucan story's implied audience, moreover, which is expected to know the biblical intertext and recognise the links, the allusion reinforces the bridge of continuity already created in the preceding co-text between Jesus and Elijah (4.25–26).[164]

Co-text

As emphasised above, the present study is interested not only in the strictly verbal dimensions of the exorcism stories but also in the various types of contextual factors – most notably, the contexts of situation and culture – that conditioned the stories' original production and reception. However, neither the implied situation nor the presupposed culture of these stories can be approached properly without due attention being given first to the relations between the stories themselves and their immediate co-text within Luke–Acts; for in addition to informing what each of these stories means, the co-text is the only part of their original discursive environment to which we have immediate access.

Select aspects of the present episode's co-text have already been discussed above, particularly in regard to questions about the story's boundaries. With 4.31–32 having been construed in that discussion not as part of the exorcism story itself but rather as a key piece of its co-text, one question worth exploring here is how this view impacts the story's relationship with its immediate verbal environment. The words ὅτι ἐν ἐξουσίᾳ ἦν ὁ λόγος αὐτοῦ in 4.32, for instance, when interpreted as part of the

---

[163] Cf. Pesch, 'Ein Tag vollmächtigen Wirkens', p. 120; Bauernfeind, *Die Worte der Dämonen*, p. 3; and Sabourin, *L'Evangile de Luc*, p. 138. The case for a conscious allusion is strengthened still further by the well-known influence of 1 Kgs 17.17–24 on Luke 7.11–17, which has no parallel in Matthew and Mark; on 1 Kgs 17.17–24 in Luke 7.11–17, see esp. J. M. Nützel, 'Elija- und Elischa- Traditionen im Neuen Testament', *BK* 41/4 (1986), p. 168; and M. H. Miller, 'The Character of Miracles in Luke–Acts', PhD dissertation, Graduate Theological Union (1971), pp. 26–7.

[164] For further discussion of the role of 1 Kgs 17 in Luke's presentation of Jesus as prophet, see Fearghail, *The Introduction to Luke–Acts*, p. 136.

exorcism's co-text, can now be read as a topical preview of all four of the pericopes that directly follow it (i.e., 4.33–37, 38–39, 40–41, and 42–44), with the motif of Jesus' authoritative word in 4.32 being echoed not only in 4.33–37 but also in each of the next three units (4.35–36, 39, 41).[165] Similarly, the spatial and temporal circumstances outlined in 4.31–32 can now serve to orientate the reader not merely to the event narrated in 4.33–37 but to all the action described in 4.33–43;[166] for the sabbath mentioned in 4.31 (ἐν τοῖς σάββασιν) is the same day whose progression is signified by the temporal clauses in verses 40 and 42 (Δύνοντος δὲ τοῦ ἡλίου and Γενομένης δὲ ἡμέρας),[167] with Capernaum – the πόλις mentioned in 4.31 – being tacitly identified in 4.43 ('I must preach . . . to *the other cities also*') as the sole location of all the action narrated in this section. And finally, the strong cohesion effected by all these features is reinforced by the repetition of several key lexemes in this section: ἐξουσία in verses 32 and 36;[168] λόγος in verses 32 and 36; δαιμόνιον in verses 33, 35 and 41; ἐπιτιμάω in verses 35, 39 and 41; and ἐάω in verses 34 and 41.[169] Thus, once 4.31–32 are recognised as offering orientation for all of 4.33–43, the cohesion and unity of this section as a whole increases considerably.

The cohesion of this same section (4.31–43), moreover, is reinforced by links between the exorcism in 4.33–37 and the episodes just before it in 4.1–30 (i.e., the temptation and the sermon in Nazareth). Most notably, in Jesus' programmatic application of Isaiah 61.1 and 58.6 to himself

---

[165] Thus, *contra* Busse, *Die Wunder des Propheten Jesus*, p. 69, the most immediate effect of ἐν ἐξουσίᾳ being repeated with ὁ λόγος in 4.32 and 36 is not to achieve a balance between wonder-working and teaching but rather to emphasise that Jesus' whole ministry – miracles and teachings – was marked by authoritative speech.

[166] By situating this single day between the imprisonment of the Baptist (3.21–22) and the call of Simon Peter (5.1–11), Luke follows a chronology that agrees neither with the other Synoptics (Matt. 3–4; Mark 1.14–39) nor with John (i.e. John 2.12; 3.22–36); for further discussion of the problem, see D. Buzy, 'Le premier séjour de Jésus à Capharnaüm', in *Mélanges bibliques: Rédigés en l'honneur de André Robert*, Travaux de l'Institut Catholique de Paris 4 (Paris, 1957), pp. 412–14.

[167] *Contra* Schürmann, *Das Lukasevangelium*, p. 244, ἐν τοῖς σάββασιν in 4.31 envisages not a period of several weeks but rather a single sabbath; otherwise, the temporal clauses in verses 40 and 42 have no clear point of reference and become unnecessarily incoherent. On the use of the plural τοῖς σάββασιν to signify a single sabbath, see BDF, p. 78; and Nolland, *Luke*, I, p. 205; for examples see esp. Matt. 12.11; Mark 2.23–24; 3.2.

[168] As ἐξουσία is associated in Luke–Acts not only with healings (e.g., Luke 4.36; 9.1; 10.19) but also with teaching (e.g., 4.32; 20.1–2) and the pronouncement of forgiveness (e.g., 5.24), it helps to effect a sense of harmony and unity between Jesus' words and his mighty deeds. Cf. H. K. Nielsen, *Heilung und Verkündigung: Das Verständnis der Heilung und ihres Verhältnisses zur Verkündigung bei Jesus und in der ältesten Kirche*, trans. R. Harbsmeier, ATDan 23 (Leiden, 1987), pp. 148–9.

[169] On ἔα as the imperative of ἐάω, see the discussion above under 'Vocabulary', p. 48.

in Luke 4.18–19, his references to liberty (ἄφεσις) for the captive and oppressed are best understood as metaphorical descriptions of exorcistic deliverance of the demonised.[170] As the episode in which these references occur is followed closely by Luke's first story of exorcism, the latter is difficult not to read as an attempt to illustrate precisely how the Isaianic prophecies were fulfilled; however, as 4.31–43 include not just one but several deeds of exorcistic deliverance (4.33–37, 39 and 41), the Isaiah citation in 4.18 is almost certainly intended to correspond to this larger section as a whole.[171] Thus, in addition to 4.33–37 being tightly linked to 4.38–43, all of 4.31–43 is tied closely to 4.16–30.

Furthermore, and widely overlooked in scholarly exegesis of Luke 4, the two occurrences of the noun ἄφεσις in the Isaiah quotation in 4.18 are echoed in 4.39 by the narrator's use of the cognate verb ἀφίημι to signify the departure of the fever from Simon's mother-in-law;[172] thus, like the exorcistic healings in verses 35 and 41, the healing at Simon's house serves to clarify how, from the narrator's point of view, the Isaiah prophecy is 'fulfilled' (4.21) in the actions of Jesus. Similarly, the use of χρίω in Jesus' portrayal of himself as having been 'anointed' by the Spirit of the Lord (4.18) anticipates the ensuing identification of Jesus as Χριστός in 4.41, where Jesus' messianic status is confirmed not only by the narrator but also by the demonic opposition.[173] And finally, reverberations of the citation in 4.18–19 can also be detected in the concluding unit of this section, 4.42–44; for just as Jesus describes himself in 4.18–19 as having been sent (ἀποστέλλω), as preaching (κηρύσσω²), and as announcing good tidings (εὐαγγελίζω), so in 4.43–44 he is portrayed

---

[170] Cf. Nolland, *Luke*, I, p. 197; Grundmann, *Das Evangelium nach Lukas*, p. 125; C. F. Evans, *Saint Luke*, TPINTC (London and Philadelphia, 1990), p. 276. As noted by J. A. Sanders, 'From Isa. 61 to Luke 4', in C. A. Evans and J. A. Sanders (eds), *Luke and Scripture: The Function of Sacred Tradition in Luke–Acts* (Minneapolis, 1993), p. 57, Isa. 61 is interpreted as envisaging eschatological release from demonic powers not only in Luke 4.18 but also in *11QMelchizedek* ii 3–16 (esp. 12); in contrast to Luke, however, *11QMelchizedek* neither speaks of exorcism per se nor sees the period of liberation as already inaugurated.

[171] Cf. Nielsen, *Heilung und Verkündigung*, pp. 138–42; G. E. Rice, 'Luke 4:31–44: Release for the Captives', *AUSS* 20 (Spring, 1982), pp. 23–5; D. L. Bock, *Proclamation from Prophecy and Pattern: Lucan Old Testament Christology*, JSNTSup 12 (Sheffield, 1987), pp. 109–10; Bovon, *Luc (1,1–9,50)*, p. 216; Goulder, *Luke*, p. 314.

[172] Kirschläger, *Jesu exorzistisches Wirken*, p. 63, e.g., in his analysis of the episode in 4.38–39, comments on the usage of ἀφίημι in the Synoptics but not on the verb's contribution to lexical strings and narrative discourse in Luke 4.16–39. The links are recognised, however, by Green, *Gospel of Luke*, p. 225.

[173] On the messianic connotations of χρίω in 4.18, see D. Seccombe, 'Luke and Isaiah', *NTS* 27/2 (1981), 54.

as having been sent (ἀποστέλλω), as preaching (κηρύσσω), and as announcing good tidings (εὐαγγελίζω).[174]

Like 4.31–44 as a whole, therefore, the story of exorcism in 4.33–37 indicates how the narrator of this section understands the programme outlined by Jesus back in 4.18–19 to have been achieved in Jesus' ministry. Yet the links that create this impression are not the only noteworthy connections between 4.33–37 and the units preceding it. First of all, as the demon's words τί ἡμῖν καὶ σοί in 4.34 echo the widow of Zarephath's conversation with the prophet Elijah (1 Kgs 17.18), their occurrence at precisely this point in Luke's narrative coheres strikingly well with the intertextual dynamics of their immediately preceding co-text; for the same story of Elijah and the widow (1 Kgs 17.1–18.1) has just been evoked in Luke 4.25–26, where Jesus compares himself to Elijah. Thus, in addition to highlighting the link between Luke's own story of Jesus and the story of Elijah in 1 Kings, this repeated use of a single intertextual resource heightens the internal cohesion of Luke's own narrative composition.

Furthermore, it is very fitting that in the sequencing of Luke's Gospel, as in that of Saint Mark, the first exorcism occurs almost directly after the temptation (Luke 4.1–13). In both cosmological and narrative terms, the rationale for this sequencing is clear: if Jesus can resist the ruler of the whole demonic realm, he should be able to overpower the ruler's underlings.[175] But just as important, this sequencing also contributes to a prominent motif that is amplified at several points later in Luke's narrative (e.g., Luke 10.17–20): the exchanges between Jesus and the demonic realm revolve chiefly around 'authority' (4.6, 36); and while the devil may claim to possess complete 'authority' (ἐξουσία) over 'all the kingdoms of the world' (Luke 4.5–6), his own minions' inability to withstand the exorcistic 'authority' (ἐξουσία) of Jesus (4.36) exposes this claim to be sheer illusion.[176]

And finally, in view of the links between Jesus' activity in 4.31–44 and the citations from Isaiah in 4.18–19, the exorcisms in this section should probably be interpreted as among 'the things which have been fulfilled' in the lives of the Lucan Jesus' earliest followers (Luke 1.1).[177] For whatever

---

[174] Busse, *Die Wunder des Propheten Jesus*, p. 85, notes the echoes of 4.18–19 in 4.43 but not those in 4.33–42.

[175] Jesus himself uses this sort of argument in Luke 11.21–23, on which see esp. Garrett, *Demise of the Devil*, pp. 40–2.

[176] Cf. Garrett, *Demise of the Devil*, pp. 40–1.

[177] The ideal reader's desire to interpret the exorcism in 4.33–37 as a fulfilment of prophecy is constituted in part by the numerous citations of and allusions to Jewish biblical

tensions might be detected between the expectations aroused by the preface on the one hand and the materials that follow it on the other, the representation of Jesus' exorcisms in Luke 4.31–44 give the impression that at least part of Luke's account will supply what the narrator of Luke 1.1 vaguely promises.[178]

Context of culture

Viewed chiefly in relation to its present Lucan co-text, the exorcism story in 4.33–37 invites the reader to interpret Jesus' action in relation not just to one but to several Jewish biblical intertexts. More specifically, the citation of Isaiah 61.1 in Luke 4.18–19, the allusion in the demon's speech to 1 Kings 17.18, and the conceptual link between the impure demon in 4.33 and the prophet Elisha's purification of Naaman the Syrian (2 Kgs 5.14) all serve to link the story tightly to biblical antecedents. Accordingly, one might expect these intertexts to refer to something like an exorcism.

From the standpoint of most critical readers of Jewish Scripture, however, nothing can be found in these intertexts that corresponds closely to the specifically exorcistic features of Luke 4.33–37. Indeed, even the well-known narrative of David's ministry to the sporadically afflicted King Saul (1 Sam. 16–19) – a text which, surprisingly, is neither cited nor echoed in any of the Lucan exorcism stories – differs from the present episode in several noteworthy ways. Nevertheless, as the David story is the nearest biblical parallel to the Synoptic exorcisms and is actually echoed in Acts 10.38–39, where it establishes an honourable precedent for Jesus' own pattern of healing, its potential significance as a source for comparative study deserves to be explored in detail.

1 Samuel 16.1–23

David is characterised in 1 Samuel 16 not only as having refreshed the demonically scourged King Saul (16.23) and benefited from a unique relationship with the Spirit of Yhwh (16.13) but also as having been specially chosen by Yhwh himself (16.8–12) and 'anointed' (16.13).

---

prophecies and patterns in Luke 1.5–4.30. On the use of Scripture in this particular section, see esp. R. C. Tannehill, 'The Story of Israel within the Lukan Narrative', in Moessner (ed.), *Jesus and the Heritage of Israel*, pp. 327–9; C. A. Evans, 'Prophecy and Polemic: Jews in Luke's Scriptural Apologetic', in Evans and Sanders (eds), *Luke and Scripture*, pp. 172–7; Bock, *Proclamation*, chs. 2 and 3 *passim*; Brawley, *Text to Text*, pp. 15–26; and P. S. Minear, 'Luke's Use of the Birth Stories', in L. E. Keck and J. L. Martyn (eds), *Studies in Luke–Acts* (Nashville, 1966), p. 111.

[178] On the vagueness of Luke 1.1, see Alexander, *Preface to Luke's Gospel*, pp. 112–16.

Since all these points have clear analogues in Luke's portrayal of Jesus, and with Jesus being repeatedly presented by Luke as a descendant of David,[179] the aforementioned allusion to the David story in Acts 10.38 coheres with much of Luke's intertextual rhetoric and its thematic content.

Nevertheless, the differences between the David story and Luke 4.33–37 are no less striking than the similarities. The 'evil spirit' that torments King Saul, for instance, so far as it is subordinate to Yhwh,[180] has more in common with 'the Satan' of Job 1.6–2.7 (cf. Zech. 3.1–2) and 'the lying spirit' of 1 Kings 22.19–23 (par. 2 Chron. 18.18–22) than with the unclean demon of Luke 4.33,[181] who, at least before being stifled by Jesus, appears to enjoy great freedom. Furthermore, to the same extent as the spirit afflicting Saul is 'upon'[182] him (vv. 16, 23) rather than inside him, the nature of the illness treated by David differs from that healed by Jesus. Third, David's mode of therapy (i.e., his playing of a lyre, 16.15–23) stands in sharp contrast to the Lucan Jesus' use of verbal rebukes and commands (Luke 4.35–36). And finally, unlike David, whose curative successes were mixed with dangerous failures (1 Sam. 18.10 and 19.9) and whose sole patient continued to suffer deeply even after treatment had begun (1 Sam. 16.23), Jesus is characterised by Luke as obtaining a swift and decisive victory over the demon in the assembly (Luke 4.35).

Digging up these sorts of incongruities is essential to a critical understanding of Luke's intertextual rhetoric. Yet in this instance as in so many others, reading with proper suspicion does not necessarily amount to contextualising with adequate complexity; for the David story in particular, like most Jewish biblical texts, would not have been read in Luke's milieu the same way it was interpreted in its original context of production – or, for that matter, in our own context by trained critics. Two texts from around Luke's time, namely Josephus *Ant.* 6.166–211 and *L.A.B.* 60.1–3, illustrate this point particularly well.

---

[179] See, e.g., Luke 2.4; 3.31; 18.38–39.

[180] The evil spirit is characterized in 1 Sam. 16.14–15 as 'from the Lord' (מאת יהוה) and 'from God'. In this regard, moreover, the MT and the LXX are in substantial agreement.

[181] On Yhwh's sovereign control of both the 'lying spirit' in 1 Kgs 22.19–22 and the evil spirit that torments King Saul, see H. W. F. Saggs, *The Encounter with the Divine in Mesopotamia and Israel* (London, 1978), p. 112. As noted by A. Caquot, 'Sur quelques démons de L'Ancien Testament (Reshep, Qeteb, Deber)', *Sem* 6 (1956), pp. 57–65, several other passages in the Hebrew Bible include references to demonic beings subordinate to Yhwh (e.g., Deut. 32.24; Ps. 78.49; Isa. 28.2; and Hab. 3.5); as these figures therefore differ significantly from the demons of Luke–Acts, they are given no attention in the present study.

[182] על in 16.16, אל in 16.23, both of which are rendered by ἐπί in the LXX.

Flavius Josephus Ant. *6.166–211*

Surprisingly, the references to demonic beings in Josephus *Ant.* 6.166–211 have been largely ignored in scholarship on the cultural context of exorcism and related phenomena in Luke–Acts.[183] This tendency almost certainly stems from the close reliance of *Antiquitates judaicae* 6 as a whole on its biblical source. To be more precise, as this larger section of Josephus' narrative follows 1 Samuel 5–31 very closely, not only in general plot but also at many points of discursive detail,[184] and as its demonological material in particular (6.166–9, 209–11) clearly derives from the account of Saul's affliction in 1 Samuel 16–19, the whole section is easy to read as telling us less about the cosmology of Josephus than, say, about the theology of his Deuteronomistic precursor.

Nevertheless, a careful comparison of *Ant.* 6.166–211 with its chief source discloses that, particularly in regard to how demons are conceptualised, Josephus diverged from his tradition in a variety of subtle but revealing ways. For instance, King Saul is portrayed in both of the key segments of *Ant.* 6.166–211 (i.e., lines 166–9 and 209–11) as having been afflicted by not one but several demons (pl. δαιμόνια in 6.166 and δαιμονίων in 6.168, 211),[185] whereas in the biblical text he is tormented by one alone.[186] Furthermore, Josephus says nothing about Saul's demons having been agents of the Israelite deity, whereas the narrator of the biblical account straightforwardly characterises the evil spirit as having proceeded 'from the Lord' (or 'from God').[187] And finally, in *Ant.* 6.209–11 the demons are mentioned not by the narrator but rather by Saul's son Jonathan, who in an effort to persuade Saul not to harm David highlights the value of the latter's exorcistic services; whereas in the biblical source of this passage (i.e. 1 Sam. 19.4–5) neither Jonathan nor any other

---

[183] Garrett, e.g., in *Demise of the Devil*, includes no discussion of this passage at all; and neither Kirschläger (*Jesu exorzistisches Wirken*, p. 57) nor Twelftree (*Jesus the Exorcist*, pp. 37, 178) comments on its demonological or cosmological significance.

[184] See, e.g., P. Bilde, *Flavius Josephus between Jerusalem and Rome: His Life, His Works, and Their Importance*, JSPSup 2 (Sheffield, 1988), p. 82.

[185] Cf. Luke 8.27–33.

[186] 1 Sam. 16.14, 15, 16, 23; 18.10; 19.9. The MT and the LXX are in complete agreement on this point.

[187] In the MT of 1 Sam. 16–19 each reference to the evil spirit includes this qualification. In the LXX, which might well have been Josephus' source for *Ant.* 6.166–9 and 209–11, the qualification is present at 1 Sam. 16.14, 15; and 19.9, but absent from 16.16, 23. On the contrast between Josephus and the biblical narrative at this point, see Twelftree, *Christ Triumphant*, p. 24.

voice in the narrative makes any retrospective reference either to David's therapeutic success or to Saul's affliction.[188]

For purposes of the present analysis, though, the most striking aspect of these differences is that at each point the Josephan version is conceptually closer to Luke 4.33–37 than the biblical account is. For instance, although the demon in the Lucan story is introduced by the narrator as a solitary figure (4.33), both the demon himself and those who testify about his departure tacitly portray him as representative of a larger demonic collective (4.34, 36). Similarly, at no point in the Lucan story is either the demoniac's affliction or the demon's role in it conceptualised as accomplishing the aims of the deity. And, by citing the exorcism's witnesses as commenting on it favourably in retrospect, Luke heightens the prominence and value of the services his hero provides. Thus, while Luke and Josephus differ from one another on a great range of religious and ideological matters,[189] their respective cosmologies overlap in a way that suggests both of them had internalised something like a demonological koine, a schema of assumptions and concepts which, in addition to differing considerably from that of their biblical heritage, was probably common both to them and to many of their Jewish contemporaries; indeed, precisely because Josephus and Luke differ in many other areas, their similarities in demonology are likely to be particularly indicative of the Lucan stories' original context of culture.[190]

L.A.B. 60.1–3

Like the Josephan passages discussed above, *L.A.B.* 60.1–3 is based on the biblical story of David's ministrations to Saul.[191] Following a brief orientation, where the 'evil spirit' is introduced as an autonomous being

---

[188] Josephus' addition of this reference to demons in *Ant.* 6.209–11 is especially noteworthy since *Antiquitates judaicae* as a whole, when compared with its biblical models, downplays the role of the supernatural in human affairs. On this and related matters, see G. Delling, 'Josephus und das Wunderbare', *NovT* 2 (1957–8), 291–309; G. W. MacRae, 'Miracles in the *Antiquities* of Josephus', in C. F. D. Moule (ed.), *Miracles: Cambridge Studies in Their Philosophy and History* (London, 1965), pp. 127–47; and L. H. Feldman, 'Josephus's Portrait of Hezekiah', *JBL* 111 (1992), 608–10.

[189] As noted by S. Mason, *Josephus and the New Testament* (Peabody, 1992), pp. 205–14, they also differ significantly in their presentation of common events (e.g., the census under Quirinius and Pilate's attack on certain Galileans).

[190] The narrator of *L.A.B.* 60.1–3, e.g., which contains yet another version of Saul's affliction, shows more agreement with Josephus *Ant.* 6.166–211 than with the biblical model.

[191] *L.A.B.* 60.1–3 is part of a larger narrative of rewritten biblical history, dated by D. J. Harrington (*OTP* II, p. 299) to around the time of Jesus.

that caused Saul to experience fits of choking (60.1), the narrator offers what he claims is the song David played to rescue the king from the demon.

> Darkness and silence were before the world was made,
> and silence spoke a word and the darkness became light.
> Then your name [i.e., the name of the evil spirit] was pronounced in the drawing together of what had been spread out, the upper of which was called heaven and the lower was called earth.
> And the upper part was commanded to bring down rain according to its season,
> and the lower part was commanded to produce food for all things that had been made.
> And after these was *the tribe of your spirits* made.
> And now *do not be troublesome* as one created on the second day.
> But if not, *remember* Tartarus where you walk.
> Or is it not enough for you to hear that, *through what resounds before you, I sing to many*?
> Or do you not remember that you were created from a resounding echo in the chaos?
> But let the new womb from which I was born *rebuke you*, from which after a time one born from my loins will rule over you. (Italics mine)

Directly after these lines the narrator concludes the unit with a short note of evaluation highlighting the composition's efficacy: namely, whenever David sang it, 'the spirit spared Saul' (60.3).

Although *L.A.B.* 60 is based on the same biblical story as Josephus *Ant.* 6.166–211, it reworks the material far more freely than Josephus does. In fact, apart from the abovementioned autonomy of the demon, only one correspondence between the retellings in *L.A.B.* 60 and Josephus illuminates the differences between Luke's cosmology and that of 1 Samuel 16–19; and that concerns whether the evil spirits act chiefly in an individual manner – as in the biblical account – or in the collective fashion exemplified in Josephus' story. In view of the song's reference to 'the tribe of your spirits', and with its inscribed audience being not just the one demon that torments Saul but rather 'many', the evil spirits in this context have a strongly group orientation; indeed, by making David's exorcistic pronouncements sound like a threat to the whole demonic realm, these same features give the song a cosmic significance that is unmatched by anything in either the 1 Samuel narrative or the Josephan version. And yet, with comparable significance being attributed to Jesus' action in Luke 4.33–37 (vv. 34, 36; cf. Luke 10.17–19; 11.14–22), this facet of *L.A.B.* 60 realises cultural potential that was almost certainly available to other, particularly Jewish, writers of the period.

Several other details of *L.A.B.* 60 are noteworthy from a comparative perspective. For instance, in both this text and Luke 4.33–37 one form or another of incantatory discourse[192] – addressed by the exorcist to the demon – is embedded in a larger frame of broadly narrative genre, giving each text as a whole a distinctively interdiscursive character,[193] whereas in 1 Samuel 16–19 no incantatory formula is cited or even alluded to. In both of the incantations (*L.A.B.* 60.1–3; Luke 4.35), moreover, as in many other ancient texts of this type, the exorcist sacrifices politeness on the altar of clarity and perlocutionary success: similarly to Jesus, who tells the demon, 'Be quiet and come out' (4.35), David commands the evil spirit in *L.A.B.* 60.2–3 not to be troublesome and to remember his base origins. Furthermore, the conventional lexicogrammar of exorcistic 'rebuke' occurs both in *L.A.B.* 60.3 and in Luke 4.35, with the demon being the target/object of the process in both cases, whereas rebuking has no place in 1 Samuel 16–19. In this latter connection, however, and as will be discussed at greater length in the chapter on Luke 9.37–43a (where verbal rebuke is once again essential to Jesus' method), a subtle but very important difference should be observed between the action of Jesus and that of David in *L.A.B.* 60.1–3: namely, Jesus issues the command directly, with no invocation of an external source of authority, whereas David approaches the demon in a less direct manner by appealing to a third-party participant (i.e., 'the new womb from which I was born') to pronounce the rebuke in their authority.

As these observations cumulatively demonstrate that the biblical story about David was being read, interpreted and rewritten around Luke's time with assumptions more comparable to those found in Luke 4.33–37 than to those in 1 Samuel 16–19, they illuminate an important facet of the Lucan story's context of culture. The same observations, though, and especially the first two, are perhaps even more interesting for what they disclose about the Lucan story's ideological context; for if Norman Fairclough is right to assert that 'the boundaries and insulations between and within

---

[192] The incantation in *L.A.B.* 60 is cited in full above, while that in the Lucan story is constituted by the utterance of Jesus in 4.35, φιμώθητι καὶ ἔξελθε ἀπ' αὐτοῦ. On the incantatory qualities of Jesus' utterance, see Twelftree, *Jesus the Exorcist*, p. 69.

[193] On interdiscursivity (i.e., the constitution of a text from diverse genres of discourse), see Fairclough, *Critical Discourse Analysis*, p. 135.

orders of discourse may be points of conflict and contestation... a part of wider social conflicts and struggles',[194] then the embedding of an exorcistic incantation within a story that identifies itself with the Jewish biblical past – where incantations are not cited with approval – cannot be void of significance. In this regard Luke's discursive practice exemplifies a willingness to transform the past in order to deal with his own agonistic present, the contours of which will be sketched in my treatment of Acts 16.16–18. Indeed, as Luke does not merely rewrite an old story from the Scriptures (as, e.g., the author of *L.A.B.* 60.1–3 does) but rather reproduces a much newer narrative of comparatively recent events, which he none the less strongly identifies with his scriptural precursor, his account resembles what Eric Hobsbawm and others have recently labelled 'invented tradition', that is, a ritual or symbolic action constructed 'to establish continuity with a suitable historic past'.[195] As in the contexts discussed by Hobsbawm, moreover, so in that of Luke–Acts the process of invention is inspired at least partly by changes in society that have undermined the social patterns for which the old traditions had originally been devised.[196]

However, despite the chasm between the sociocultural context of 1 Samuel and that of Luke–Acts, all the texts cited above agree on a couple of very fundamental assumptions: malevolent spirit beings exist and, whether independently or as agents of some higher divine power, can invade human bodies so as to cause illness or disease. In fact, this pair of interlocked assumptions constitutes by far the most commonly invoked aetiology of illness attested in sources from the Graeco-Roman world; for as documented impressively by Dale Martin in *The Corinthian Body*, the only aetiological alternative – namely, that which attributes illness not to invasion by hostile forces but rather to imbalance in the body's own internal elements – was embraced solely by intellectuals familiar with philosophy or professional medical theory.[197] Indeed, when Martin argues that philosophers and medical theorists had, by the early Imperial period, succeeded in creating 'a relatively new common sense

---

[194] Ibid., p. 132.

[195] E. Hobsbawm, 'Introduction: Inventing Traditions', in E. Hobsbawm and T. Ranger (eds), *The Invention of Tradition* (Cambridge, 1992), p. 1.

[196] Ibid., pp. 4–5. On the particular kinds of social and political changes that contributed to the formation of the Synoptic tradition in general, see esp. E. W. Stegemann and W. Stegemann, *The Jesus Movement: A Social History of Its First Century*, trans. O. C. Dean (Minneapolis, 1999), pp. 126–36, 170–86; G. Theissen, *The Gospels in Context: Social and Political History in the Synoptic Tradition*, trans. L. M. Maloney (Minneapolis, 1991), pp. 151–65, 258–80.

[197] D. B. Martin, *The Corinthian Body* (New Haven, 1995), pp. 152–62.

that portrayed disease as imbalance rather than invasion, at least among the educated class',[198] he almost certainly underestimates the degree to which the invasionist model continued to hold sway even in the upper strata. Josephus, for instance, clearly accepts the invasionist aetiology not only when he is rewriting biblical material (e.g., *Ant.* 6.166–211) but also in his presentation of events from his own lifetime (e.g., *Ant.* 8.42–49), even though he was aristocratic, well educated and conversant with a wide range of contemporary philosophical opinion;[199] and, against any temptation we might have to see Josephus as exceptional in this matter, say, on grounds of his Jewishness, the same invasionist perspective is discernible in Flavius Philostratus' biography of the first-century CE pagan philosopher Apollonius of Tyana,[200] to whom Philostratus attributes various healings that presuppose demonically caused illness.[201]

Apollonius of Tyana and the rarity of exorcism in pagan narrative

Philostratus' portrayal of Apollonius is pertinent to our analysis in several ways,[202] most of which are discussed in the next chapter; but one aspect of Philostratus' narrative merits at least brief attention here. The issue in

---

[198] Ibid., p. 153.

[199] As noted by Bilde, *Flavius Josephus*, pp. 200–1, Josephus' belief in the miraculous and related phenomena is undoubtedly less rhetorical and formal than his frequently discussed rationalism is. On Josephus' social status, educational background and philosophical proclivities, see Mason, *Josephus*, pp. 36–40, 66–70.

[200] Flavius Philostratus (*c.* 170–250 CE), sophist and member of a circle patronised by the emperor Septimius Severus and his wife Julia Domna, was commissioned by the empress to produce an account about Apollonius, who, before perishing during the reign of Nerva (96–98 CE), performed extraordinary deeds that were derided by his ancient critics as 'magical' in character. Although most scholars interested in the *Life* accept that it contains a historical core, most also judge it to be highly propagandistic and more indicative of the second- and third-century world of its author than of the first-century milieu of his hero. For further discussion of Philostratus' narrative and the historical difficulties it poses, see E. L. Bowie, 'Apollonius of Tyana: Tradition and Reality', in *ANRW* II.16.2, pp. 1655, 1665–7, 1686; Graf, *La magie dans l'antiquité gréco-romaine*, pp. 114–15; C. A. Evans, 'Apollonius of Tyana', in C. A. Evans and S. E. Porter (eds), *Dictionary of New Testament Background* (Downers Grove, IL, 2000), pp. 80–1; G. Bowersock, 'Introduction', in *Philostratus: Life of Apollonius* (Harmondsworth, 1970), pp. 11–19; R. MacMullen, *Enemies of the Roman Order: Treason, Unrest, and Alienation in the Empire*, paperback edn (London, 1966; London, 1992), pp. 112–15.

[201] See, e.g., Philostratus *VA* 3.38. While the invasionist assumptions in this passage may be less indicative of the first-century beliefs of Apollonius than of the third-century ones of Philostratus, the text still causes trouble for Martin's thesis since his position is that 'the invasion etiology' came increasingly to be rejected by the educated class in this period. Martin, *Corinthian Body*, p. 155.

[202] As noted by W. Kahl, *The New Testament Miracle Stories in Their Religious-Historical Setting: A Religionsgeschichtliche Comparison from a Structural Perspective*

question involves the temporal distance between the historical Apollonius and Philostratus' own time of writing – a gap which, in addition to being far greater than that between Jesus and Luke, entails a much larger historical problem in regard to the ancient comparative materials. More specifically, although a handful of narratives about exorcism or closely related activities survives in Jewish sources from the first century CE or earlier, narrative parallels in pagan sources from the same era are more rare, with almost all the relevant material coming from the second century CE or later.[203]

As others have suggested, this pattern in our evidence probably says less about the realities of pre-Antonine pagan religious practice than about the snobbishness of the Classical literary tradition.[204] Yet this latter factor should not be allowed to blind us to other, potentially more powerful, explanations. In this connection a frequently overlooked contrast between the assumed cosmologies of the Jewish and pagan stories possesses particular importance. To be precise, because Luke had absorbed a cosmological schema whose demons form a unified hierarchy with Satan at the top, he is able to interpret a single exorcistic healing by Jesus as a victory of cosmic magnitude against the entire house of 'Beelzebul, the ruler of the demons';[205] by contrast, in Philostratus' *Vita Apollonii* – as in Lucian's story of the Syrian exorcist (*Philops.* 16) and in a variety of pagan materials of non-narrative genres (e.g., spells, curses and incantations) – demons are represented as working either individually or in small groups (sometimes in sevens),[206] never as agents of a demonic empire, so that exorcism in these contexts lacks most of the high cosmic drama and significance present in the NT accounts.[207]

Another reason then for the absence of exorcism stories in pagan narratives from earlier than the second century CE is that wherever exorcisms

---

(Göttingen, 1994), p. 230, Apollonius is one of only two 'immanent bearers of numinous power' (i.e., personalities that combine both divine and human qualities) about whom *several* stories of miracle were told in antiquity. This consideration by itself makes Philostratus' account especially important for contextualising the Lucan stories.

[203] Cf. F. E. Brenk, 'In the Light of the Moon: Demonology in the Early Imperial Period', *ANRW* II.16.3, p. 2108; K. Thraede, 'Exorzismus', *RAC* VII, cols 48–9; and McCasland, *By the Finger of God*, pp. 65–9.

[204] See, e.g., M. Q. Smith, 'Prolegomena to a Discussion of Aretalogies, Divine Men, the Gospels and Jesus', *JBL* 90 (1971), 174–99.

[205] See, e.g., Luke 4.36; 10.17–18; 11.14–23. For further discussion of this aspect of the exorcisms, see esp. Garrett, *Demise of the Devil*, pp. 42, 45–6.

[206] See, e.g., *PGM* 4.1235–49; 5.333–8; 7.430–2; *DT* 237.1–19 (*CTBS* 9).

[207] Cf. M. Q. Smith and E. W. Smith, '*De Superstitione* (*Moralia* 164E–171F)', in H. D. Betz (ed.), *Plutarch's Theological Writings and Early Christian Literature* (Leiden, 1975), p. 26.

in this period *were* performed or narrated among pagans, the cosmological framework within which they were interpreted militated against their acquiring any great significance. To pagan audiences of written narratives in this era, therefore, accounts of exorcism had little to make them tellable or remarkable. That tales of allegedly successful exorcisms could even invite ridicule, moreover, at least among intellectuals, is well illustrated by the aforementioned story in Lucian about the popular exorcist from Syria. And, while Philostratus includes several episodes of broadly exorcistic activity in his *Vita Apollonii*,[208] none of these stories shows any interest in whether the miraculous deed impacted demonic beings in general.

The wildly heterogeneous and unorganised character of the demons in Graeco-Roman paganism therefore helps to explain the lack of close narrative parallels in pagan sources from earlier than the second century. Yet this insight does very little to help us understand how demonic beings and exorcistic practices were conceptualised by the non-literate masses of the wider Mediterranean and Oriental world.[209] For purposes of acquiring this latter sort of information, in fact, reliance on narrative sources can be extremely misleading; for as soon as we look beyond the narrative materials to consider sources similar to the embedded discourse of Jesus in Luke 4.35 – that is, exorcistic incantations, apotropaic formulas and the like – a strikingly different picture emerges. One example of this type of material has already been discussed above in my treatment of *L.A.B.* 60.1–3, and later I shall comment on others in connection with the rebuking motif in Luke 9.42; but at least a few points about this sort of discourse ought to be made here.

Incantations, exorcistic violence and fever demons

Texts written on various kinds of materials (e.g., wooden tablets, earthenware bowls and thin metal sheets) and designed either to expel demons from the afflicted or to prevent the former from attacking in the first place have survived in abundance from a wide range of ancient periods, places and religious systems.[210] While much of this material was produced two

---

[208] Six episodes in *Vita Apollonii* revolve around contests between evil spirits and Philostratus' hero: 3.38; 4.10, 20, 25; 6.27, 43.

[209] On the distance between popular belief and the outlook reflected in the ancient Greek literary tradition, see Smith, 'Prolegomena', p. 179.

[210] See, e.g., D. L. Penney and M. O. Wise, 'By the Power of Beelzebub: An Aramaic Incantation Formula from Qumran (4Q560)', *JBL* 113 (1994), 627–50; M. J. Geller (ed.), *Forerunners to Udug-hul: Sumerian Exorcistic Incantations*, Freiburger Altorientalische

or more centuries after the time of Luke, an equally impressive volume of it survives from earlier times – in some instances as early as the third millennium BCE – deriving from cultural systems which, through the long and multifaceted intercourse between ancient Israel and her Near Eastern neighbours (e.g., Egypt, Assyria and Phoenicia), contributed in various ways to the formation of Judaism in general and its demonologies in particular in the centuries leading up to the Common Era. But just as important, comparative studies that have considered both the early and the late materials have uncovered a striking degree of continuity between these sources in content, mode and tenor;[211] indeed, of the many contributions made by the Dead Sea Scrolls to our understanding of Judaism and primitive Christianity in their historical and cultural contexts, the least is by no means the scrolls' inclusion of apotropaic and exorcistic incantations which strengthen the discursive bridge between the incantatory texts of earlier and later provenance.[212] Thus, while utterances like that in Luke 4.35b have no positive precedent in Jewish Scripture, they fit very well into the range of incantatory practices attested both in pagan and extrabiblical Jewish sources.[213]

To be sure, the comparatively large volume of extant material of this kind affords us no guarantee of its familiarity to or use by a substantial portion of the population that concerns us here; but other texts offer a

---

Studien 12 (Stuttgart, 1985); Thompson (ed.), *Devils and Evil Spirits*; Y. Avishur, 'The Second Amulet Incantation from Arslan Tash', *UF* 10 (1978), 29–36; Y. Avishur, 'The Ghost-Expelling Incantation from Ugarit (Ras Ibn Hani 78/20)', *UF* 13 (1981), 13–25; J. C. de Moor, 'An Incantation against Evil Spirits (Ras Ibn Hani 78/20)', *UF* 12 (1980), 429–32. The following corpora include numerous examples of the same kind of material: J. Naveh and S. Shaked, *Amulets and Magic Bowls: Aramaic Incantations of Late Antiquity*, 2nd edn (Jerusalem, 1987); Isbell (ed.), *Aramaic Incantation Bowls*; E. M. Yamauchi (ed.), *Mandaic Incantation Texts*, AOS 49 (New Haven, 1967); J. F. Borghouts (ed.), *Ancient Egyptian Magical Texts*, Religious Texts Translation Series, Nisaba 9 (Leiden, 1978); M. Meyer and R. Smith (eds), *Ancient Christian Magic: Coptic Texts of Ritual Power* (San Francisco, 1994); K. Preisendanz and A. Heinrichs (eds), *Papyri Graecae Magicae: Die griechischen Zauberpapyri*, rev. 2nd edn, 3 vols. (Leipzig, 1973–4).

[211] See, e.g., J. W. Wesselius, 'Notes on Aramaic Magical Texts', *BO* 39 (1982), p. 250; P. Michalowski, 'On Some Early Sumerian Magical Texts', *Or* 54 (1985), pp. 224–5; and A. Green, 'Beneficent Spirits and Malevolent Demons: The Iconography of Good and Evil in Ancient Assyria and Babylonia', *Visible Religion* 3 (1984), pp. 84–5; Penney and Wise, 'By the Power of Beelzebub', pp. 629–30; and Naveh and Shaked, *Amulets and Magic Bowls*, p. 13; L. H. Schiffman and M. D. Swartz, *Hebrew and Aramaic Incantation Texts from the Cairo Genizah: Selected Texts from Taylor-Schechter Box K1*, Semitic Texts and Studies 1 (Sheffield, 1992), p. 28; C. C. McCown, *The Testament of Solomon* (Leipzig, 1922), pp. 53–4.

[212] See esp. *4QSongs of the Sage^a* frag. 1 lines 4–6; *4QExorcism ar*; and *11QApocryphal Psalms* v–vi.

[213] Cf. Aune, 'Magic', p. 1532; Twelftree, *Jesus the Exorcist*, p. 206; *Christ Triumphant*, pp. 66, 71.

few useful clues. On the Jewish side, for instance, Josephus' representation of the exorcistic talents possessed by a certain Jewish contemporary of his named Eleazar, who is said to have used 'incantations' (ἐπῳδάς) and 'modes of exorcisms' (τρόπους ἐξορκώσεων) bequeathed by King Solomon for the benefit of the demonically afflicted, emphasises that this type of therapy was well known and widely employed amongst Jews in his own day.[214] While Josephus' desire in this context to elevate the honour of his own nation by extolling the virtue of their great ancestral ruler, Solomon, should alert us to the possibility of exaggeration in these matters, neither the reputation of Solomon for demonological wisdom nor the impression that incantations were widely used in exorcistic therapy amongst the Jews lacks support from other sources.[215]

As for the use of incantations in pagan contexts, moreover, an impression broadly similar to this emerges from the Hippocratic essay *De morbo sacro* and from Lucian's *Philopseudes sive incredulis*, both of which shed considerable light on folk health care in the process of subjecting it to ridicule. The former, composed anonymously some time between 430 and 330 BCE, was written specifically in order to correct the popular Greek diagnosis and treatment of the so-called 'sacred disease', a category best understood as including a whole family of illnesses (not limited, as sometimes asserted without support, to what modern medicine calls 'epilepsy') whose symptoms[216] closely resemble those of the NT accounts of demon-possession. The essay's anonymous author, moreover, in arguing that the cause of these illnesses is not, *contra* the popular aetiology, either divine or demonic[217] but rather phlegmatic blockage of vessels running

---

[214] Josephus *Ant.* 8.45–9. Note esp. the first reference in this passage to exorcistic skill, i.e., παρέσχε δ' αὐτῷ μαθεῖν ὁ θεὸς καὶ τήν κατά τῶν δαιμόνων τέχνην ('God enabled him [i.e., Solomon] to learn the anti-demon skill', 8.45), where the article τήν probably has a well-known nuance.

[215] On the reputation of Solomon see, e.g., Wisd. 7.15–22; *11QApocryphal Psalms* ii 2; Luke 11.31 (par. Matt. 12.42). On Jewish use of incantations see, in addition to the Qumran texts cited above, *b. Meil.* 17b; *b. Shab.* 61a–b; *b. Pes.* 112a–b; Acts 19.13–14; Str-B, vol. IV.1, pp. 273–6; for further discussion of the latter topic see E. Ferguson, *Demonology of the Early Christian World*, Symposium Series 12 (Lewiston, 1984), p. 92; Goodenough, *Jewish Symbols*, II, p. 209; J. Neusner, *The Wonder-Working Lawyers of Talmudic Babylonia: The Theory and Practice of Judaism in Its Formative Age* (New York, 1987), pp. 194–208.

[216] The symptoms include shouting, loud cries, loss of voice, convulsions, foaming at the mouth, clenching of the teeth, fear, panic, falling to the ground, wild running, and insane behaviour (Hippocrates *Morb. Sacr.* 1.81–90; 7.1–25; and 12.6–8).

[217] Although δαιμόνιον in *Morb. Sacr.* 1.65 and 12.6 can be construed as roughly synonymous with θεός, which would leave demons completely outside the diagnostic picture, the co-text of 1.65 in particular suggests that demonic beings are also in view. Most notably, the terms μαγεύω and σελήνη, which occur repeatedly in 1.52–100, have such strong

to and from the brain,[218] simultaneously provides a clear description of the therapeutic methods which the usual diagnosis is normally accompanied by, namely the use of incantations in conjunction with ritual purification.[219]

Thus, in addition to testifying to the popularity of incantatory discourse in the healing of spirit-afflictions amongst pagans in pre-Hellenistic times, the author of *De morbo sacro* provides a valuable corrective to the distorted impression created by the absence of exorcism in the classical tradition of Greek narrative. But just as significant, by implying that the incantatory elements of therapy were normally embedded in a larger symbolic frame of ritual purification, his treatise anticipates a seldom-noticed feature of Jesus' actions in Luke 4.33–37: as the addressee of Jesus' incantational rebuke is described not only as a demon (4.35) but also as a spirit of 'impurity' (4.33, 36), the larger frame of narrated symbolic action in which the rebuke is embedded looks very much like a purification rite, an impression strongly reinforced, moreover, by the allusion in the immediately preceding co-text (4.27) to the prophet Elisha's paradigmatic cleansing of Naaman the Syrian.

Much closer to Luke's day, Lucian's criticism of exorcistic and related therapies demonstrates that folk intervention in his context was very similar to that attacked by Hippocrates. The method routinely used by the famous exorcist from Syria, for instance, is described as consisting chiefly of oaths (ὅρκους) and threats addressed directly to the demon,[220] while the sole device employed by Arignotus the Pythagorean consists of a binding formula recited in the Egyptian tongue (αἰγυπτιάζων τῇ φωνῇ συνήλασα κατᾴδων αὐτόν).[221] The general proximity here to the incantatory praxis of Jesus, however, should not be allowed to obscure significant differences of detail: in particular, the 'oaths' used by Lucian's Syrian should probably be understood as including the invocation of one divine being or other (cf. Acts 19.15),[222] whereas the incantatory utterance

---

demonological overtones that early readers probably would have thought of demons even if the noun δαιμόνιον had been absent from the passage; not without reason, therefore, J. Chadwick and W. N. Mann (eds), *The Medical Works of Hippocrates* (Oxford, 1950) translate δαιμόνιον in 1.65 as 'devil'.

[218] Hippocrates *Morb. Sacr.* 2.8–17 and 5.1–7, 19.

[219] Ibid., 1.8, 23, 32, 52, 60–5, 100; 18.19.

[220] Lucian *Philops.* 16. As in Luke 4.33–35, it is worth adding, so in this essay the healer's use of an interpersonally direct formula of expulsion constitutes the final step in a process of conversation between exorcist and demon.

[221] Lucian *Philops.* 31.

[222] LSJ, s.v. 'ὅρκος'. On the conventionality of invoking divine assistance in the context of exorcism, see pp. 252–60 below.

by the Lucan Jesus conspicuously lacks reference to external sources of power or authority.[223]

Formal and generic aspects of Jesus' utterance in Luke 4.35 constitute only one of several areas in which comparative study of ancient incantations can enrich our understanding of the Lucan episode. Other areas worthy of comment in this connection are the narrator's representation of the exorcism as having been achieved without the patient suffering harm (4.35) and the relationship between this episode as a whole and the one directly following it (i.e., the healing of Peter's mother-in-law of 'fever' in 4.38–39).

As for why the author of Luke–Acts wished to emphasise the non-injurious character of Jesus' intervention, at least part of an answer can be deduced without recourse to comparative sources by means of a close reading of the Lucan story itself. More specifically, the Lucan episode's frontgrounding of Jesus' authority, discussed earlier in this chapter, would be undermined by a denouement in which either the exorcist's own technique or the departing demon brought harm to the patient.[224] That such a resolution was more than a theoretical possibility in this context, moreover, can be seen both in the parallel story in Mark's Gospel, where prior to taking its leave the demon is able to convulse the patiently violently (Mark 1.26), and in Mark 9.26, where the exorcism's climax is so violent that for an unspecified time afterwards the patient was thought by many of the action's witnesses to be dead (indeed, even the story's narrator says the patient was ὡσεὶ νεκρός).

As Mark's Gospel clearly provides the less flattering portrayal of Jesus in these matters, it should almost certainly be regarded as offering the more accurate image of Jesus' actual performance. But just as important, several other lines of evidence converge to suggest that not only the exorcisms of Jesus but also those performed by other healers in antiquity sometimes involved one form of violence or another. Recent anthropological research into the cross-cultural phenomenon of shamanism, for instance, indicates that some of the procedures used by shamans in healing

---

[223] Cf. Klutz, 'Grammar of Exorcism', pp. 157–8; Twelftree, *Jesus the Exorcist*, pp. 159–63; J. P. Meier, *A Marginal Jew: Rethinking the Historical Jesus*, II, *Mentor, Message, and Miracles* (New York, 1994), p. 406. In addition to implying that Jesus himself is somehow an embodiment of divine authority, this feature of his utterance is reinforced by the grammar of the rebuking process narrated earlier in the same verse: Jesus does not merely mediate, indirectly, a rebuke issued ultimately by God but rather functions himself as the originator and sayer of the rebuke; on this latter point see below, pp. 192–4.

[224] Cf. Loisy, *L'Evangile selon Luc*, p. 165. *Contra* Twelftree, *Jesus the Exorcist*, p. 71, the kind of violence included in the Marcan parallel (1.26) is unlikely to have heightened Jesus' authority and simultaneously embarrassed the early church.

and related activities (e.g., inducing altered states of consciousness) involve extreme forms of pain and punishment, in some cases to the point of bodily injury.[225] Philostratus, moreover, narrates a broadly exorcistic intervention in which a demon disguised as an old man is brought to a violent end – in accordance with Apollonius' instructions – by public stoning.[226] And in an incantatory text from ancient Sumer, a figure who identifies himself as 'the incantation priest' and the 'chief exorcist' describes his own procedures as including not only the laying of his hands on the patient's head[227] but also shouting at the patient, frightening them and even striking them on their cheeks.[228] Thus, while violent and even painful procedures in shamanic and other systems of health care have probably facilitated healing in more instances than we might care to imagine, the evidence surveyed here nevertheless contributes to the construction of a context in which Luke's note about the non-injurious resolution of Jesus' intervention (4.35) would have had immediate relevance and appeal.[229]

Finally, incantatory and related documents from antiquity shed potentially decisive light on an exegetical difficulty that bears weightily on the present episode's relation to its immediate co-text. More specifically, while most scholars interested in this story recognise at least some of the features that tie it closely to the healing narrated in the immediately ensuing unit (4.38–39),[230] none has utilised the ancient incantatory evidence to anything like its full potential for solving one of the latter unit's main interpretative problems – namely, how the 'fever' rebuked by Jesus would have been understood in Luke's own context of culture – a question which in turn affects the degree of cohesion to be seen between the two accounts of healing in this context.

On the whole, modern exegesis has interpreted πυρετός as signifying either (1) a fever in the familiar physiological sense, albeit personified as a demon in this instance by virtue of the word's intra-clausal relation to ἐπιτιμάω, whose occurrence in 4.39, then, is best understood not as an

---

[225] Winkelman, *Shamanism*, pp. 84, 92, 150–1.   [226] Philostratus *VA* 4.10.
[227] *FUH* 3.4–11; cf. Luke 13.13–16, where Jesus lays hands on a woman to liberate her from an ailment caused by Satan.
[228] *FUH* 3.93–7. On the possible use of these methods by Jesus and other ancient healers, see M. Q. Smith, *Jesus the Magician* (London, 1978), p. 32.
[229] Cf. Theissen, *Miracle Stories*, pp. 87–8, who in support of a similar interpretation cites Josephus *Ant.* 8.47: the exorcism performed by Eleazar in the presence of Vespasian results in the patient falling violently to the ground (πεσόντος εὐθὺς τ'ἀνθρώπον). See also Acts 19.16, however, where the violence is suffered by the exorcists at the hands of the demoniac. On violence in exorcism, see also Van der Loos, *Miracles of Jesus*, p. 375; Twelftree, *Jesus the Exorcist*, pp. 70–1.
[230] See, e.g., Bovon, *Luc (1, 1–9,50)*, p. 218.

exorcistic command addressed to a spirit of illness but rather as a literary-poetic strategy for effecting a sense of parallelism between this and the preceding unit;[231] or (2) the familiar variety of physical illness but in this instance with connotations of broadly satanic oppression (cf. Acts 10.38), and thus as a phenomenon 'comparable to demon possession but not to be identified with it';[232] or (3) a particular demonic spirit, signified here by a metonymy of effect, that specialises in causing fever.[233]

Significantly, no advocate of either of the first two positions has demonstrated more than a second-hand familiarity with the ancient sources in which fever is actually identified as a demon; indeed, nothing more than this has been demonstrated even by commentators who opt for the third interpretation.[234] This unfortunate state of affairs is almost certainly due in part to the now famous delays in the editing and publication of much of the Qumran material, which includes one text of very critical significance for the present problem; yet it is also partly due, I think, to a tendency amongst many New Testament scholars to fish in text-comparative waters whose shallowness minimises the chance for a prize catch. But more to the point, in an Aramaic incantation (*4QExorcism ar*) first made publicly accessible in the early 1990s,[235] references to indisputably demonic phenomena such as the one 'who enters the flesh, the male penetrator and the female penetrator', 'he who crushes the male and she who passes through the female', and unspecified spirits that are directly adjured and enchanted by the narrator (רוח, 1 ii 5–6) sandwich a striking reference to 'fever and chills' (אשא וערית, 1 i 4), indicating that at least for this author 'fever' could function as a metonym for a type of demon.[236] The proximity of this text's register to that of Luke 4.33–39, moreover, and thus its relevance to the matter that concerns us here, must be estimated as very high, particularly in view of the two texts' shared interest in patients of both genders. And finally, in order to establish still more firmly that πυρετός

---

[231] Marshall, *Gospel of Luke*, pp. 194–5; Bovon, *Luc (1, 1–9,50)*, p. 218.
[232] Nolland, *Luke*, I, p. 212. Similar positions are taken by Kirschläger, *Jesu exorzistischen Wirken*, pp. 63, 68, who characterises the Lucan unit as an 'exorzismusartigen Krankheitsbannung'; and J. B. Green, *Gospel of Luke*, p. 225 n. 79.
[233] Theissen, *Miracle Stories*, p. 86; Schürmann, *Das Lukasevangelium*, p. 252.
[234] See, e.g., Theissen, *Miracle Stories*, p. 86, whose effort to support this position consists solely of a reference to an earlier study by R. Hengel and M. Hengel.
[235] See R. Eisenman and M. Wise (eds), *The Dead Sea Scrolls Uncovered: The First Complete Translation and Interpretation of Fifty Key Documents Withheld for Over 35 Years* (Shaftesbury, 1992), pp. 265–7.
[236] For further discussion of these lines and their interpretation, see Penney and Wise, 'By the Power of Beelzebub', pp. 640–2; and M. Wise, M. Abegg and E. Cook, *The Dead Sea Scrolls: A New Translation* (San Francisco, 1996), p. 443.

does indeed signify a demonic being in the Lucan passage, only a moderate burden of evidentiary weight needs to be placed on the incantation from Qumran; for as an example of the sort of discursive bridge discussed at the beginning of this section, the Qumran text merely confirms what could have been deduced from the continuity in this same matter between texts of earlier and later provenance, one of which refers not only to 'the spirit... called fever (and) shivering' (רוחה דמתקריה אשתה אוריתה) but also to the process of rebuking whereby the noxious entity is expelled.[237]

Consequently, and especially with the co-meronymy of the 'impure spirit(s)' and 'the fever-demon' reinforcing the cohesion produced by the repetition of ἐπιτιμάω in verses 35 and 39, the two episodes of healing stick together in their Lucan narrative context even more tightly than is usually recognised; and one result of this is that the emphasis in 4.31–44 on Jesus' authority over the demonic spirits of illness acquires even greater salience than it possesses without support from the reading just defended.

Finally, in regard to wider implications of this reading and scholarly objections that might be raised against it, an issue of primarily meta-critical significance ought to be raised before this section is brought to a close. More specifically, by resulting not only in greater emphasis being placed on Jesus' authority over the demons but also in a more emphatic nexus being established between the demons and common forms of illness, the reading just defended gives demonic beings a more conspicuous place in Luke's world-view than they have according to the alternative interpretations. This fact, I believe, is not unrelated to the pattern of reluctance on the part of many interpreters, especially in the Anglo-American tradition of exegetical commentary, to grapple seriously with this reading's increasingly evident strengths; after all, in a context of reception where even the most ardent Christians find it almost impossible to treat their experiences of fever and related ailments as instances of demonic affliction, this interpretation implicitly relegates much of the Lucan Jesus' activity and its presuppositions to a position of irrelevance. And why invest substantial portions of one's life analysing and commenting on a narrative that is no longer relevant?

In this light, genuine sympathy must be felt for the interpreter who would modernise passages like Luke 4.38–39 by minimising their demonological features and pre-modern concepts of health care. If we, however, are to allow ourselves to be confronted (and potentially enriched) by

---

[237] *AMB* amulet 9.1–4.

these stories in all their foreignness and apparent impertinence, we must resist the temptation posed by such strategies. And ironically, by trying instead to contextualise these narratives as fully and on as many levels as contemporary methods allow, we may just find that other, less theoretically objectionable, ways of relativising their stubbornly prominent demonology emerge. One of these ways, in fact, will begin to take shape in my treatment of the Lucan Gospel's third story of exorcism (9.37–43a), and it will be explored in greater detail in relation to the exorcism attributed to Paul in Acts 16.16–18.

Ethnicity, polyphony and the body in a synagogal exorcism

As noted above in the treatment of vocabulary, an audience familiar with the use of δαιμόνιον and πνεῦμα ἀκάθαρτον in the LXX could easily have associated the demon in this story with notions of Gentile religion and idolatry.[238] Such associations would have rung even louder, moreover, in the ears of listeners who recognised the allusion in 4.34 to 1 Kings 17.18, where a precursor to the utterance inspired by the demon is found on the lips of the Gentile widow of Zarephath. Indeed, in the setting of a Jewish assembly in Capernaum, and with the echo of the Gentile woman being 'shouted in a loud voice' (4.33), this demon sounds the way a proud New Englander with a strong Bostonian accent might have sounded on a Sunday morning in 1865 in the First Baptist Church of Atlanta; and, as the dislodging of the demon unfolds, the individual human body he had once invaded and then held captive becomes a synecdoche for the much larger field of struggle over the integrity of Jewish identity in a world of pagan empire.

As the impure spirit in this story therefore represents on a vertical axis almost everything that was dangerous to Jewish identity and distinctiveness on the concrete level of socioreligious and political experience, the 'holy' figure that successfully expels it can be viewed as a zealous champion of traditional Jewish boundaries and modes of self-definition. Moreover, since impurity in the context of a Jewish assembly in Galilee would probably have been understood by many of those present to be

---

[238] The association is apparent in a wide range of Jewish texts from the Second Temple, Tannaitic and Amoraic periods; see esp. *T. Jud.* 23.1–4; *T. Dan.* 5.5–8; *T. Naph.* 3.3; *T. Jos.* 20.2; *1 Enoch* 53.1–5; 55.3–4; *T. Sol.* 6.4; 8.10; *Mart. Isa.* 1.9; 2.4–5; *m. Shab.* 2.5; *m. Erub.* 4.1; *Gen. Rab.* 36.1; 52.7; *Ex. Rab.* 10.7; 30.16; *Lev. Rab.* 5.1. For further discussion of the relationship between demonic influence and Gentiles in ancient Jewish thought, see Böcher, *Das Neue Testament*, p. 16; O. Böcher, *Dämonenfurcht und Dämonenabwehr: Ein Beitrag zur Vorgeschichte der christlichen Taufe*, BWANT 90 (Stuttgart, 1970), pp. 139–43.

transferable either by touch or through the air in an enclosed space,[239] the exorcism in this context not only heals the individual patient but also removes a potential source of pollution from the entire community.

Despite the multiplicity of strategies that contribute to this impression, however, and as Bakhtin's dialogical principle would encourage us to expect, this story has room for other voices, registers, and ideological orientations. For alongside the centripetal energy that, at least on the surface, speaks for Jewish boundaries and particularity, a centrifugal movement can also be felt, speaking in a register that crosses traditional boundaries and expressing an implicit claim of cosmic and universal proportions. Jesus' brief incantatory utterance, to be precise, which is his sole method of exorcism in this context, not only lacks the conventional invocation of external divine aid, an appeal which, had it been included, would have indicated the identity of the god whose authority was needed; it furthermore has no feature that could even begin to distinguish it as a distinctively Jewish formula.

If emphasis is placed chiefly on the latter of these two instances of absence, the interpretative result will consist largely of a proper recognition of a specific instance of ideational polyphony or even incoherence, which would stand in tension with the various sources of textual cohesion analysed above but by no means cancel their effect. If on the other hand the emphasis is put primarily on the former case of absence (i.e., that of appeal to external sources of authority), the interpretation will need to entertain a possibility which much exegesis of the Synoptic Gospels in general has been largely unwilling to entertain, namely that by behaving in this context as if all the power and authority necessary to expel the demon were resident within his own person, Jesus tacitly plays the role of God himself.[240] The best option, of course, is probably to embrace both of these emphases, a choice that would allow (but not require) us to chasten the unruly heteroglossia of absence two by subordinating it to the potentially unifying force of absence one.[241] As these same two

---

[239] See, e.g., Lev. 14.43–47; 15.2b–27. My primary assumption here is neither that Pharisaic precursors to the rabbis would have been present in this assembly nor that the assembly was necessarily held in a building; rather, it is that synagogues in Palestine, like the Jewish prayer-houses in the diaspora, had as one of their several functions 'the reading of the law and the teaching of the commandments' (B. Lifshitz, *Donateurs et fondateurs dans les synagogues juives* (Paris, 1967), pp. 70–1, no. 79, a first-century CE inscription from Jerusalem cited in S. J. D. Cohen, *From the Maccabees to the Mishnah*, Library of Early Christianity (Philadelphia, 1987), pp. 112–13), including the laws of purity.

[240] An exception is Twelftree, *Jesus the Exorcist*, p. 173, and the handful of scholars mentioned there in n. 4.

[241] I.e. the divine power that Jesus makes present in the context of exorcism is none other than that of Yhwh, the God of Israel and of the Jewish people.

tendencies are also collocated in the Lucan writings' other stories of exorcism, comparative evidence related to each will be used in the ensuing chapters to enrich the interpretation and contextualisation begun here.

Conclusion

The present chapter has achieved a couple of overarching aims, both of which are important for the remaining parts of this study. In the first place, it has outlined a broadly sociolinguistic framework of concepts and techniques that integrates literary-stylistic and sociocultural dimensions of interpretation and allows them to illuminate one another. Simultaneously, by applying the framework to the story in Luke 4.33–37, it has demonstrated how attending to a text's multiple levels of language and context helps us to distinguish what is prominent in the text from what is not.

In regard to Luke 4.33–37 in particular, the most significant findings of this analysis relate to the episode's boundaries, its frontgrounding of Jesus' authority and power, tensions between its biblical-intertextual rhetoric and its cosmological assumptions, and the semantic and ritual implications of the conflict between 'the Holy One of God' and the 'unclean demon'. More specifically, by identifying the unit of analysis as 4.33–37 rather than 4.31–37, my interpretation construes 4.31–32 as an orientation for everything that follows up to the end of 4.44; consequently, the cohesion between the constituent units of 4.31–44 – and especially between the exorcism story and the episode of healing in 4.38–39 – already hints at what the comparative evidence in *4QExorcism ar* confirms, namely that Jesus' authority over the unclean spirits (i.e., not just 'diabolic power') is a prominent concern not only in 4.33–37 but also in 4.38–39. Furthermore, the analysis has demonstrated that the authority and power of Jesus in this story constitute not merely one overt motif among many but rather are presupposed, entailed and implicated on so many different levels of textual and contextual reality (e.g., information structure, repetition, transitivity, verbal aspect, intertextuality et al.) that together they constitute the episode's most prominent emphasis. Indeed, by implying that the divine authority essential for exorcistic victory is present and active in Jesus' own person, the story significantly deviates from its own biblical intertexts and thus poses an interpretative dilemma, which readers invariably negotiate according to ideological interests and other factors that are not my primary interest here. And finally, both through the lexis of holiness and impurity within the story itself and through the link between this emphasis and the reference in the antecedent co-text to

Conclusion

Elisha's cleansing of Naaman, potentially significant but largely ignored interfaces emerge in this story between demonology and impurity on the one hand, and between exorcism and rituals of purification on the other, which have not received the attention they deserve in critical exegesis. As these interfaces have even greater salience in Luke 8.26–39, they receive extensive treatment in the following chapter.

2

PURITY AND THE EXORCISM IN LUKE 8.26–39

To a degree which many interpreters have underestimated at their peril, the Synoptic tradition of the Gerasene demoniac (Luke 8.26–39; par. Matt. 8.28–34; Mark 5.1–20) is an interpretative mine-field. The multiplicity of demonic powers that possess the man from Gerasa (Luke 8.27, 30–33), for instance, has been taken by some interpreters as evidence that the man was suffering from multiple personality disorder,[1] a diagnosis that imposes a modern medical category on the ancient Mediterranean world-view of the text and requires Jesus to heal an illness which comparable folk healers probably never heal.[2] The same feature, moreover, in conjunction with the demons' disclosure of their collective name as 'Legion' (Luke 8.30), has enticed several other analysts into interpreting the story as a repudiation of 'the Roman military garrison',[3] a reading which overlooks the ultimately intertextual function of the story's military lexis and underestimates the importance of Jewish systems of impurity in the assumed context of culture.[4] And the request by Jesus for the demonic power's name (Luke 8.30) has led still other interpreters to worry about how Jesus' method of exorcism can escape being viewed as less 'Christian' than 'magical',[5] a problem that dissolves as soon as the distinction between 'magic' and 'Christianity' (or religion) is recognised as less substantive than perspectival.[6]

---

[1] E.g., S. L. Davies, *Jesus the Healer: Possession, Trance, and the Origins of Christianity* (London, 1995), pp. 88–9.
[2] On the difference between curable cases of 'possession sickness' and potentially incurable cases of 'madness', see L. A. Sharp, *The Possessed and the Dispossessed: Spirits, Identity, and Power in a Madagascar Migrant Town*, Comparative Studies of Health Systems and Medical Care (Berkeley, 1993), pp. 246–51.
[3] C. Myers, *Binding the Strong Man: A Political Reading of Mark's Story of Jesus* (Maryknoll, 1988), pp. 191–4; cf. P. W. Hollenbach, 'Help for Interpreting Jesus' Exorcisms', in E. H. Lovering (ed.), *SBLSP* 32 (1993), pp. 124–5.
[4] See discussion and notes below, pp. 111; 125–33.
[5] See, e.g., Bovon, *Luc (1.1–9,50)*, p. 425.
[6] In support of this view, see T. E. Klutz, 'Reinterpreting Magic in the World of Jewish and Christian Scripture: An Introduction', in T. E. Klutz (ed.), *Magic in the Biblical World:*

But more importantly, these kinds of difficulties and the desire to solve them have become so distracting in scholarly commentary on this story that several important aspects of the text's style and cultural context have suffered neglect. The ensuing analysis therefore reflects an effort to be less concerned about solving problems than about inferring meanings, identifying emphases, and recovering cultural contexts, an effort which, even where it leaves problems unsolved, may at least allow them to be seen in a new or more revealing light. This kind of attempt furthermore matches very well the use of concepts and techniques such as those employed in the preceding chapter. The Greek text to which they are applied below reads as follows:

26 Καὶ κατέπλευσαν εἰς τὴν χώραν τῶν Γερασηνῶν, ἥτις ἐστὶν ἀντιπέρα τῆς Γαλιλαίας. 27 ἐξελθόντι δὲ αὐτῷ ἐπὶ τὴν γῆν ὑπήντησεν ἀνήρ τις ἐκ τῆς πόλεως ἔχων δαιμόνια καὶ χρόνῳ ἱκανῷ οὐκ ἐνεδύσατο ἱμάτιον καὶ ἐν οἰκίᾳ οὐκ ἔμενεν ἀλλ' ἐν τοῖς μνήμασιν. 28 ἰδὼν δὲ τὸν Ἰησοῦν ἀνακράξας προσέπεσεν αὐτῷ καὶ φωνῇ μεγάλῃ εἶπεν· Τί ἐμοὶ καὶ σοί, Ἰησοῦ υἱὲ τοῦ θεοῦ τοῦ ὑψίστου; δέομαί σου, μή με βασανίσῃς. 29 παρήγγειλεν γὰρ τῷ πνεύματι τῷ ἀκαθάρτῳ ἐξελθεῖν ἀπὸ τοῦ ἀνθρώπου. πολλοῖς γὰρ χρόνοις συνηρπάκει αὐτὸν καὶ ἐδεσμεύετο ἁλύσεσιν καὶ πέδαις φυλασσόμενος καὶ διαρρήσσων τὰ δεσμὰ ἠλαύνετο ὑπὸ τοῦ δαιμονίου εἰς τὰς ἐρήμους. 30 ἐπηρώτησεν δὲ αὐτὸν ὁ Ἰησοῦς· Τί σοι ὄνομά ἐστιν; ὁ δὲ εἶπεν· Λεγιών, ὅτι εἰσῆλθεν δαιμόνια πολλὰ εἰς αὐτόν. 31 καὶ παρεκάλουν αὐτὸν ἵνα μὴ ἐπιτάξῃ αὐτοῖς εἰς τὴν ἄβυσσον ἀπελθεῖν. 32 Ἦν δὲ ἐκεῖ ἀγέλη χοίρων ἱκανῶν βοσκομένη ἐν τῷ ὄρει· καὶ παρεκάλεσαν αὐτὸν ἵνα ἐπιτρέψῃ αὐτοῖς εἰς ἐκείνους εἰσελθεῖν· καὶ ἐπέτρεψεν αὐτοῖς. 33 ἐξελθόντα δὲ τὰ δαιμόνια ἀπὸ τοῦ ἀνθρώπου εἰσῆλθον εἰς τοὺς χοίρους, καὶ ὥρμησεν ἡ ἀγέλη κατὰ τοῦ κρημνοῦ εἰς τὴν λίμνην καὶ ἀπεπνίγη. 34 Ἰδόντες δὲ οἱ βόσκοντες τὸ γεγονὸς ἔφυγον καὶ ἀπήγγειλαν εἰς τὴν πόλιν καὶ εἰς τοὺς ἀγρούς. 35 ἐξῆλθον δὲ ἰδεῖν τὸ γεγονὸς καὶ ἦλθον πρὸς τὸν Ἰησοῦν καὶ εὗρον καθήμενον τὸν ἄνθρωπον ἀφ' οὗ τὰ δαιμόνια ἐξῆλθεν ἱματισμένον καὶ σωφρονοῦντα παρὰ τοὺς πόδας τοῦ Ἰησοῦ, καὶ ἐφοβήθησαν. 36 ἀπήγγειλαν δὲ αὐτοῖς οἱ ἰδόντες πῶς ἐσώθη ὁ δαιμονισθείς. 37 καὶ ἠρώτησεν αὐτὸν ἅπαν τὸ πλῆθος τῆς περιχώρου τῶν Γερασηνῶν

From the Rod of Aaron to the Ring of Solomon, JSNTSup 245 (London, 2003), pp. 1–9, and the scholarly literature cited there.

ἀπελθεῖν ἀπ' αὐτῶν, ὅτι φόβῳ μεγάλῳ συνείχοντο· αὐτὸς δὲ ἐμβὰς εἰς πλοῖον ὑπέστρεψεν. 38 ἐδεῖτο δὲ αὐτοῦ ὁ ἀνὴρ ἀφ' οὗ ἐξεληλύθει τὰ δαιμόνια εἶναι σὺν αὐτῷ· ἀπέλυσεν δὲ αὐτὸν λέγων· 39 Ὑπόστρεφε εἰς τὸν οἶκόν σου καὶ διηγοῦ ὅσα σοι ἐποίησεν ὁ θεός. καὶ ἀπῆλθεν καθ' ὅλην τὴν πόλιν κηρύσσων ὅσα ἐποίησεν αὐτῷ ὁ Ἰησοῦς.

Cohesion and boundaries

Unlike the story discussed in the preceding chapter, Luke's second exorcism narrative possesses relatively uncontroversial boundaries, leaving little room for doubt about where the episode begins and ends. This clarity stems chiefly from the presence of particular thematic structures which, in addition to effecting cohesion among the clauses and sentences of Luke 8.26–39, are demonstrably absent from the surrounding episodes. The noun χώρα, for instance, which is used in 8.26 and echoed by περίχωρος in 8.37, occurs not once between Luke 3.2 and 8.25, and makes no further appearance in the ensuing co-text prior to Luke 12.16.[7] Similarly Γερασηνός, which occurs once near the beginning of this story (8.26) and again near its end (8.37), appears nowhere else in Luke–Acts.[8] The repetition of the noun πόλις (8.27, 34 and 39), moreover, whose precise referent can be determined only by construing a connection back to Γερασηνῶν in 8.26, not only strengthens the sense of cohesion among these verses but also helps to distinguish them from the surrounding materials since it is not used either in the immediately preceding episode (8.22–25, the Stilling of the Storm) or in those that directly follow (8.40–56). This understanding of the unit's boundaries is reinforced by several other considerations, some of which are treated below in my examination of the story's structure.

---

[7] The cognate noun περίχωρος does not occur in Luke's Gospel after 8.37, though it does occur in Acts 14.6.

[8] The textual problem concerning which city Jesus and the disciples travelled to is treated in detail in my unrevised PhD thesis (T. E. Klutz, 'With Authority and Power: A Sociostylistic Investigation of Exorcism in Luke–Acts', University of Sheffield (1996), pp. 78–9), where I defend the reading adopted by the UBS and Nestle-Aland texts, i.e. Γερασηνῶν (8.26, 37). For further discussion of the difficulty see J. McRay, *Archaeology and the New Testament* (Grand Rapids, 1991), pp. 166–8; T. Baarda, 'Gadarenes, Gerasenes, Gergesenes and the "Diatessaron" Traditions', in E. E. Ellis and M. Wilcox (eds), *Neotestamentica et Semitica: Studies in Honour of Matthew Black* (Edinburgh, 1969), pp. 188–94; C. Masson, 'Le démoniaque de Gérasa: Marc 5:1–20 (Matthieu 8:28–34; Luc 8:26–39)', in *Vers les sources d'eau vive: Études d'exégèse et de théologie du Nouveau Testament*, Publications de la Faculté de théologie, Université de Lausanne (Lausanne, 1961), pp. 20–1; Schmid, *Das Evangelium nach Lucas*, p. 162; Fitzmyer, *Luke I–IX*, pp. 736–7.

As just demonstrated, the particular features that give a story its lines of demarcation can also contribute much to its unity and cohesion. In terms of cohesion, for instance, two of the most important referents in Luke 8.26–39 are the man and the group of demons, both of which are denoted for the first time in 8.27 (ἀνήρ τις ἐκ τῆς πόλεως ἔχων δαιμόνια). Following their initial appearance, they are almost constantly in view until the end of 8.39, where they leave Luke's narrative as abruptly as they entered it. Their referential prominence therefore strongly enhances the cohesion of 8.26–39 while simultaneously confirming the normal understanding of the unit's boundaries.[9]

Numerous other factors contributing to the cohesion of this story could be mentioned – the referential salience of Jesus, for instance, and the typically frequent use of the conjunctions καί, δέ, γάρ, and ὅτι – but the evidence summarised above is sufficient to confirm that Luke 8.26–39 is both internally cohesive and a distinct unit of text.

Story structure

Although this story does not provide a fully developed 'abstract', it does supply something of a preview in its 'orientation' (8.26–27); for 8.26–27 hints that the story will revolve primarily around an encounter between Jesus and 'a man from the city who had demons' (8.27). As a proper orientation, moreover, 8.26–27 also discloses *who* was involved in the action (i.e., Jesus, the man, and the demons), *when* the action occurred (i.e., after the stilling of the storm, as indicated by Καὶ κατέπλευσαν, and after Jesus had stepped from the boat onto the land, as indicated by the temporal participle ἐξελθόντι), and *where* it took place (i.e., τὴν χώραν τῶν Γερασηνῶν, ἥτις ἐστὶν ἀντιπέρα τῆς Γαλιλαίας).

However, the orientation provided by 8.26–27 is not as complete as it may at first seem; for some of the story's participants – the pigs, the herdsmen, and the people from the surrounding area – are not introduced until 8.32–34. Two discursive effects of this delay are worth noting. On the one hand, although the introduction of new characters momentarily decelerates the progress of narrated action, it simultaneously sets the stage for dramatic events that sharply increase the pace: the destruction of the swine, for instance, happens to 'characters' who do not appear until the story is half finished and, almost immediately after their introduction, are

---

[9] In addition, the impression that all the clauses of 8.26–39 cohere around one unifying topic is reinforced by the two instances of ὅσα ... ἐποίησεν in 8.39, which implicitly encapsulate the entire story: it concerns what God, acting through Jesus, did for the demoniac.

driven by the demons to a mass death. On the other hand, since neither the swine nor the herdsmen are foregrounded by any feature of the narrative, neither of them appears to have been central to the rhetorical interests of the implied author; nor for that matter does either of them play as important a role as that filled by the people who hear the herdsmen's report (8.34–37), whose function is treated below in relation to the evaluative aspects of narrative structure.

Following the first phase of orientation, 8.28–32 consists primarily of 'complicating action'.[10] In 8.28, for instance, the demoniac falls before Jesus and addresses him. In 8.30 Jesus asks the possessing agent for its name[11] and receives the startling reply (i.e., λεγιών). In 8.31–32b the demons beg Jesus not to command them to depart to the abyss, and to permit them to enter the nearby swine instead. And in 8.32c he grants their request. This whole set of developments, however, is only the first of two cycles of complicating action; for further complications in the plot arise after the climax narrated in 8.33.

The 'resolution' of the cycle of events just summarised is narrated in 8.33, where, after the demons enter the pigs, the latter rush down the bank and drown. The climactic quality of these events, moreover, is intensified by the dramatic placement of the verb ἀποπνίγω at the end of the sentence. In view of this extraordinary denouement, and in light of the relatively simple plot of the exorcism story in Luke 4.33–37, the present episode might seem to have reached its end, opening up the possibility that a new episode is just about to be introduced.

Instead of any fulfilment of these expectations, however, a new cycle of complicating action is introduced (8.34–39a) and the same story is continued. The herdsmen, for instance, having witnessed the newsworthy events, bolt to the city and the nearby farms, spreading news about 'what had happened' (8.34). Next, the people from these areas come out to see 'what had happened', discover the former demoniac completely transformed, and find themselves overwhelmed by fear (8.35). The frightened newcomers are then told by the herdsmen how the man had been healed

---

[10] The only exception is the explanatory aside in 8.29, which momentarily suspends progress in the assumed sequence of events and functions as 'evaluation'.

[11] As noted by Twelftree, *Christ Triumphant*, p. 64, Jesus' request for the demonic power's name could have been understood by ancient readers as an effort to obtain tactical advantage, especially since (1) the enemy has just displayed knowledge of Jesus' identity (8.28), and (2) Jesus' use of the singular pronoun in τί σοι ὄνομά ἐστιν entails that he may have underestimated his opponents' number. On the other hand, the request need not have only one function; and by prompting a disclosure of the enemy's multiplicity – a legion in the Roman army consisted of around 5,500 men – the question also draws attention to the magnitude of Jesus' eventual victory.

(8.36). The newcomers, however, despite the healing, respond by asking Jesus to get away from them (8.37a), and Jesus begins to comply with their request (8.37b). Before Jesus is able to get away, though, and in contrast to the awestruck people from the surrounding region, the former demoniac communicates a desire to remain near Jesus (8.38a); but the latter, having alternative plans for the man, sends him back to his home and instructs him to declare how much God had done for him (8.38b–39a). With the second cycle of complicating action having thereby reached its end, the story's second and final resolution is narrated: the one who had once been controlled by demons now obeys the command of Jesus and proclaims 'throughout the whole city how much Jesus had done for him' (8.39b).

Scattered throughout these parts of the story are elements of 'evaluation', which momentarily interrupt the chronological sequence of narrated events in order to explain the present relevance of the action to the audience. For instance, immediately after narrating the approach of the demoniac (8.27a), the storyteller briefly suspends the progress of action in order to give some background information about the man: 'for a long time', says the narrator, the man 'had not worn clothes and was not staying in a house but among the tombs' (8.27b, trans. mine). As Roger Spielmann has observed, information about 'what didn't happen' (or about what a given character did not do) often both anticipates and highlights subsequent narration of what did take place;[12] and here in 8.27b, the description of the man as not wearing clothes and not living in a house both anticipates and underscores Jesus' eventual reversal of these privations (8.34–36, 39). As this same sense of reversal is adumbrated further by several other features discussed below (e.g., verbal aspect and intertextuality), it will emerge by the end of this analysis as one of the story's most prominent emphases.

Similar effects are generated by the aside in 8.29b, where the narrator explains why Jesus commanded the spirit to depart: 'For many a time it had seized him [i.e., the man]; he used to be kept under guard, being bound with chains and fetters, but breaking apart the bonds he was repeatedly driven by the demon into the desert.' By providing these details, the storyteller highlights the extremity of the man's illness: prior to his encounter with Jesus, numerous attempts had been made to constrain him, but all these had failed. Indirectly, the image of not just one but multiple failures also serves to underscore the extraordinary power and

---

[12] R. Spielmann, 'Collateral Information in Narrative Discourse', *Journal of Literary Semantics* 16 (1987), pp. 207–9.

success of the subsequent intervention by Jesus. And finally, since Jesus' exorcistic command (παρήγγειλεν...τῷ πνεύματι τῷ ἀκαθάρτῳ, 8.29a) is implied by the ensuing conjunction in πολλοῖς γὰρ χρόνοις συνηρπάκει αὐτόν (8.29b) to be motivated simply by consideration of the man's pitiable bondage, this same information simultaneously focuses attention on Jesus' compassion. To an audience that had no doubts about the ability of demons to cause illness and other forms of misfortune, this combination of features would have made the relevance of this story abundantly clear.

Another noteworthy instance of 'evaluation' is present in the words τὴν χώραν τῶν Γερασηνῶν, ἥτις ἐστὶν ἀντιπέρα τῆς Γαλιλαίας (8.26),[13] which imply an audience that knows the location of Galilee but not that of Gerasa.[14] From the standpoint of story structure, though, the chief import of this construction resides not in its contribution to the image of the text's audience but rather in what it might be understood to imply about the religious and cultural affinities of the Gerasenes: living 'opposite Galilee' (i.e., in the geographical area of the Decapolis), the people of Gerasa were thoroughly Hellenised and predominantly Gentile.[15] As for the interpretative implications of this point, however, we should proceed only with the utmost caution. What contemporary scholarship knows about the Decapolis around 30–40 CE should not be equated with what the author or audience of Luke–Acts knew,[16] especially since the author in particular seems to have been confused about the whereabouts of Gerasa.[17] Thus, to assert unequivocally, as J. Fitzmyer does, that the demoniac was a Gentile[18] is to underestimate the complexity of this matter; after all,

---

[13] The relative clause is without parallel in the Matthaean and Marcan versions of the story.

[14] Similarly Luke's first reference to Galilee, in Luke 1.26, presupposes a reader who knows the location of Galilee but not that of Nazareth. On the implied reader's geographical knowledge, see esp. Tyson, *Images of Judaism*, pp. 24–5.

[15] C. H. Kraeling, *Gerasa: City of the Decapolis* (New Haven, 1938), pp. 27–32; and E. Schürer, *The History of the Jewish People in the Age of Jesus Christ (175 B.C.–A.D. 135)*, ed. G. Vermes et al., rev. edn (Edinburgh, 1979), II, pp. 125–6, 149–55.

[16] E. Hilgert, 'Symbolismus und Heilsgeschichte in den Evangelien: Ein Beitrag zu den Seesturm- und Gerasenererzählungen', in F. Christ (ed.), *Oikonomia: Heilsgeschichte als Thema der Theologie* (Hamburg, 1967), p. 56, interprets the reference to Gerasa in 8.26 as signalling a preview of the Gentile mission; but since Luke, unlike Matthew and Mark, never even refers to the 'Decapolis' (of which Gerasa was a part), his implied audience cannot be assumed to know about the area's strongly Hellenistic character, knowledge they would need in order to understand the proposed signal.

[17] As Gerasa is thirty-seven miles southeast of the Sea of Galilee, which is the 'lake' Jesus crosses in Luke 8.22–27, it cannot be the historical site of Jesus' encounter with the demoniac. Cf. McRay, *Archaeology*, pp. 167–8; P. Perkins, 'Gerasa', *HBD*, p. 340.

[18] Fitzmyer, *Luke I–IX*, p. 735. Cf. F. Annen, *Heil für die Heiden: Zur Bedeutung und Geschichte der Tradition vom besessenen Gerasener (Mk 5, 1–20 parr.)*, FTS 20 (Frankfurt,

according to Josephus (*J.W.* 2.480), the inhabitants of Gerasa included not only Gentiles but also Jews,[19] and several aspects of the demoniac's character (e.g., his apparent knowledge of Jewish Scripture and his possible hostility to the Romans) are more appropriate to a Jew than to a Gentile.[20]

Only one other instance of evaluation merits attention here. In 8.37, having just narrated the request of the local population that Jesus go elsewhere, the storyteller pauses briefly to explain their unreceptiveness: ὅτι φόβῳ μεγάλῳ συνείχοντο. Due perhaps to the powerful influence of emotion on the formation of memory, any event that arouses intense fear among a large group of people (e.g., natural disasters and wars) has good potential for development into an entertaining story.[21] But just as important, in this particular situation the description of hostility to Jesus as stemming from 'fear' may also have fulfilled an ideological function: to be precise, it could have been understood to imply that repudiation of Jesus often stems from a shameful lack of courage.[22] Strong support for this reading is given below in my treatment of repetition.

As for the object of this fear, nothing explicit is said either by the narrator or by any of the characters. Nevertheless, by attending especially to patterns of repetition and their sequencing, we may be able to fill this gap in a way that respects the complexities of the text and illuminates the force of its rhetoric.

Repetition

Several morphemes, words and phrases that are employed repeatedly in Luke's version of this story occur either less frequently or not at all in the Matthaean and Marcan parallels (Matt. 8.28–34; Mark 5.1–20). A noteworthy example of this phenomenon is Luke's repetition of the substantive τὸ γεγονός (8.34, 35), which occurs only once in the Marcan parallel (5.14) and not at all in the Matthaean. On the level of reference

---

1976), pp. 182–3; P. Lamarche, 'Le Possédé de Gérasa (Matt. 8, 28–34; Mc 5, 1–20; Lc 8, 26–39)', *NRT* 90 (1968), p. 590; and Van der Loos, *Miracles of Jesus*, p. 387. For a more cautious assessment, see Sabourin, *L'Evangile de Luc*, p. 190.

[19] Cf. Kraeling, *Gerasa*, pp. 33–4; Schürer, *History of the Jewish People*, II, p. 150.

[20] Cf. J. D. M. Derrett, 'Contributions to the Study of the Gerasene Demoniac', *JSNT* 3 (1979), pp. 6, 13; and Busse, *Die Wunder des Propheten Jesus*, p. 206.

[21] On the relationship between human emotion, memorability and narrative, see M. Freeman, *Rewriting the Self: History, Memory, Narrative* (London, 1993), pp. 92–4.

[22] While 'fear' is not usually portrayed negatively in Luke–Acts, in some contexts it is the antithesis of faith, as, e.g., in Luke 8.25, 50. On the relationship between fearlessness and honour among ancient Mediterranean males, see B. J. Malina, *The New Testament World: Insights from Cultural Anthropology*, 3rd edn (Louisville, 2001), pp. 47, 49.

and cohesion, the two occurrences in the Lucan account have almost identical functions: in each case the article is anaphoric, pointing back to the events just narrated and linking the new cycle of complications to the one preceding. However, on the level of perceptual point of view, they differ significantly: most notably, in 8.34 the phrase denotes what had been seen by the swineherds, whose chief interest surely would have been the drowned swine, whereas in 8.35 the phrase denotes what was seen subsequently by other people from the surrounding area, whose sole object of interest (at least initially) is the transformed state of the former demoniac. The repetition of τὸ γεγονός in these verses therefore enables Luke's audience to view the exorcism from two very different perspectives, one focusing on the destruction of property and the other on the transformation of the patient.

This same contrast, moreover, contributes to a significant but seldom noticed pattern in the plot and structure of 8.35–39. In 8.37–39, for instance, the contrast in responses to Jesus – the people ask him to go away (8.37), whereas the former demoniac wants to stay with him (8.38) – reads very much like an elaboration of the antithesis between the destructive and salvific aspects of the exorcism. This two-sided quality of the event is developed still further by means of the fear motif in verses 35 and 37, which is noteworthy not only for its contribution to the tension just noted but also as another distinctively Lucan instance of repetition.

Although both Luke and Mark characterise the people from the surrounding region as having been frightened by the man's miraculous transformation (ἐφοβήσαν, Luke 8.35; Mark 5.15), only Luke describes the people's subsequent repudiation of Jesus as arising from 'great fear' (φόβῳ μεγάλῳ, 8.37). As the morpheme φοβ- furthermore does not occur anywhere else in the Marcan parallel, its greater prominence in Luke's account invites comment. In 8.35 the short clause in which the verbal form occurs (καὶ ἐφοβήσαν) presents no unusual difficulties: the paratactic structure of 8.35 as a whole, the shift in transitivity from behavioural processes (e.g., ἦλθον) to a mental one, and the frontgrounding of the immediately preceding description of the man's transformation all work together to envisage a state of awe caused by the occurrence of something extraordinary or divine[23] – in this context, Jesus' dramatic reversal of the man's condition.

Perhaps owing to the morphological correspondence between the verb ἐφοβήσαν and the noun used in 8.37, many commentators have construed

---

[23] Cf. Kirschläger, *Jesu exorzistisches Wirken*, p. 118 n. 182; Schneider, *Das Evangelium nach Lucas*, p. 195; Nolland, *Luke*, I, p. 412.

them in this context as having an almost identical semantic architecture, with the supramundane transformation of the man being both the cause of fear in 8.35 and the unexpressed object of the 'great fear' in 8.37.[24] Several details in 8.35–37, however, militate strongly against this reading. Most notably, in the summary of the herdsmen's speech in 8.36 (πῶς ἐσώθη ὁ δαιμονισθείς), and thus between the first and second occurrences of φοβ- (8.35, 37), the adverb πῶς ('in what manner') implies that what the herdsmen reported had less to do with the dramatic transformation of the demoniac – a reality their audience had already deduced for themselves (8.35) – than with the event's visible circumstances and material consequences, with special emphasis probably having been placed on the destruction of the swine. Consequently, the local people's hostile response to Jesus (8.37) is represented both temporally and logically as arising not from awestruck recognition of the miraculous but rather from the implied report about the swine.

In 8.37, moreover, a strong sense that the people's response to this report involves something qualitatively different from the innocent fear mentioned in 8.35 – indeed, something shameful and very negative – is created by the lexicogrammatical pattern of the clause ὅτι φόβῳ μεγάλῳ συνείχοντο, for συνέχω in the passive voice with a simple dative of instrument is used earlier in Luke's Gospel to denote the experience of being 'gripped' by a demonically caused illness (Luke 4.38).[25] And finally, as indicated by the presence of ὅτι just before the noun in 8.37, the fear in that context is central to the narrator's explanation of the people's rejection of Jesus, a response whose impropriety is underscored by its resemblance to the repudiation of Jesus in the synagogue of Nazareth (Luke 4.25–30).[26]

In Luke 8.36–37, therefore, the people's agitation over the loss of the swine causes their initial awe in the presence of divine power to transmute

---

[24] Cf. R. Pesch, *Der Besessene von Gerasa: Entstehung und Überlieferung einer Wundergeschichte*, SBS 56 (Stuttgart, 1972), p. 63; Schürmann, *Das Lukasevangelium*, p. 486; Kirschläger, *Jesu exorzistisches Wirken*, p. 118 n. 182. Taken this way, the Lucan account would differ at this point from the Marcan parallel, where the local people's repudiation of Jesus directly follows an explicit reference to the herdsmen to the swine (Mark 5.16–17), and which therefore is widely recognised as insinuating that anxieties over the destruction of the swine lead to the repudiation. For further discussion of this facet of the Marcan account, see Masson, 'Le démoniaque de Gérasa', p. 29.

[25] Cf. also Matt. 4.24 (ποικίλαις νόσοις καὶ βασάνοις συνεχομένους); Acts 28.8 (πυρετοῖς καὶ δυσεντερίῳ συνεχόμενον).

[26] Eleven of the twelve contexts where φόβος occurs in Luke–Acts connect the experiences denoted by this noun to supramundane events of one kind or another. See Luke 1.12, 65; 2.9; 5.26; 7.16; 8.37; 21.26; Acts 2.43; 5.5, 11; 19.17; Acts 9.31 is the only exception. As the fear that overwhelms Zechariah in Luke 1.12 is accompanied by unbelief (1.20), it is especially comparable to that in 8.37.

into a monstrous externality whose effects, ironically, are not unlike those produced by demons. The rhetorical impact of this and similar connections between demonic influence and economic interest in Luke–Acts as a whole is discussed further in the chapter below on Acts 16.16–18, where the co-occurrence of these same motifs contributes to a striking parallel between that episode and the one treated here.

Just as the repetition of φοβ- foregrounds the greatness of Jesus' power by highlighting the diverse effects it has on people, so the exclusively Lucan repetition of ἐπιτρέπω (8.32) highlights Jesus' authority over the demons. Luke 8.32b in particular, like its parallel in Mark 5.13, contains a brief note about Jesus 'permitting' the demons to enter the pigs: καὶ ἐπέτρεψεν αὐτοῖς. As in Mark, moreover, so in Luke the reference to the process of permitting is made by the narrator, and in each case a hierarchy of authority is entailed, with the position of Jesus tacitly being above that of the demons.[27] In Luke's version of the story, however, this is not the first occurrence of this idea (as it is in Mark's) but rather the second; for in the immediately preceding sentence of the Lucan account (Luke 8.32a), the demons themselves are described as begging Jesus to 'permit' (ἐπιτρέψῃ) them to enter the pigs. Thus, by repeating ἐπιτρέπω so as to suggest that not only the story's narrator but also the demons themselves see Jesus as standing above them in the cosmic order, Luke emphasises the authority of Jesus to a degree that is unmatched by the parallels in Mark and Matthew.[28]

This emphasis on Jesus' authority over the demons is underscored yet further by Luke's repetition of παρακαλέω (in the sense of 'to beg',[29] as in the RSV). Occurring twice in 8.31–32, in both instances it denotes a verbal action which the demons perform on Jesus. And since beggars are typically inferior in rank to their beggees, these two instances of παρακαλέω tacitly confirm what the uses of ἐπιτρέπω and ἐπιτάσσω in the same story imply: as one who holds power and authority over an entire 'legion' of demons, Jesus occupies a very lofty position in the cosmic hierarchy.

Also worthy of comment is Luke's repetition of the morpheme ἱματ- (8.27, 35), which, like τὸ γεγονός, is utilised only once in the Marcan version (Mark 5.15) and not at all in the Matthaean. By itself, though, the repetition of this form in the Lucan account is scarcely indicative of its weighty contribution to the episode's overall force, for it not only adds

---

[27] See, e.g., Matt. 19.8 (par. Mark 10.4); John 19.38; Acts 21.39, 40; 26.1; 27.3; 28.16.
[28] Cf. Pesch, *Der Besessene von Gerasa*, p. 61.
[29] BAGD, s.v. 'παρακαλέω'. Inequality in status between speaker and hearer is implied by the same term in Luke 7.4; 8.41; Acts 9.38; 13.42; 16.15; 21.12; 24.4; 25.2.

salience to the clothing motif but also strengthens the story's dramatic power and intertextual rhetoric. More specifically, unlike Mark, whose reference to the healed demoniac as 'clothed' (Mark 5.15) is that account's only hint that the man was ever naked, Luke explicitly asserts at the outset that 'for a long time the man had worn no clothes [ἱμάτιον, 8.27]'; consequently, the subsequent portrayal of the man in Luke as 'clothed' (ἱματισμένον, 8.35) stands out as an especially spectacular reversal of his previously naked and miserable condition.[30] Furthermore, and as discussed at greater length below, this same instance of repetition contributes to an intertextual link between Luke's version of the story and LXX Isaiah 58.6–7, where the 'day acceptable to the Lord' is pictured as a time when the hungry are fed and the naked are clothed (Isa. 58.7).

Effects similar to those produced by the occurrences of ἱματ- are generated by Luke's repetition of the morpheme οἰκ- (οἰκία in 8.27, οἶκος in 8.39), which occurs twice in Mark's rendition (5.3, 19) but not at all in Matthew's. Once again, comparing Luke with Mark proves very illuminating, and particularly significant contrasts emerge when the first use of οἰκ- in Luke's account is compared with its Marcan parallel. Immediately after his reference to the demoniac's nakedness (8.27), for instance, Luke comments on the man's customary encampment: καὶ ἐν οἰκίᾳ οὐκ ἔμενεν ἀλλ᾽ ἐν τοῖς μνήμασιν. In terms of basic content, this description differs little from the parallel in Mark, whose relative clause ὅς [i.e., the demoniac] τὴν κατοίκησιν εἶχεν ἐν τοῖς μνήμασιν portrays the man as having a 'dwelling' among the tombs. Despite the ideational similarities between the two versions, however, there are notable differences between them in terms of stylistic effect. To be precise, whereas the construction in Mark represents the man as actually having a 'dwelling'[31] – a dwelling, that is, among the tombs – in Luke the adversative ἀλλά, placed between ἐν οἰκίᾳ οὐκ ἔμενεν and ἐν τοῖς μνήμασιν, conventionally implicates that 'tombs' cannot rightly be considered a 'dwelling' at all. Consequently, in contrast to Mark, Luke pictures the man as having been deprived not only of clothes but also of a bona fide dwelling; and as a result, the wretchedness of the man's condition is more pronounced in Luke than it is in Mark.

---

[30] Cf. Pesch, *Der Besessene von Gerasa*, p. 59; Schneider, *Das Evangelium nach Lucas*, I, p. 193; Bovon, *Luc (1,1–9,50)*, p. 419; Kirschläger, *Jesu exorzistisches Wirken*, p. 103. On the reversal of fortunes as one of Luke's favourite descriptions of salvation, see J. B. Green, '"The Message of Salvation" in Luke–Acts', *ExAud* 5 (1989), pp. 27–30.

[31] Although τὴν κατοίκησιν εἶχεν can be rendered into idiomatic English as 'he lived' (BAGD, s.v. 'κατοίκησις'), the noun κατοίκησις overlaps semantically with οἰκία and denotes a dwelling or home.

This same divergence also anticipates a difference in literary effect between the second occurrences of οἰκ- in the two accounts (Luke 8.39; Mark 5.19). Most notably, since the demoniac in Mark does actually have a dwelling of sorts (i.e., in the tombs), Mark's subsequent reference to Jesus instructing the man to go to his 'home' (τὸν οἶκον, 5.19) allows the reader to see the man's transformation as consisting simply of a relocation from one home to another, from a home in the tombs to a home with his friends. By contrast, as the demoniac in Luke is initially characterised as not having a home, Luke's subsequent reference to Jesus instructing the man to return to his 'home' (τὸν οἶκον) invites the audience to interpret the man's transformation not merely as a move from one home to another but rather as a change from homelessness to the lodgings he had enjoyed before he fell prey to Legion. The effects of Luke's repetition of οἰκ- are therefore more dramatic than Mark's and convey a stronger sense of reversal: the naked have been clothed, the homeless have been given shelter.[32] And once again the Lucan account corresponds to LXX Isaiah: the fast acceptable to the Lord, according to LXX Isaiah 58.7, requires not only clothing the naked but also bringing 'the homeless poor into your house' (πτωχοὺς ἀστέγους εἴσαγε εἰς τὸν οἶκόν σου).

The probability that our story contains a deliberate allusion to LXX Isaiah 58.6–7 is increased still further by an instance of repetition not yet mentioned. The morpheme δεσ-, which occurs twice in Luke's version of the story (the verb δεσμεύω and the noun δεσμός in 8.29), is completely absent from the Matthaean and Marcan accounts, though Mark does use the morphologically cognate verb δέω once (the infinitive δεδέσθαι in Mark 5.4). Like the motifs of clothing and housing, the motif of oppressive 'bonds' occurs both in this story and in LXX Isaiah 58.6–7, helping to build an intertextual bridge which is especially strong in the Lucan version due to its repeated use of the Isaiah text's vocabulary.

Only one other instance of repetition in this story merits attention. In 8.39, the exclamatory correlative ὅσος occurs twice with the verb ἐποίησεν – first, in Jesus' instruction to the former demoniac, 'Return to your home and declare *how much God has done for you*' (ὅσα σοι ἐποίησεν ὁ θεός), and second, in the narrator's summary of what the man actually proceeded to proclaim, namely, 'how much *Jesus* had done for him' (ὅσα ἐποίησεν αὐτῷ ὁ Ἰησοῦς). Due not only to the repetition but also to the nearness of the two constructions to one another, a striking

---

[32] Cf. Kirschläger, *Jesu exorzistisches Wirken*, p. 116.

parallelism emerges, with the salvific action of God being tacitly equated with the exorcistic deed of Jesus.[33] The Matthaean version of this story, it is worth noting, omits this material altogether; whereas Mark, although he includes it, makes the parallelism between the intervention of 'the Lord' and the action of Jesus considerably less salient. This latter difference in prominence becomes almost immediately apparent when the relevant clauses of each account are printed next to one another as parallel lines, with features of metre and word order and tense form all contributing to the Lucan structure's greater schematic intensity:

Luke 8.39: ὅσα σοι ἐποίησεν ὁ θεός
ὅσα ἐποίησεν αὐτῷ ὁ Ἰησοῦς.

Mark 5.19–20: ὅσα ὁ κύριός σοι πεποίηκεν καὶ ἠλέησέν σε (5.19)
ὅσα ἐποίησεν αὐτῷ ὁ Ἰησοῦς (5.20).

Word order and information structure

Immediately after referring in 8.27 to the demons, the story's narrator begins his summary of the demoniac's condition with the independent clause καὶ χρόνῳ ἱκανῷ οὐκ ἐνεδύσατο ἱμάτιον καὶ ἐν οἰκίᾳ οὐκ ἔμενεν ἀλλ' ἐν τοῖς μνήμασιν. The adverbial group χρόνῳ ἱκανῷ, by preceding the main verb of its clause, stands out as a marked theme and thereby foregrounds the extensive duration of the man's sufferings.[34] Perhaps, since the man has been afflicted for a long time, other healers have tried to help but found no success; whatever assumptions we make in this connection, the man comes to Jesus with no minor illness. But most importantly, by emphasising the longevity of the man's condition, this fronting of χρόνῳ ἱκανῷ indirectly serves to heighten the power and authority of Jesus' subsequent expulsion of the demons (8.33).

Above, my treatment of the fear motif suggested that the people's rejection of Jesus in 8.37 is best understood as stemming directly from

---

[33] Cf. Schneider, *Das Evangelium nach Lucas*, p. 195: 'Was Gott tun will, tut er durch Jesus'.

[34] Cf. Pesch, *Der Besessene von Gerasa*, p. 59. A similar effect is achieved in 8.29, where πολλοῖς ... χρόνοις is placed before the verb συνηρπάκει for special emphasis.

the healing's destructive aspects. The importance of this connection in its Lucan context, however, is indicated not only by the distinctiveness of the Lucan account's repetition of φοβ- (8.35, 37) but also by the thematic location of φόβῳ μεγάλῳ in its clause (8.37). More specifically, by placing it ahead of the verb on which it depends (i.e., συνείχοντο), Luke makes φόβῳ μεγάλῳ a marked theme,[35] which coincides with the instance of repetition to frontground the people's fear of additional material loss. Furthermore, since this same construction is situated in a clause that highlights the relevance of the story for its audience, it hints that the fear inside the world of the narrative is not without parallel outside the text, in the social world of the implied author and audience: as in the one, Luke hints, so in the other, those who oppose Jesus do so because their fear of economic loss is greater than their love of neighbour.[36]

Lexis: collocations and connotations

In this text as in many others, certain kinds of semantic potential are realised not simply by the presence of an individual term or grammatical structure but rather by the co-occurrence of a whole set of terms which, because they belong to a recognisable register of discourse, create a whole atmosphere of connotative effects and associative meanings. As several instances of this collocative level of meaning contribute to septuagintal allusions, they can be treated most satisfactorily in the section below on intertextuality; but two others are best considered here.

The first collocational cluster consists of the words μνῆμα (8.27), χοῖρος (8.32, 33), and the noun phrase τῷ πνεύματι τῷ ἀκαθάρτῳ (8.29). To any reader familiar with the LXX, each of these items would have had associations with the phenomenon of impurity. The adjective ἀκάθαρτος, for instance, is used with great frequency in the LXX to denote objects that either cause or are associated with physical, moral or ritual

---

[35] In the NT Gospels and Acts, the normal position of a simple dative of instrument within its clause is *after* the verb on which it depends (see, e.g., Matt. 8.16; 13.15; Mark 6.13; Luke 9.32). Departures from this pattern, like that in Luke 8.37, often result in the foregrounding of the noun and its qualifiers (e.g. Luke 7.38²) – especially when the verb is, like συνείχοντο, in the passive voice; see, e.g., Matt. 4.24; Mark 9.49; Luke 21.5; Acts 22.24; 28.8.

[36] In order to maintain the churches' plausibility, Luke had to explain why they and their founder had encountered so much opposition; and Luke's way of explaining it in this context is to nihilate it, i.e., attribute it to base or ignoble motives such as fear. On nihilation as a technique of legitimation more generally, see P. Berger and T. Luckmann, *The Social Construction of Reality: A Treatise in the Sociology of Knowledge* (Harmondsworth, 1967), pp. 130–3.

contamination;[37] included among these objects are spirits, tombs and swine.[38] The structure of the story as a whole, moreover, is strongly shaped by the antithetic relation of all these elements to Jesus. By the unclean spirits, for instance, Jesus is recognised as someone disposed to torment them (8.28); at least implicitly, he also sets himself against the tombs (8.27) by eventually replacing these with a proper home for the man (8.39); and finally, by allowing the swine to be destroyed even though their involvement in the performance was presumably not essential to its success, Jesus shows himself to be no friend of unclean animals.[39]

The co-occurrence of these lexemes and the collective antipathy between their referents and Jesus, therefore, helps to characterise the latter as one who is diametrically opposed to things unclean and who upholds traditional Jewish distinctions between pure and impure.[40] Furthermore, as this characterisation involves too many features in the passage to be dismissed, say, as a 'fossil' that has no discernible relevance for the text's original audience, we would do well to ponder, as indeed the chapter below on Acts 16.16–18 does ponder, what sort of situation this feature of the story would have been relevant to; for it presupposes an audience that is not only familiar with the Levitical distinctions between clean and unclean but also at least partly in sympathy with them.[41]

---

[37] See, e.g., Lev. 5.2; 11.4–47; 12.2–5; 13.36–55; 14.36–47; 15.2–27; Num. 19.7–22; Isa. 6.5; 52.1, 11; Ezek. 4.13; Zech. 13.2.

[38] *Unclean spirits*: Zech. 13.2. *Tombs*: Num. 19.16, 18; Isa. 65.4. *Swine*: Lev. 11.7; LXX Ps. 79.14; Isa. 65.4; 66.3, 17; 1 Macc. 1.47; 2 Macc. 6.18; 7.1; 4 Macc. 5.2 and 6.15. For further discussion of the swine in particular, see Annen, *Heil für die Heiden*, pp. 162–73, who puts special emphasis on the association of swine in Second Temple Jewish thought with paganism and idolatry.

[39] *Contra* F.-J. Leenhardt, 'An Exegetical Essay: Mark 5:1–20', in R. Barthes et al. (eds), *Structural Analysis and Biblical Exegesis*, trans. A. M. Johnson (Pittsburgh, 1974), p. 100, neither the transferral of the demons into the swine nor the drowning of the latter is essential to therapeutic success; for in every other Synoptic exorcism (e.g., Mark 7.24–30; Luke 4.33–37; 9.37–43a) victory is achieved without the demon being relocated to a specified place. More persuasive is Annen, *Heil für die Heiden*, pp. 177–8, who reads the fate of the swine as part of a polemic against paganism and idolatry.

[40] Cf. C. Tassin, 'Jésus, exorciste et guérisseur', *Spiritus* 120 (1990), p. 286; Annen, *Heil für die Heiden*, pp. 183–4; J. Vencovsky, 'Der gadarenische Exorzismus: Matt. 8, 28–34 und Parallelen', *CV* 14/1 (1971), p. 16; and J. D. M. Derrett, 'Spirit-possession and the Gerasene Demoniac: An Inquest into History and Liturgical Projection', *Man* 14/2 (1979), pp. 287, 290.

[41] This observation constitutes not so much a refutation as a necessary adjustment of the view espoused by J. Starobinski, 'The Gerasene Demoniac: A Literary Analysis of Mark 5:1–20', in Barthes et al. (eds), *Structural Analysis*, p. 60, who, in commenting on Mark's version of the story, astutely notes that 'the absence of a precise addressee' in the text gives the story a symbolic character which enables 'readers of all times to recognize themselves in it', but fails to observe the various context-specific qualities that none the less tie the text to a particular set of historical constraints.

The second collocational group is composed primarily of the forms δεσμεύω (8.29), ἅλυσις (8.29), πέδη (8.29), and δαιμ- (8.27, 29, 30, 33, 35, 36 and 38), though other forms such as ἐξέρχομαι (8.29, 33), δεσμός (8.29), ὄνομα (8.30), φυλάσσω (8.29), μνῆμα (8.27), and -τασσω (8.31) can be seen as belonging to the same semantic field. The particular field I have in mind here is the vocabulary of demon management and control in the so-called 'magical' spells and incantations of Graeco-Roman Egypt. In the verbal co-texts of *PGM* 4.1227–64, 3007–86,[42] 3092; 5.304–69,[43] 459–89; and 13.293–7, for example, at least two and usually three or more of the lexemes mentioned above occur together. A particularly striking example is *PGM* 4.1227–64 (entitled 'Excellent rite for driving out demons',[44] 4.1227), which includes not only δεσμεύω (4.1246) and δεσμός (4.1246) but also φυλάσσω (4.1262), δαιμ- (4.1227, 1239, 1243, 1254), and ἐξέρχομαι (4.1243, 1245). Lines 1245a–1248, moreover, which read ἔξελθε, ἔξελθε, δαίμων, ἐπεί σε δεσμεύω δεσμοῖς ἀδαμαντίνοις ἀλύτοις, καὶ παραδίδωμί σε εἰς τὸ μέλαν χαός ἐν ταῖς ἀπολείαις, merit special attention.

As all the terms underlined above have close analogues in Luke 8.26–39, the collocational similarity between the two texts is arresting by itself. But just as striking is a more specific conceptual parallel between what the narrator of the formula just cited threatens to do, namely deliver the demon 'into the black chaos of perdition', and what the demons in Luke's story ask Jesus not to do, namely 'command them to depart into the abyss' (Luke 8.31). The inference to be drawn from all this, of course, is not that Luke obtained his lexical stock or ideas from this particular incantation but rather that much of the lexis collocated in both *PGM* 4.1227–64

---

[42] As in Luke 8.26–39 so also in *PGM* 4.3065–81, which is part of 'a tested charm of Pibechis [a legendary practitioner of magico-medical healing, according to Betz, *GMPT*, p. 96 n. 386] for those possessed by daimons' (4.3007), the forms ἄβυσσος, δαιμόνιον, πνεῦμα and χοιρ- all co-occur in a relatively brief stretch of text. The charm presents itself as 'Hebraic' (4.3084–86) and conditions its own effectiveness on the user's abstinence from pork (χοιρίον, 4.3079–81). The link between swine consumption and vulnerability to demons, it is worth noting, antedates not only *PGM* 4.3007–86 (fourth century CE) but also the present story; for in the LXX of Isa. 65.3–4, the Lord describes himself as being constantly provoked by the Judahites, whom he accuses of burning incense 'to demons' and eating 'swine's flesh'.

[43] In *PGM* 5.304–69, classified by M. Q. Smith (*GMPT*, p. 107) as a *defixio*, i.e., an attempt to employ an underworld power for the purpose of controlling or injuring some designated person, the forms δαιμ-, δεσμεύω, μνῆμα ὄνομα and -τασσω all occur together in one relatively brief passage (5.304–34). The user of this formula, in order to achieve their desired goal, must first of all write on a papyrus or a lead lamella a secret name (5.311) along with what they wish not to happen, and then deposit the finished *defixio* in the grave of 'someone untimely dead' (5.332–3).

[44] *GMPT*, p. 62.

and Luke 8.26–39 was probably part of an already conventional style of communication in the world of spells and incantations by the time of Luke's composition. To be sure, there are many formal and functional differences between the two texts – for instance, Luke 8.29 gives several of the key terms a literal sense, whereas *PGM* 4.1227–64 employs them metaphorically; yet the appearance of this kind of vocabulary in Luke 8.26–39 increases the likelihood that Luke was familiar with the language of spells and incantations, as indeed the occurrence of still other terms and constructions from this register in Acts 19.13–19 confirms.[45]

In addition to these collocative meanings, the associations effected by several individual words in this story also deserve consideration. As in Luke 4.33–37, for instance, so also in the present episode a distinctively Lucan preference is shown for the noun δαιμόνιον instead of πνεύμα ἀκάθαρτον as a way of denoting the spirits that afflict human beings. Although all three Synoptic accounts include the verb δαιμονίζομαι (Matt. 8.28, 33; Mark 5.15, 16, 18; and Luke 8.36), only the Lucan account uses the noun, which occurs six times in this passage alone (Luke 8.27, 29, 30, 33, 35 and 38). The basic sense of δαιμόνιον in its New Testament occurrences is relatively clear – it signifies evil spirit beings 'who occupy a position somewhere between the human and the divine'[46] – and as in Luke's first exorcism story so also here the term has potential to associate Jesus' battle against the demons with the Israelite prophets' warfare against pagan idols.[47] Indeed, these associations are even more conspicuous in the present episode since the Latin loanword λεγιών, absent from 4.33–37, could certainly have been read in a post-70 CE setting as connoting alien soldiers or even the political reality of Roman dominance.[48]

---

[45] Note especially ἐξορκιστής (cf. *PGM* 4.1239), ὁρκίζω (cf. *PGM* 4.3045), and ὀνομάζειν... τὸ ὄνομα (cf. Plutarch *Table Talk* 706.e) in 19.13; πρᾶξις (cf. *PGM* 4.1227) in 19.18, and τῶν τὰ περίεργα πραξάντων (cf. *PGM* 12.404) in 19.19. For further discussion of the lexical and ideational correspondence between Acts 19.13–20 and the formulas preserved in the Greek magical papyri, see R. Kotansky, 'Greek Exorcistic Amulets', in Meyer and Mirecki (eds), *Ancient Magic*, pp. 243–5.

[46] BAGD, s.v. 'δαιμόνιον'.

[47] Cf. Theissen, *Miracle Stories*, pp. 255–6; and see the discussion of vocabulary in my treatment of Luke 4.33–37, pp. 44–5.

[48] Cf. Annen, *Heil für die Heiden*, pp. 173, 183–4. As noted by J. D. M. Derrett, 'Legend and Event: The Gerasene Demoniac: An Inquest into History and Liturgical Projection', in E. A. Livingstone (ed.), *Studia Biblica 1978: Sixth International Congress on Biblical Studies, Oxford 3–7 April 1978*, JSNTSup 2 (Sheffield, 1980), pp. 63 and 70 n. 4, the words ἐπιτρέπω (8.32), ὁρμάω (8.32), and ἐπιτάσσω (8.31) can also be read as possessing military connotations; thus, in conjunction with the links discussed below (under 'intertextuality') between the Lucan account and LXX Ps. 105.7–12, which itself alludes to earlier accounts of the destruction of Pharaoh's army (Exod. 14.1–29), Derrett's observation greatly strengthens the case for attributing military overtones to λεγιών.

However, as Luke in particular was far less interested in challenging imperial military power than in identifying his heroes with the story of Israel's God, these connotations ought to be read as serving chiefly this latter interest.

Also worthy of attention is the uniquely Lucan employment of ἐνδύω, which occurs in the portrayal of the afflicted man as wearing no clothes (8.27). While the clausal co-text of ἐνδύω clearly commends the ordinary sense of 'to wear', the word's nuances on a connotative level, especially for an audience familiar with the LXX, are potentially radial and diffuse; for among the septuagintal contexts in which ἐνδύω occurs are *several* passages that have striking lexical and conceptual correspondences to Luke 8.26–39. In general terms, just as NT authors sometimes use ἐνδύω to refer to the 'putting on' of spiritual protection for the purpose of succeeding in conflicts against the spirits of wickedness,[49] so also the LXX sometimes uses ἐνδύω to refer to an act of clothing that equips one for success either in priestly service, prophetic ministry, or situations of conflict.[50] In connection with priestly service, for example, ἐνδύω occurs five times in Leviticus 16.4–32, where Yhwh stresses that Aaron must be clothed in his proper priestly garments (ἱμάτια, 16.4) if the Yom Kippur ritual is to fulfil the expiatory purpose for which it was designed.[51] In relation to prophetic ministry, moreover, a notable use of ἐνδύω is found in 2 Chronicles 24.20, where Zechariah the son of Jehoiada is characterised as performing a powerful prophetic ministry in Judah after he has been 'clothed' by the Spirit of Yhwh.[52] And finally, in Codex Sinaiticus of LXX Esther 5.1, ἐνδύω is used in connection with the 'putting on' of Esther's royal robes, which help her to protect her people from the schemes of a wicked Gentile. All of these contexts evince thematic resemblances to Luke's story of the undressed demoniac who, after being healed and clothed by Jesus (8.33–35), engages in a preaching ministry to the primarily pagan city of Gerasa.

However, because ἐνδύω in Luke 8.27 is used not to picture the man as properly clothed but rather, with the negative particle, to depict him

---

[49] See Rom. 13.12, 14; 1 Cor. 15.53–54; Eph. 6.11, 14; 1 Thess. 5.8.

[50] See, e.g., Exod. 28.41; 29.5–8; Lev. 8.5–13; 16.4–32; 21.10; Num. 20.26, 28; 1 Chron. 12.18; 2 Chron. 6.41; 24.20–22; Esther 5.1; Isa. 59.17–19; 61.10–11; Ezek. 16.8–10; Zech. 3.3–4(4–5); and Judith 10.3.

[51] Note also that, in contrast to the LXX of Lev. 16.8, 10, where the term used for the Lord's enigmatic antithesis (ἀποπομπαῖος, 'a sending away', LSJ, s.v.) has no demonological overtones, the MT of these verses (and 16.26) includes several references to עזאזל (Lev. 16.8, 10, 26), a demonic being who haunts the desert and inspires the Israelites to sin. On the clothing motif, cf. also Zech. 3.1–9; and 2 Chron. 6.41.

[52] See also 2 Chron. 28.15 and Isa. 61.10–11.

as wearing *nothing*, his condition resembles that of Esther in the passage just noted less than it does that of her cousin Mordecai in LXX Esther 4.1. Most notably, when Mordecai learns of Haman's plan to annihilate the Jewish people, he 'rends his clothes' (διαρρήγνυμι, which occurs in Luke 8.29, and ἱμάτιον, which occurs in Luke 8.27), 'puts on' (ἐνδύω) sackcloth, and wails in a 'loud voice' (φωνῇ μεγάλῃ, cf. Luke 8.28) about the injustice being plotted against his people. Similar clusters of motifs also occur in the literary co-texts of Judith 9.1; 10.3; and Baruch 4.20, where ἐνδύω is used with σάκκος to denote the wearing of sackcloth by Jews in response to threats from Gentile enemies.

In the LXX, then, the verb ἐνδύω is repeatedly collocated with concepts and motifs that also co-occur in Luke 8.26–39. Thus, while it is possible that only one of the texts noted above was on Luke's mind when he edited this story, it is just as likely that the general pattern of usage was loosely imitated by Luke in order to produce a septuagintal effect; but more importantly, however this latter question is settled, Luke's unique choice of ἐνδύω to depict the demoniac as wearing no clothes has powerful connotative effects. It suggests vulnerability, defencelessness against alien oppression, and unfitness for any kind of divine service. It evokes images of those Jews such as Mordecai, Judith and Baruch who, when their ethnic and religious identities were severely threatened by the politics of foreign rule, took off their normal attire and 'put on' sackcloth. By clothing this man (Luke 8.35), the Lucan Jesus performs an action that has both political and religious connotations: he reverses the harsh effects of the demonic legion's presence and equips the man to speak, with his own voice, about how much God has done for him.[53]

The aforementioned potential of the word λεγιών (8.30) to convey associations both with pagan military power and with the story of Israel's God is strengthened by the co-occurrence of several other terms in this story with similar connotations.[54] The placement of ὕψιστος on the lips of the demon-inspired man (8.28; par. Mark 5.7),[55] for example, recalls the regular occurrence of the same term on the lips of Gentiles depicted in the LXX.[56] A comparable effect is fostered by the demoniac's use of

---

[53] For further discussion of the significance of clothing in this story, see especially Leenhardt, 'Mark 5:1–20', pp. 103–4.

[54] Cf. Van der Loos, *Miracles of Jesus*, p. 388; Theissen, *Miracle Stories*, p. 255.

[55] As υἱὸς ὑψίστου clearly carries messianic overtones earlier in Luke's Gospel (1.32–33), and as υἱὲ τοῦ ὑψίστου τοῦ θεοῦ recalls the messianic title the demons assign to Jesus back in 4.41, the appellation in 8.28 should likewise be understood in a messianic sense. Cf. Schürmann, *Das Lukasevangelium*, pp. 47–8, 483.

[56] See Gen. 14.19, 20; Num. 24.16; Isa. 14.14; Dan. 3.26; and 1 Esd. 6.31; 8.19, 21. Although Luke's use of ὕψιστος as a substantive (Luke 1.32, 35, 76; 2.14; 6.35; 19.38; and

βασανίζω (in the request μή με βασανίσῃς, 8.28, par. Mark 5.7), a term which in all of its septuagintal contexts involves conflict between Jews and Gentiles.[57] Furthermore, the distinctively Lucan selection of σώζω, which occurs in the summary of the swineherds' speech in 8.36 (πῶς ἐσώθη ὁ δαιμονισθείς), contributes to an allusion to LXX Psalm 105.8–10, where the Lord is praised for having saved the Psalmist's progenitors from their Egyptian enemies.[58] And, like his use of σώζω, Luke's employment of ἄβυσσος (8.31), which denotes the underworld place of punishment for God's enemies,[59] elicits on a connotative level memories of the Exodus victory over the Egyptians; for ἄβυσσος often refers in the LXX to the waters which the Lord led the Israelites through but which suffocated their Egyptian adversaries.[60] Finally, and especially in view of this latter point, ἐσώθη in 8.36 should probably be heard as an echo of Luke 3.6, where τὸ σωτήριον τοῦ θεοῦ echoes the 'Second Exodus' motif of Isaiah 40.3–5.[61]

Transitivity

As Luke 8.26–39 contains over fifty clauses, my aim in this section is not to analyse the transitivity nuances of each clause but rather to comment

---

Acts 7.38) has no pagan connotations, his use of the term as an adjective has a significantly different flavour, with its meaning on the lips of the pagan soothsayer in Acts 16.17 being very similar to that found in the septuagintal passages just cited.

[57] In many of these contexts Gentiles are portrayed as tormenters of Jews (e.g. 2 Macc. 7.13; 9.6; 4 Macc. 6.5, 10, 11; 8.2, 5, 27, 32; 11.16, 20; 12.4, 13; 13.27; 15.22; 16.3, 15), whereas in most of the others the God of Israel is portrayed as tormenting and punishing the Gentile enemies of his people (1 Sam. 5.3; Wisd. 11.9; 12.23; 16.1, 4; 2 Macc. 1.28; 7.17; 4 Macc. 9.32).

[58] Nearly identical usage of σώζω can be observed in LXX Isa. 37.20, 35; 38.6; 49.24, 25, where deliverance of Jews from their Gentile oppressors is envisaged. On the contribution of σώζω to the allusion to LXX Psalm 105, see below under 'Intertextuality', pp. 110–11; for further discussion of σώζω in Luke 8.36, see W. C. van Unnik, 'L'usage de σώζειν "sauver" et des dérivés dans les évangiles synoptiques', in *Sparsa Collecta: The Collected Essays of W. C. van Unnik, Part One: Evangelia, Paulina, Acta*, NovTSup 29 (Leiden, 1973), p. 27; and B. H. Throckmorton, 'Σώζειν, σωτηρία in Luke–Acts', *SE* 6 (1973), pp. 516–17.

[59] Cf. BAGD, s.v. 'ἄβυσσος'; Bovon, *Luc (1,1–9,50)*, p. 426. See, e.g., Rev. 9.1, 2, 11; 11.7; 17.8; and 20.1, 3.

[60] See LXX Ps. 76.16; 105.9; Isa. 44.27; 51.10; 63.13. Note also LXX Hab. 3.10 and Ezek. 26.19, where 'the deep' is represented as an instrument of judgement on pagan enemies other than the Egyptians.

[61] Cf. R. C. Tannehill, *The Narrative Unity of Luke–Acts*, II, *The Acts of the Apostles* (Minneapolis, 1990), p. 197. While Throckmorton, 'Σώζειν, σωτηρία', 516–17, rightly stresses that σώζω in 8.36 denotes the healing of historical, physical life, his assertion that the term is 'de-eschatologized' in this context ignores the whole word group's contribution to Luke's theme of fulfilment and exaggerates the distance between Luke's salvation-historical schema and other varieties of New Testament eschatology; for further elaboration of this criticism, see Fitzmyer, *Luke I–IX*, pp. 20–2.

more generally on how transitivity contributes to the characterisation of the story's key participants. Towards this goal let us begin by considering the demoniac.

Surprisingly, when the demoniac makes his first appearance in the narrative, he is portrayed as the performer of a material process: ὑπήντησεν ἀνήρ τις ἐκ τῆς πόλεως ἔχων δαιμόνια (8.27). Thus, unlike the first demoniac portrayed in Luke's narrative (4.33–37), who is introduced merely as an 'existent' in the synagogue (4.33), the man from Gerasa is represented at the outset as actually doing something: he meets Jesus (8.27). The verbs of the next two clauses, however, which also have the man as their subject and denote material and behavioural processes (ἐνεδύσατο and ἔμενεν, 8.27) respectively, are negative in polarity and therefore represent the man not by what he does but rather by what he does not do; thereby he begins to look severely limited in his capacity for independent action.

In 8.28, moreover, where any effort to distinguish between the man and the demons is undermined by the logic of possession, nothing is said that might palliate this sense of constriction; indeed, the same image is strongly reinforced by several other clauses in 8.29–37. In 8.29, for example, the man is the 'goal' denoted by the pronoun αὐτός in the clause συνηρπάκει αὐτόν, which represents a material action performed by the demon(s). Furthermore, although he is the implied grammatical subject of the material processes denoted by ἐδεσμεύετο and φυλλασσόμενος (8.29), he fills an affected role in these processes as well, with the agent(s) of δεσμεύω being ἁλύσεσιν καὶ πέδαις and that of φυλλάσσω being deleted. Similarly, in ἠλαύνετο ὑπὸ τοῦ δαιμονίου εἰς τὰς ἐρήμους, the man is the 'goal' of material action undertaken by the demon. And later, after he is said to have been 'found' by the people from the surrounding area (8.35), the herdsmen's explanation of πῶς ἐσώθη ὁ δαιμονισθείς (8.36) puts the man in two more affected roles, first in ἐσώθη and then in the nominalized process implied by ὁ δαιμονισθείς (i.e., 'the one who had been demon-possessed').

However, after being repeatedly characterised as a 'recipient' rather than as a doer of the story's main actions, the man assumes a more autonomous role in the narrative's concluding clauses. In 8.38a, for example, while the types of processes denoted by ἐδεῖτο and εἶναι are clearly not material but rather verbal and relational, the participant roles of 'sayer' and 'carrier' in these clauses are filled by the former demoniac, whose new scope for action is hinted further through the shift from ὁ δαιμονισθείς in 8.36 to ὁ ἀνὴρ ἀφ' οὗ ἐξεληλύθει τὰ δαιμόνια in 8.38 (cf. ὁ δαιμονισθείς in Mark 5.18); but even more remarkably, in describing him in 8.39b as going away (ἀπέρχομαι) and preaching (κηρύσσω) throughout the city of Gerasa,[62] Luke pictures the man as participating in behavioural and verbal processes that entail a high degree of independence.

Like the characterisation of the man, the portrayal of the demons in this story is powerfully shaped by choices of transitivity. The preceding analysis of the man, in fact, has already given us a significant portion of the demons' transitivity profile; for they not only have 'seized' and 'driven' the man into the desert (8.29) but also have 'entered' and 'demonised' him (8.30, 36). Still, the man is not the only participant the demons interact with in this story. In 8.28, for instance, speaking and acting through the man, the demons see Jesus (ἰδὼν δὲ τὸν Ἰησοῦν), cry out (ἀνακράξας), fall down before him (προσέπεσεν αὐτῷ), speak with a loud voice (φωνῇ μεγάλῃ εἶπεν), and beseech him (δέομαί σου).[63] Significantly, though, not once in these five clauses are the demons portrayed as affecting Jesus in any material sense; and just as important, the embedded clause μή με βασανίσῃς actually serves to characterise them as assuming (correctly) that Jesus has the power and inclination not only to affect them but to cause them serious harm. In 8.29a, moreover, where the narrator explains why the demons ask Jesus not to torment them (παρήγγειλεν γὰρ τῷ πνεύματι τῷ ἀκαθάρτῳ ἐξελθεῖν ἀπὸ τοῦ ἀνθρώπου), the action denoted by παραγγέλλω – a process of commanding which, though verbal, often possesses material implications for its addressee[64] – has Jesus as its 'sayer' and the unclean spirit as its 'target'.

Like 8.29a, all the other clauses that depict exchanges between the demons and Jesus (8.30–32) involve what are fundamentally verbal processes; yet they differ from each other in regard to their implications. The demons, for instance, are twice represented in 8.31–32 as 'begging' (παρακαλέω) Jesus; and, while begging might be interpreted as having material overtones, the structure of the process itself normally assumes

---

[62] The circumstantial element καθ' ὅλην τὴν πόλιν is echoed by καθ' ὅλης ('throughout') in Acts 9.42 and 13.49, where the dissemination of the Christian message is envisaged; thus, *contra* Schneider, *Das Evangelium nach Lucas*, p. 193, the mission to the Gentiles is anticipated less by Jesus' ministry to the man (who for reasons given above under 'Story structure' should not be assumed to be a pagan) than by the man's subsequent preaching throughout Gerasa. For further discussion of the missionary aspects of Jesus' healings in Luke, see Nielsen, *Heilung und Verkündigung*, p. 153.

[63] Occurring fifteen times in Luke–Acts but only once in Matthew and not at all in Mark, δέομαι is a Lucan favourite. As noted by Bovon, *Luc (1,1–9,50)*, p. 424, the grammatical object of δέομαι is often God when it is not Jesus (cf. Luke 10.2; 21.36; 22.32; Acts 4.31; 8.22, 24; and 10.2); see also Acts 21.39 and 26.3, where the word clearly connotes the hierarchy of authority in the political domain.

[64] As indicated by the entry in BAGD, παραγγέλλω usually refers to processes such as directing, commanding, ordering and instructing, whose 'sayers'/'actors' are typically recognised to be persons in authority.

inequality of power in the relationship between the participants, with the 'sayer' assuming a subordinate role vis-à-vis the addressee.

By contrast, Jesus does not participate in any verbal process that puts him in an inferior position in relation to other characters. Rather, in three of the four clauses in 8.31–32 where he is the 'sayer', Jesus' utterances are described in a fashion which implies that the speaker has authority over his audience, notwithstanding the numerical advantage and cosmic power of the latter. Indeed, by begging Jesus 'not to *command* [ἐπιτάξῃ] them to depart into the abyss' and 'to *permit* [ἐπιτρέψῃ] them to enter' the swine, the demons themselves tacitly acknowledge that whatever directive he eventually issues to them, it will undoubtedly achieve his aims. And immediately thereafter, this estimation of Jesus' commands is reinforced by the narrator, whose use of ἐπιτρέπω to denote Jesus' act of permission (καὶ ἐπέτρεψεν αὐτοῖς, 8.32) echoes the wording of the demons' request and confirms their understanding of the situation. In summary, then, Luke's transitivity choices help to portray the demons (1) as having more than enough power to control the man from Gerasa, but (2) as having virtually no power either to affect Jesus or to prevent him from impacting them.

Much of what needs to be said about the participant profile of Jesus is implicit in the preceding analysis. More specifically, whereas both the man and the demons are repeatedly described as being influenced materially by other participants in the story, the Lucan Jesus possesses something like a static dynamism: other participants in this story register no significant effect on him, but he makes a lasting impact on them. The man, for example, is transformed from wildness and nakedness to sobriety and clothing; the demons find themselves ripped from their human host and trapped in the swine, who promptly take them precisely where they had hoped not to go; yet the only change Jesus undergoes is a spatial one, from the boat to the land and back to the boat, and this Jesus brings about himself. Indeed, the transitivity of the Lucan account's concluding clause, ὅσα ἐποίησεν αὐτῷ ὁ Ἰησοῦς, concisely summarises what the story's whole set of transitivity selections say cumulatively. Although the legion of demons had more than enough energy to reduce the man from Gerasa to a pitiable embodiment of impurity, their strength paled into impotent resignation when they met the Lucan Jesus, whose authoritative actions for the benefit of this man constitute the outstanding feature of this story's transitivity patterns.[65]

---

[65] Although several other participants (e.g., the swine, the herdsmen, and the people from the city and farms) are indispensable to the plot of the story, nothing in Luke's

Transitivity, however, involves not only processes and participants but also circumstances (as shown, for example, by adverbial groups and prepositional phrases). As for the circumstantial elements in the present story, one particularly notable pattern emerges from an analysis of these as a group: a large number of them denote spatial locations.[66] Spatial categories of one nuance or other are suggested repeatedly in this passage by Luke's use of ἀντιπέρα (8.26), ἐπί (8.27), ἐκ (8.27), ἐν (8.27, 32), ἀπό (8.29, 33, 37, 38), κατά (8.33, 39), πρός (8.35), and παρά (8.35); but perhaps most remarkably, the preposition εἰς occurs with one spatial sense or other eleven times in this passage.[67]

These observations alone are sufficient to indicate that space in general and how it is parcelled in particular have high importance in this story; and on closer inspection, a variety of ideological assumptions can be discerned in these references. For instance, when the narrator notes that the man ἐν οἰκίᾳ οὐκ ἔμενεν ἀλλ' ἐν τοῖς μνήμασιν (8.27), he implies that it is unusual – indeed, deviant and disgraceful – for a man to live among tombs rather than in a house; in other words, the narrator has an implicit ideology of human habitation, a point of view about where people should and should not dwell. When moreover he discloses that Jesus commanded the unclean spirit ἐξελθεῖν ἀπὸ τοῦ ἀνθρώπου (8.29), he insinuates that it is a bad thing for unclean spirits to be located inside a person; thus, he has a theory about where these spirits belong and where they do not. Similarly, when he mentions at the end of 8.29 that the demon drove the man εἰς τὰς ἐρήμους, he assumes that the desert is not a suitable place for human beings to be. Likewise, when he portrays the demons as begging not to be sent εἰς τὴν ἄβυσσον (8.31),[68] he assumes that the abyss is not a place demons long to inhabit. And finally, when the narrator depicts Jesus as allowing the demons to come out 'from' (ἀπό, 8.33) the man and to go 'into' (εἰς, 8.33) the swine, he indirectly

---

characterisation of them significantly alters his representation of the more prominent participants analysed above.

[66] Cf. Starobinski, 'Gerasene Demoniac', pp. 61–5, 68.

[67] See Luke 8.26, 29, 30, 31, 32, 33², 34², 37, 39. No other single pericope or stretch of fourteen verses in Luke's Gospel has as many occurrences of εἰς as the present story. As the word furthermore occurs only twice in Luke's first exorcism story and not at all in his third (9.37–43a), its high frequency in the present narrative cannot be explained as a predictable feature of the genre; in the Marcan parallel (Mark 5.1–20), moreover, which is lengthier than Luke's version, the word occurs only ten times.

[68] Compared with the request in Mark not to be sent ἔξω τῆς χώρας (Mark 5.10), the request in Luke not to be sent εἰς τὴν ἄβυσσον results in a more authoritative Jesus; for indirectly it portrays Jesus not as a mere exorcist but as a doer of deeds that have cosmic, eschatological significance. On the eschatological connotations of ἄβυσσος, see Twelftree, *Christ Triumphant*, pp. 101–2; Schmid, *Das Evangelium nach Lucas*, p. 162.

suggests that swine provide a more appropriate abode for demons than humans do.[69]

Not all the references to spatial locations in this story can be examined here. But solely on the basis of those just noted, Luke 8.26–39 can be read as instantiating an ideology of space. The author of this story has a prescriptive cosmological grammar that specifies where things should and should not be; and in view of this rulebook's weighty contribution to the story's ideological point of view, interpretations that completely overlook it while concentrating at length on the reference to 'the region of the Gerasenes, which is opposite Galilee' (8.26) are guilty of an exegetical imbalance and selectivity that is difficult to justify.[70]

Verbal aspect

Unsurprisingly, the tense form that occurs most frequently in this text is the aorist,[71] which in most cases draws no special attention to the events it signifies.[72] Yet several of the verbs, participles and infinitives in this story have non-aorist forms, and a few of these have aspectual significance that merits comment.

In 8.27, for instance, the present tense participle ἔχων and the imperfect tense verb ἔμενεν are imperfective in aspect, drawing special attention to the durative facet of the demoniac's misfortune. Both the present and the imperfect highlight the fact that these elements of the man's suffering had been with him for an extended period of time. Similar effects are achieved by the imperfect forms ἐδεσμεύετο ('he used to be kept under guard') and ἠλαύνετο ('he used to be driven'), which highlight what had regularly happened to the man before he met Jesus. Even more arresting, though, is the pluperfect tense form συνηρπάκει ('it [i.e., the demon] had seized'), which in conjunction with πολλοῖς... χρόνοις[73] frontgrounds what the man's state had been prior to Jesus' exorcistic command. Collectively,

---

[69] Cf. Schürmann, *Das Lukasevangelium*, p. 484, who rightly stresses that the relocation has special appropriateness from a Jewish point of view.

[70] E.g., Kirschläger, *Jesu exorzistisches Wirken*, pp. 97–8; J. B. Green, *Gospel of Luke*, pp. 335–7; Marshall, *Gospel of Luke*, p. 335; and Fitzmyer, *Luke I–IX*, pp. 735, 737, all highlight the ethno-theological potential of ἀντιπέρα τῆς Γαλιλαίας (8.26) yet say nothing about the larger pattern constituted by the text's other circumstantial elements of space.

[71] Of the seventy-one words in this passage that have tense as a feature of their form, forty-four are aorist.

[72] Porter, *Idioms*, pp. 23, 35.

[73] As noted by R. Girard, *The Scapegoat*, trans. Y. Freccero (Baltimore, 1986), p. 168, this construction implies not a continuous case of affliction but rather intermittent bouts, which led the man and his community into a vicious circle of physical bindings and demon-inspired escapes.

these selections from the Greek system of tense forms strongly accentuate the gravity of the man's illness and therefore elevate, indirectly, the greatness of Jesus' power in the ensuing performance of exorcism.

Earlier in this chapter, it was observed that the authority of Jesus derives part of its salience in this story from the repetition of verbs such as παρακαλέω (8.31, 32) and δέομαι (8.38), which in these contexts are used to portray various characters 'begging' Jesus. This emphasis is underscored even further, however, by the tense forms that have been selected for these words, with the imperfective aspect of both παρεκάλουν ('they [i.e., the demons] were begging him', 8.31) and ἐδεῖτο ('the man... was begging him', 8.38) suggesting that repeated petitions were involved.[74] Choice of tense form reinforces the effect of repetition yet again in 8.34–35, where the events summarised by the participle γεγονός are spotlighted not only by the reiteration of this term but also by the complex, stative aspect of its perfect tense form.

Finally, 8.35–38 contains four words whose tense forms draw special attention to the dramatic transformation that Jesus effected in the life of his patient. Two of these words, the present tense participles καθήμενον and σωφρονοῦντα (8.35), foreground the contrast between how the man was perceived to behave *after* the exorcism – he was 'found... sitting at the feet of Jesus[75]... and being in his right mind' – and how he had behaved previously, as outlined by the narrator back in 8.29. The same contrast is also accentuated by the perfect tense form of ἱματισμένον, whose stative aspect underscores the change from nakedness (8.27) to a condition of having been clothed. And lastly, representing a state of affairs that is explicitly linked to the man's desire to stay with Jesus (8.38), the pluperfect verb ἐξεληλύθει not only frontgrounds the demons' departure but also, in view of its connection to the imperfective main verb ἐδεῖτο in the same clause, helps to emphasise the impact this departure had on the man's aspirations and behaviour; namely, it inspired him to engage in an extended plea to remain near his liberator.

In an indirect but none the less striking way, therefore, the features that are highlighted by the author's choices of tense forms correspond to those emphasised by his manipulations of the transitivity system. Foregrounded by both sets of selections, and even without the lexis of ἐξουσία and

---

[74] Cf. J. A. Kleist, 'The Gadarene Demoniacs', *CBQ* 9 (1947), p. 101; Kirschläger, *Jesu exorzistisches Wirken*, p. 125.

[75] As noted by Schneider, *Das Evangelium nach Lucas*, p. 195, the construction παρὰ τοὺς πόδας connotes discipleship in this context, with the man's submission to Jesus being symbolised by his posture. Luke shows unique fondness of this particular symbol, using it also in Luke 7.38; 8.41; 10.39; 17.16; Acts 4.35, 37; 5.2; 22.3.

Intertextuality 109

δύναμις (cf. Luke 4.36), the power and authority of Jesus in this story are just as prominent as they are in Luke 4.33–37.

Intertextuality

Like the story about the demoniac in the synagogue (Luke 4.33–37), Luke 8.26–39 derives much of its force from allusions to the LXX. Both stories, in fact, include an allusion to the words Τί ἐμοὶ καὶ σοί spoken by the distressed widow of Zarephath to Elijah (LXX 1 Kgs 17.18; cf. Luke 4.34; 8.28).[76] Although this expression occurs in a variety of septuagintal contexts,[77] a special link between Luke 8.28 and 1 Kgs 17.18 in particular is suggested by several lines of evidence. First, and as already noted in my treatment of intertextuality in Luke 4.34, a clear and uniquely Lucan allusion to the story of Elijah and the widow occurs in the account of Jesus' teaching in Nazareth (1 Kgs 17.9 in Luke 4.26), serving not only to effect a typological correspondence between Jesus and Elijah but also to constrain interpretation of Luke's first exorcism narrative. Second, like Luke 4.33–37 and 8.26–39, in genre-critical terms 1 Kings 17.17–24 constitutes a miracle story,[78] whereas other septuagintal passages in which Τί ἐμοὶ καὶ σοί or comparable constructions occur belong to other genres. And third, at yet another point of resemblance to the story in 4.33–37, the present episode includes several items that are also collocated in LXX 1 Kings 17.17–24: οἶκος, -ερχομαι, πνεῦμα, and τοῦ θεοῦ with a *nomen regens* in the vocative (ἄνθρωπε in 1 Kgs 17.18, and υἱέ in Luke 8.28). The Elijah typology seen earlier in Luke's narrative should therefore probably be seen in this context as well, where it would serve chiefly to widen the bridge of continuity between the ideological commitments of the implied author and the authoritative traditions of Judaism.

1 Kings 17.18, however, is not the only biblical text that produces echoes in Luke's version of this story. Indeed, Luke 8.26–39 resembles a well-used palimpsest, with traces of a variety of biblical passages being

---

[76] Cf. Theissen, *Miracle Stories*, p. 255; and Bauernfeind, *Die Worte der Dämonen*, pp. 3, 23–4. As noted by Bauernfeind (p. 24) in particular, the occurrence of singular ἐμοί distinguishes the utterances in Luke 8.28 and 1 Kgs 17.18 from that in Luke 4.34 (where we find instead plural ἡμῖν), giving the echo extra strength in the present story.

[77] E.g., Josh. 22.24; Judg. 11.12; 2 Sam. 16.10; and 2 Kgs 3.13. Although Τί εμοὶ καὶ σοί literally means 'What to me and to you?', its usage in these septuagintal contexts, as well as in Luke 4.34 and 8.28, suggests an atmosphere of interpersonal conflict between the 'sayer' and the addressee; thus the expression might be best rendered 'What do you and I have in common?', which suggests that the 'sayer' perceives his or her addressee to be an enemy.

[78] Cf. P. K. McCarter, '1 Kings', in *HBC*, p. 319.

discernible beneath Luke's own composition.[79] Perhaps the most conspicuous of these traces have been left by LXX Psalm 105.7–12, which not only includes a whole constellation of terms and motifs that likewise co-occur in Luke 8.26–39 but also contains patterns that are present in our story's immediately preceding co-text (i.e., the stilling of the storm, Luke 8.22–25).[80] More specifically, in recalling the salvific power which the Most High displayed at the Red Sea, verses 7–12 of LXX Psalm 105 read:

> οἱ πατέρες ἡμῶν ἐν Αἰγύπτῳ οὐ συνῆκαν τὰ <u>θαυμάσιά</u> σου
> οὐκ ἐμνήσθησαν τοῦ πλήθους τοῦ ἐλέους σου
> καὶ παρεπίκραναν ἀναβαίνοντες ἐν τῇ ἐρυθρᾷ θαλάσσῃ.
> καὶ <u>ἔσωσεν</u> αὐτοὺς ἕνεκεν τοῦ <u>ὀνόματος</u> αὐτοῦ τοῦ γνωρίσαι
>   τὴν δυναστείαν αὐτοῦ·
> καί <u>ἐπετίμησεν</u> τῇ ἐρυθρᾷ θαλάσσῃ, καὶ ἐξηράνθη,
> καὶ ὡδήγησεν αὐτοὺς ἐν <u>ἀβύσσῳ</u> ὡς ἐν <u>ἐρήμῳ</u>·
> καὶ <u>ἔσωσεν</u> αὐτοὺς ἐκ χειρὸς μισούντων
> καὶ ἐλυτρώσατο αὐτοὺς ἐκ χειρὸς ἐχθροῦ.
> καὶ ἐκάλυψεν <u>ὕδωρ</u> τοὺς θλίβοντας αὐτούς,
> εἷς ἐξ αὐτῶν οὐχ ὑπελείφθη.
> καὶ <u>ἐπίστευσαν</u> ἐν τοῖς λόγοις αὐτοῦ
> καὶ ᾖσαν τὴν αἴνεσιν αὐτοῦ.

In regard to vocabulary, the narrator of these verses not only uses σῴζω, ὄνομα, ἄβυσσος and ἔρημος, which likewise co-occur in the Lucan exorcism story, but also employs θαυμασ-, ἐπιτιμάω, ὕδωρ and πιστ-, which appear together again in Luke's narrative about the storm. As three of these terms (σῴζω, ἄβυσσος and ἔρημος), moreover, do not occur in

---

[79] In addition to the passages discussed below, see LXX Isa. 65.3–4, where the motifs of swine and demons and tombs are collocated; and LXX Ps. 90.1–16, where ὕψιστος, the φόβος/φοβέω group, and δαιμόνιον co-occur with the motifs of protection, hostile armies, and salvation. On the heavy contribution of Scripture to the parallel account in Mark 5.1–20, see Annen, *Heil für die Heiden*, pp. 177–8, 182; and Derrett, 'Legend and Event', pp. 64–5. On the echoes of Isa. 65.3–4 in particular, see Derrett, 'Contributions to the Study of the Gerasene Demoniac', pp. 9–10; Bovon, *Luc (1,1–9,50)*, pp. 423–4; W. Wink, *Unmasking the Powers: The Invisible Forces That Determine Human Existence* (Philadelphia, 1986), pp. 44, 183 n. 3; Schürmann, *Das Lukasevangelium*, pp. 480, 482 n. 65. Surprisingly, Busse (*Die Wunder des Propheten Jesus*, pp. 204–19) says nothing about any of these allusions (including 1 Kgs 17.18!) and therefore neglects one of the most important levels of meaning in the story.

[80] While several commentators have noted the influence of LXX Psalm 105 on Luke 8.22–25 (e.g. Schürmann, *Das Lukasevangelium*, p. 476; Nolland, *Luke*, I, pp. 400–1), none to my knowledge has entertained the possibility that the psalm can be heard in both 8.22–25 and 8.26–39.

either of the Synoptic parallels (Matt. 8.28–34; Mark 5.1–20), their presence in Luke 8.26–39 looks very much like a deliberate attempt to echo LXX Psalm 105.7–12. Furthermore, as in LXX Psalm 105.7–12 so also in Luke 8.22–39, the motifs of salvation from pagan 'armies', the powerful word of rebuke which controls the mighty waters, the use of the waters to destroy the hostile forces, and the importance of belief in the authoritative word are highly prominent. And finally, the existence of three widely recognised allusions to this same psalm in Luke 1.68–72 firmly establishes that Luke was both familiar with this text and uniquely inclined to weave it into his own story.[81]

Inferring an allusion to LXX Psalm 105.7–12 in the present episode generates a complex series of communicative effects, a couple of which are worth describing. First, and on the level of particulars, a connection of this kind encourages the construction of a multifaceted correspondence between (a) Jesus and ὁ κύριος of the psalm, (b) deliverance from evil spirits and deliverance from the Egyptians, and (c) the army of demons and the forces of Pharaoh.[82] But just as important, it also functions more generally to amplify the same sense of continuity noted above in connection with the allusion to 1 Kings 17.18, with the new (and thus vulnerable) movement of Jesus' followers being closely identified with the ancient (and thus venerable) traditions of Israel.

Another Jewish-biblical voice that can be heard in the Lucan account is LXX Isaiah 58.6–7. In this latter context the Lord himself is the speaker, and having described the kind of religious observance he cannot endure (Isa. 58.3–5), he proceeds to outline the contours of a more acceptable service:

<u>λῦε</u> πάντα σύν<u>δεσμον</u> ἀδικίας,
διάλυε στραγγαλιὰς βιαίων συναλλαγμάτων,
ἀπόστελλε τεθραυσμένους ἐν ἀφέσει
καὶ πᾶσαν συγγραφὴν ἄδικον διάσπα·
διάθρυπτε πεινῶντι τὸν ἄρτον σου
καὶ πτωχοὺς ἀστέγους εἴσαγε εἰς τὸν <u>οἶκόν</u> σου·
ἐὰν ἴδῃς γυμνόν, περίβαλε,
καὶ ἀπὸ τῶν <u>οἰκείων</u> τοῦ σπέρματός σου οὐχ ὑπερόψῃ.

[81] The three connections consist of LXX Ps. 105.10 (ἔσωσεν... ἐκ χειρός μισούντων) in Luke 1.71 (σωτηρίαν... ἐκ χειρός πάντων τῶν μισούντων ἡμᾶς); v. 45 of the psalm (καὶ ἐμνήσθη τῆς διαθήκης αὐτοῦ) in Luke 1.72 (καὶ ἐμνησθῆναι διαθήκης ἁγίας αὐτοῦ); and v. 48 of the psalm (Εὐλογητὸς κύριος ὁ θεὸς Ἰσραήλ) in Luke 1.68 (Εὐλογητὸς κύριος ὁ θεὸς τοῦ Ἰσραήλ). Cf. Nolland, *Luke*, I, pp. 85–7.

[82] Cf. Derrett, 'Legend and Event', pp. 63–4.

Although several items that co-occur in this passage are also collocated in Luke 8.26–39, the most striking connection between the two texts is conceptual in nature. Most notably, just as the Lord in Isaiah 58.6–7 prescribes the loosing of every bond of unrighteousness, the clothing of the naked, and the sheltering of the homeless, so in the present episode Jesus releases, clothes, and arranges shelter for one who, in addition to having been bound by literal chains (8.29), had been reduced to nakedness and deprived of his home (8.27). Like LXX Psalm 105.7–12, moreover, this same Isaianic oracle creates echoes in other parts of Luke's narrative, as it does for instance in Luke 4.18 where Jesus defines himself partly in terms taken from Isaiah 58.6 (ἀποστεῖλαι τεθραυσμένους ἐν ἀφέσει). Furthermore, by virtue of the distinctive repetition of the morphemes οἰκ- (8.27, 39) and ἱματ- (8.27, 35) in the Lucan version of the story, the reverberations of the Isaianic text are considerably louder in Luke than they are in Mark.[83] The author of Luke's Gospel, therefore, almost certainly understood Jesus' healing of this demoniac as a fulfilment of the programme commended in Isaiah 58.6–7.[84]

Those who approach this story with a hermeneutic of suspicion, however, will detect a certain ungrammaticality in some (or perhaps all) of these intertextual strategies: in 1 Kings 17, for instance, Elijah does not expel a demon from the widow or her son; and, despite their intrinsic impurity, the swine who drown in the lake are never shown to have posed the same kind of threat to the well-being of God's people that the army of Pharaoh did. In this light, not to mention that provided by numerous other incongruities that could be discussed, Luke's willingness to represent an exorcism by Jesus as corresponding to prophecies and patterns which ostensibly have nothing at all to do with exorcism, demons, or anything of the sort would seem to deserve whatever suspicious readings it gets.[85] Indeed, as soon as these fissures between the Lucan text and its biblical intertexts are brought into the open, Nietzsche's observation that 'every word is a mask'[86] may seem to have been confirmed here with a vengeance, with the intertextual face worn by Luke's Jesus decomposing, right before our eyes, into a tissue of ideological expediency

---

[83] In the Matthaean parallel, it is worth noting, no trace of Isa. 58.6–7 can be found.

[84] On the eschatological flavour of the passage as a whole, see F. Mussner, *Die Wunder Jesu: Eine Hinführung* (Munich, 1967), pp. 50–1; Twelftree, *Christ Triumphant*, pp. 105–6; and Kirschläger, *Jesu exorzistisches Wirken*, p. 127.

[85] Note the similar use of Isa. 29.18; 35.5–6; 42.18; 26.19; and 61.1 in Luke 7.18–23, whose interest in exorcism in particular as fulfilment of Isaianic prophecy is absent from the parallel in Matt. 11.2–6.

[86] F. Nietzsche, *Beyond Good and Evil: Prelude to a Philosophy of the Future*, trans. R. J. Hollingdale (repr., London, 1990), p. 216.

and illusion.[87] And yet, as should become increasingly apparent in my treatments of the Lucan stories' cultural context, this sort of judgement can be nothing more than the beginning of any explanation that aims for a satisfying measure of complication.

Presuppositions, implicatures and entailments

As in Luke 4.33–37 so also in the present narrative, belief in the existence of demonic beings is neither defended nor even asserted but rather taken for granted as a piece of cosmological common sense (8.27). This type of belief is attested in a wide range of ancient comparative materials, many of which are discussed in my treatments of the Lucan stories' cultural context.

Less typical of the exorcism genre is the reference in 8.31 to the 'abyss' (ἄβυσσος), which in this context is the underworld place of punishment for wicked spirits.[88] Like the reality of the demons, the existence of this place is not a matter of debate for any of the voices that speak in the story. In view of the word's association with torment, moreover, the demons' petition not to be sent there conveys almost the same meaning as their request back in 8.28, μή με βασανίσῃς. But perhaps more important, by portraying the demons as assuming that Jesus might indeed wish to consign them to such a place, the narrator implies that the relationship between Jesus and the demons is one of extreme hostility; indeed, since Jesus is perceived to be adamantly anti-demonic by the demons themselves, it would be senseless to view him (as did some of his movement's early opponents[89]) as one of the demons' allies. And since this same image of antipathy is also suggested by the demons' cry Τί ἐμοὶ καὶ σοί (8.28),[90] Jesus' opposition to the forces of evil should be recognised as another prominent theme in this text.

Even more emphatic than Jesus' hostility towards the demons, however, are his authority and power over them. For instance, in addition to the overtones of hierarchy noted above in connection with ἐπιτρέπω and παρακαλέω, the constructions μή με βασανίσῃς (8.28) and ἵνα μὴ ἐπιτάξῃ αὐτοῖς εἰς τὴν ἄβυσσον ἀπελθεῖν (8.31) presuppose a power

---

[87] The problem is no less serious in the allusion to Isa. 65.1–7 than in the one just discussed; for as noted by Annen, *Heil für die Heiden*, p. 183, the divine voice in the Isaianic intertext threatens those 'who sit in tombs' with a frightful punishment, whereas Luke portrays the man from the tombs as a recipient of God's mercy.

[88] BAGD, s.v. 'ἄβυσσος'; and see above, p. 98.

[89] See, e.g., Mark 3.20–30; Luke 11.14–23 (par. Matt. 12.22–30). For discussion of the key passages, see esp. M. Q. Smith, *Jesus the Magician*, pp. 31–3.

[90] See the discussion and notes above under 'Intertextuality', p. 109.

structure in which the one who torments and commands possesses higher rank than those on the receiving end of these processes;[91] but just as important, by embedding these constructions in the demons' own speech (direct discourse in 8.28, indirect in 8.31), the narrator also implies that Jesus' supremacy in this order is not merely a product of his own point of view but was actually acknowledged by the demons themselves. Similar connotations are engendered by the speech act verb δέομαι (8.28), which introduces the request μή με βασανίσῃς. Used regularly to denote a petition from a subordinate to a superior,[92] δέομαι encodes an attitude of respect that is well suited to this context, especially with Jesus having just subdued the wind and waves by his word (8.24). The position of Jesus is elevated still higher, moreover, when Luke discloses that this urgent pleading comes not just from one demon but rather from an entire legion of them (8.30). And finally, by virtue of the linear, phonemic and conceptual proximity of ἐπιτρέψῃ in 8.32 to ἐπιτάξῃ in 8.31, a widely overlooked but powerful instance of paronomasia is created, underscoring not only the overtones of authority implicit in both words but more specifically the superior position of Jesus in the processes they denote.[93]

A variation of this same theme can also be heard in 8.38, though in that context the inferior party is not the group of demons but rather the former demoniac. Jesus' authority over the man in particular is implied by the narrator's use of the verbs δέομαι in 8.38a and ἀπολύω in 8.38b. As in 8.28, where the unclean spirit 'begs' Jesus not to torment him, so also in 8.38a the transitivity framework surrounding δέομαι has Jesus in the role of 'receiver', putting him in superior position vis-à-vis the 'sayer' in the implied hierarchy. As for ἀπολύω, although it differs significantly

---

[91] Note, e.g., the use of βασανίζω in Josephus *Ant.* 16.232; LXX 1 Sam. 5.3; Wisd. 11.9; 12.23; 16.1, 4; 2 Macc. 1.28; 7.13, 17; 9.6; 4 Macc. 6.5, 10, 11; 8.2, 5, 27; 9.7, 15, 27, 32; 11.16, 20; 12.4, 13; 13.27; 15.22; 16.3, 15; Rev. 9.5; 11.10; 14.10; 20.10; and the use of ἐπιτάσσω in Herodotus 4.83; 5.111; Sophocles *Ant.* 664; LXX Gen. 49.33; Esther 1.8; 3.2, 12; LXX Ps. 106.29; Ezek. 24.18; Dan. 1.18; 2.2, 46; 3.19, 20; Tobit 3.6, 15; Ep. Jer. 1; 1 Esd. 2.26, 28; 4.57; 5.51; 6.19, 28; Judith 10.9; 12.6; Bel & Dr. 14; 1 Macc. 4.41; 5.49; 9.54; 10.81; 12.27; Mark 6.27; Luke 14.22; Acts 23.2; Philem. 8.

[92] See, e.g., Plato *Ap.* 17.c; Josephus, *Ant.* 9.9; LXX Gen. 19.18; 44.18; Matt. 9.38; Luke 5.12; 8.38; 9.38, 40; 10.2; 22.32; Acts 4.31; 8.22, 24; 10.2; 21.39; 26.3; Rom. 1.10; and 1 Thess. 3.10.

[93] On the hierarchical connotations of ἐπιτάξῃ in this context, cf. Pesch, *Der Besessene von Gerasa*, p. 61. Neither ἐπιτάξῃ nor ἐπιτρέψῃ, it is worth noting, is found in either of the Synoptic parallels, so the wordplay they create is probably Luke's own innovation. Its prominence is heightened by the distinctively Lucan parallelism of the words' respective sentences (8.31, 32), both of which evince the sequence: καὶ [παρακαλέω] αὐτὸν ἵνα + [third person singular aorist subjunctive] αὐτοῖς εἰς + [substantive in the accusative] + [aorist infinitival form of prefixed -ερχομαι]; cf. Kirschläger, *Jesus exorzistisches Wirken*, p. 113.

from δέομαι in sense, it none the less shares the potential of the latter to evoke connotations of hierarchy and authority: in the sociocultural milieu of Luke–Acts, masters 'release' slaves (Matt. 18.27), Roman governors 'release' Jewish prisoners (Luke 23.16, 17, 18, 20, 22, 25, and par.), and husbands 'release' their wives (Luke 16.18 and par.). The narration of Jesus 'releasing' this man (8.38), therefore, constitutes yet another hint that Jesus possesses very high authority, honour and status.[94]

Co-text

Luke 8.26–39 has strong thematic bonds to its immediate co-text, contributing in particular to the emphasis in 8.22–56 on Jesus' authority over misfortune.[95] Much of this emphasis is realised through instances of repetition that become apparent only when 8.22–56 is read as a whole.

In 8.31, for instance, the demons' assumption that Jesus might 'command' (ἐπιτάξῃ) them to depart echoes the observation made by the disciples in the preceding unit, where they marvel that Jesus 'commands [ἐπιτάσσει] even wind and water' (8.25). Similarly, the prostration of the healed demoniac παρὰ τοὺς πόδας τοῦ Ἰησοῦ[96] in 8.35 anticipates the gesture of the synagogue ruler Jairus in 8.41, whose stance before Jesus is described in identical phraseology. The portrayal of Jairus in this latter context, it should be noted, contributes to the cohesion of this section in still another way so far as his request that Jesus 'come' to his house (εἰσελθεῖν, 8.41) derives part of its significance from its relation to the entreaty back in 8.37, where the people of Gerasa, by contrast, beg Jesus to go away (ἀπελθεῖν). Other links between two or more of the units in this section are established by the recurrence of σώζω (8.36, 48, 50); πίστις/πιστεύω (8.25, 48, 50); and φόβος/φοβέω (8.25, 35, 37, 50).

Formal repetition, however, is not the only type of device that gives this larger section a sense of cohesion. As discussed above under 'Intertextuality', for instance, both the exorcism narrative and the story in 8.22–25 allude to LXX Psalm 105.7–12, which therefore gives 8.22–39 a layer of inter-pericope cohesion on top of the ties just outlined. But just as important, since this same psalm also implies a close relationship between the demonic realm and conditions of impurity (106.37–39), its intertextual presence in the exorcism story does more than merely reinforce the link between these same motifs within the pericope itself; it also

---

[94] Similar connotations of hierarchy are conveyed by ἀπολύω in Acts 3.13; 4.21, 23; 5.40; 16. 35, 36; 17.9; 19.40; 23.22; 26.32; and 28.18.
[95] Cf. Busse, *Die Wunder des Propheten Jesus*, p. 205.
[96] This construction is absent from the Marcan and Matthaean parallels.

helps to give the impurity motif a high level of salience in the larger structure of Luke 8.26–56, which includes references not only to an unclean spirit (8.29) and tombs (8.27) and swine (8.32–33) but also to a human corpse (8.49, 53) and a gynaecological discharge (8.43–44). The relationship between impurity and demonology in this story therefore deserves fuller treatment, which it receives below in my discussion of cultural context.

Here, though, a few other aspects of this story's co-text ought to be considered. First, the strong linkage in 8.26–56 between impurity on the one hand and diverse types of illness on the other, including demon-possession, closely parallels several ideational complexes found earlier in the Gospel. A similar pattern can be seen for instance in the relations between Jesus' expulsion of 'the impure spirit' in 4.33–37 and that story's immediate co-text, which includes references both to Elisha's purification of Naaman the Syrian of 'leprosy' (4.27) and to Jesus' exorcistic healing of Simon's mother-in-law (4.38–39). Furthermore, as this latter reference in particular raises the question of how Luke understood the relationship between illness in general and demon possession – are they different but related states of being? Genus (illness) and species (possession)? Two sides of a single phenomenological coin? – it is worth asking at this juncture whether the antecedent co-text of Luke 8.26–39 contains anything else that might shed light on this matter.

In this connection Luke 6.17–19 deserves special consideration. In addition to giving orientation for the sermon on the plain (Luke 6.20–49), this unit refers to a group of persons who, prior to being healed by Jesus, had been 'troubled by unclean spirits' (6.18b). This reference clearly reinforces the link noted above between demonology and impurity in the narrator's world-view; but for my present purposes the most noteworthy feature of this line is its relationship with the construction immediately preceding it, namely 'a great multitude of people . . . who had come to hear him [i.e., Jesus] and to be healed of their diseases' (6.18a). More specifically, although the phrase οἱ ἐνοχλούμενοι ἀπὸ πνευμάτων ἀκαθάρτων (6.18b) has been understood by some interpreters as denoting only a subset of the group that approached for healing,[97] several grammatical features of these verses support an alternative interpretation. Most notably, whereas 6.18a (οἳ ἦλθον ἀκοῦσαι αὐτοῦ καὶ ἰαθῆναι ἀπὸ τῶν νόσων αὐτῶν) does not assert that these people were actually healed but only that finding therapy was one of their main reasons for approaching, the immediately ensuing line (καὶ οἱ ἐνοχλούμενοι ἀπὸ πνευμάτων ἀκαθάρτων

---

[97] E.g., J. B. Green, *Gospel of Luke*, p. 262.

ἐθεραπεύοντο, 6.18b) does assert that healing – indeed, healing of an entire 'crowd' of people – eventually took place. By thus encouraging the reader to view the therapeutic process in the second line as a fulfilment of the hopes mentioned in the first, this particular sequence entails that the group which actually experienced healing (6.18b) was identical to that which came to Jesus for precisely this purpose (6.18a);[98] but just as important, this also means that from the standpoint of the narrator, all the illnesses envisaged in this context stemmed from the activity of 'unclean spirits'.

Once this link between illness and impure spirits is recognised, moreover, the immediately ensuing description of Jesus' therapeutic technique as involving physical contact between the healer and the clients (Luke 6.19) can be seen to contribute to a pattern that is also apparent in Luke 8.26–48. To be precise, as in the latter passage so also here in 6.19 exorcistic healing is juxtaposed with Jesus' touch (πᾶς ὁ ὄχλος ἐζήτουν ἅπτεσθαι αὐτοῦ) and the power this touch conveys (δύναμις παρ' αὐτοῦ ἐξήρχετο καὶ ἰᾶτο πάντας). This kind of repetition has significance even if it is read on a strictly intratextual level; but equally noteworthy is the same pattern's lexical and ideational correspondence to the fifth and sixth chapters of Leviticus. For the capacity of Jesus' touch to transform the impure into the holy recalls the remarkable properties of the grain and sin offerings in Leviticus 6.14–18, 24–30, which transmit holiness to anything that happens to touch them. In this light, the description of physical contact between Jesus and the impure as resulting not in the contamination of Jesus (cf. Lev. 5.2–3) but rather in the holiness of his patients may well be based on the representation of these offerings in Leviticus.

The next reference to a demonic being in Luke's narrative is found in Luke 7.18–23, where Jesus responds to John the Baptist's disciples by healing many persons of νόσων καὶ μαστίγων καὶ πνευμάτων πονηρῶν (7.21). As Jesus proceeds immediately thereafter to imply that all these actions correspond to various oracles found in Isaiah – 'the blind receive sight, the lame walk, the lepers are cleansed, the deaf hear, the dead are raised, the poor are brought good news' (7.22)[99] – none of which is associated in Isaiah itself with demons,[100] the three substantives in 7.21

---

[98] Cf. Kirschläger, *Jesus exorzistiches Wirken*, p. 178.
[99] Cf. Isa. 29.18; 35.5–6; 42.18; 26.19; 61.1.
[100] While it is possible that the translators of LXX Isaiah could have understood these phenomena in a demonological sense without employing overtly demonological lexis (e.g. δαιμόνιον), in this particular instance the absence of explicit lexical support weighs against the idea; for LXX Isaiah is one of the few septuagintal texts that includes explicit references

should probably not be understood as denotatively distinct; rather, as in Luke 6.18–19 so also here νόσος and πνεῦμα signify different aspects (e.g., the physical and the cosmological) of a single negative state of being. And with μάστιξ also being added to the string, the effect of the whole trio is to portray the healings as having been multifaceted and complete.[101] In Luke 7.21, therefore, as in Luke's first and second stories of exorcism, evil spirits are implicitly associated with impurity ('the lepers are cleansed', 7.22) and exorcistic healing is presented as fulfilling Isaianic expectation.

If my reading of νόσων καὶ μαστίγων καὶ πνευμάτων πονηρῶν in 7.21 is correct, then Jesus' use of Isaiah 61.1 in the ensuing verse (πτωχοὶ εὐαγγελίζονται) to interpret his healing activity has further narrative consequences that deserve our attention. For first of all it entails that those who are harassed by evil spirits are understood by Jesus to overlap those who are designated as 'the poor' (πτωχοί); otherwise Jesus' use of this particular intertext loses all its relevance. But furthermore, this unit (i.e., 7.18–23) is not the first in Luke's Gospel to have these motifs interlaced. In Luke 6.20, for instance, immediately after Jesus heals many persons of demoniacal afflictions, his first of several macarisms is Μακάριοι οἱ πτωχοί, his audience clearly including those he has just delivered from diabolical oppression (cf. 7.1). Similarly, and as noted in my analysis of Luke 4.33–37, the citation of Isaiah 61.1 in Luke 4.18-19 (and in particular the words εὐαγγελίσασθαι πτωχοῖς) directly precedes and anticipates an account of Jesus' teaching and healing in which deliverance of the demonised is especially prominent (4.33–37, 38–39, 41). Consequently, the collocation of demon-possession, healing, and the poor in Luke 8.26–39 should occasion no surprise; for although the noun πτωχός does not occur in this episode, the related motifs of homelessness and nakedness and bondage do find expression, working together to recall the oracle of LXX Isaiah 58.6–7, where one aspect of the Lord's acceptable fast is to bring the πτωχοὺς ἀστέγους . . . εἰς τὸν οἶκόν σου.

Situated immediately after Jesus' response to the disciples of John (7.18–23), his witness concerning the Baptist (7.28–35) sheds valuable light on the experience of demon-possession in the assumed context

---

to demons at points where a demonological reading of the Hebrew Vorlage is intended by the translator. See, e.g., LXX Isa. 65.3, 11.

[101] μάστιξ is used in the LXX to render נגע in Ps. 90(91).10, a psalm used apotropaically not only in Luke 4.10–11 and 10.17–20 but also at Qumran in *11QApocryphal Psalms* vi 3–14 and in Late Antique incantations such as *AMB* bowl 11.6–7. Similar in effect to νόσων καὶ μαστίγων καὶ πνευμάτων πονηρῶν in Luke 7.21, moreover, is the paratactic presentation of the healing in Luke 9.42 – ἐπετίμησεν δὲ ὁ Ἰησοῦς τῷ πνεύματι τῷ ἀκαθάρτῳ καὶ ἰάσατο τὸν παῖδα καὶ ἀπέδωκεν αὐτὸν τῷ πατρὶ αὐτοῦ – where the three verbs capture different aspects of a single therapeutic intervention.

of culture; for when Jesus says, 'John the Baptist has come eating no bread and drinking no wine, and you say, "He has a demon"' (7.33), his utterance presupposes that in the culture shared by John, his opponents, and Jesus himself, unconventional behaviour like John's ascetic diet had the potential to be interpreted as the work of a demonic being. Since someone in this milieu could therefore be labelled as a demoniac entirely on the basis of unconventional behaviour, many of the demoniacs encountered by Jesus were probably suffering chiefly from socioreligious degradation and marginalisation, and only secondarily from the psychological and physiological consequences of these processes.

Several features of the story about the man from Gerasa, moreover, are anticipated in Luke 8.1–3, which, in addition to including Luke's first reference to the demonic realm after that in 7.33, also summarises Jesus' most typical activities (e.g., going 'through cities and villages . . . bringing the good news of the kingdom of God', 8.1) and connects what precedes the summary (i.e., 7.36–50) to what follows (8.4–21). As for the linking function, the characterisation of those who accompany Jesus as including not only 'the twelve' but also 'some women . . . who provided for them [i.e., Jesus and the twelve] out of their means' (8.2–3) develops the interest shown in the preceding co-text in Jesus' association with women of marginal status (7.36–50).[102] Similarly, the demonological motif in 8.2, where Jesus is implied to have healed all these women of possession illness (i.e., 'evil spirits and infirmities'), is developed further in the immediately ensuing section, where he explains that the birds in his parable of the sower (8.5) actually represent 'the devil' (8.12). But for purposes of contextualising Luke's second exorcism story, the most important features of the summary in 8.1–3 are the characterisation of Mary of Magdala as having been possessed by multiple demons, and the portrayal of her and all these other formerly demonised women as having become sources of economic support for Jesus' whole itinerant outfit; for the first of these items highlights the cosmic authority and power of Jesus in a way that anticipates his victory over the legion of spirits in 8.26–39 (cf. also 11.24–26 and Acts 19.13–20), while the latter is paralleled by the implicitly contractual relationship that develops between Jesus and the

---

[102] As neither Mary of Magdala nor Susanna is identified in this context in relation to a husband or son, both probably would have been understood to have been unmarried; as they are also described (along with the other women) not only as having once been demon-possessed but also as having later travelled in public with Jesus, their social status and reputation would be very low by conventional Graeco-Roman standards. T. K. Seim, *The Double Message: Patterns of Gender in Luke–Acts*, Studies of the New Testament and Its World (Edinburgh, 1994), pp. 34–7.

man from Gerasa (8.35, 38–39).[103] Indeed, with the women's provision of support therefore functioning as a positive example of how to respond to Jesus' gift of healing, they also stand in conspicuous contrast to the Gerasene demoniac's ungracious neighbours (8.35–37), whose negative response to Jesus has already been interpreted above as deriving from fear of material loss.

Finally, Jesus' identification of the metaphorical birds of 8.5 as 'the devil' (8.12) not only develops the demonological motif of 8.1–3 in a new register but also has significant connections to the exorcism of 8.26–39 and its immediate co-text. Perhaps most noteworthy in this regard is Jesus' discourse on why the devil 'takes away' the word of the gospel from the hearts of many who have heard: the devil's purpose, Jesus says, is that those who have heard 'may not believe and be saved' (8.12). As noted above at the beginning of the present section, the motifs of faith and salvation function as a key source of cohesion for all of Luke 8.22–56, in some instances occurring together as a thematic complex (8.48, 50) but in other cases separately (8.25, 36).

In this light, and as the purpose clause that contains these motifs in Luke 8.12 (i.e., ἵνα μὴ πιστεύσαντες σωθῶσιν) is absent from the Matthaean and Marcan parallels (Matt. 13.19; Mark 4.15), the degree of lexical and thematic cohesion exemplified by Luke 8.4–56 is comparatively striking; but just as important, since faith and salvation are joined by several other motifs that connect 8.22–56 to 8.4–15 – most notably the lexeme βίος (8.14, 43) but also different compounds from the πνίγω group (8.7, 14, 33, 42)[104] – the string of marvels in the latter section is easy to see *en masse* as an illustration of Jesus' teachings in 8.4–15. The disciples' worry about perishing in the storm (8.22–25), for instance, narrated as it is only shortly after Jesus' teaching in 8.11–15, serves very well as an example of the 'cares ... of life' (8.14), while the fear of further material loss in Gerasa (8.33–37) nicely illustrates how the 'riches of life' can lead to an inappropriate response to divine intervention.

---

[103] Viewed in relation to Jesus' 'gift' of healing, the women's provision of support is part of what Pilch and Malina and others call a 'dyadic contract', with Jesus' provision of exorcistic therapy having informally obligated the recipients to enter a relationship with him of reciprocal support. See Pilch, 'Sickness and Healing', pp. 193–4; Malina, *New Testament World*, pp. 94–6.

[104] As neither βίος nor the various compounds of πνίγω occur often in Luke's writings, the contribution of their repetition in Luke 8.4–56 to this section's cohesion is greater than it may at first seem. Βίος, e.g., is not used in Luke prior to this section, where its two occurrences (8.14, 43) are without parallel in Matthew and Mark; and neither ἀποπνίγω (8.7, 33) nor συμπνίγω (8.14, 42) are used by Luke outside this section of the narrative.

Context of culture

With its demonic legion, naked demoniac, drowned swine and tacit allusions to ancient Jewish systems of impurity, this story requires a massive effort of contextualisation if it is to be understood in a manner that does justice to the historically particular assumptions, values and knowledge of its earliest producers and consumers. Sources that shed light on the interface between demonology and impurity, especially in Second Temple Judaism but also in other ancient religious systems, deserve special consideration in this connection; yet, in terms of comparative and genre-critical interpretation of this story, the exorcism narratives in Philostratus' *Vita Apollonii* – and especially that found in *VA* 4.20 – merit first place in the analysis to be pursued here, for reasons that will emerge in the process of comparison.

Apollonius the exorcist

In a society rife with conflict between slave and free, oppressed provincials and beneficiaries of Roman rule, those of high birth and those of low,[105] the amply documented assumption that spirit beings were behind a wide range of human misfortunes and could even be coerced, by means of verbal formula or ritual action, into taking the side of one antagonist against that of another must have contributed to the demonophobic mood attested in various types of ancient documents.[106] These same assumptions, moreover, must also have nurtured a felt need (or at least helped to maintain existing markets) for the services provided by magico-religious practitioners who could manage and, where necessary, drive away the spirits of misfortune. The cult of the Neopythagorean philosopher Apollonius of Tyana, like the early church, undoubtedly owed at least some of its popularity to its hero's ability to overpower these beings, who on several occasions in Philostratus' *Vita Apollonii* are depicted as succumbing to the sage's clever tactics.[107] As the particular misfortunes that the Philostratean demons inspire in these contexts include not only seafaring calamities (3.56) but also an unhealthy preference on the part of the

---

[105] On the social divisions and conflicts in the Late Republic and early Imperial period, see G. Alföldy, *The Social History of Rome*, trans. D. Braund and F. Pollock, rev. edn (London, 1988), pp. 65–85.

[106] See, e.g., *CTBS* nos 18, 19, 20, 45, 48.

[107] See Philostratus *VA* 3.38, 56; 4.10, 20, 25, 44; 6.27, 43; and 7.3. As noted however by Brenk, 'In the Light of the Moon', p. 2140, the supernatural enemies of Apollonius include a malevolent mermaid, a satyr, a ghost, and a lamia, none of which has close parallel in Luke–Acts.

possessed for wilderness regions (3.38),[108] the importance of Philostratus' narratives for comparative study of the Lucan story is difficult to overestimate. Since one of Philostratus' stories, in fact, namely that in *VA* 4.20, is closer in register to Luke 8.26–39 than is any other narrative preserved from antiquity outside the NT,[109] it deserves special consideration here.

One feature or other of *VA* 4.20 has attracted attention in a variety of modern studies of Jesus' exorcisms.[110] Nevertheless, because these studies have tended to operate at a relatively high level of abstraction (e.g., comparing Jesus and Apollonius in general as exemplars of the divine man construct),[111] none of them to my knowledge has compared this story in a systematic fashion with the Synoptic unit about the Gerasene demoniac in particular.[112] The following survey of the parallels between the two gives a generally accurate sense of the Philostratean story's plot.

First, like the demoniac in the Lucan account, the youth healed by Apollonius is characterised as not merely afflicted by a demon but actually indwelt and thus possessed by one.[113] Second, both narratives include features that emphasise the severity of the demon's ill-effects on the victim.[114] Third, in each case the demon manifests its presence partly through the loudness of the utterances it inspires.[115] Fourth, both narratives contain a reference to the demon driving its victim, with the verb ἐλαύνω

---

[108] Cf. Luke 8.22–25, 29.

[109] *Contra* C. A. Evans, 'Apollonius of Tyana', p. 80–1, who, in arguing that the deeds of Philostratus' Apollonius have less value for comparative study of the Gospels than do the relevant Jewish materials, ignores the multiple correspondences between *VA* 4.20 and Luke 8.26–39.

[110] See, e.g., Twelftree, *Jesus the Exorcist*, pp. 74, 81, 95, who erroneously implies (p. 95 n. 17) that the exorcistic convention of acquiring and using the demon's name is depicted in *VA* 4.20.

[111] On the similarities between Luke–Acts and *Vita Apollonii* on the one hand, and between the historical Jesus and the historical Apollonius on the other, see M. Q. Smith, *Jesus the Magician*, pp. 84–7. See also J. Z. Smith, 'Good News Is No News: Aretalogy and Gospel', in J. Neusner (ed.), *Christianity, Judaism, and Other Greco-Roman Cults*, Part I, *New Testament* (Leiden, 1975), pp. 26–8, who compares the Marcan Jesus and Peter to the Philostratean Apollonius and Damis (an alleged contemporary of Apollonius and source for much of Philostratus' story).

[112] P. Fiebig, *Jüdische Wundergeschichten des neutestamentlichen Zeitalters* (Tübingen, 1911), pp. 86–9, hints at a few of the similarities but offers no sustained comparison of the two accounts.

[113] Apollonius' diagnosis, e.g., implies that the youth's speech is inspired by the demon; cf. Luke 8.28–33.

[114] The narrator in *VA* 4.20 emphasises, e.g., how much damage the demon had done to the young man's reputation: 'he was at that time the subject of crude wagoner's songs' (my trans.); cf. Luke 8.27, 29.

[115] In *VA* 4.20 the youth interrupts Apollonius' speech on libations with 'loud and rude laughter'; cf. Luke 8.28.

serving to denote the process in both cases.[116] Fifth, like the demons in Luke's story, the evil spirit in *VA* 4.20 is described not only as being expelled from its victim but also as acknowledging beforehand its inferiority vis-à-vis the exorcist.[117] Sixth, in both cases the method of healing consists chiefly of verbal command. Seventh, the agent of possession is portrayed in both accounts as visibly affecting a material object in the immediate environment of its departure. Eighth, the narrator of each account represents the healing as an instance of dramatic reversal.[118] Ninth, both patients undergo a change in their mode of dress as a consequence of the healing.[119] And finally, the teaching and values of the healer are adopted by the former demoniac in each case as further evidence of the healing's success.

Although a few of these motifs (e.g., the prominence of verbal commands and the visibility of the demon's departure) are sufficiently common to the genre that no great significance can be attached to their presence in each account,[120] the co-occurrence of all ten features in the two stories constitutes a very heavy volume of correspondence. Furthermore, while no other pair of units from Luke's Gospel and the *Vita* exemplify a cluster of parallels comparable in weight to this one, their larger narrative co-texts do correspond in ways that are increasingly well recognised. In an impressive contribution to our understanding of the genre of the Gospels, for instance, Richard Burridge has shown that Luke and the *Vita* share several macro-generic features that are not common to all other examples of Graeco-Roman βίοι. Most notably, both narratives consist of smaller episodes whose seams are relatively easy to identify; both include complexes of material in which travel and change in setting are conspicuous;

---

[116] In *VA* 4.20 the demon 'drives' (ἐλαύνει) the boy to behave outrageously; cf. Luke 8.29.

[117] When Apollonius fixes his gaze on the demon, the latter cries out in fear (δεδοικότως) and promises not only to leave its victim but also to cease its harmful activities in general; cf. Luke 8.28, 31–32.

[118] According to Philostratus, the youth 'returned to his own disposition' (ἐπανῆλθεν εἰς τὴν ἑαυτοῦ φύσιν); on reversal in the Lucan episode, see the discussion above under 'Story structure', p. 87.

[119] The youth in Philostratus gave up his habit of wearing 'light and effeminate garments' (τε τῶν χλανιδίων καὶ ληδίων) in exchange for the austere style of Apollonius.

[120] E.g., the role of verbal utterances in the exorcist's technique can also be seen in *b. Meil.* 17b, where the second-century rabbi Simeon ben Yohai is said to have healed the possessed daughter of the emperor by means of the simple command 'Ben Temalion [the name of the demon], get out! Ben Temalion, get out!' (As noted moreover by M. J. Geller, 'Jesus' Theurgic Powers: Parallels in the Talmud and Incantation Bowls', *JJS* 28 (1978), pp. 141–2, Ben Temalion is portrayed, like the pythian spirit of Acts 16.18, as obeying the exorcist's command without delay.) And the motif of the demon's visible departure is also found in Lucian *Philops.* 16; and Josephus *Ant.* 8.48.

and both have material in which uncanny happenings associated with the birth and death of the central character are narrated.[121]

In order to use all these findings properly for the interpretation of Luke's story, however, we need to take into account several other factors. In regard to the two episodes of exorcism in particular, for instance, the similarities noted above are accompanied by significant differences: unlike Jesus, who neither in this story nor in Luke's other exorcism narratives ever deviates from the local diagnostic consensus (i.e., that the patient is demon-possessed), Apollonius overtly contradicts community opinion in his Athenian setting, where, at least prior to the sage's postulation of a demonic presence, most people had attributed the patient's licentious conduct to 'the boisterous humour of youth'; and unlike the violent effect of the demons on the swine – a development Jesus undeniably permits but which neither he nor the narrator presents as proof of therapeutic success – the demon's spectacular toppling of a nearby statue in Philostratus' story is explicitly represented as a response to Apollonius' injunction that the demon give 'a visible sign' of his exit. Furthermore, and in regard to the larger narrative frameworks of these two episodes, the *Vita Apollonii* as a whole is more than four times longer than the Gospel of Luke, the latter being far closer in this regard to the generic norm.[122] And finally, although the similarities just canvassed suffice to indicate an area of overlap in Luke and Philostratus' cultural resources and assumptions, their overt ideological agendas disagree very deeply, with the Pythagorean heritage that clothes Apollonius being clearly at odds with the Jewish-biblical tradition in which Luke firmly places Jesus.

On the one hand, then, by combining the broad areas of macro-generic correspondence noted by Burridge and the largely unnoticed but very striking parallels between the Lucan episode and *VA* 4.20, the foregoing analysis increases the likelihood that one of these traditions has influenced the other. In view of the documents' respective dates of composition, moreover, and with Philostratus' claim to knowledge of written testimony transmitted by an eyewitness (i.e., Damis) continuing to invite scholarly

---

[121] R. A. Burridge, *What Are the Gospels?*, SNTSMS 70 (Cambridge, 1992), pp. 173, 177–80. The correspondences on the level of macro-genre become even more impressive than Burridge allows as soon as Luke's Gospel is viewed as part of the larger two-volume composition Luke–Acts; for the Acts of the Apostles has its own distinctive set of parallels to the Philostratus narrative, on which see A. Reimer, 'Virtual Prison Breaks: Non-Escape Narratives and the Definition of "Magic"', in Klutz (ed.), *Magic*, pp. 130–3, 136–9; R. I. Pervo, *Profit with Delight: The Literary Genre of the Acts of the Apostles* (Philadelphia, 1987), pp. 38–9, 109.

[122] Burridge, *What Are the Gospels?*, pp. 169, 199.

suspicion,[123] any literary influence in this case is more likely to run from Luke (or related Synoptic traditions) to Philostratus than vice versa.

On the other hand, the observations above neither prove that Luke or related Synoptic tradition has influenced Philostratus nor disprove that early traditions about Apollonius could have influenced Luke or his sources.[124] Nevertheless, and especially when assessed in relation to the best available hypotheses regarding rates of conversion and Christian growth to the time of Constantine, these observations do tell us something important about the cultural context of the Lucan story's earliest reception: almost a century before the conversion of Constantine, and thus when probably less than one per cent of the empire's total population had converted to Christianity,[125] a story as close in register to Luke 8.26–39 as *VA* 4.20 could be expected by its author to be intelligible and persuasive to an audience that probably included not only the imperial court but also a wider circle of interested pagan consumers.[126] Furthermore, as none of the motifs shared by Luke 8.26–39 and *VA* 4.20 in particular are present in Jewish biblical texts that deal with evil spirits, the cultural universe of the Lucan story has just as much in common with the wider magico-religious conglomerate of the Imperial age as it does with Jewish Scripture in particular; thus, while the prominence of specifically biblical forms of intertextual rhetoric in Luke's story clearly implies an audience that knows and appreciates Jewish Scripture, the structure and main emphases of his account would have been intelligible and potentially appealing to a much wider audience.

Unclean spirits and systems of impurity

As noted in the last chapter, the exorcism narrated in Luke 4.33–37 functions like a purification rite. Concerns about impurity are even more

---

[123] See, e.g., Bowie, 'Apollonius of Tyana', pp. 1655, 1665–7, 1686; Bowersock, 'Introduction', in *Philostratus*, pp. 10, 17–19; Graf, *La magie dans l'antiquité gréco-romaine*, pp. 114–15; MacMullen, *Enemies of the Roman Order*, p. 115; C. A. Evans, 'Apollonius of Tyana', p. 81; and H. C. Kee, *Miracle in the Early Christian World: A Study in Sociohistorical Method* (New Haven, 1983), p. 256.

[124] Cf. G. Petzke, *Die Traditionen über Apollonius von Tyana und das Neue Testament*, SCHNT 1 (Leiden, 1970), pp. 68–72.

[125] If we accept the figures proposed by R. Stark, *The Rise of Christianity: A Sociologist Reconsiders History* (Princeton, 1995), pp. 4–13, who defends a model of steady Christian growth of around 40% per decade, then the number of Christians in the empire at the time of the *Life*'s composition (*c.* 216–20 CE) was almost certainly less than 500,000, i.e., less than one per cent of an estimated population of sixty million.

[126] Note esp. Philostratus *VA* 1.2–3, which shows an explicit interest in correcting *widespread* misconceptions about the narrative's central character (1.2–3).

pronounced in the present narrative, with allusions to Jewish purity codes being apparent not only within the story itself (e.g., tombs, impure spirits, swine) but also in its immediate co-text (the menstrual disorder and the corpse in 8.40–56) and in one of its biblical intertexts (Ps. 106.7–12, 34–39). Although this facet of the story can be understood satisfactorily without an exhaustive knowledge of ancient Jewish systems of impurity, it can also lead us into some fascinating and largely overlooked levels of meaning if it is contextualised merely in relation to one oft-neglected facet of these systems, namely the evidence for an interface between demonology and impurity in early Judaism.

Evidence for the existence of this interface comes in various forms. The most obvious type of support for it is the present story's own presupposition pools, which, like those found in Luke 4.33–37, include references to 'unclean spirits' where the reader has been given no explanatory aid towards understanding the existence or character of these beings. Since these references furthermore take for granted the audience's assent not only to the realities of impurity and spirit beings but also to the existence of a nexus between the two, they exemplify very well what the literary critic William Empson had to say about words and phrases becoming 'compact doctrines', that is, implicit and normally unnoticed propositions about what is 'really there and worth naming';[127] and here, specifically in regard to the nexus aspect of the doctrine, what is 'really there and worth naming' should probably be understood as analogous to Luke's subsequent references to a 'dumb demon' (δαιμόνιον κωφόν, Luke 11.14) and 'a spirit of infirmity' (πνεῦμα... ἀσθενείας, Luke 13.11), where narrative logic in both cases implies a relation of demonic cause to symptom-effect. Moreover, as this relation directly entails that a demonic aetiology was assumed in Luke's milieu for at least some (probably many) cases of impurity, the possibility that some Jewish groups in Luke's day understood impurity in general to be intrinsically demonic merits serious consideration, especially since the newly accessible scrolls from Qumran add a substantial body of material to that previously available and known to be relevant to the question.[128]

Notwithstanding the prominence of the demon–impurity nexus in our exorcism account, brief consideration of its occurrence and distribution

---

[127] W. Empson, *The Structure of Complex Words* (London, 1951; repr., 1985), p. 39.
[128] See, e.g., *1QRule of the Community* iv 9–10, 20–2; *Damascus Document*^{d} iv 13–18; *4QEnoch*^{a} ar iii 13–14; *4QPseudo-Ezekiel*^{b} 1 ii 3–4; but esp. *4QDamascus Document*^{a} 6 i 6–13 (par. *4QDamascus Document*^{d} frag. 7 lines 1–8 et al.), where the various skin disorders denoted by צרעת are attributed to the malevolent action of a רוח (cf. Lyons and Reimer, 'Demonic Virus', pp. 29–31; Avalos, *Illness and Health Care*, p. 375).

elsewhere in the Synoptic tradition and in Acts indicates that it must have been present in earlier gospel materials and was probably presupposed by Jesus himself. The Gospel of Mark, for instance, which almost certainly was composed earlier than Luke even if it did not serve as a source for it, has nearly twice as many occurrences (eleven) of πνεῦμα ἀκαθάρτον and its formal variants as Luke does (six), even though Mark's total length is only 57.9% that of Luke's.[129] Mark also uses these constructions more frequently than Luke does specifically in their shared exorcism stories (seven occurrences to four); but perhaps most significantly, in the Lucan composition's second volume, whose lexical choices were probably constrained less by written sources than the first volume's were, the phrase occurs only twice (Acts 5.16; 8.7) – notably, in stories whose settings are Palestinian – with πνεῦμα being qualified repeatedly by πονηρόν in another episode (Acts 19.11–20) where ἀκάθαρτον might have been the more appropriate choice.[130] These observations on their own, then, suggest that the link between demons and impurity was neither invented nor given special salience by the author of Luke–Acts, even though the phrase does carry ideological freight for him as observed earlier in this chapter.

Furthermore, since the exorcisms narrated in Mark's Gospel provide a more realistic image of the role of violence in Jesus' praxis than do their Lucan parallels, the Marcan accounts might also provide greater insight into how the demon–impurity nexus was understood by some of Jesus' followers between his time and the date of the Lucan writings' composition. Is it possible, for instance, that in some settings the impurity behind which the demons were perceived to be lurking, and which Jesus' exorcisms removed, consisted of neither psychopathology (e.g., multiple personality disorder) – a medico-centric explanation often assumed in modern research but seriously flawed in ways discussed below – nor what might today be called an immoral lifestyle, but rather ritual impurity? Mark 7.1–30 contains several clues that point to a positive

---

[129] The percentage is based on figures given in R. Morgenthaler, *Statistik des neutestamentlichen Wortschatzes* (Zurich, 1958), p. 164.

[130] In an episode where Jewish itinerants of priestly status are so decisively overpowered by a demoniac that they cannot escape with their purity intact (Acts 19.16), a description of the demon as ἀκάθαρτον may have underscored the irony of the itinerants' humiliation more effectively than πονηρόν; however, as ἀκάθαρτον is used in both of the Acts episodes that involve exorcism in a Palestinian setting (5.16; 8.7), the employment of πονηρόν to describe a demon in a non-Palestinian setting (i.e. Ephesus) may well have been encouraged by the expectation that, in the age to come, the unclean spirit (רוח טמאה) would be removed – not from all the earth – but rather 'from the land' (מן־הארץ, Zech. 13.2), i.e., the land of Israel.

answer to this question. Most notably, by placing the story of Jesus' expulsion of an 'impure spirit' (πνεῦμα ἀκάθαρτον, 7.25) from the daughter of a Gentile woman directly after a block of materials on ritual purity (7.1–23), which Jesus decentres in typically charismatic fashion,[131] the author of Mark undoubtedly expected his audience to interpret Jesus' exorcistic purification of the Gentile girl in the light of his preceding reconceptualisation of purity;[132] for the morphological repetition instanced by the use of ἀκάθαρτον in 7.25, just after the occurrence of the cognate form καθαρίζων in 7.19, creates a form of inter-pericope cohesion that strongly promotes precisely this kind of reading.

Thus, in addition to suggesting that demon-possession may have been construed in this context (certainly in Mark's interpretation, but perhaps also in the milieu of Jesus himself) as somehow involving the application of Jewish codes of impurity, this particular juxtaposition of traditions also hints that Jesus' exorcisms may have been interpreted as instantiating certain aspects of his unconventional teaching on purity. Hence, in Mark's version of the exorcism in the synagogue, the bystanders' interpretation of Jesus' performance as constituting a διδαχὴ καινή (Mark 1.27) may point to a valid and historically useful insight on at least two levels: in content if not altogether in form, Jesus' exorcisms did in fact stand in continuity with his teaching; and the content of his teaching concerning exorcism in particular (e.g., Luke 11.24–26), which in one fashion or other had to subvert the demon–impurity nexus, was perceived to be non-traditional and threatening to the established order.[133]

Although Burton Mack and others have persuasively warned against readings that take Mark's Gospel to be an ideologically innocent record of historical facts about Jesus,[134] the general validity of these warnings scarcely requires us to take a negative view of the historicity of the particular Marcan evidence summarised above. For in the first place, in strongly tradition-orientated societies like those in which the Gospels were first read and heard, the author of Luke would have had far greater incentive to exaggerate Jesus' loyalty to Jewish ancestral custom than the author of Mark would have had to overstate his innovativeness. But just as

---

[131] Cf. G. Vermes, *Jesus the Jew: A Historian's Reading of the Gospels* (London, 1973), pp. 80–2.

[132] Cf. C. M. Tuckett, 'Mark', in J. Barton and J. Muddiman (eds), *The Oxford Bible Commentary* (Oxford, 2001), p. 900; R. P. Booth, *Jesus and the Laws of Purity: Tradition History and Legal History in Mark 7*, JSNTSup 13 (Sheffield, 1986), pp. 28–9.

[133] Cf. M. Q. Smith, *Jesus the Magician*, pp. 31–2.

[134] See, e.g., B. Mack, *A Myth of Innocence: Mark and Christian Origins* (Philadelphia, 1988), pp. 15–24.

importantly, evaluating Mark's Gospel as broadly reliable in its representation of Jesus' teaching and practice in this particular area helps us to explain, in a manner the alternative cannot, another portion of Mark's narrative that clarifies the link between demonology and impurity in the cultural context of the Gospels.

The material in question is found in Mark 3.20–35, where notes of conflict between Jesus and his family immediately surround the Beelzebul controversy. As Twelftree and others have observed, both the reference in 3.21 to people saying Jesus was mad and the accusations cited in verses 22 and 30 (i.e., that Jesus himself was possessed and performed his exorcisms only by the power of Satan) are very unlikely to have been invented by the earliest churches.[135] Furthermore, and as the accusations themselves imply, not only the charge regarding the source of Jesus' power but also the challenge regarding his 'madness' arose in response to one of his exorcisms (3.21–22). Less obvious, however, and even more important for the present discussion, is the way these features cohere with a couple of other details that likewise have good claim to authenticity. More specifically, as the summary of what people were saying about Jesus (i.e., 'He has gone out of his mind', 3.21b) is presented as an explanation of his family's attempt 'to take charge of him' (3.21a), which initially is presented as a response to rumours that Jesus and the twelve were abstaining to an unusual degree from eating (3.20), the rumour of madness and the abstinence from food are intriguingly interconnected: in addition to constituting a type of unconventional behaviour that elsewhere is judged to be symptomatic of demon-possession (Luke 7.33; Matt. 11.18), abstemious conduct is widely attested as a technique of inducing altered states of consciousness, which from an emic standpoint are often interpreted as a positive variety of spirit-possession.[136]

Not surprisingly, therefore, in Jesus' ensuing response to the charge of being an agent of Satan, he implicitly characterises his exorcism(s) not as his own work but rather as the work of the Holy Spirit (Mark 3.28–29). This characterisation, moreover, entails not only that Jesus' self-understanding in exorcistic settings was dramatically altered by his own experiences of spirit-possession – in such settings his persona was not that of Jesus of Nazareth but rather that of 'Holy Spirit' or the divine presence itself[137] – but also that, like other advanced shaman-healers

---

[135] Twelftree, *Jesus the Exorcist*, pp. 100, 177; M. Q. Smith, *Jesus the Magician*, p. 32.
[136] For discussion and bibliography, see the next chapter, pp. 204–5.
[137] Cf. Davies, *Jesus the Healer*, pp. 23–36, 74–7.

discussed in the recent anthropological literature, he had developed a high level of meta-experiential skill in reflecting on and controlling these experiences for his own socioreligious aims.[138]

The atmosphere of general unconventionality, abstemious behaviour and altered states of consciousness surrounding Jesus' exorcistic performance furthermore coheres very well with another noteworthy feature of the Marcan account. In 3.30, to be more precise, where the narrator explains why Jesus said what he said about the unpardonable sin (i.e., blaspheming the Holy Spirit by attributing his role in Jesus' exorcisms to Satan), he cites the charge of the opponents as being that Jesus was possessed by 'an unclean spirit'. Although the latter phrase broadly fits into one of Mark's favourite patterns of usage,[139] its function in this context deviates in significant ways from the normal pattern and, especially since it helps in this instance to represent a perspective hostile to Jesus, it has a strong claim to authenticity.[140] But just as important, if as seems likely Jesus did in fact derive his exorcistic authority from altered states of consciousness and ecstatic experiences of spirit-possession rather than from traditional channels of therapeutic power (e.g., incantations in the Solomon tradition),[141] his performance of exorcism probably showed scant regard for the distinctions between pure and impure that must have been at play in most Jewish settings of illness; indeed, Jesus' exorcisms may have worked precisely by either implicitly or explicitly subjecting this system of differences to a kind of ritual-symbolic critique.[142]

In the eyes of those committed to maintaining these distinctions, this type of disregard would have looked like the work of a pagan or impure spirit (Mark 3.22). This same kind of unconventionality would also help to explain why, in the Matthaean and Lucan parallels, Jesus' relation to

---

[138] See, e.g., Walsh, 'Psychological Health of Shamans', pp. 116–17; I. M. Lewis, *Religion in Context: Cults and Charisma* (Cambridge, 1986), pp. 85, 90–3; F. Bowie, *The Anthropology of Religion: An Introduction* (Oxford, 2000), pp. 199–201, 207; Winkelman, *Shamanism*, pp. 79–80, 84–6.

[139] πνεῦμα occurs with ἀκάθαρτον in Mark 1.23, 26, 27; 3.11, 30; 5.2, 8, 13; 6.7; 7.25; 9.25.

[140] Cf. M. Q. Smith, *Jesus the Magician*, pp. 32–3.

[141] Cf. ibid., p. 32. On the therapeutic value of the shamanic healer's charismatic and authoritarian self-representation, cf. Davies, *Jesus the Healer*, pp. 75–7; Winkelman, *Shamanism*, pp. 268–9.

[142] In her cross-cultural analysis of rites of affliction, Catherine Bell, *Ritual: Perspectives and Dimensions* (Oxford, 1997), p. 117, observes that possession and exorcism 'often involve elements of rebellion against social constraints' and undermine 'other dimensions of the religious and social order'; the relevance of Bell's observations to the context of Jesus is supported by my reading below of Luke 11.24–26 (par. Matt. 12.43–45).

Solomon is defined more by difference than by similarity,[143] and also why Jesus' practice is not mentioned in the writings of Flavius Josephus but his contemporary Eleazar's is: unlike Jesus, Eleazar and most other Jewish exorcists from around this time probably utilised traditions of incantatory utterance and ritual performance associated with Solomon or David.[144] By identifying themselves with an established Jewish tradition of therapeutic praxis, these other figures posed no serious threat either to Jewish tradition or to established groups identified with it. Jesus, by contrast, had acquired a reputation for healing in a manner that had nothing distinctively Jewish about it,[145] in addition to having been disgraced by the manner of his death; consequently, traditions about his exorcistic prowess had nothing whatsoever to contribute to Josephus' rhetorical project.

Finally, in this same complex of materials surrounding the Lucan and Matthaean versions of the Beelzebul controversy is another unit of tradition which, since it contributes to the demonology–impurity nexus in a uniquely illuminating way, merits comment here. In Luke 11.24–26 and Matthew 12.43–45, Jesus produces a sapiential utterance which, although it coheres broadly in topic with its exorcistic co-text, is less at home in the agonistic setting provided for it by the evangelists than in the situation to which it was probably first addressed, namely a context of demonological instruction for Jesus' followers.[146] Although the ambiguities presented by this unit are too numerous and complex to discuss in detail here,[147] three relatively straightforward aspects of it are especially relevant to our interests.

First of all, by referring at the outset to the central participant in the action as 'the unclean spirit' (11.24), Jesus presupposes, like the narrators of the exorcism stories, the reality of an interface between demonology and impurity, signalling thereby that what he is about to say pertains as much to the movement of impurity as to that of demonic beings; indeed, by describing 'the impure spirit' in a manner that closely resembles the way impurity on its own could be described – you can get rid of it but it has a nasty way of coming back in one form or other (11.26) – Jesus

---

[143] See Luke 11.31 (par. Matt. 12.42), where Jesus claims καὶ ἰδοὺ πλεῖον Σολομῶνος ὧδε.

[144] See, e.g., Josephus *Ant.* 8.46–8; *11QPsalms*^{a} xxvii 9–10; *11QApocryphal Psalms* v 2–14. For discussion of exorcistic incantations in the Solomon tradition, see pp. 257–60 and the literature cited there.

[145] See pp. 79–80.   [146] C. F. Evans, *Saint Luke*, p. 494.

[147] For summary and evaluation of the interpretative options, see esp. R. Piper, *Wisdom in the Q-Tradition*, SNTSMS 61 (Cambridge, 1989), pp. 123–4, 129–30.

adds here to the evidence adduced above for a very tight interlocking of the two fields of meaning. Furthermore, although Jesus' description of unclean spirits returning to their hosts after expulsion is not inconsistent with assumptions attested in a variety of other ancient sources on the topic,[148] the degree of abstraction in Jesus' comments differs markedly from that in other extant references to the phenomenon;[149] more specifically, by repeatedly using present tense verb forms with gnomic force in the main clauses describing the actions of the unclean spirit and his victim,[150] Jesus speaks in this unit like someone who had observed numerous exorcistic interventions and had reflected theoretically on why they so often failed to provide lasting relief. And third, although the scope of Jesus' critique in this saying is so encompassing that it could be construed as including his own exorcistic practice,[151] it should probably be understood rather as directed exclusively at the practices of others; for if as seems likely the sayings in verses 20 and 24–26 go back to Jesus himself, they would entail that Jesus saw these healers as giving their patients no reorientation of eschatology, no reconceptualisation of impurity, and no programme of post-exorcism resocialisation comparable to what he himself provided.[152] Thus, although these figures could expel an impure spirit here and there (Luke 11.19), they neither criticised nor offered alternatives to the larger religio-medical system that had defined and produced their patients' spirit-impurity illnesses in the first place, leaving their patients therefore with the dreadfully high likelihood of recontamination in the near future.

Hence, although these other exorcists are not represented negatively in Luke 11.19 ('by whom do your sons cast them out?'), they certainly do belong to that general system of care which Jesus indirectly criticises

---

[148] See, e.g., 1 Sam. 16.23; 18.10; Tobit 8.3; Mark 9.25; Josephus *Ant.* 8.45, 47; Philostratus *VA* 4.20; *Acts of Thomas* 5.46.

[149] *Contra* J. B. Green, *Gospel of Luke*, p. 459, whose description of this teaching as 'standard' and 'common' ignores both the demon–impurity nexus and the unusually high level of abstraction in the saying.

[150] τὸ ἀκάθαρτον πνεῦμα...διέρχεται...λέγει...εὑρίσκει...πορεύεται...παραλαμβάνει...κατοικεῖ. If indeed Jesus said something like this, he almost certainly would have said it in Aramaic, whose verbal system is fully capable of expressing the gnomic nuance sometimes conveyed by various forms in the Greek system. (Gnomic force is realised, e.g., by the aphel participles in the following clauses of Dan. 2.21: והוא מהשנא עדניא וזמניא מהעדה מלכין ומהקים מלכין, 'He [i.e., the God of heaven] *changes* times and seasons, *deposes* kings and *sets up* kings'.)

[151] See, e.g., C. F. Evans, *Saint Luke*, p. 494.

[152] On Jesus' own practice in these areas, see esp. Twelftree, *Jesus the Exorcist*, p. 173 (eschatology); Vermes, *Jesus the Jew*, pp. 80–2 (impurity); Booth, *Jesus and the Laws of Purity*, pp. 207, 213–19 (impurity); and Davies, *Jesus the Healer*, pp. 107–12 (resocialisation).

in 11.24–26. *Contra* Twelftree, therefore, who understands these practitioners as receiving exclusively favourable treatment (i.e., as those who are with Jesus rather than against him) in 'Q',[153] their image in the sayings tradition as a whole is in fact tinged with ambiguity:[154] while they admirably drove out unclean spirits in certain cases (Luke 11.19), they unfortunately did nothing to prevent them from returning and causing an even worse state of affairs (Luke 11.24–26).

Key features on the demonology–impurity interface

Due chiefly to scholarly neglect of the nexus discussed above, my treatment of it to this point has focused chiefly on establishing the mere existence of the interface and demonstrating its presence in multiple sources and layers of the Synoptic tradition. The discussion above therefore provides a general framework for probing the interface for more specific points of intersection that might shed further light on the cultural context assumed by Luke 8.26–39.

As noted above, one type of impurity alluded to in the present story is that of corpse defilement. More specifically, since the man from Gerasa was actually dwelling among the tombs (8.27), which could convey impurity either through direct contact or vertically to objects above them,[155] he would have been viewed by audiences familiar with the dominant impurity systems as someone suffering not only from demon-possession but also from corpse impurity. On the surface, and especially for most modern readers, these two aspects of the man's condition appear to be clearly distinguishable, with the former undoubtedly seeming far more severe and traumatic than the latter. For reasons worth exploring at least briefly, however, this perception probably owes more to modern psychoanalytic reinterpretation of demon-possession (e.g., William Peter Blatty's *The Exorcist*) than it does to detailed knowledge

---

[153] Twelftree, *Jesus the Exorcist*, pp. 106–8. One reason Twelftree understands 'Q' in this fashion is that he devotes no attention to the saying in Luke 11.24–26 and Matt. 12.43–45, which he excludes from his analysis because he understands it to involve possession not of persons but rather of places (pp. 13–14); against this, the use of ἄνθρωπος at the beginning and end of the saying (11.24, 26) to denote what the demon comes out of and subsequently returns to strongly suggests that the intervening domestic lexis (e.g. οἶκος, Luke 11.24), which Twelftree takes literally, ought rather to be understood metaphorically.

[154] As recognised, e.g., by A. E. Harvey, *Jesus and the Constraints of History* (London, 1982), p. 109, cited disapprovingly by Twelftree, *Jesus the Exorcist*, p. 107.

[155] See Num. 19.14–16; *m. Ohal.* 18.1–2. On the substantive continuity between the biblical and the rabbinic teachings in this area, see H. K. Harrington, *The Impurity Systems of Qumran and the Rabbis: Biblical Foundations*, SBLDS 143 (Atlanta, 1993), pp. 153–6; and Booth, *Jesus and the Laws of Purity*, pp. 128–9.

of ancient Jewish demonology and its intersection with the codes of impurity.

Although Jewish Scripture itself contains no evidence for a close relationship between demons and corpse defilement, several items of evidence from around the first century CE suggest that Jewish biblical passages about death in general and corpse defilement in particular were coming to be read in ways that exemplify a demonisation of death and of things associated with it. Most of our best evidence for this hermeneutical process comes from the New Testament, whose key passages are treated briefly below; but the source that relates most directly to the demonisation of corpse impurity in particular comes from a rabbinic anecdote about the great first-century CE sage Yohanan ben Zakkai, who is cited as having once interpreted the red heifer ritual of Numbers 19.1–10 as a type of exorcistic performance that treats this type of defilement as equivalent to demon-possession. While the anecdote in question is perhaps best known for its relevance to debates about the relationship between properly religious ritual and 'magic',[156] it is no less pertinent to the present discussion, as becomes especially clear towards the end of the extract cited below.

> A heathen questioned Rabban Yohanan ben Zakkai, saying: The things you Jews do appear to be a kind of sorcery. A heifer is brought, it is burned, is pounded into ash, and its ash is gathered up. Then when one of you gets defiled by contact with a corpse, two or three drops of the ash mixed with water are sprinkled upon him, and he is told, 'You are cleansed!'
>
> Rabban Yohanan ben Zakkai asked the heathen: 'Has the spirit of madness ever possessed you?' He replied: 'No.' 'Have you ever seen a man whom the spirit of madness has possessed?' The heathen replied: 'Yes.' 'And what do you do for such a man?' 'Roots are brought, the smoke of their burning is made to rise about him, and water is sprinkled upon him until the spirit of madness flees.' Rabban Yohanan ben Zakkai then said: 'Do not your ears hear what your mouth is saying? It is the same with a man who is defiled by contact with a corpse – he, too, is possessed by a spirit, the spirit of uncleanness, and, [as of madness], Scripture says, *I will cause [false] prophets*

---

[156] See e.g., P. S., Alexander, 'Incantations and Books of Magic', in Schürer, *History of the Jewish People*, III.1, p. 343.

Context of culture 135

as well as the spirit of uncleanness to flee from the Land'
(Zech. 13.2).[157]

The immediately ensuing co-text of this exchange, moreover, sheds additional light on the broader cultural context; for when the Gentile challenger has gone away and Yohanan is pressed by his pupils for a deeper and more scholarly solution, the rabbi's answer diverges sharply from the reply given to the Gentile.

> 'The corpse does not have the power by itself to defile, nor does the mixture of ash and water have the power by itself to cleanse. The truth is that the purifying power of the Red Heifer is a decree of the Holy One. The Holy One said: "I have set it down as a statute, I have issued it as a decree. You are not permitted to transgress my decree. This is the statute of the Torah"' (Num. 19.1).

This latter saying complicates the immediately preceding dialogue in ways that should not be overlooked. On one level, for instance, it demonstrates that what some of the most learned rabbis believed about such matters probably differed appreciably from what was accepted by the uninstructed;[158] but on another plane, and precisely by virtue of the leading rabbis' exceptional learning in these areas, the saying also entails that corpse impurity may well have been understood by the less scholarly as a form of demonic affliction or even as possession by 'the spirit of madness'.

Furthermore, if Yohanan's glib identification of 'the spirit of madness' and the demon of corpse impurity has any analogue to how categories of illness are employed in Luke and earlier Jesus traditions, then the denotative boundaries between these categories should probably be understood

---

[157] *Pesiq. Rb. Kah.* 4.7, whose conversation between Yohanan and the heathen is transmitted in nearly the same form in several other rabbinic works including *Num. Rab.* 19.8. Although the extant texts are late and their relation to earlier traditions difficult to define, their witness to the hermeneutical process of including demonic beings in biblical passages which make no explicit mention of them coheres with developments attested in much earlier sources (e.g., LXX Isa. 65.11; LXX Ps. 95.5).

[158] To interpret Yohanan's ambivalence as utterly ironic, however, would undoubtedly be to modernise him in a historically inappropriate way. As both J. Neusner and J. Goldin have shown, the rabbis in general shared most of the demonological and related beliefs held by other Jews at this time; see J. Goldin, 'The Magic of Magic and Superstition', in E. S. Fiorenza (ed.), *Aspects of Religious Propaganda in Judaism and Early Christianity* (South Bend, 1976), p. 131; Neusner, *Wonder-Working Lawyers*, pp. 194, 198, 207–8, 251–2, 260–1.

as imprecise and potentially overlapping except where good evidence to the contrary is available. Two Synoptic passages outside Luke, in fact, exemplify a fluidity comparable to Yohanan's precisely in the semantic field where demon-possession and corpse impurity intersect. In Mark 9.14–29, for instance, Jesus' exorcistic healing of the possessed youth reaches its successful conclusion, not with the departure of the unclean spirit (9.25–26), but rather only after the shattered patient has first become like a corpse and then been physically raised – as if from the dead – by the hand of Jesus (9.26–27). And similarly, in immediate anticipation of Jesus' instruction in Matthew 10.8 that the twelve 'heal the ill, *raise the dead*, cleanse the lepers, cast out demons', the narrator of the Gospel implies that 'authority over unclean spirits' is essential for success not just in exorcism but in all forms of healing (10.1), which by implication would include the raising of the dead mentioned shortly afterwards.[159]

Although the demonological assumptions and vocabulary of the Synoptics differ from those attested in Paul's writings, the Synoptic association of corpse impurity and unclean spirits finds an area of broad correspondence in Paul's personification of death as a demonic ruler that exercises dominion over entire periods of human history (Rom. 5.12–21) and which therefore must be subjected – along with the other demonic rulers, authorities and powers – to the authority of Christ at the end (1 Cor. 15.26).[160] As numerous interpreters of Paul have observed, his conceptualisation of death in these passages strikingly resembles that found in Wisdom of Solomon 2.23–24, where death is explicitly characterised as having entered the world through the arch-demonic agency of the devil.[161] To be sure, none of these latter passages relate directly to the demonisation of corpse impurity in particular; but since both Romans 5.12–21 and Wisdom of Solomon 2.23–24 do have direct intertextual ties to Genesis 3, they instantiate the mythic dimension of a dialectic whose ritual aspects are found in the Jewish-biblical laws of impurity, and whose generative criteria primarily revolve around either proximity to death or relation to femininity.[162]

---

[159] In ἔδωκεν αὐτοῖς ἐξουσίαν πνευμάτων ἀκαθάρτων ὥστε ἐκβάλλειν αὐτὰ καὶ θεραπεύειν κ.τ.λ. (Matt. 10.1), the infinitive of purpose θεραπεύειν is just as dependent on ἔδωκεν . . . ἀκαθάρτων as ἐκβάλλειν is.

[160] See esp. Rom. 5.12–21 and 1 Cor. 15.26, but also perhaps Rom. 8.38–39; for discussion see B. Byrne, *Romans*, Sacra Pagina 6 (Collegeville, 1996), pp. 277–80.

[161] See, e.g., ibid., p. 176; D. E. H. Whitely, *The Theology of St. Paul* (Oxford, 1964), p. 23.

[162] For discussion of these and other general criteria, see esp. Avalos, *Illness and Health Care*, pp. 300–7.

Thus, with death in general and corpse impurity in particular having probably had demonic associations in the minds of many people in Luke's cultural milieu, the reference to the tombs in the exorcism story (8.27) and the immediately ensuing portrayal of Jesus touching and raising the corpse of Jairus' daughter (8.49–55) are far more tightly interconnected than is usually recognised. Furthermore, and for reasons that involve the impurity code but also transcend it, the account of Jesus' healing of the woman with the haemorrhage in 8.43–48 likewise coheres even better with its immediate co-text than is normally appreciated; for in *4QExorcism ar*, whose content has been demonstrated by M. Wise and D. Penney to be highly conventional and thus typical of the incantatory genre,[163] concern is expressed not only about the activities of the fever demon (1 i 4) but also about 'he who crushes the male and she who passes through the female' (1 i 5), unclean spirits whose main activity was probably understood to be crushing testicles and causing irregular vaginal discharges respectively.[164] Hence, the woman with the vaginal haemorrhage in 8.43–48 may well have been understood as suffering attack from a spirit that specialised in producing her particular kind of affliction; and so all three healings narrated in Luke 8.26–56 should probably be understood as having depended on what the narrator of Matthew 10.1 calls 'authority over impure spirits'.

Of course, none of this proves that first-century Jews in general always thought of demons when they thought about impurity or vice versa. And fortunately, in order to demonstrate and interpret the link between the two in Luke 8.26–39, a pervasive association of this kind need not have existed; instead, all that is necessary for my purposes here is evidence for the availability of the semantic potential to be used and recognised in texts and contexts where the link would have been appropriate. Both the co-text and the cultural context of the Lucan story, I suggest, would have strongly encouraged the text's earliest readers to make this connection.

Possession, unconventionality and socioreligious change

As hinted above in connection with the Synoptic evidence, one form of impurity in particular appears to have had a measure of shame and blame attached to it that was either largely or entirely missing from the other forms. The type of impurity I have in mind is unconventional speech and behaviour.

---

[163] Penney and Wise, 'By the Power of Beelzebub', pp. 629–30.
[164] The victims would therefore be unfit for participation in the cult (Lev. 15.19–32; 21.16–23).

In regard to the demonisation of unconventionality in the ancient Mediterranean world, it has become commonplace to use Mary Douglas' 'group and grid' schema as a way of understanding the fundamental differences between the cultural context of this particular type of deviance labelling and the world of the western reader.[165] According to this approach, biblical societies are distinguished by the strong pressure they exert on their members to conform to societal norms (i.e., they are 'strong' as opposed to 'weak' on the group axis) and by a high degree of congruity between those norms on the one hand and the actual experience of most members of the society on the other (i.e., they are 'high' rather than 'low' on the grid axis). Although this approach is helpful to the extent that it foregrounds real differences between the two contexts in terms of sociocultural constraints and their implications for identity construction and perceptions of deviance, it has rightly been criticised for overgeneralising in ways that hinder or even misguide interpretation rather than enriching it.[166] The observations made in this section, therefore, are designed not so much to argue in favour of a particular application of Douglas' approach as to look afresh at certain pieces of ancient evidence that broadly cohere with it.

Above, in regard to the link between demons and impurity in the Synoptic Gospels, it was noted that Jesus himself behaved in ways that encouraged some of his contemporaries – not only on the narrative level of the Gospels but also in Jesus' own historical setting – to consider him demon-possessed (cf. Mark 3.20–30). As the particular form of unconventionality that occasioned the charge in Mark 3.22 was probably an intense form of fasting,[167] which most likely was undertaken with the conscious aim of inducing an altered state

---

[165] See M. Douglas, *Natural Symbols: An Exploration in Cosmology* (New York, 1973), pp. 95–7; and B. J. Malina and J. Neyrey, 'Jesus the Witch: Witchcraft Accusations in Mt. 12', in *Calling Jesus Names: The Social Value of Labels in Matthew* (Sonoma, CA, 1988), pp. 3–32.

[166] See, e.g., Avalos, *Illness and Health Care*, pp. 304–5; and Lewis, *Religion in Context*, pp. 83–4.

[167] Although the construction from which I draw this inference (i.e. καὶ συνέρχεται πάλιν ὁ ὄχλος, ὥστε μὴ δύνασθαι αὐτοὺς μηδὲ ἄρτον φαγεῖν, Mark 3.20) does not ground Jesus' behaviour in the sort of intentionality one normally associates with fasting, the ensuing clauses (3.21) clearly imply that rumours about his not eating are precisely what lead his family to judge him mad and to come out to take charge of him; thus Jesus' kin interpret his behaviour the same way the opponents of the Baptist evaluated his fasting regimen, i.e., as a form of unconventionality symptomatic of demon-possession (Matt. 11.17–19; Luke 7.24–35). On the role of fasting and other forms of ascetic discipline in the life of Jesus, see esp. D. C. Allison, *Jesus of Nazareth: Millenarian Prophet* (Minneapolis, 1998), pp. 172–216, esp. pp. 172–5.

of consciousness that would increase Jesus' own exorcistic authority,[168] other Gospel units in which accusations of demon-possession co-occur with references to fasting or disputes about authority might be expected to illuminate the dynamics of demon-possession in Luke's milieu.

Particularly in regard to fasting, the double tradition of Jesus' testimony concerning John the Baptist (Matt. 11.17–19; Luke 7.24–35) has special significance. In that context Jesus responds to those who dishonoured John for his ascetic habits but also criticised Jesus for his allegedly less abstemious ways. More significantly, in the course of this response Jesus implies that John's asceticism had been the trigger for an accusation by the opponents that John was demon-possessed: 'John came neither eating nor drinking, and they say, "He has a demon"' (Matt. 11.18; par. Luke 7.33). As in Mark 3, therefore, so also here, the road to becoming a demoniac begins with unconventional behaviour; indeed, in these contexts the whole phenomenon is very much a socially constructed process, having less to do with individual psychopathology (e.g., multiple personality disorder) than with challenges to local religious authority, rhetorical efforts to shame the challengers, and strategies of social control.

This understanding of Luke's cultural context, moreover, is both reinforced and enriched by evidence found in the Fourth Gospel, whose controversy dialogues include three separate exchanges in which Jesus is accused of being demon-possessed (John 7.20; 8.48–52; 10.20). While none of these accusations occur in contexts where fasting is also mentioned, they do occur alongside strong claims to authority by Jesus in settings marked by intense social conflict. In John 10.20, for instance, the assertion by one Jewish faction in Jesus' audience that he 'has a demon and is out of his mind' (Δαιμόνιον ἔχει καὶ μαίνεται) is presented as a response to Jesus' emphatic claim to have received special authority from the Father both to lay down his life and to take it up again (John 10.17–19); thus, in addition to demonstrating the link between accusations of demon-possession and conflict over religious authority, this exchange also shows that attributions of madness in this milieu are less indicative of substantive efforts to diagnose disease than of rhetorical attempts to shame one's opponents as deviant. Similarly, in John 8.48–52 Jesus is accused twice by his Jewish opponents of being demon-possessed, once after he implies that they are children of

---

[168] On fasting as a method of inducing altered states of consciousness, see the next chapter, pp. 202–5.

the devil (8.44), and again after he claims that anyone who keeps his word will never see death (8.51); in the opponents' first accusation in this setting, moreover, the charge that Jesus 'has a demon' closely parallels an insinuation that he is a Samaritan – a description whose pejorative character is unmistakable in light of the wider co-text (e.g., John 4.9)[169] – providing yet further evidence that perceptions of demon-possession tended to arise in settings where socioreligious conflict was involved.

Although the Fourth Gospel's date of composition is probably later than that of Luke–Acts, its witness to powerful ties between perceptions of the demonic and differences of religion is scarcely evidence of recent innovation. For in the first place, the relationship in question lies closer to the Gospel's underlying cultural assumptions than to its overt Christological rhetoric; but just as important, the same connection can be discerned in a range of widely divergent sources from antiquity,[170] the most relevant being the exorcism narrated in Acts 16.16–18 and analysed later in the present study. For my present purposes, what is most noteworthy about this latter story is that, although neither its narrator nor Paul as exorcist shows any doubt that the Philippian slave-girl's pythian spirit was an evil demonic entity fully deserving of the eviction it eventually suffers, unconverted pagan readers of this story (or pagan observers of events like the one it narrates) almost certainly would have found this evaluation utterly baffling; for in their eyes, as in those of the slave-girl herself and her owners, the pythian spirit that inspired her utterances would have been at worst a morally neutral intermediary being, a daimonic subordinate of Apollo that inspired oracles for people seeking information from the gods.[171] Like Jesus and John the Baptist in the Gospel texts just surveyed, therefore, the slave-girl from Philippi is a demoniac only to people who represent a different religious ideology.

Very significantly, therefore, this latter analysis suggests that, on the way to becoming the sort of person whose demon-possessed status could be unproblematically taken for granted by the narrator of Luke–Acts, the future demoniac first had to go through the same kind of agonistic process that Jesus and John the Baptist underwent: in brief, they had to experience

---

[169] Cf. Böcher, *Dämonenfurcht und Dämonenabwehr*, pp. 143–4.

[170] In addition to the episode in Acts 16.16–18, the stories in Philostratus *VA* 4.20; *1QGenesis Apocryphon* xix–xx; and *4QPrayer of Nabonidus ar* frags 1–3 lines 1–8, contain evidence for this same view of possession, with the perception of possession being situated in a setting of either intense interpersonal conflict or strong religious difference.

[171] See below, pp. 243–5.

conflict with their socioreligious environment and eventually be labelled by their antagonists as deviant and demon-possessed. Thus, unlike people suffering from other forms of impurity that may have had demonic associations (e.g., Peter's mother-in-law and the woman with the haemorrhage), the full-fledged demoniac probably acquired their particular status at least partly by deviating from group norms in a fashion that was evaluated in morally negative terms. For instance, and as discussed in greater detail in the chapter on Acts 16.16–18, the Philippian slave-girl is treated by the Lucan Paul as a demoniac because she repeatedly misrepresents the character of Paul's gospel. Similarly, the 'young dandy' healed by Apollonius in *VA* 4.20 had acquired a bad reputation for his licentious style of living. And in the *Damascus Document*^{a}, 'every man over whom the spirit of Belial dominates' is closely associated with the preaching of apostasy and judged as deserving far harsher treatment (i.e., execution) than that befitting people who simply need to be 'cured' of imperfection in ritual observance.[172]

As the process of becoming a demoniac therefore involves social dynamics that are largely hidden from view in Luke 8.26–39, we might anticipate that exorcism, as the reversal of this process, likewise involves far more than this story straightforwardly depicts. And ironically, one of the best pieces of evidence for this is found in the story itself. The detail I have in mind here is the characterisation of the former demoniac as sitting at the feet of Jesus (8.35), a posture which, as discussed earlier in this chapter, is rightly interpreted by many commentators as symbolising an attitude of discipleship. Although the main function of this symbol on a literary-rhetorical level is to help create a sense of dramatic reversal and thereby foreground Jesus' power to effect change, the same image invites us to hear an alternative story about the social realities of exorcistic therapeutics; to be precise, since no former demoniac could have brought honour to Jesus as healer without becoming one of his disciples, and since becoming a disciple could scarcely be achieved in any substantive sense within the temporal frame of the exorcism story itself, the note about the man's posture points in a richly symbolic but also realistic way beyond this story's immediate setting of tombs and sea and into his future, and beyond that into the future of every demoniac who would find in Jesus a true release from the grips of the demon–impurity system. What this symbol suggests, therefore, is that an experience of discipleship – of leaving behind the local structures which applied the demon–impurity labels in the first place, adopting the patterns of culture and practice that defined

---

[172] *Damascus Document*^{a} xii 2–5.

a new group of itinerant charismatics, and in effect undergoing a process of resocialisation into the life world of a mobile religious alternative – was not merely the *result* of effective therapy but rather an essential *component* of it.[173]

As all this leaving, adopting and undergoing entails far more active participation on the part of the patient than the surface structures of the narrative itself would suggest, questions may properly be raised about what sort of person would have been ready to sign up for such a life-rearranging programme. While an acceptance of the story's own cosmological framework affords an easy response to this question – namely, someone indwelt and dominated by a demonic being – recent studies in the social psychology of religious conversion may offer us a complementary and more historically interesting way of understanding the change from demoniac to disciple, even if we are not entirely happy to think of the demoniac's transformation as a conversion experience.[174]

On the basis of research into the backgrounds of modern converts to new religious movements, for instance, Rodney Stark and others have recently emphasised that these movements attract nearly all of their new recruits from situations of religious discontent and accommodationist tendencies.[175] Similarly, in a fascinating ethnography of spirit-possession in the Madagascar town of Ambanja, Lesley Sharp has observed that effective exorcistic therapy in that context typically involves patients whose ties to their own local kinship and religious structures have already been seriously weakened, who have desperately sought therapy from indigenous healers but found no cure, and who – after undergoing an exorcistic rite that accepts many of the features of the indigenous cosmology but simultaneously subverts the cultural logic that produces the illness – often relocate to a retreat where they concentrate on building a new identity.[176] These latter patients, moreover, significantly resemble I. M. Lewis' category of persons who experience spirit-possession

---

[173] Cf. Davies, *Jesus the Healer*, pp. 107–12. As hinted above in the discussion of Philostratus *VA* 4.20, Apollonius' exorcistic healing of the boisterous youth includes a similar but more explicit note of discipleship near its end, strengthening the impression that successful exorcism in this milieu involved far more than a quick word of rebuke.

[174] On the possibility that conversion played an instrumental role in the healings performed by Jesus and his followers, see L. Wells, *The Greek Language of Healing from Homer to New Testament Times*, BZNW 83 (Berlin, 1998), pp. 138, 141–3, 161, whose value would have been enhanced by critical reflection on what 'conversion' might mean with reference to the ministry of Jesus.

[175] Stark, *Rise of Christianity*, pp. 19, 55.   [176] Sharp, *The Possessed*, pp. 245–75.

as a positive and health-enhancing phenomenon, whom Lewis himself memorably characterises as not suffering from serious mental disease but rather as 'ordinary "normally" neurotic people'.[177] But most importantly, the patterns of pre-conversion religious experience of the converts studied by Stark and Sharp may help us to imagine the backgrounds of those demoniacs who underwent Jesus' full programme of discipleship therapy. Like Jesus himself, many of the demoniacs who experienced healing in his context probably contributed to their own prior marginalisation by behaving in a deviant fashion that arose out of religious discontent.

In many of these cases, moreover, patient dissatisfaction with local religious structures would have been aggravated further by limitations in the available systemic resources for dealing with their kinds of difficulties. The Israelite temple and priestly establishment, for instance, had never served the specifically therapeutic functions fulfilled by certain other ancient temple systems (e.g., that of Greece).[178] Furthermore, although several ancient sources confirm that first-century Palestinian society had ample space for various types of local magico-religious healers,[179] the relief provided by the vast majority of their interventions must have been highly ephemeral at best; for all the available evidence suggests that these figures operated inside the parameters of the very system that constructed their patients' illnesses in the first place (Luke 11.24–26).[180] By giving the various types of polluted ill so few options for effective intervention and hope, the cities and villages of Palestine in this period would have given a sizable portion of their population ample reason for religious dissatisfaction. Indeed, the particular combination of impurity systems, demonological beliefs, and health care constraints found together in Palestinian society at the time of Jesus could easily have created a golden opportunity for an itinerant charismatic healer with an alternative concept of purity.[181]

---

[177] I. M. Lewis, *Ecstatic Religion: A Study of Shamanism and Spirit Possession*, 2nd edn (London, 1989), p. 176.

[178] Avalos, *Illness and Health Care*, pp. 316–17, 365–6.

[179] See, e.g., Luke 11.19 (par. Matt. 12.27); Acts 19.13–20; Josephus *Ant.* 8.45–49; *4QExorcism ar* ii 5.

[180] E.g., although the Qumranians were demonstrably interested in practices of an apotropaic nature (e.g. *4QSongs of the Sage*^{b} frags 8, 10, 35, 48, 49 and 51), it is far less evident that they performed exorcisms on afflicted members of their own group; and the exorcistic performance described in Josephus *Ant.* 8.45–49 stands very prominently in continuity with the established therapeutic tradition of Solomon.

[181] Cf. Avalos, *Illness and Health Care*, pp. 368, 393–4; and *Health Care and the Rise of Christianity*, pp. 68–71.

Ritual of relocation and 'anti-rite' in Jesus' performance of exorcism

Above, in trying to recover the socioreligious processes that constituted possession and exorcism in the world of Jesus, I have implied that Jesus' own exorcistic practice probably stood in what might be best characterised as a partly countercultural and partly contracultural position vis-à-vis the Jewish ethnic subculture of Palestinian society; that is, it consisted partly of a prophetic opposition to existing methods of managing the human costs of the demon–impurity nexus (e.g., Luke 11.24–26 and par.), and partly of an alternative approach that summoned the demoniacs to a new and potentially more promising future (e.g., Luke 8.1–3).[182] Undeniably, this understanding of Jesus' position entails that he must have been blessed by a rare combination of critical acumen and religious creativity. Yet it need not be construed as entailing either that Jesus must have possessed qualities of a supramundane character or even that his ability to subvert old structures and create new ones was fundamentally different from that found by students of religious healing in other contexts. Catherine Bell, for instance, in her stimulating and much praised cross-cultural study of ritual, has pointed out that the most effective ritual responses to illness very often instantiate some kind of historical or structural opposition to other varieties of ritual expertise institutionalised in the cultural context.[183] More specifically she observes:

> Analyses of female shamans in Korea, the infamous Salem witch trials, or modern ecstatic Hindu saints suggest that these phenomena [i.e., rites of affliction and healing] involve elements of rebellion against social constraints; they may even institutionalise methods of inverting, reversing, or undermining other dimensions of the religious and social order.[184]

Accordingly, and especially since certain features of Luke 8.26–39 are comparable to essential elements of one of the most important and authority-imbued rituals in the ancient Jewish calendar, namely the Yom Kippur ceremony (Lev. 16.1–34), this story deserves to be probed more carefully than it has been hitherto for potentially oppositional stances vis-à-vis other ritual performances known from the same cultural milieu.

---

[182] On the differences between countercultural and contracultural types of rhetoric, see, e.g., Robbins, *Exploring the Texture of Texts*, p. 87.
[183] Bell, *Ritual*, p. 117.   [184] Ibid.

Although good reasons will be given below for excluding Leviticus 16 from the specifically intertextual analysis offered earlier in this chapter, several features of the ritual outlined in that section of Leviticus correspond to particular facets of Luke 8.26–39 and cumulatively contribute to a case for the present exercise in comparison. For instance, as Jesus' transferral of the impure spirits from the demoniac to the bodies of the swine is similar to the Levitical ritual's removal of iniquity from Israel to the wilderness outside the camp (Lev. 16.20–22), both actions correspond to what J. Z. Smith has defined as a 'ritual of relocation', that is, a process that symbolises the transferral of a hostile power or a negative state of being to a place outside the subjectively defined socioreligious order of the formerly contaminated entity.[185] Second, both processes assign important participant roles to animals, with the function of the swine in transferring the demons into the lake (Luke 8.31–33) being similar to that of the live goat which takes the iniquities of Israel into the wilderness (Lev. 16.10, 20–22). Furthermore – and the significance of this point cannot be overestimated when one recalls how sparse the references to demons are in Jewish Scripture – the actantial position of 'opponent' in both processes is fulfilled primarily by demonic powers, with the demon Azazel in Leviticus 16 being no less instrumental in the cyclical contamination of Israel than the army of impure spirits is in the pollution of the man from Gerasa.[186] Fourth, both actions not only involve the employment of water in the functional role of 'helper', they also agree on the fundamental importance of the clothing worn (or not worn) by select participants.[187] And finally, like the immediately ensuing co-text of the Lucan story (8.40–56), the antecedent co-text of Leviticus 16 evinces a pronounced interest in impurity in general (chs 11–15) and the more specific variety of pollution caused by gynaecological processes – whether regular or irregular – in particular (15.19–30, 32–33).

---

[185] J. Z. Smith, 'Towards Interpreting the Demonic Powers in Hellenistic and Roman Antiquity', *ANRW* II.16.1, pp. 428–9. A similar example is pictured in Tobit 8.1–3, where the evil demon Asmodeus is ritually separated from Sara of Ecbatana and transferred to 'the remotest parts of Egypt'.

[186] Cf. B. A. Levine, *In the Presence of the Lord: A Study of Cult and Some Cultic Terms in Ancient Israel*, SJLA 5 (Leiden, 1974), pp. 81–2; A. Jirku, *Die Dämonen und Ihre Abwehr im Alten Testament* (Leipzig, 1912), pp. 32–4. B. Janowski, 'Azazel עזאזל', in *DDD*, cols 240–6, argues that in the earliest form of Leviticus 16 עזאזל was not intended to denote a demonic being, but acknowledges that this interpretation arose early in the history of the text's reception.

[187] Water: Lev. 16.4, 24–28; Luke 8.33. Clothing: Lev. 16.4, 23–28, 32; Luke 8.27, 35. On the role of water in ancient exorcistic and related rituals, see Böcher, *Dämonenfurcht und Dämonenabwehr*, pp. 11–13.

In view of this high volume of correspondence, and with Luke having been demonstrably interested in exploiting this sort of intertextual potential, it might be tempting to see in this linkage some kind of deliberate rhetorical strategy at work in the Lucan text. Yielding to this temptation, however, would probably be a mistake; for in the first place no exegete in the history of interpretation has to my knowledge ever proposed such a reading and, while at least in theory a lack of intertextual imagination could be the cause of this long silence, more persuasive reasons for it can be offered. Most notably, alongside the parallels just summarised run deep incongruities and oppositions that require the relationship between the two texts to be defined in some other way. As for the oppositions, the following seem especially noteworthy: (a) whereas the scapegoat ritual overtly serves the collective interest of atoning for the holy place and expiating the sins of all Israel (Lev. 16.15–22), the rite performed by Jesus implicitly subordinates the collective purity of the community to the healing of the individual patient (Luke 8.35–39); (b) whereas the scapegoat ritual proceeds on the assumption that the demonic power (i.e., Azazel) is itself stationed *outside* the community and pursues its contaminating aims from there (Lev. 16.10, 21–22), the exorcistic rite of Jesus starts from the presupposition that the demonic powers have already broken through the walls and are now *inside* the house (Luke 8.27–33); (c) whereas the scapegoat ritual is conceptualised as an iterative event to be performed once each year 'for ever' (Lev. 16.29–34), the exorcistic performance of Jesus has an eschatological, climactic and once-for-all flavour about it, especially since the demons' fear of being sent to the abyss appears to be symbolically realised by their ultimate transferral to the watery grave of the swine;[188] (d) whereas the animal whose death is prescribed by the sacrificial logic of Yom Kippur is a goat (i.e., not the one for Azazel but the one for Yhwh, Lev. 16.9, 15), the type of creature whose death is effected by the exorcism is the notoriously impure swine (Luke 8.32–33); and (e) whereas it is the aristocratic figure of the high priest whose change of clothing is featured in the scapegoat ceremony (Lev. 16.3–4, 23–24), it is the lowly demoniac whose transition in attire is highlighted in the exorcism (Luke 8.35).

Although questions about the origins of the Yom Kippur ritual and the precise nature of its observance in late Second Temple times are too complex to be handled satisfactorily here, the event's importance as one of the central festivals of Israel cannot be doubted.[189] Its annual repetition

---

[188] Cf. Bovon, *Luc (1,1–9,50)*, pp. 425–6.
[189] See, e.g., Schürer, *History of the Jewish People*, II, pp. 275–6; Wise, Abegg and Cook, *Dead Sea Scrolls*, p. 452.

must have impressed its logic on the minds of many people in Palestinian society at the time; and certainly by the era of Jesus and probably much earlier, it was understood to counteract the noxious influence of a demonic being.[190] As it furthermore had to be officiated by the high priest, whose high authority in both the religious and the political domains entailed unique honour and aristocratic privilege,[191] its symbolism could easily have been inverted by critics of the cultic establishment so as to lampoon either the Yom Kippur ritual itself or those who officiated it.[192] The task of exploring whether the exorcism narrated in Luke 8.26–39 was understood this way either by Jesus himself or by later pre-Synoptic traditionists cannot be taken up here; but the possibility certainly merits further consideration, especially since the macrostructural parallel to this story in Acts 19.11–20 (discussed in the chapter on Acts 16.16–18) transforms several of the motifs found in the present narrative precisely into a lampooning of the high priest's family.[193]

Whatever conclusions a full diachronic study of this matter might reach, these same observations have several noteworthy implications for interpreting the Lucan story in its own context. First, although no direct or causal link has been established here between the Lucan story and Leviticus 16, the set of similarities and differences just outlined certainly does point to the existence of a shared cultural repertoire; and it is one in which ritual-symbolic action plays a far more important role than has been recognised to date by scholarship on Jesus' exorcisms.[194] Furthermore,

[190] Cf. L. Grabbe, 'Leviticus', in Barton and Muddiman (eds), *Oxford Bible Commentary*, p. 101; M. J. Gruenthaner, 'The Demonology of the Old Testament', *CBQ* 6 (1944), p. 24; M. Q. Smith, 'Jewish Religious Life in the Persian Period', in W. D. Davies and L. Finkelstein (eds), *The Cambridge History of Judaism*, I, *Introduction; The Persian Period* (Cambridge, 1984), p. 266; Jirku, *Die Dämonen*, pp. 32–3; S. Mowinckel, *Religion und Kultus* (Göttingen, 1953), p. 36; Y. Kaufmann, *The Religion of Israel: From Its Beginnings to the Babylonian Exile*, translated and abridged by M. Greenberg (London, 1960), p. 64.

[191] Schürer, *History of the Jewish People*, II, pp. 275–6.

[192] As Jesus' threat against the temple in his last week (Mark 13.1–2 and parr.) was very probably indicative of his attitudes to its associated priesthood, the possibility that he may previously have enacted a ritual-symbolic critique of the priesthood's privileged role in one of the Jewish calendar's most sacred ceremonies is by no means inconceivable.

[193] Although exorcism in the context of Jesus and his earliest followers has not often been interpreted as a laughing matter, its performance in other contexts certainly has been; on the comic aspects of exorcistic therapy in a modern Sri Lankan context, e.g., see B. Kapferer, *A Celebration of Demons: Exorcism and the Aesthetics of Healing in Sri Lanka*, 2nd edn (Oxford and Washington, 1991), pp. 285–90, 315–19. Within Luke–Acts itself, moreover, exorcism's potential for humour and dramatic irony has already been seen above in my comments on the curious presence of a demoniac in a synagogue (Luke 4.33), and will be seen in a more overt form below in my comments on Acts 19.11–20, which looks in many respects like an inversion of the present narrative.

[194] In Twelftree's *Jesus the Exorcist*, e.g., no discussion is devoted either to the Yom Kippur ritual or to the potential relevance of recent studies of ritual in general.

in trying to interpret the exorcism narratives in relation to their original context of culture, scholarship needs to give more attention than it customarily does, not merely to how each narrative relates to its historically reconstructed event and its various written intertexts, but to ceremonial actions and ritual performances which likewise could have contributed to the story's range of interdiscursive effects for its earliest audiences. Third, in view especially of the *contrasts* that emerged in the course of the comparison above, and since many details of this story probably reflect a historical event in the life of Jesus,[195] this analysis confirms that Jesus was probably more critical of traditional Jewish codes of impurity – at least in symbolic or indirect ways – than a number of recent contributions to historical Jesus research have been willing to allow.[196] But most important, as the evidence that supports this latter judgement scarcely lies on the surface of Luke's story but rather is almost buried in it, its recovery helps us to appreciate how passionate Luke was to soften the deviance of Jesus and to bring him as far as possible into line with the biblical heritage of Israel.

Master of the storm demon

Above, in dealing with matters of co-text, I pointed out the existence of strong cohesive ties between the present story and the episode that directly precedes it (i.e., 8.22–25, Jesus' stilling of the storm). One point bearing on this matter, however, has been reserved for discussion until now since it simultaneously involves an aspect of the story's cultural context. To be precise, just as this narrative's original cultural milieu provided semantic potential for construing the different forms of impurity in 8.40–56 as manifestations of the demonic, so it also provided resources adequate to warrant a demonological interpretation of 'the wind and the raging waves' in 8.22–25.

In an incantatory text from ancient Sumer, for instance, one demon in particular is characterised as specialising in the causation of terrible storms.[197] Later Mesopotamian incantations from Asshurbanipal's

---

[195] Twelftree, *Jesus the Exorcist*, pp. 72–87.
[196] See, e.g., P. Fredriksen, 'Did Jesus Oppose the Purity Laws?', *BibRev* (June 1995), pp. 22–5; E. P. Sanders, *Jewish Law from Jesus to the Mishnah: Five Studies* (London and Philadelphia, 1990), pp. 39–42; and G. Vermes, *The Religion of Jesus the Jew* (London, 1993), pp. 18–26, each of which minimises the tension between Jesus and his Jewish contemporaries in regard to the laws of purity.
[197] *FUH* 5.365. On the conceptualisation of misfortune as demonic in ancient Mesopotamian religion, see P. Michalowski, 'Carminative Magic: Towards an

time, moreover, witness to a similar identification of evil spirits with destructive storms and mighty winds.[198] Much later (c. third or fourth century CE), in one of the numerous dialogues found on the lips of King Solomon and his various demonic discussants in the *Testament of Solomon*, the demon Lix Tetrax describes himself as stirring up among other things 'whirlwinds' (στρόφους, 7.5), while the two spirits whose discourses take up most of chapters 22–5 are closely associated with deadly blasts of wind (22.2, 9–15) and the Red Sea (23.2; 25.5–7) respectively. And finally, in LXX Psalm 105.7–12, whose echoes can be heard in both of the Lucan episodes being considered here (i.e., 8.22–25 and 8.26–39), the representation of the Lord as rebuking the Red Sea already reverberates with its own demonological echoes from still earlier Near Eastern and biblical myths of the primeval battle against chaos.[199]

Thus, while potentially diabolic overtones of the storm in Luke 8.22–25 have been vaguely noted by a number of interpreters, a widely unacknowledged wealth of comparative material suggests that – particularly in a context like this one where exorcism clearly has a prominent place – the wind and waves should probably be construed more specifically as either a particular evil spirit or a demonic pair.[200] As a result, the story in 8.26–39 has considerably stronger cohesive ties to the storm narrative in 8.22–25 than most analyses of these units indicate; and, in view of the demonic overtones of the phenomena confronted by Jesus in 8.40–56, the whole multi-unit sequence stretching from verse 22 to verse 56 can now be appreciated as having layers of implicit and culture-specific cohesion and coherence which neither the surface levels of linguistic structure nor much of modern exegesis would suggest.

Understanding of Sumerian Poetics', *ZA* 71 (1981), p. 5; T. Jacobsen, *The Treasures of Darkness: A History of Mesopotamian Religion* (New Haven, 1976), pp. 12–13; and Saggs, *Encounter with the Divine*, p. 104.

[198] See, e.g., *DESB* tablet 16, pl. xix, lines 4, 13–14, 25–44; cf. Luke 8.22–25.

[199] F. Stolz, 'Sea, ים', in *DDD*, col. 1400; and S. Mowinckel, *The Psalms in Israel's Worship*, trans. D. R. Ap-Thomas (Oxford, 1962), I, pp. 152–4. The demonisation of the Red Sea in particular is apparent in several Psalms passages other than Ps. 106.7–12, including Pss 74.13–14; 89.9–10; 104.4–9; 107.23–30.

[200] Thus neither Bovon's talk of the natural elements' *personification* (*Luc 1–9*, p. 412) nor J. B. Green's assertion that Jesus 'confronts these . . . forces . . . *as though* they were demonic powers' (*Gospel of Luke*, p. 333, italics mine) is strictly accurate; for both imply that what is being represented as demonic in this unit is actually thought by Luke not to be, a reading which, in light of the comparative material summarised above, looks like a domestication of the text's alien world-view. In both cases, I would suggest, the interpretation is not unrelated to the commentator's silence regarding the ancient incantatory tradition.

Conclusion

As in Luke's first narrative of exorcism so in Luke 8.26–39, the power and authority of Jesus are strongly foregrounded, even though the terms δύναμις and ἐξουσία do not occur in this story. The emphasis on these motifs in the present narrative derives primarily from correspondences between features found on several different levels of the text's style. Jesus' power, for instance, is accentuated indirectly through the narrator's description of the demoniac's condition (8.27, 29b), the severity of which is highlighted not only by features of word order but also by transitivity and verbal aspect. The worse the affliction, the greater the power required for its healing; and the affliction of this particular demoniac is very bad indeed.

Both the name and the number of the demons, moreover, strengthen the impression that the opponent whom Jesus defeats is a mighty force whose powers are manifold. The stronger the enemy, the greater the strength required for victory; and the power of this particular enemy is very great indeed. The emphasis on Jesus' triumph and power is underscored yet further by (1) the contrast between the failure of the demoniac's community to help him (8.29b) and the dramatic success of Jesus, (2) the foregrounded fear which Jesus' suprahuman abilities occasion among the people of the surrounding region, (3) the contribution of Luke's transitivity choices to the impression that Jesus effects change in other participants in the story but is not affected or changed by them, (4) the parallelism in 8.39 between the action of God and the action of Jesus, and (5) the repeated reference to verbal/symbolic processes in which Jesus is tacitly characterised as having authority over other participants in the narrative.

Due to these mutually reinforcing features, Jesus looks more like a god in this episode than like a mere charismatic healer or prophet. And the story is not void of clues regarding which god Jesus should be compared to; for the allusions to Scripture in this narrative encourage the reader to compare Jesus not only to the prophet Elijah but even to the Lord God himself, whose paradigmatic destruction of the Egyptian army in the Red Sea is re-enacted in the descent of Legion and the pigs into the lake. Indeed, when the impact of Luke's allusion to LXX Psalm 105.7–12 is combined with the echoes of Isaiah 58.6–8; 65.3–4; and 1 Kings 17.18, the communicative force of Scripture in this story is comparable to that in Luke 4.33–37: it suggests that Jesus' mighty deed of exorcism not only fulfills eschatological hopes but also derives from the same divine power that wrought salvation in the past for the Israelites.

Conclusion

But finally, and despite the Jewish-biblical tradition in which Luke firmly plants his hero, the comparative analysis of this story indicates that several of its assumptions and motifs have more in common with those found in various extrabiblical and ancient pagan sources than with those attested in Jewish Scripture. Some of these sources, moreover, illuminate the story's relations to its immediate co-text, either by clarifying the implicit effects of the demonology–impurity nexus in 8.40–56 or by confirming that Jesus' authority over the demonic realm is also pictured in 8.22–25. Others enable us to fill in certain gaps in our understanding of spirit affliction by elucidating its relations to impurity and deviance. And still others help us to imagine the exorcistic performance of the historical Jesus as a potentially subversive ritual of purification, whose substantial deradicalisation in the present story is consonant with the intertextual rhetoric treated at length above.

3

DISCIPLESHIP AND THE EXORCISM IN LUKE 9.37–43A

Like the tradition of the Gerasene demoniac, the story of Jesus' encounter with a man and his demonically afflicted son is found in all three Synoptics (Matt. 17.14–21; Mark 9.14–29; Luke 9.37–43a). In all three the man discloses that some of Jesus' disciples had already proved themselves incapable of correcting the boy's condition; in all three Jesus responds with a lament over the faithlessness of his generation; and in all three Jesus himself ultimately succeeds against the demon and liberates the boy. Not without reason, therefore, the three accounts are normally read by scholars of the Gospels as variant renderings of a single unit of tradition.

Yet, like many other units in the triple tradition, this one has been shaped into three markedly different performances. Indeed, as detailed at several points below, the particular configuration of agreements and disagreements between the three accounts is sufficiently tangled to cause serious headaches for anyone bent on having a tidy solution to the Synoptic problem.[1] Even more than the stories analysed in the last two chapters, therefore, Luke 9.37–43a welcomes a reading that is released from the bonds of the source-critical yoke. By taking full advantage of the methodological jubilee, and more specifically by shifting critical focus

---

[1] On the tradition-historical relationships between the three versions of the story, see esp. X. Léon-Dufour, 'L'Episode de l'enfant épileptique', in *Etudes d'Evangile* (Paris, 1965), pp. 187, 210–27, who argues that the earliest form of the story is preserved by Luke; L. Vaganay, 'Les Accords négatifs de Matthieu-Luc contre Marc: L'épisode de l'enfant épileptique (Mt. 17,14–21; Mc. 9,14–29; Lc 9,37–43a)', in *Le problème synoptique: Une hypothèse de travail* Bibliothèque de théologie 3/1 (Tournai, 1954), p. 413, who uses the story as evidence of Matthew and Luke's use of a pre-canonical Greek version of Matthew's Gospel; Goulder, *Luke*, pp. 445–6, who interprets the minor agreements (e.g., Ἰησοῦς εἶπεν ... καὶ διεστραμμένη ... ὧδε in Matt. 17.17 and Luke 9.41) as evidence of Luke's dependence on Matthew; and H. Aichinger, 'Zur Traditionsgeschichte der Epileptiker-Perikope Mk 9,14–29 par Mt 17,14–21 par Lk 9,37–43a', in A. Fuchs (ed.), *Probleme der Forschung*, SNTU 3 (Vienna, 1978), pp. 114–26, who posits the existence of a 'Deuteromarkus' to explain the data. See also Kollmann, *Jesus und die Christen*, pp. 209–11; G. Petzke, 'Die historische Frage nach den Wundertaten Jesu: Dar gestellt am Biespiel des Exorzismus Markus IX.14–29 par.', *NTS* 22/2 (1976), p. 198.

Boundaries and cohesion

away from the elusive interaction between tradition and redaction to the interplay between story and co-text, the reading below has implications that ripple powerfully throughout the remainder of this study, impacting my understanding of everything from the structure of Luke 9.1–50 as a whole and the relative prominence of exorcism in it to the macrostructural function of the story in Acts 16.16–18 and the implied situation of all four Lucan narratives of exorcism. To be sure, as the cumulative effect of this shift is difficult to appreciate without full knowledge of the Acts episode, only part of it can be delineated in my analysis of the Gospel story below; but certainly by the end of the next chapter, the account in Luke 9.37–43a will have begun to look less like a sibling of the renderings in Matthew 17.14–21 and Mark 9.14–29 than like a second cousin once removed.

The same heuristic tools used in the previous two chapters are instrumental in my interpretation of the present narrative, whose Greek text reads as follows:

> 37 Ἐγένετο δὲ τῇ ἑξῆς ἡμέρᾳ κατελθόντων αὐτῶν ἀπὸ τοῦ ὄρους συνήντησεν αὐτῷ ὄχλος πολύς. 38 Καὶ ἰδοὺ ἀνὴρ ἀπὸ τοῦ ὄχλου ἐβόησεν λέγων· διδάσκαλε, δέομαί σου ἐπιβλέψαι ἐπὶ τὸν υἱόν μου, ὅτι μονογενής μοί ἐστιν. 39 καὶ ἰδοὺ πνεῦμα λαμβάνει αὐτὸν καὶ ἐξαίφνης κράζει καὶ σπαράσσει αὐτὸν μετὰ ἀφροῦ καὶ μόγις ἀποχωρεῖ ἀπ' αὐτοῦ συντρῖβον αὐτόν· 40 καὶ ἐδεήθην τῶν μαθητῶν σου ἵνα ἐκβάλωσιναὐτό, καὶ οὐκ ἠδυνήθησαν. 41 ἀποκριθεὶς δὲ ὁ Ἰησοῦς εἶπεν· ὦ γενεὰ ἄπιστος καὶ διεστραμμένη, ἕως πότε ἔσομαι πρὸς ὑμᾶς καὶ ἀνέξομαι ὑμῶν; προσάγαγε ὧδε τὸν υἱόν σου. 42 ἔτι δὲ προσερχομένου αὐτοῦ ἔρρηξεν αὐτὸν τὸ δαιμόνιον καὶ συνεσπάραξεν· ἐπετίμησεν δὲ ὁ Ἰησοῦς τῷ πνεύματι τῷ ἀκαθάρτῳ καὶ ἰάσατο τὸν παῖδα καὶ ἀπέδωκεν αὐτὸν τῷ πατρὶ αὐτοῦ. 43 ἐξεπλήσσοντο δὲ πάντες ἐπὶ τῇ μεγαλειότητι τοῦ θεοῦ.

Boundaries and cohesion

As nearly all modern exegesis of Luke 9.37–43a recognises seams between verses 36 and 37 on the one hand and verses 43a and 43b on the other,[2] my aim in this section is not so much to identify the boundaries of this story as it is to explain, in linguistic terms, why they are as

---

[2] See, e.g., Kirschläger, *Jesu exorzistisches Wirken*, pp. 131–2; Fitzmyer, *Luke I–IX*, pp. 805–6.

uncontroversial as they are. Part of the explanation offered below involves the story's own internal cohesion, which therefore is treated under the same heading.

One clear indicator of this episode's boundaries is the introduction of new participants in 9.37–38 and their subsequent exit from the narrative in 9.43. In terms of information structure, for instance, the most newsworthy clause in the story's first sentence is not κατελθόντων αὐτῶν ἀπὸ τοῦ ὄρους (9.37), whose frame of reference is utterly dependent on the immediately preceding unit (9.28–36), but rather συνήντησεν αὐτῷ ὄχλος πολύς, whose subject/'actor' appears in Luke's Gospel for the first time at this point. Although the noun ὄχλος occurs many times in Luke's Gospel prior to this juncture, it does not occur in the two episodes that immediately precede this one, and its anarthrous character in 9.37 clearly signals that a new participant is in view.

In 9.38, however, the focus of the narrator shifts away from the crowd as a whole to one of its members, a certain man who, the reader subsequently learns, has a possessed son (9.39). As the noun used in the initial reference to the man (ἀνήρ, 9.38) is anarthrous, it signals that he too has been absent from the action narrated up to this point. His newness to the larger narrative, moreover, is reinforced by the septuagintism καὶ ἰδού (9.38), which directly precedes ἀνήρ and fulfils its usual function of signalling the introduction of new information.[3] From this initial reference in 9.38 until the end of 9.42, the man plays a prominent role, first by referring to himself several times when he speaks to Jesus (9.38–40), then by functioning as the primary addressee of Jesus' response (9.41), and finally by being portrayed as an explicit 'beneficiary' of Jesus' intervention (ἀπέδωκεν αὐτὸν τῷ πατρὶ αὐτοῦ, 9.42). Indeed, by playing an overt part in all three of these segments of the episode, the man serves as one of the story's main sources of referential cohesion.

With the man's role as beneficiary in 9.42 being his final appearance in the story (and in the Gospel as a whole), the focus shifts at the beginning of 9.43 back to the collective entity of which he is implicitly a part. As a result, the grammatical subject of the clause ἐξεπλήσσοντο δὲ πάντες ἐπὶ τῇ μεγαλειότητι τοῦ θεοῦ (9.43a) parallels the phrase ὄχλος πολύς at the end of 9.37, completing an inclusio around the man's exchange with Jesus (9.38–42).[4] The most immediate effect of this device is its enhancement of the unity and cohesion of the material within the frame; at the same time, though, the elements of the frame itself, in verses 37 and 43, also help to signal the location of the story's boundaries.

---

[3] BAGD, s.v. 'ἰδού'.   [4] Cf. Bovon, *Luc (1, 1–9,50)*, p. 493.

In this light, and as none of the new participants introduced in 9.37–43a is envisaged in the main clauses of the ensuing unit (Jesus' second prediction of his passion, 9.43b–45), the scholarly consensus on where this story begins and ends has strong support. But just as important, in trying to understand in linguistic terms why this consensus exists in the first place, the analysis above has identified some widely overlooked clues to the rhetorical force of the episode as a whole. Most notably, as the framing device created by ὄχλος πολύς (9.37) and πάντες (9.43a) gives special salience to the story's last clause (ἐξεπλήσσοντο δὲ πάντες ἐπὶ τῇ μεγαλειότητι τοῦ θεοῦ), it ultimately serves to heighten both the aspectual prominence of the imperfective verb ἐξεπλήσσοντο and the implicit identification of Jesus' deed of exorcism with 'the majesty of God'. These features therefore merit further attention, which they receive in the appropriate sections below.

Story structure

Although Luke 9.37–43a includes neither an 'abstract' nor a 'coda', it does have a fully developed 'orientation', indicating when the action occurred (the day after Jesus' transfiguration), where it occurred (near the foot of the mountain), and who was involved (Jesus, the three disciples who had been on the mountain with him, and a 'great crowd' that included the father of the demoniac). All this information is given at the story's beginning (9.37–38), which is a less than remarkable location for this kind of material.[5]

More noteworthy is what directly follows, namely the 'complicating action', which stretches from the beginning of 9.38 to the end of 9.42a and specifies the difficulties and tensions that arose when Jesus was met by the crowd. Tensions begin to rise, for instance, when a man from the crowd begs Jesus 'to look upon' his only son (9.38), who is described as suffering almost continuously from a demonically caused affliction (9.39). By this point in Luke's larger narrative, though, the implied audience well recognises that Jesus is fully capable of dealing with such difficulties; for he has already been characterised as possessing authority and power to vanquish not just individual demonic beings (e.g., Luke 4.33–37) but an entire legion of them (Luke 8.26–39).

The father's disclosure that his son has a demon (9.39), however, is only the beginning of this story's complicating action. Narrative tension increases significantly in 9.40 when the father adds that the demon has

---

[5] Toolan, *Narrative*, p. 155.

already proved itself more than a match for Jesus' own disciples (presumably the nine who were not privy to the transfiguration), who are implied to have intervened in the case when Jesus was absent. The capacity of this information to heighten interest, it should be noted, stems primarily from developments narrated in this unit's antecedent co-text, where the disciples are portrayed not only as having received exorcistic 'power and authority' from Jesus himself (9.1–2) but also as having used it to good effect prior to the present case (9.6, 10). In view of these earlier tastes of success, their more recent failure to help this man generates a number of narrative questions and uncertainties. Most notably, if the demon afflicting this boy has been able to resist the efforts of Jesus' disciples, whose power for such ministry had been given by Jesus himself, might he not be able to ward off any therapeutic intervention made by Jesus as well?[6]

This new tension in the story is neither resolved nor even reduced by what immediately follows the man's report about the disciples. Indeed, the plot only thickens when, in 9.41, Jesus responds to the man's revelations by saying something so utterly impenetrable that interpreters have been mystified by it ever since: ὦ γενεὰ ἄπιστος καὶ διεστραμμένη, ἕως πότε ἔσομαι πρὸς ὑμᾶς καὶ ἀνέξομαι ὑμῶν; προσάγαγε ὧδε τὸν υἱόν σου. Here we encounter the ultimate semiotic puzzle, a linguistic garden of forking paths which, as soon as it is entered, presents a number of challenging questions. Why does Luke's hero respond with such venom to this pitiable human being? Who does Luke understand to be included among Jesus' addressees here?[7] And what happens to the overall force of these words when the impact of their allusions to LXX Deuteronomy 32.5, 20 and Isaiah 46.4 is mapped onto the already opaque sense of the words themselves?[8] Each of these matters will be addressed by the end of the present chapter; but most important for understanding the story's structure, Jesus' utterance in 9.41 does not resolve narrative tension but only increases it.

The final piece of complicating action in this unit comes in 9.42 when the possessed youth, having been summoned by his father, is violently torn and convulsed by the demon in the presence of Jesus. Here the tension reaches its peak. With the demon still showing no sign of yielding, and in view of the questions raised by the complicating actions outlined above,

---

[6] Cf. Kirschläger, *Jesu exorzistisches Wirken*, p. 139.

[7] After mentioning the disciples and the boy's father as the two main options, which are not mutually exclusive, Loisy, *L'Evangile selon Luc*, p. 278, illustrates how difficult the problem is by frankly acknowledging he cannot solve it.

[8] On the allusions to Deut. 32.5, 20 and Isa. 46.4, see Schürmann, *Das Lukasevangelium*, p. 570.

Luke's audience could easily expect the upcoming 'resolution' to involve at least a bona fide struggle, even though they (unlike the boy's father, perhaps) can predict the winner. But a struggle is definitely not what the reader finds in the Lucan denouement; rather, Luke says: ἐπετίμησεν δὲ ὁ Ἰησοῦς τῷ πνεύματι τῷ ἀκαθάρτῳ καὶ ἰάσατο τὸν παῖδα καὶ ἀπέδωκεν αὐτὸν τῷ πατρὶ αὐτοῦ (9.42b).[9] Thus, despite the prior failure in this case by the disciples, which Luke (unlike Matthew and Mark) never directly explains, the Lucan Jesus disposes of this fiend just as easily as he disposed of the demonic opponents back in Luke 4.33–37 and 8.26–39. Moreover, by representing Jesus' victory here as being so decisive that the readership's expectation of a genuine struggle is frustrated,[10] Luke achieves a dramatic heightening of Jesus' power: Jesus, Luke seems to say, wins masterfully even when the foe appears uniquely formidable.

The only structural element that remains to be analysed is 'evaluation', of which there are only three instances that warrant attention here. Two of these involve what Toolan labels 'exaggerative quantifiers'.[11] In Luke 9.37, for example, the crowd that meets Jesus near the base of the mountain is characterised as 'large' (πολύς), a description whose imprecision and generality encourage the reader to see this meeting as an event of great importance with consequences that impact a large number of people. Comparable to this is the instance of exaggerative quantification that appears in 9.43a, where the narrator describes the effect of the exorcism on those present: 'And *all* [πάντες]', he says, 'were astonished [ἐξεπλήσσοντο] at the majesty of God'. As is true of Luke's use of πολύς in 9.37, so also here the interpreter cannot be absolutely certain that Luke is exaggerating. Yet, as the action represented by the verb ἐξεπλήσσοντο is fundamentally a mental process of the affective variety, a literal understanding of πάντες would implicitly characterise the narrator as claiming to know what had happened in the minds of everyone present; indeed, in order to have possessed this sort of knowledge, the narrator would need to be virtually ominiscient. A better account of what is happening here, therefore, is that πάντες is simply a narrative-enlivening exaggeration,

---

[9] As the departure of the demon is not explicitly narrated, the effectiveness of the intervention represented by ἐπετίμησεν is apparently taken for granted; cf. Kirschläger, *Jesu exorzistisches Wirken*, p. 147.

[10] By portraying Jesus' exorcistic command as not achieving its aim until the demon has first cried out, convulsed the boy violently, and abused him so severely that bystanders think he is dead, the parallel in Mark 9.25–27 comes much closer than Luke's does to fulfilling the reader's expectations of a genuine struggle.

[11] Toolan, *Narrative*, p. 160.

whose main function is to guide the reader into the preferred interpretation of the unit as a whole: namely, if everyone in the large crowd that witnessed this exorcism construed it as a revelation of the majesty of God, then surely the reader should do likewise.[12]

The final instance of evaluation to be treated here is signalled by the explicative ὅτι in 9.38,[13] which occurs on the lips of the demoniac's father and introduces his explanation of why Jesus should 'look upon' his son.[14] In a note without parallel in the Matthaean and Marcan versions, the father discloses that the son in question is in fact his μονογενής.[15] Consequently, when he then indicates that the child's sufferings are almost continuous (πνεῦμα... μόγις ἀποχωρεῖ ἀπ' αὐτοῦ, 9.39), he implies what most ancient Mediterranean listeners would have been able to infer without interpretative guidance, namely that this illness involved not merely the physical limitations of an individual child but rather the continuation and status of a whole family line.[16] Yet the sufferings of the youth himself are by no means backgrounded in his father's plea, for in the single complex of clauses that describe the boy's sufferings (9.39) the child himself is explicitly referred to no less than five times, chiefly as a passive victim of the demon's violent power (e.g., καὶ ἰδοὺ πνεῦμα λαμβάνει αὐτόν... καὶ σπαράσσει αὐτὸν μετὰ ἀφροῦ καὶ μόγις ἀποχωρεῖ ἀπ' αὐτοῦ συντρῖβον αὐτόν). By highlighting in this fashion the power of the demon, the father's speech ultimately underscores the power implicit in Jesus' eventual victory; and indirectly, by implying that the illness posed a threat to the whole family line, the same speech also elevates the value of Jesus' therapeutic gift.

---

[12] On the tendency of other-directed, dyadic personalities to imitate the observed or narrated actions of others, cf. J. Rockwell, 'A Theory of Literature and Society', in J. Routh and J. Wolff (eds), *The Sociology of Literature: Theoretical Approaches*, Sociological Review Monograph 25 (Keele, 1977), pp. 37–40.

[13] On the use of explicatives to enhance a story's tellability, see Toolan, *Narrative*, p. 161.

[14] As ὅτι introduces a similar explanation in Matthew's account (ὅτι σεληνιάζεται, Matt. 17.15) but is absent from the Marcan parallel, it constitutes a positive agreement between Matthew and Luke against Mark; on this and other minor agreements, see Vaganay, 'Les accords négatifs', pp. 407–8; and Aichinger, 'Zur Traditionsgeschichte der Epileptiker-Perikope', pp. 117–26.

[15] Here Luke differs notably from Matthew and Mark, neither of whom characterises the boy as an only child. Indeed, neither Matthew nor Mark uses the word μονογενής even once in their entire narrative, whereas Luke employs it not only here but also in the stories about Jairus' daughter (Luke 8.42) and the widow of Nain's son (Luke 7.12). The latter story in particular and the present episode have in common a significant volume of stylistic features and motifs, on which see Aichinger, 'Zur Traditionsgeschichte der Epileptiker-Perikope', pp. 141–3; Kirschläger, *Jesu exorzistisches Wirken*, p. 147 n. 94; Goulder, *Luke*, pp. 445–6; Busse, *Die Wunder des Propheten Jesus*, p. 267.

[16] Cf. B. J. Malina and R. L. Rohrbaugh, *Social-Science Commentary on the Synoptic Gospels* (Minneapolis, 1992), p. 344; and Bovon, *Luc (1, 1–9.50)*, pp. 496–7.

Repetition

A couple of instances of repetition in this story are noteworthy from a stylistic point of view. As in 9.38, for instance, so in 9.39 the construction καὶ ἰδού prepares the reader for the introduction of a new participant,[17] in this instance the demonic spirit; but far more importantly, as the construction possesses a distinctively septuagintal flavour,[18] its occurrence on the lips of two different speakers – first the story's narrator (9.38), and then the man (9.39) – creates a chain of discursive effects that go far beyond its basic grammatical function. On the one hand, its occurrences in this context fit neatly into a larger intertextual strategy to paint the whole episode in the colours of Jewish biblical narrative: the narrator, for instance, uses not only the septuagintism καὶ ἰδού but also septuagintal narrative syntax in 9.37 (i.e., Ἐγένετο δὲ . . .); Jesus utilises phraseology in 9.41 that almost certainly derives from LXX Deuteronomy 32.5, 20 and Isaiah 46.4; and the demoniac's father not only echoes the narrator by using καὶ ἰδού but also employs septuagintal phraseology, namely the construction ἐπιβλέψαι ἐπί,[19] in his request for Jesus' intervention.[20] On the other hand, by associating this particular style not only with Jesus and the voice of the narrator but also with the demoniac's father, whose

---

[17] BAGD, s.v. 'ἰδού'.

[18] Cf. BDF, p. 3. In contrast to the LXX, where ἰδού is used to render nearly all the Hebrew Bible's 1,057 occurrences of הנה (cf. B. K. Waltke and M. O'Connor, *An Introduction to Biblical Hebrew Syntax* (Winona Lake, 1990), p. 675 n. 4), ancient Greek historians and biographers such as Thucydides, Cassius Dio, Diodorus Siculus, Dionysius of Halicarnassus, and Plutarch never use it. As the word is therefore a true septuagintism, and with its seventy-nine occurrences in Luke–Acts being matched in frequency by no other writing of the NT except the Gospel of Matthew (fifty-six occurrences), it does a great deal to give this and other parts of Luke's narrative the biblical effect that was apparently suitable for the situation.

[19] On the septuagintal character of ἐπιβλέπω + ἐπί, cf. Busse, *Die Wunder des Propheten Jesus*, p. 256 n. 4. ἐπιβλέπω occurs frequently in the LXX, being linked in forty-seven different contexts to the preposition ἐπί, whereas it does not occur at all – either with or without the preposition – in a large group of non-Jewish Greek authors, including Homer, Herodotus, Thucydides, Apollonius Rhodius, Aelius Aristides, the historian Appianus, Chariton, Dio Cassius, Marcus Aurelius, Philostratus, Philumenus the medical writer, and anonymous medical writers (on *TLG* disk C) whose combined works are approximately the length of Luke–Acts (i.e., 40,000 words). Although ἐπιβλέπω does occur *without* independent ἐπί in a few pagan authors (e.g., in Diogenes Laertius *Vitae philosophorum* 5.71.5; in Plutarch *Marc.* 7.2.1; in Athenaeus *Deipnosophistae* 9.69.8; Galen *De methodo medendi libri xiv* 10.81.17; 10.213.16; 10.214.7 et al.), its occurrence with the independent preposition in tow is very rare outside biblical Greek, exceptions being Plutarch *De liberis educandis* 2.D.3; and Galen *De sanitate tuenda libri vi* 6.392.6.

[20] The effect of all this, it is worth noting, is that Luke's version of the story has a far more septuagintal flavour than either Matthew's or Mark's does; for the Matthaean and Marcan accounts (Matt. 17.14–21; Mark 9.14–29) lack not only καὶ ἰδού (Luke 9.38–39) but also Ἐγένετο δὲ (9.37) and ἐπιβλέψαι ἐπί (9.38).

subsequent shaming by Jesus (9.41) implicitly depicts him as a less than exemplary character, the storyteller inadvertently dilutes the ideological force of his own intertextual rhetoric.

The only other interesting instance of repetition is the occurrence of the verb δέομαι in verses 38 and 40. In both of its occurrences it appears on the lips of the man, who begins his speech with the plea, διδάσκαλε, δέομαί σου ἐπιβλέψαι ἐπὶ τὸν υἱόν μου (9.38), and concludes by adding, καὶ ἐδεήθην τῶν μαθητῶν σου ἵνα ἐκβάλωσιν αὐτό [i.e., the demon], καὶ οὐκ ἠδυνήθησαν (9.40). By portraying the man as one who describes his own behaviour as a begging of his prospective benefactors, Luke presents him as possessing an appropriate politeness, humility and understanding of his own position before Jesus and the disciples; indeed, the father is considerably more respectful in Luke's account than he is in the Matthaean and Marcan parallels.[21] But due to these same distinctives, the response the man receives from the Lucan Jesus – ὦ γενεὰ ἄπιστος καὶ διεστραμμένη... προσάγαγε ὧδε τὸν υἱόν σου (9.41) – is marked by a measure of directness which, in addition to exceeding that of the parallel utterance in Matthew and Mark, seems contextually inappropriate or even impolite in its own dialogical context. Whether Jesus' utterance is as inappropriate as it seems is discussed further below, in my treatment of the story's cultural context.

Iconicity

The way Jesus' triad of responses in Luke 9.42b (ἐπετίμησεν δὲ ὁ Ἰησοῦς... καὶ ἰάσατο... καὶ ἀπέδωκεν...) frustrates the reader's anticipations of a struggle between exorcist and demon is given due attention above in connection with story structure. Analysis of the same sentence's internal structure and sequencing, however, indicates that 9.42b contributes to the force of this narrative in several other noteworthy ways. More specifically, these clauses constitute one tri-colonic unit in which all three lines manifest the same pattern of transitivity and sequencing: all three involve material processes, all three portray Jesus as 'actor', and all three exemplify conventional word order by placing the main verb at the head of the clause and the affected participants near the clause's end.[22]

---

[21] Especially sharp is the contrast to the parallel material in Mark 9.17–18, where the man begins by complaining, ἤνεγκα τὸν υἱόν μου πρὸς σέ (9.17), and concludes by imperiously adding, εἶπα τοῖς μαθηταῖς σου ἵνα αὐτὸ ἐκβάλωσιν, καὶ οὐκ ἴσχυσαν (9.18). As the father in Mark therefore almost upbraids Jesus for the failure of the disciples, Jesus' firm reply (9.19) is more clearly appropriate to its conversational setting in Mark than it is to that in Luke.

[22] The climax in Mark's account contains nothing similar to the parallelism in Luke 9.42b, while that in Matthew, although it does have three parallel clauses in a single

Since this pattern is without analogue in the Matthaean and Marcan versions of the story, we may wish to look more closely at the possible effects and motivations of this construction. For instance, by repeatedly presenting Jesus not as a 'goal' but rather as an 'actor' in several consecutive processes of a material kind, the Lucan version tacitly reinforces the high authority and power which, earlier in the Gospel, have been attributed to him in precisely this kind of setting (e.g., Luke 4.36; 8.31–32). Furthermore, by uniting these three clauses into a single sentential complex, the Lucan version gives the impression that the removal of the demon, the healing of the boy, and the reunion with the father are all accomplished in one mighty stroke. And by placing not only the verbal processes but also the passive participants (i.e., τῷ πνεύματι τῷ ἀκαθάρτῳ, τὸν παῖδα, τῷ πατρὶ αὐτοῦ) in parallelism with each other, the Lucan version foregrounds the impact of Jesus' intervention on others in his environment: the demon is no longer 'in' but 'out', the boy is no longer ill but well, and the status of the father is no longer threatened by the extinction of his family line.

Thematic organisation and information structure

Apart from the group of clauses just discussed, the only construction in Luke 9.37–43a whose word order invites special attention is ὅτι μονογενής μοί ἐστιν, which marks the beginning of the father's explanation of why Jesus should 'look upon' his son. As ὅτι in this context is inherently thematic and thus incapable of exhausting the entire thematic potential of the clause,[23] the construction that immediately follows it – μονογενής μοί – must also be regarded as part of the clause's theme, leaving the position of rheme to be filled by the verb ἐστιν on its own. Now because the clause in question is brief, and because grammatical complements in New Testament Greek often precede the predicate of their

---

paratactic complex (καὶ ἐπετίμησεν αὐτῷ ὁ Ἰησοῦς καὶ ἐξῆλθεν ἀπ' αὐτοῦ τὸ δαιμόνιον καὶ ἐθεραπεύθη ὁ παῖς ἀπὸ τῆς ὥρας ἐκείνης, Matt. 17.18), lacks the striking symmetry of the Lucan construction, e.g., uniformity in process type (ἐξῆλθεν is behavioural, not material) and in grammatical subject across the three clauses. Furthermore, by making no reference to how Jesus' intervention affects the father, Matthew portrays Jesus as influencing only two participants, the demon and the boy.

[23] As explained by Halliday, *Functional Grammar*, p. 51, inherently thematic items are those which 'in the evolution of the language . . . have as it were floated to the front of the clause and stayed there'. ὅτι fits this description perfectly because, whenever it occurs, it always stands at the beginning of its clause; but just as important, like other inherently thematic elements of the language, ὅτι by itself cannot exhaust the thematic potential of any clause in which it occurs, because it says too little about the topic of the clause it introduces.

respective clauses,[24] we cannot be certain that this particular sequence was chosen in order to accentuate μονογενής μοί, that is, the special value the boy had as his father's only son. Yet, if in fact this emphasis was intended, the appropriate word order was selected to produce it; and just as important, had this stress not been desired, the verb ἐστιν could easily have been placed ahead of μονογενής μοί.[25] Consequently, μονογενής μοί should probably be interpreted as a marked theme in this context, signalling that the relevance of this story as a whole has as much to do with the horizontal dynamics of ancient Mediterranean structures of kinship as it does with the vertical combat between Jesus and the unclean spirit.[26]

Lexis

As the overall flavour of a text's vocabulary generates effects that are greater than the sum of its lexical parts, the items chosen for special discussion below are treated not so much as isolated lexical problems as bundles of communicative potential, whose actual force is powerfully shaped by the collocational patterns and genre of the story as a whole.

συναντάω

In addition to being absent from the Matthaean and Marcan versions of this story, the verb συναντάω, used by the narrator in 9.37, is found in no writing of the NT other than Luke–Acts and Hebrews.[27] For these and other reasons that emerge below, it deserves special consideration.

Viewed first in relation to its clausal co-text in 9.37 (συνήντησεν αὐτῷ ὄχλος πολύς), the word is relatively unproblematic in sense: it means, quite simply, 'met'. However, when the lexicogrammatical pattern of this entire clause – that is, συναντάω followed directly by the dative αὐτῷ and then by the nominative subject/actor of the clause[28] – is compared

---

[24] Porter, *Idioms*, pp. 293–5.
[25] In Luke–Acts and the Fourth Gospel, e.g., the predicate does precede the complement in five clauses whose length and structure are comparable to this one (i.e., ὅτι + εἰμί without an expressed subject + any complement), and in none of these cases is any special emphasis apparent; see John 10.26; 11.15; 17.14; Acts 11.24; 22.15. However, when the predicate is preceded by the complement, as it is here and in seventeen comparable constructions in Luke–Acts and the Fourth Gospel (e.g., Luke 5.8; 7.39; 9.12; John 1.15; 5.27; Acts 2.25), the complement can be seen to possess special prominence in each case.
[26] Cf. Pilch, 'Sickness and Healing', pp. 186–7, 195–8.
[27] συναντάω appears on five occasions in Luke–Acts (Luke 9.18, 37; 22.10; Acts 10.25; and 20.22) and twice in Hebrews (7.1, 10).
[28] Patterns either identical or very similar to this are exemplified by four of the five clauses in which συναντάω occurs in Luke–Acts, the sole exception being Acts 20.22.

with that of clauses in which συναντάω is used by other ancient writers, an additional set of associations comes into view: in general, the collocational pattern exemplified in Luke has much less in common with those found in pagan biographers, historians and composers of other types of texts than with those reflected in the Greek translation of Jewish Scripture.

Thucydides, for instance, to whom Luke has often been compared,[29] does not use συναντάω even once in his writings. Plutarch, moreover, whose extant corpus is vastly larger than the whole NT, uses it only four times,[30] and in only one of these occurrences do the syntax and sequencing of the verb's clausal co-text resemble the pattern found in Luke.[31] Similarly, Xenophon uses it in only two contexts (*An.* 1.8.15.3 and 7.2.5.1), neither of which manifests syntactical structures similar to the pattern of the Lucan clause.[32] Likewise, in its two occurrences in Diogenes Laertius and its single appearance in Dionysius of Halicarnassus, the syntactical formations differ significantly from Luke's usage.[33] Apart from Plutarch, in fact, the only pre-third century CE pagan biographers and historiographers in the canon of *TLG* disk C whose employment of this term ever resembles its usage in Luke 9.37 are Dio Cassius and Diodorus Siculus.[34] In order to find other ancient examples that are comparable to the Lucan construction, one must turn away from pagan writers to Josephus and the LXX.

There are twelve occurrences of συναντάω in Josephus' writings,[35] and several of these contribute to syntactical patterns which are either

---

[29] See, e.g., B. Witherington, 'Editor's Addendum', in *History, Literature, and Society in the Book of Acts* (Cambridge, 1996), pp. 25–7; C. Hemer, *The Book of Acts in the Setting of Hellenistic History*, ed. C. H. Gempf (Tübingen, 1989; repr., Winona Lake, 1990), pp. 65–7; I. H. Marshall, *Luke: Historian and Theologian* (Grand Rapids, 1970), p. 55.

[30] Plutarch *Sull.* 2.4.2; *Pomp.* 33.1.3; *De amore prolis* 494.C; and *De vitioso pudore* 530.F.

[31] See Plutarch *Sull.* 2.4.2: καὶ συνήντησεν αὐτῷ τὸ τοιοῦτον.

[32] Xenophon *An.* 1.8.15.3 well illustrates the distance from the Lucan pattern, reading πελάσας ὡς συναντῆσαι ἤρετο εἴ τι παραγγέλλοι.

[33] See Diogenes Laertius *Vitae Philosophorum* 4.3; 6.38; and Dionysius Halicarnassensis *Ant. Rom.* 4.67.

[34] See Dio Cassius *Historiae Romanae* 59.19; versio 1 in volumine 1, 175.6; Xiphilini epitome, vol. 3, 164.10; Petri Patricii excerpta Vaticana sive Maiana, vol. 3, 24.5; and Diodorus Siculus *Bibliotheca historica* (lib. 1–20) 3.65; 14.104; 17.13; and (lib. 21–40) 23.9. συναντάω also occurs in Diodorus Siculus *Bibliotheca historica* (lib. 1–20) 14.75; 18.28; and (lib. 21–40) 34/35.24, but in these contexts the usage and syntax differ markedly from that of Luke 9.37; lib. 1–20, 14.75 illustrates especially well the stylistic distance of Diodorus' usage from Luke's, reading οἱ δὲ πλεῖστοι τὰ ὅπλα ῥιπτοῦντες συνήντων, δεόμενοι φείσασθαι τοῦ βίου.

[35] Josephus *Ant* 6.50; 7.203, 205; 8.331; 9.132; 14.377; 15.111; and *J.W.* 2.16; 4.620, 634; 5.40, 42.

similar or identical to that in Luke 9.37.[36] However, whenever we compare Luke with Josephus, it is important to remember that *both* writers drew deeply from their knowledge of the LXX;[37] accordingly, and since scholarly arguments for either Luke or Josephus knowing the other's work have so far not won wide support,[38] wherever their respective usages of συναντάω fit the same stylistic mould the first explanation we ought to explore is that the shared pattern stems from septuagintal influence.

As it turns out, συναντάω is used with relatively high frequency in the LXX, often being followed, as in Luke 9.37, first by a dative of association and then by an expressed subject of the verb.[39] However, as none of the LXX's parallels corresponds to the Lucan construction in any other significant way, the conclusion to be derived from these observations is not that the words συνήντησεν αὐτῷ ὄχλος πολύς in Luke 9.37 were deliberately designed to generate intertextual echoes from a particular passage in Jewish Scripture; rather, the point to be made is that when this construction is plotted on a stylistic continuum whose range includes both pagan writers and Judaeo-Hellenistic authors and translators, it can be seen to lie closest to septuagintal and related patterns of usage. Thus, while neither the verb συναντάω nor the clause of which it is a part contributes to an allusion to a particular passage of Jewish Scripture, they do help to effect a biblical mood and register which, as discussed more fully below in connection with intertextuality, shape the overall force of this story.

---

[36] See, e.g., Josephus *Ant.* 7.203; 9.132; and *J.W.* 2.16.

[37] On the influence of the LXX on Josephus, see Bilde, *Flavius Josephus*, pp. 80–3, 92–7; Schürer, *History of the Jewish People*, III.1, pp. 479–80.

[38] Recent comparative study of the relationship between Luke–Acts and Josephus tends to emphasise one set or another of shared generic conventions, without either assuming or asserting direct influence by one author on the other; see, e.g., the following contributions to Moessner (ed.), *Jesus and the Heritage of Israel*: G. E. Sterling, ' "Opening the Scriptures": The Legitimation of the Jewish Diaspora and the Early Christian Mission', pp. 209–11; D. D. Schmidt, 'Rhetorical Influences and Genre: Luke's Preface and the Rhetoric of Hellenistic Historiography', pp. 38–9, 49–51; W. S. Kurz, 'Promise and Fulfillment in Hellenistic Jewish Narratives and in Luke and Acts', pp. 159–64. A valuable but ultimately unpersuasive exception is Mason, *Josephus*, pp. 214–25, which argues that the author of Luke–Acts probably had access to Josephus *Antiquitates Judaicae* 18–20.

[39] Of the sixty-two occurrences of συναντάω in the LXX, twenty-eight are immediately followed by a direct object in the dative (often αὐτῷ), resulting in a pattern similar to that of Luke 9.37. Twelve of these are immediately followed not only by a dative direct object but also by a nominative subject (in that order) and therefore correspond to the pattern in Luke 9.37 even more closely. Of this latter group, Exod. 4.24 bears the most detailed resemblance to the Lucan pattern: 'Ἐγένετο δὲ ἐν τῇ ὁδῷ ἐν τῷ καταλύματι συνήντησεν αὐτῷ ἄγγελος κυρίου.

σπαράσσω, ἐκπλήσσω and μεγαλειότης

Like συναντάω, the terms σπαράσσω (9.39), ἐκπλήσσω (9.43a) and μεγαλειότης (9.43a) contribute to the distinctiveness of the Lucan account vis-à-vis its Synoptic parallels. For instance, although the verb σπαράσσω does occur in the Marcan version of this story, as does the cognate form συσπαράσσω (Mark 9.20),[40] neither of these terms functions the way σπαράσσω does in Luke 9.39. Most notably, whereas in Luke σπαράσσω is used by the demoniac's father to describe what the demon habitually had been doing to the boy up to the present time (Luke 9.39), in Mark it is used by the narrator to denote what the demon did to the boy (i.e., convulse him violently) even *after* it had been rebuked by Jesus (Mark 9.26). Thus, in contrast to the Marcan usage, which entails that the demon did not submit to Jesus' commands without a struggle (Mark 9.25–26), the function of the term in Luke ultimately reinforces that account's emphasis on the supreme authority of Jesus' exorcistic word; furthermore, by forging a correspondence between the father's description of his son's illness and the subsequent manifestation of the illness in the presence of Jesus, the morphemic correspondence between σπαράσσει (9.39) and συνεσπάραξεν (9.42) implicitly aligns the world-view of the narrator with that of the father, not only in relation to the diagnosis of this particular instance of misfortune but more generally in terms of the cosmology this diagnosis presupposes.[41]

The verb ἐκπλήσσω (9.43a), on the other hand, is absent from both of the Synoptic parallels to this account. Its function in 9.43a is to denote the effect which the exorcism had on those who witnessed it: ἐξεπλήσσοντο

---

[40] The σπαράσσω, συσπαράσσω group makes only five appearances in the NT: Mark 1.26; 9.20, 26; and here in Luke 9.39, 42. All five signify the material process of 'convulsing', and in each instance the actor that causes the convulsion is a demonic being. In the LXX this group is represented on only four occasions (2 Sam. 22.8; Jer. 4.19; Dan. 8.7; and 3 Macc. 4.6) and none of these involve demonic agents, though in Dan. 8.7 and 3 Macc. 4.6 the causative agents are wicked Gentiles, who in many Jewish sources of the period are understood to be the evil spirits' earthly instruments (cf. Böcher, *Dämonenfurcht und Dämonenabwehr*, pp. 139–43). The absence of the σπαράσσω group from the Hippocratic essay *De morbo sacro*, which is normally understood to describe a range of epileptic ailments, should make us hesitant to accept the proposal of Dunn and Twelftree ('Demon-Possession and Exorcism', 222) that the boy's condition be demythologised as epilepsy. As emphasised by J. Pilch, 'Insights and Models for Understanding the Healing Activity of the Historical Jesus', in E. H. Lovering (ed.), *SBLSP* 32 (1993), p. 154, equating the boy's illness with epilepsy is an example of hermeneutical 'medicocentrism', whereby the medical categories of the interpreter are mapped isomorphically onto and given priority over those of the text's ancient author.

[41] Cf. Pilch, 'Sickness and Healing', p. 199. Neither in the present story nor elsewhere in Luke's Gospel does Jesus or the narrator ever reject the participants' folk diagnosis and its cosmological assumptions.

δὲ πάντες ἐπὶ τῇ μεγαλειότητι τοῦ θεοῦ. As in all its other occurrences in the NT Gospels so also here, it designates a mental-affective response to something said or done by Jesus and perceived by the 'senser' to be remarkable or unusual in some way.[42] There is, moreover, nothing particularly septuagintal about its use in this context: none of its five occurrences in the LXX[43] demonstrates noteworthy linguistic or thematic correspondences to Luke 9.37–43a; and, apart from a common predilection for passive forms of this verb, its occurrences here and elsewhere in Luke–Acts share no more semantic ground with those attested in the LXX than with those found in pagan authors.[44]

Along with ἐκπλήσσω, the noun μεγαλειότης is found in the story's last clause, where it is part of the syntagm τῇ μεγαλειότητι τοῦ θεοῦ. In general, the occurrence of this word in ancient texts is rare;[45] but where it does occur, it typically denotes either the perceived sublimity of some deity or the majestic honour of some human being whose relationship to the divine is uniquely intimate.[46] More specifically, in both the NT and the LXX it usually has explicit associations with power, strength and royal rule.[47] Clearly, then, the word belongs to the general semantic domain of honour, so that its use in a story that highlights the authority of Jesus in so many other ways is, from a stylistic point of view, highly appropriate. The nature of the honour Jesus is portrayed as acquiring in this context, moreover, should probably be read as heightened both by the rarity of

---

[42] In Luke 4.32 (par. Matt. 7.28; Mark 1.22), e.g., crowds are said to have been 'amazed at his teaching' (ἐξεπλήσσοντο ἐπὶ τῇ διδαχῇ αὐτοῦ); see also Matt. 13.54; 19.25 (par. Mark 10.26); Matt. 22.33 (par. Mark 11.18); Mark 6.2; 7.37; Luke 2.48; 9.43; Acts 13.12.

[43] Eccles. 7.17[16]; Wisd. 13.4; 2 Macc. 7.12; 4 Macc. 8.4; 17.16.

[44] See, e.g., Aeschylus *Pers.* 430; *PV* 360; Sophocles *Trach.* 253; *Phil.* 759; and Herodotus 1.43.8; 1.91.4; 1.199.24; 3.148.8.

[45] It makes only three appearances in the NT (here in 9.43a; Acts 19.27; and 2 Pet. 1.16), four in the LXX (Jer. 40[33].9; Dan. 7.27; and 1 Esd. 1.4; 4.40), and three in Josephus (*Ant.* 1.24.3; 8.111.6; and *Ap.* 2.168.4). But more strikingly, it does not occur even once in Homer, Herodotus, Thucydides, Dio Cassius, Diodorus Siculus, Dionysius of Halicarnassus, Aeschylus, Sophocles, Euripides, Plutarch, Lucian, and a great many other writers.

[46] See, e.g., 1 Esd. 1.4 (τὴν μεγαλειότητα Σαλωμων); Josephus *Ant.* 1.24 and *Ap.* 2.168, where the majestic character of the deity himself is in view; and 2 Pet. 1.16, where μεγαλειότης denotes the messianic majesty of Jesus that was revealed to the implied author at Jesus' transfiguration. As noted by Léon-Dufour, 'L'épisode de l'enfant épileptique', p. 209 n. 16, this third occurrence is particularly relevant to interpretation of Luke 9.43a since the tradition about the transfiguration is situated more closely to the Lucan rendition of this exorcism than it is to either the Matthaean or Marcan versions, neither of which, it should be noted, employ μεγαλειότης.

[47] See, e.g., LXX Dan. 7.27, where μεγαλειότης is conjoined with βασιλεία, ἐξουσία and ἀρχή; 1 Esd. 4.40, where μεγαλειότης is parallel to ἰσχύς, βασίλειον and ἐξουσία; and 2 Pet. 1.16, where it appears to overlap semantically with δύναμις.

Lexis 167

this term's occurrence in general and by its phrasal collocation in this instance with τοῦ θεοῦ.

ἐκβάλλω

Having described the characteristic features of his son's affliction in the presence of Jesus, the father concludes his speech with a note concerning the most recent development in the case: καὶ ἐδεήθην τῶν μαθητῶν σου ἵνα ἐκβάλωσιν αὐτό, καὶ οὐκ ἠδυνήθησαν (9.40). The verb ἐκβάλλω here not only explicitly summarises the content of the father's prior request (i.e., 'expel' the demon) but also implicitly denotes both what the disciples were unable to do and what Jesus, by contrast, eventually did do. The term occurs with relatively high frequency in both the NT and the LXX. In the NT, for example, it is found no less than eighty-one times, twenty of these occurring in Luke's Gospel and five in the Acts of the Apostles; several of its occurrences in Luke–Acts, moreover, involve the eviction of evil spirits from the demonised.[48] In the context of Luke 9.40, then, as in many of its other occurrences in the Gospels, the term's basic sense is unambiguously 'to drive out, expel, or throw out more or less forcibly'.[49]

Due chiefly, perhaps, to the paucity of references to exorcism and related practices in Jewish Scripture, the verb ἐκβάλλω is never used in the LXX to denote the expulsion of an evil spirit. However, in several septuagintal contexts the term is employed in ways that, both grammatically and conceptually, resemble its usage in Luke 9.40; to be more precise, in these contexts ἐκβάλλω serves to denote the Israelite deity's expulsion of pagan peoples, or their gods, or both, from the land promised to the children of Israel.[50] Thus, with the deities of Israel's neighbours having been increasingly demonised in Jewish biblical interpretation during the Hellenistic age,[51] the use of ἐκβάλλω in the present story to denote the relocation of an unclean spirit is by no means inappropriate; indeed, if the original audience of Luke–Acts was as steeped in the LXX as the

---

[48] E.g., Luke 9.49 (par. Mark 9.38); 11.14, 15, 18, 19, 20 (par. Matt. 12.24–28; Mark 3.22–23); and 13.32.

[49] BAGD, s.v. 'ἐκβάλλω'. The term occurs in several other ancient texts dealing with the same general field; see, e.g., the 'Excellent rite for driving out daimons' in *PGM* 4.1227–64, whose collocation of ἐκβάλλω, δαιμόνιον, ἀκάθαρτος, δύναμις and θεός significantly resembles the lexis of the present story and partially instantiates a pattern that by Luke's time may well have been an established register of exorcistic discourse. Cf. Kotansky, 'Exorcistic Amulets', pp. 243–5 nn. 1, 3.

[50] See, e.g., LXX Exod. 23.18, 28, 29, 30, 31; 33.2; 34.11, 24; Num. 21.32; Deut. 11.23; 33.27; Josh. 24.12, 18; Judg. 6.9; 2 Sam. 7.23; 1 Chron. 17.21; Pss 77.55; 79.8; Judith 6.14, 16; 1 Macc. 11.66; 13.11.

[51] See, e.g., LXX Pss 90.6; 95.5; Isa. 65.3, 11.

implied reader appears to have been, they may well have understood ἐκβάλλω in this context to imply a correspondence between Jesus' victory against the unclean spirit and the Israelite deity's victories against the unclean nations surrounding his people.

Transitivity

As in Luke 4.33–37 and 8.26–39 so in the present story, the characterisation of the various participants in the action is significantly shaped by patterns of transitivity that emerge only as the text is experienced as a linear whole. The 'great crowd' (9.37), for instance, functions as 'actor' in the material process denoted by συνήντησεν, a happening whose 'goal' in this instance is Jesus (αὐτῷ).[52] While the positioning of Jesus in a non-actor role at the story's outset is notable in itself, the significance of this feature derives mainly from its relations to subsequent clauses in the same unit. Three aspects of these clauses are particularly worthy of comment. First, the crowd plays no further role in the action until the very last clause of the narrative, ἐξεπλήσσοντο δὲ πάντες ἐπὶ τῇ μεγαλειότητι τοῦ θεοῦ (9.43a). Furthermore, in that context, where the crowd is implicitly included in πάντες, it functions as a passive 'senser' in the mental process signified by ἐξεπλήσσοντο,[53] whose 'phenomenon' is τῇ μεγαλειότητι τοῦ θεοῦ. But most importantly, since the majesty of God is implied in this context to have been present in the deed just performed by Jesus, its active function here contributes to a striking contrast between the first and last clauses of the unit: while the story begins with the crowd affecting Jesus (9.37), it concludes with Jesus affecting the crowd, in addition to everyone else included in πάντες.

In terms of transitivity the disciples must be understood as consisting of two sub-groups, neither of which is presented as exerting much influence on its environment. The first sub-group, understood from the antecedent co-text (9.28) to be Peter, James and John, constitutes with Jesus the collective 'behaver' in the clause κατελθόντων αὐτῶν ἀπὸ τοῦ ὄρους (9.37),

---

[52] As noted by W. Radl, *Paulus und Jesus im Lucanischen Doppelwerk: Untersuchungen zu Parallelmotiven im Lukasevangelium und in der Apostelgeschichte*, Europäische Hochschulschriften 23/49 (Berne, 1975), pp. 300–1, the favourable connotations of ὄχλος in this passage are typical of how Luke usually employs the term prior to Luke 22.47, where it is used to denote a group allied with the Satan-possessed Judas (cf. 22.3).

[53] As mental processes can be realised with either the senser or the phenomenon in the position of grammatical subject (Halliday, *Functional Grammar*, p. 110), the same state of affairs signified by ἐξεπλήσσοντο πάντες ἐπὶ τῇ μεγαλειότητι τοῦ θεοῦ could have been represented by ἐξεπλήσσεν ἡ μεγαλειότης τοῦ θεοῦ πάντας, which makes the functionally passive role of the senser more obvious.

where, in addition to affecting no other participant, they make their sole appearance in the story. The second sub-group, on the other hand, consisting of those not present on the mountain when Jesus' glory was disclosed (9.28–36), does participate in several of the processes depicted in the immediately ensuing verses (9.38–40); none the less, in regard to transitivity the most striking feature of their portrayal is not what they do but rather what they lack, namely the exorcistic ability necessary to expel the demon (9.40).[54]

In comparison with both the crowd and the two groups of disciples, whose function in this unit is chiefly to form a backdrop – partly neutral, partly negative – against which Jesus can stand out, the father of the demoniac plays a more prominent and interesting role in the story. In terms of transitivity, the most significant aspect of his role is that all the processes he participates in except one are verbal (i.e., symbolic or communicative). In 9.38, for instance, ἐβόησεν and λέγων designate communicative processes in which the father is the 'sayer'. This same pattern, with the father filling the role of 'sayer' on two more occasions, is evident in the clauses δέομαί σου (9.38) and καὶ ἐδεήθην τῶν μαθητῶν σου (9.40). On a superficial reading, Jesus' subsequent instruction, προσάγαγε ὧδε τὸν υἱόν σου (9.41), may seem to be a departure from this pattern since the father is the unexpressed subject of προσάγαγε, which represents a process of the material variety; yet the imperative mood of this verb entails that the man's participation in the designated process is to this point only potential, not actual.[55] And finally, in the story's climax (9.42b) the father functions merely as an oblique participant in the material process signified by καὶ ἀπέδωκεν αὐτὸν τῷ πατρὶ αὐτοῦ, where he is cast in the role of what Halliday calls a 'beneficiary/recipient';[56] that is, he is one to whom goods (in this case, his son) are given. In summary, the transitivity pattern of the clauses in which the father is a participant serves cumulatively to depict him as someone whose range of participation is tightly restricted.

Yet the father is not nearly as limited in his range of involvement as his demonised son, who in nine of the twelve processes in which he has

---

[54] The unflattering portrayal of the disciples in the present story is consistent with how they are portrayed at several other points in 9.1–50 (esp. 9.32–33, 45–46, and 49–50); cf. D. Moessner, 'Luke 9:1–50: Luke's Preview of the Journey of the Prophet like Moses of Deuteronomy', *JBL* 102 (1983), pp. 591–5; and Schürmann, *Das Lukasevangelium*, pp. 569–70.

[55] The relationship between this same clause (προσάγαγε ὧδε δὲ τὸν υἱόν σου) and the transitivity of that directly following it, i.e., ἔτι δὲ προσερχομένου αὐτοῦ, is perfectly consistent with the characterisation just noted of the father, whose role in the boy's coming is conveyed not by the grammar of the clause but rather by implicature.

[56] See Halliday, *Functional Grammar*, pp. 132–3.

a role occupies the affected position in material actions. He is portrayed in this manner in 9.38, for example, where his father pleads with Jesus to 'look upon' his son (ἐπιβλέψαι ἐπὶ τὸν υἱόν μου).[57] In 9.39, moreover, the son is represented in three different clauses as the powerless object of the demon's recurrent and violent aggression: the demon 'seizes him' (λαμβάνει αὐτόν), 'convulses him' (σπαράσσει αὐτόν), and 'shatters him' (συντρῖβον αὐτόν). And in 9.42a, where the boy is depicted by the narrator as finally coming into the presence of Jesus, he is impacted not only by the demon, who tears and convulses him (ἔρρηξεν αὐτὸν . . . καὶ συνεσπάραξεν), but also by Jesus, who heals him and gives him to the father (καὶ ἰάσατο τὸν παῖδα καὶ ἀπέδωκεν αὐτὸν τῷ πατρὶ αὐτοῦ).

In five of the clauses just summarised, the son and the spirit function together as the sole participants in the action (9.39, 42a); and strikingly, in all five instances the spirit is described as performing material actions that powerfully impact his human environment. As the demon moreover is mentioned in only four other clauses, three of which do nothing but reinforce the image just noted,[58] he is clearly understood to have options and power which the other participants discussed thus far do not enjoy.

One other process in which the demon is a participant, however, calls for attention. In 9.42b, in a striking departure from his normally active role in the story's happenings, the demon is characterised by the narrator as having been 'rebuked' (ἐπετίμησεν) by Jesus. While ἐπιτιμάω here undeniably denotes a symbolic process, it also has material overtones, with Jesus' speech being less a communication *to* the demon than a verbal action *on* him. In terms of Halliday's nuanced grammar of symbolic processes, the demon is not merely a receiver or audience in this process but a 'target'.[59] This shift in characterisation from the demon's usual role of actor to that of target helps to signal the shift in story structure, discussed earlier, from complicating action to climax. But perhaps more significantly, the same shift in transitivity marks the demon's last appearance in the story: the moment he changes from actor to object

---

[57] As the discourse sense of ἐπιβλέψαι ἐπί in this context is very close to that of ἰᾶσθαι in Luke 5.17 and 9.2, the process it denotes is best understood not in a literal sense, as mental, but rather as a metonymy of the cause, and thus as material.

[58] In καὶ μόγις ἀποχωρεῖ ἀπ' αὐτοῦ (9.39) the demon is the sole participant in a behavioural process (ἀποχωρεῖ) that further highlights his relative liberty to control himself and shape his immediate surroundings; in ἵνα ἐκβάλωσιν αὐτό (9.40), the demon is the goal of action not in the world of real events but only in the domain of the man's projected wishes; and in the elliptical καὶ οὐκ ἠδυνήθησαν (i.e., to expel the demon, 9.40), the clause's negative polarity only underscores in yet another way the superiority of the demon's might.

[59] See Halliday, *Functional Grammar*, p. 130.

Verbal aspect 171

is the moment he disappears, literally, from the unfolding discourse of the text.[60]

As indicated therefore by the structure and location of this instance of rebuking (9.42), Jesus wields power and authority that neither the demon nor the other participants in this story can match. However, just as the characterisation of the demon is shaped by developments and even reversals in the linear unfolding of his participant profile, so too the portrayal of Jesus is anything but static in terms of transitivity, notwithstanding the predictability of his eventual emergence as the mightiest actor on the stage. As noted at the beginning of this section, for instance, he functions as the 'goal' in the narrative's first material process (συνήντησεν αὐτῷ ὄχλος πολύς, 9.37); and from that point until the end of the story's complicating action in 9.42a, not once does Jesus occupy the role of 'actor' in a material process that is presented as having actually taken place. Indeed, in this same stretch of text the transitivity patterns of the clauses cumulatively attribute far greater dynamism to the unclean spirit than they do to Jesus.

Consequently, the clause ἐπετίμησεν δὲ ὁ Ἰησοῦς τῷ πνεύματι τῷ ἀκαθάρτῳ (9.42b) signals a dramatic transition not only in the portrayal of the demon but also in the depiction of Jesus and in the movement of the story. More specifically, in addition to marking the point where the demon is transformed from frenetic 'actor' to decimated 'target', these same words also effect Jesus' transition from being a 'goal' (9.37), a 'target' (9.38), a 'sayer' (9.41) and so on, to being a performer of material action. And the semantic burden of this construction is made even heavier by its foundational position in the instance of iconicity treated above; for on top of its pivotal role in the characterisation of both Jesus and the demon, it also initiates a pattern of transitivity that is replicated in the two clauses that directly follow it – καὶ ἰάσατο τὸν παῖδα and καὶ ἀπέδωκεν αὐτὸν τῷ πατρὶ αὐτοῦ – with Jesus as 'actor' in all three material processes. In this light, the words ἐπετίμησεν δὲ ὁ Ἰησοῦς τῷ πνεύματι τῷ ἀκαθάρτῳ should undoubtedly be attributed an exceedingly high degree of prominence in this context.

Verbal aspect

As in Luke's first two stories of exorcism so in this one, the aorist tense form predominates, occurring more frequently than all the other tense

---

[60] Note the contrast to the parallels in Matt. 17.18–21 and Mark 9.25–29, where the success of the rebuke is not taken for granted but rather narrated subsequently, requiring a post-rebuke reference to the demon.

forms combined.[61] Although none of these aorists is particularly noteworthy in itself, as a group they provide a background against which other forms and processes are allowed to stand out and be seen as more prominent.

Like Luke 8.26–39 in particular, the present episode includes a section in which the severity of the patient's affliction is strongly foregrounded by the tense forms chosen for use in the description. More specifically, in all five of the clauses that picture the demon's effects on the youth (9.39), the chosen form is the present tense: the demon 'seizes' (λαμβάνει) the boy, 'convulses' (σπαράσσει) him, 'scarcely leaves' (μόγις ἀποχωρεῖ) him, 'shatters' (συντρῖβον) him, and makes him suddenly 'cry out' (κράζει). By means of these selections, the boy is depicted not only as suffering repeated attacks but also as continuing to be under the demon's punishing influence at the time of the father's utterance. With the illness therefore being no minor case, the reader is prodded to rate Jesus' eventual expulsion of the demon (9.42) as no ordinary achievement.

The sole occurrence of the perfect tense form in this story is the adjectival participle διεστραμμένη in 9.41, where Jesus describes the generation of his day as faithless and 'perverse'. Unlike ordinary adjectives, the use of the participle as a modifier grammaticalises verbal aspect;[62] and in this particular instance, the complex, stative nuance of the perfect tense form frontgrounds the spiritually perverted condition which, according to the Lucan Jesus, had been evident in the prior interaction between the father and the disciples. To be sure, the morphological agreement of διεστραμμένη with the final word of LXX Deuteronomy 32.5 is part of a larger allusion to Deuteronomy 32.5, 20, and thus on a superficial reading could be dismissed as a mere duplication of what Luke found in his source. However, the biblical intertext is scarcely followed in a slavish manner at this point; and, since the phrase in which the Lucan Jesus uses διεστραμμένη is actually foregrounded by devices other than verbal aspect – most notably, by the emphatic vocative of address ὦ γενεά – διεστραμμένη should likewise be construed here as emphatic, perhaps having been designed precisely to draw attention to the biblical tenor of Jesus' utterance.

Finally, as the imperfect tense form ἐξεπλήσσοντο is used in 9.43 where the less significant aorist could have been employed, this verb too draws special attention to the process it represents. Signifying progressive action that resulted from the exorcistic healing ('all were being

---

[61] Of the thirty-one words whose form includes tense in this passage, eighteen are aorist.
[62] Porter, *Idioms*, p. 186.

astonished'), ἐξεπλήσσοντο highlights the mental and affective impact that Jesus' intervention registered on those who witnessed it. And indirectly, it reinforces this story's image of Jesus as one whose therapeutic power and effectiveness are unique.

Intertextuality

Earlier in this chapter, my analysis of repetition observed that septuagintal style colours the discourse not only of this story's narrator but also of Jesus and the father of the demoniac. As the features most responsible for this effect – namely Ἐγένετο δὲ in 9.37, καὶ ἰδού in 9.38–39, and ἐπιβλέψαι ἐπί in 9.38 – are found in neither the Marcan parallel nor the Matthaean, they contribute to the distinctiveness of Luke's version of this unit; indeed, as noted below, they cohere well with a different but related set of features whose motivations are rather more conspicuous. What I have in mind here are three allusions to specific passages of Jewish Scripture.

In response to the father of the demoniac, the Lucan Jesus begins by exclaiming, ὦ γενεὰ ἄπιστος καὶ διεστραμμένη (9.41). While the meaning and implications of this exclamation are problematic, most Lucan scholars agree on at least one issue concerning its interpretation: it alludes to either the fifth verse of Deuteronomy 32, or the twentieth verse of the same chapter, or both of these verses.[63] Linguistic support for the third of these options is particularly strong. In LXX Deuteronomy 32.5, for example, Moses denounces the Israelites as 'a crooked and perverse generation' (γενεὰ σκολιὰ καὶ διεστραμμένη), a construction whose internal syntax, sequencing and vocabulary are almost identical to that of the last four words of Jesus' exclamation. The co-occurrence of γενεά and διαστρέφω in LXX Deuteronomy 32.5, moreover, is highlighted in the immediately ensuing co-text of the same passage (32.20), where a term cognate to διαστρέφω, namely ἐκστρέφω, is used with γενεά to accuse the Israelites yet again of being 'a perverse generation' (γενεὰ ἐξεστραμμένη). Furthermore, with Moses describing the Israelites as 'sons in whom there is no faithfulness' (υἱοί οἷς οὐκ ἔστιν πίστις, LXX Deut. 32.20), the Lucan Jesus' use of ἄπιστος should probably be construed as yet another echo produced by the septuagintal text. And finally, between the two references in Deuteronomy to the Israelites as a 'perverse generation' (Deut. 32.5, 20), Moses accuses his audience of having 'sacrificed to demons [δαιμονίοις] and not to God, to gods whom they had not known' (LXX

---

[63] Cf. Vaganay, 'Les accords négatifs', p. 413; J. B. Green, *Gospel of Luke*, pp. 388–9; Busse, *Die Wunder des Propheten Jesus*, p. 257; Fitzmyer, *Luke I–IX*, p. 809.

Deut. 32.17); as δαιμόνιον occurs only eight times in the LXX outside Tobit and Baruch, and only once in the entire Hexateuch, its occurrence in both LXX Deuteronomy 32.17 and Luke 9.42a adds considerable strength to the intertextual bond between these two contexts.[64]

One effect of this allusion is to foster a powerful sense of continuity between Jesus and Moses, who very appropriately have just been portrayed conversing with one another (9.30–31); indeed, in the Lucan transfiguration Jesus is probably to be understood as the prophet like Moses of Deuteronomy 18.15.[65] Furthermore, because γενεὰ ἄπιστος καὶ διεστραμμένη in its Lucan context characterises not only the father of the demoniac but also the disciples,[66] a scathing analogy between the idolatrous Israelites of Deuteronomy and Jesus' disciples comes into view: as the Lucan account of the transfiguration clearly echoes the story of Moses on the mountain (esp. LXX Exod. 24.9–25.9),[67] Jesus' ensuing confrontation with perversion and faithlessness in the exorcism story corresponds to what Moses too had encountered at the foot of a mountain (Exod. 32.1–35).

Another text that has almost certainly shaped the production and original reception of the present unit is the biblical story of Elisha's raising of the Shunammite woman's son (2 Kgs 4.8–37).[68] The two stories share the following motifs: (1) the theme of the only child, highly valued by the parent (2 Kgs 4.14–17; Luke 9.38), (2) the illness that threatens the child's life and distresses the parent (2 Kgs 4.18–24; Luke 9.38–40), (3) the conveyance of the sick child to the locale of a wonder-working man of God (2 Kgs 4.22–25; Luke 9.41–42a), (4) the wonder-worker's proximity to a mountain associated with revelatory phenomena (2 Kgs

---

[64] As the Marcan version of this story has neither δαιμόνιον nor διαστρέφω, it should not be understood as alluding to Deut. 32 at all; ἰάομαι (LXX Deut. 32.39; Luke 9.42b), moreover, which occurs in neither the Matthaean nor the Marcan version of this story, constitutes yet another link between Luke 9.37–43a and Moses' Song.

[65] Note especially αὐτοῦ ἀκούετε in 9.35, which is probably an echo of LXX Deut. 18.15, αὐτοῦ ἀκούσεσθε; cf. Moessner, 'Luke 9:1–50', pp. 588–9; and D. A. Ravens, 'Luke 9:7–62 and the Prophetic Role of Jesus', *NTS* 36 (1990), p. 124.

[66] Cf. Moessner, 'Luke 9:1–50', p. 592. Interpreting γενεά as including the disciples has stronger support from the immediate co-text (esp. 9.32–33, 45–46, 49–50) than from the Lucan account's divergences from Mark and Matthew, whose second person plural command φέρετε (Matt. 17.17; Mark 9.19) and concluding dialogue (Matt. 17.19–21; Mark 9.28–29) draw more attention to the disciples' failure than do the parallel elements in Luke's account.

[67] Cf. Bovon, *Luc (1, 1–9,50)*, p. 479.

[68] Cf. F. W. Danker, *Jesus and the New Age*, rev. edn (Philadelphia, 1988), p. 203; and Marshall, *Gospel of Luke*, p. 391. Neither 2 Kgs 4.8–37 nor Deut. 32.5, 20 is mentioned even as a potential intertext by Kirschläger, *Jesu exorzistisches Wirken*, pp. 131–57, who therefore neglects an important layer of the story's meaning for its first audience.

4.25, 27; Luke 9.37), (5) the failure of the wonder-worker's disciple(s) to carry out instructions and to heal the child (2 Kgs 4.29–31; Luke 9.1–2, 40), (6) the remarkable success of the master wonder-worker in eventually healing the child (2 Kgs 4.32–35; Luke 9.42b), and (7) the transfer of the healed child to the parent (2 Kgs 4.36–37; Luke 9.42b).

While none of these motifs by itself amounts to a significant connection, the co-occurrence of all seven of them in both 2 Kings 4.8–37 and Luke 9.37–43a creates a strong case for reading the latter as modelled on the former. Furthermore, although 2 Kings 4.8–37 had probably impressed itself on the present unit of tradition by the time it reached the author of Luke–Acts, its impact on the Lucan version shows signs of having been deliberately amplified; for three of the links just mentioned – the only child, the mountain, and the transference of the child to the parent – are not shared by either the Matthaean or the Marcan version of this story. The Lucan account in particular, then, looks like a serious attempt to portray Jesus as a prophet in the honourable mould of Elisha.

As suggested in the last two chapters, the oracles of Isaiah (e.g., LXX Isa. 58.6–7 and 61.1–2) contribute much to the force of Luke's first two exorcism narratives. Finding that Isaiah has influenced the present episode as well should therefore be less surprising than to find no Isaianic influence here at all. In this regard LXX Isaiah 65.1–14 (esp. vv. 8–14) deserves special attention.

In LXX Isaiah 65.14 the Lord God warns those who fail to honour him: 'You shall *scream* [κεκράξεσθε] on account of your pain of heart and shall cry aloud from the *shattering of spirit* (συντριβῆς πνεύματος)'. The collocation in this passage of κράζω and συντρίβω suggests a provocative similarity between the sufferings of those who dishonour the God of Isaiah and the afflictions of Luke's demoniac, who is described as crying out wildly (κράζει) and being shattered (συντρῖβον).[69] In the immediately preceding co-text of the Isaiah oracle (65.8–14), moreover, the Lord characterises the same rebellious mob as not only forgetting his holy 'mountain' (ὄρος, 65.11) but also preparing a table for τῷ δαίμονι (65.11),[70] a term whose lexical kinship with Luke's δαιμόνιον (Luke 9.42) significantly heightens the sense of an intertextual bond. And finally, in

---

[69] As both of the key terms here are absent from the parallels in Matt. 17.14–21 and Mark 9.14–29, only the Lucan account has potential to be heard as an echo of Isaiah.

[70] The demonological lexis in 65.11 is peculiar to the LXX, and in particular to codices A and B. As the reading attested by the MT (i.e., גד, the god of fortune named in numerous inscriptions from Canaan and Phoenicia; S. Ribichini, 'Gad גד', *DDD*, cols 642–4) is probably closest to the original, the use of δαιμόνιον in mss A and B of the LXX looks very much like an example of the tendency of Second Temple Jewish sources to demonise the deities of others.

the Isaiah text's opening accusation (65.1–7), the same disloyal crowd is depicted as habitually burning incense to τοῖς δαιμονίοις (65.3),[71] so that they are warned by the Lord: 'Their sins and those of their <u>fathers</u> [πατέρων] . . . I shall repay [ἀποδώσω]' (65.7).

With the Isaianic motifs of demon-worship, tomb-dwelling, and swine-consumption (LXX Isa. 65.3–4) having clearly influenced the story of the Gerasene demoniac, Luke has already demonstrated familiarity with this section of Isaiah. In this light, and in view of the cumulative force of the links outlined above, a deliberate allusion to Isaiah 65.1–14 in the present story can be deduced without great effort. On careful inspection, though, and despite Luke's rhetoric of eschatological fulfilment, the events of this third story of exorcism do not correspond very closely to the expectations of Isaiah 65.1–14: unlike the possessed youth in Luke, for instance, the disobedient people of Isaiah 65.1–14 have nothing to await except divine retribution and certain destruction (65.15). What therefore seems to matter most to Luke is not some tidy scheme of ideational correspondences but rather the overtone of continuity and fulfilment.

Presuppositions and implicatures

In Luke 9.42, when the narrator juxtaposes Jesus' rebuking of the unclean spirit and his healing of the youth, he implicitly endorses the assumptions made earlier by the father, who not only takes for granted the existence of spirits but also presupposes spirit causation in his son's illness (9.39–40).[72] Indeed, as the validity of these same assumptions is not questioned in any way by Jesus, whose actions suggest that he too endorsed this cosmology, the scheme in question functions as a firm set of givens, as components of a religious world whose reality for the narrator and his characters is as solid as the mountain Jesus descends at the beginning of the story. In this regard the presuppositional framework of the present story is almost identical to that of Luke 4.33–37 and 8.26–39.

However, and particularly in view of the confidence all the participants in the story apparently have in the assumptions just discussed,

---

[71] As in 65.11 so here in 65.3, δαιμόνιον is attested only in the LXX. The MT of 65.3 reads, simply, ומקטרים על־הלבנים ('burning incense on bricks').

[72] As noted by A. George, 'Le miracle dan l'oeuvre de Luc', in X. Léon-Dufour (ed.), *Les miracles de Jésus selon le Nouveau Testament* (Paris, 1977), p. 251, the assumption that illness is caused by demonic beings is expressed more frequently in the writings of Luke (e.g., Luke 4.39, 40–41; 6.18; 7.21; 8.2; 9.1–6, 42; 10.1–20; 13.11–14; Acts 5.16; 10.38) than in other writings of the NT; but unlike Hippocrates and Lucian of Samosata, none of the latter show any sign of taking exception to the idea (see, e.g., Matt. 10.1; John 10.20; 2 Cor. 12.7–10).

the father's tacit acknowledgement in 9.40 that he himself has recently made an erroneous assumption about these matters is truly remarkable. More specifically, when the father reports that he has already asked Jesus' disciples for assistance but found them powerless, he implicitly judges his prior assumption that the disciples would be able to heal his son as having been mistaken. Thus, while it may be clear to everyone in this context that the boy's illness is the work of a malevolent spirit, far greater uncertainty surrounds the question of who is capable of dealing with this kind of crisis. This same sense of uncertainty furthermore heightens, at least marginally, the impact of Jesus' eventual victory over the evil creature.

Earlier, when the father pleads, δέομαί σου ἐπιβλέψαι ἐπὶ τὸν υἱόν μου (9.38), his illocutionary goal is not difficult to ascertain: he wants his son to be healed by Jesus. The transparency of the father's aim, however, should not be allowed to obscure an interesting incongruency between this utterance's ultimate force and its strictly grammatical sense; for the difference in question generates additional meanings in the form of implicatures. For example, although the use of δέομαι in this context contributes almost nothing to the force of the father's utterance, it does significantly affect what Halliday and others would call the 'tenor' of the discourse, and more specifically the respective positions of the father and Jesus on a continuum of power;[73] to be more precise, by describing the request he addresses to Jesus as an instance of begging, the father not only wraps himself in appealing humility but also implicitly presents himself as Jesus' social inferior. In neither the Matthaean parallel nor the Marcan, moreover, is the father depicted as adopting this sort of stance.[74]

At least one other implicature in the discourse of the father merits our attention. In 9.38b, where the father begins to explain his request for Jesus' help, the first reason he offers (ὅτι μονογενής μοί ἐστιν) is no more semantically opaque than the request that precedes it: with unimpeachable clarity and economy, the man is saying that the son in question is his only child. The illocutionary force of this disclosure, however, is by no means exhausted by the vague inference that the boy had special importance as his father's only child; rather, and in view of the value attached in this culture to child-bearing as a source of honour and a means

---

[73] On the role of power and tenor in discourse, see esp. Eggins, *Systemic Functional Linguistics*, pp. 63–4. Of the different Synoptic versions of this story, only Luke's employs δέομαι, which is used with similar connotations in Luke's second exorcism story (8.28, 38) and Luke 5.12 (par. Matt. 9.38); 10.2; 21.36; Acts 4.31; 8.22, 24; 10.2; 21.39; 26.3; Rom. 1.10; and 1 Thess. 3.10.

[74] E.g., where the father in Luke uses the infinitive ἐπιβλέψαι, which helps to give his request an indirect and polite quality, the father in Matthew (17.15) employs a more direct imperative of request, ἐλέησον.

of preserving the family name,[75] the ultimate point must be that the status and preservation of the father's family line are threatened far more gravely in the case as it stands than they would be, say, by the illness of a child that had one brother or more. A corresponding increase in the value of Jesus' subsequent intervention therefore needs to be recognised: in addition to vanquishing an unclean spirit and healing a wretched youth, Jesus saves a whole family line from the dust of death and restores its current generation of members to their appropriate honour.

Finally, in the last clause of the story, presupposition and implicature work in concert to convey one of this unit's most rhetorically important messages. Having just narrated Jesus' climactic reversal of the situation (9.42b), the storyteller evaluates Jesus' success through the eyes of the crowd that witnessed it: 'And all were astonished', he comments, 'at the majesty of God' (9.43). What is particularly noteworthy about this comment is the relationship between the construction τῇ μεγαλειότητι τοῦ θεοῦ and its antecedent co-text. Most notably, with the article τῇ serving to particularise μεγαλειότητι, 'the majesty of God' is simply presupposed to have been evident somehow in the happenings just narrated (9.37–42), even though neither μεγαλειότης nor θεός has been explicitly mentioned in these verses. In order to make sense of this assumption, the reader needs to identify 'the majesty of God' with the activity of Jesus that has just been narrated, and especially with the exorcistic climax of 9.42. But just as important, by merely implying this connection rather than asserting it, the storyteller maximises the likelihood that his audience might adopt this high view of Jesus for themselves.

Co-text

Although Luke 9.37–43a constitutes a discrete unit of text with relatively clear boundaries, it also has significant connections to the materials that come immediately before and after it. The temporal circumstance signified by τῇ ἑξῆς ἡμέρᾳ (9.37), for instance, situates the action of the ensuing clauses in relation to what has just been narrated, namely the transfiguration of Jesus in 9.28–36. Similarly, in the construction κατελθόντων αὐτῶν ἀπὸ τοῦ ὄρους (9.37), the anaphoric use of the article with ὄρος refers back to the mountain envisaged in 9.28. The resultant cohesion with the transfiguration scene is strengthened further by the septuagintisms Ἐγένετο δὲ and καὶ ἰδού in 9.37–39, which perpetuate the strongly

---

[75] Cf. Malina and Rohrbaugh, *Social-Science Commentary*, p. 344; R. Wilson, 'Child, Children', in *HBD*, pp. 161–2.

biblical flavour of 9.28–36.[76] The exorcism, therefore, is closely tied to the transfiguration not only in terms of spatio-temporal setting but also in regard to style and register.[77]

Directly following the exorcism story, the words Πάντων δὲ θαυμαζόντων ἐπὶ πᾶσιν οἷς ἐποίει (9.43b) tightly link the unit it introduces back to 9.37–43a. Indeed, since this same construction is very similar in both transitivity and content to the last clause of the exorcism story (i.e., ἐξεπλήσσοντο δὲ πάντες ἐπὶ τῇ μεγαλειότητι τοῦ θεοῦ, 9.43a), it might be best understood as a co-referential transformation of the latter, functioning chiefly to orientate the reader to the ensuing words of Jesus (i.e., 9.44). With the exorcism and the ensuing passion prediction (9.43b–45) therefore being strongly interlocked, Luke is able to underscore what the disciples – at least at this point in the narrative – can experience only as an unfathomable incongruity: although Jesus has power and authority to vanquish robust demons, heal the ill and restore interpersonal peace, he nevertheless 'is to be delivered into the hands of men' (9.44). As teaching very similar to this is also ascribed to Jesus in two different sections of the immediately preceding co-text (9.18–22, 30–36), the idea that he possessed clear foreknowledge of his passion has special prominence in this chapter.[78]

Luke's distinctive placement of the commissioning of the twelve (9.1–6), moreover, plays an important co-textual role which Matthew and Mark's arrangements of the same traditions do not allow.[79] Most notably, in Luke 9.1–2, and thus directly after a section in which Jesus has been depicted as the sole performer of therapeutic deeds (8.26–56), Luke represents Jesus as giving the twelve δύναμιν καὶ ἐξουσίαν ἐπὶ πάντα τὰ

---

[76] Cf. Aichinger, 'Zur Traditionsgeschichte der Epileptiker-Perikope', pp. 137–8. Ἐγένετο δὲ occurs in 9.28, καὶ ἐγένετο in vv. 29 and 33, and καὶ ἰδού in 9.30. Only the third of these items is found in the Synoptic parallels (Matt. 17.3).

[77] Cf. Kirschläger, *Jesu exorzistisches Wirken*, p. 136. Since Luke omits the dialogue about the coming of Elijah, which in Matthew and Mark stands between the transfiguration and the exorcism (Matt. 17.10–13; Mark 9.11–13), the connection between these two episodes is much tighter in Luke than it is in the parallels. Thus, as noted by A.A. Trites, 'The Transfiguration in the Theology of Luke: Some Redactional Links', in L. D. Hurst and N. T. Wright (eds), *The Glory of Christ in the New Testament: Studies in Christology in Memory of George Bradford Caird* (Oxford, 1987), p. 74, for Luke 'the "glory" of God on the mountain-top is matched by the "majesty" of God in the valley, where Christ meets human need'.

[78] On τὴν ἔξοδον αὐτοῦ in 9.31 as including Jesus' death, see Marshall, *Gospel of Luke*, pp. 384–5.

[79] Matthew, e.g., has the commissioning in ch. 10 of his narrative (10.1, 7–11, 14), which stands very far from his version of the present exorcism (17.14–21), while Mark has two versions of it (3.13–19; 6.6b–13), neither of which directly impacts how his rendition of the exorcism is read.

δαιμόνια καὶ νόσους θεραπεύειν and commissioning them 'to proclaim the kingdom of God and to heal'. By thus creating expectations that at some point soon in the ensuing narrative the twelve will be doing what Jesus is presented in 8.26–56 as having just done,[80] these two verses foster a sense of macrotextual linkage between the sections that directly precede and follow.[81] The reference in 9.1 to the exorcistic 'power and authority' given to the disciples, to the extent that it echoes the testimony of the bystanders in Luke's first exorcism story (4.36), reinforces and extends this linkage. And finally, the expectations aroused by these features in 9.1–2 are immediately fulfilled in verses 6 and 10, where the kerygmatic and therapeutic successes of the disciples are summarised in a style that recalls some of Jesus' accomplishments in earlier segments of the narrative (e.g., 8.1, 39).

Cumulatively, therefore, these features of 9.1–6 and 10 build up a very positive and promising image of the disciples. Consequently, the careful reader/hearer of the immediately ensuing units is likely to experience at least a minor sense of dissonance and surprise at the speech of the demoniac's father (9.38–40), whose unfavourable characterisation of the disciples as having been unable (οὐκ ἠδυνήθησαν, 9.40) to expel the demon from his son appears to undermine the prior account of the disciples receiving δύναμιν (9.1) for precisely this kind of intervention. Indeed, in this earlier context the twelve not only receive 'power and authority' to heal the demonised (9.1–2) but employ these endowments so effectively that they become a cause for concern to Herod the tetrarch (9.6–9). Notwithstanding these developments in 9.1–9, however, the father's unflattering portrayal of the disciples is disputed neither by Jesus nor by any other voice in the narrative, even though it has potential indirectly to bring dishonour to Jesus.[82]

Furthermore, if the implied sequence of actions taken by the demoniac's father up to his interchange with Jesus is to make any sort of narratological sense – why, most importantly, did he approach the disciples before coming to Jesus? – then knowledge of the disciples' prior successes has to be recollected by the reader from back in 9.1–10 and attributed to the

---

[80] Nolland, *Luke*, I, p. 425, rightly stresses the link between 9.1–3 and 8.1–56 but says nothing about the role of 9.1–3 in creating expectations of parallels (i.e., between Jesus and his followers).

[81] On the topical unity of Luke 9.1–50 (esp. 9.7–50), see J. A. Fitzmyer, 'The Composition of Luke, Chapter 9', in C. H. Talbert (ed.), *Perspectives on Luke–Acts* (Edinburgh, 1978), pp. 140, 144–50.

[82] Cf. Malina and Rohrbaugh, *Social-Science Commentary*, p. 234. As in Matt. 17.16 and Mark 9.18 so in Luke 9.40, the father describes those who failed as τῶν μαθητῶν σου.

father; but precisely because these latter moves are made so easy by virtue of the numerous referential and lexical strings that cut across 9.1–40,[83] they do nothing to mitigate the apparent tension between Jesus' gift and the disciples' failure. In fact, they only make it more conspicuous.

This tension produces a host of interpretative effects and possibilities. The most obvious response to it, perhaps, is to see it as an instance of incoherence and thus as an invitation to deconstruction. Particularly as the adjective πάντα is used by the narrator with τὰ δαιμόνια back in 9.1 to indicate the extent of the disciples' power and authority,[84] the subsequent disclosure that some of these same disciples had failed to manage this particular demon (9.40) certainly seems to undermine the narrator's reliability. But just as important, in addition to raising questions about the reliability of the narrator, this same tension also serves both to highlight the power of Jesus, whose therapeutic success stands out by contrast to the disciples' failure, and to intensify doubts about the disciples' readiness for ministry.[85]

The relevance these doubts about the disciples have to Luke's larger narrative programme, moreover, increases sharply when, immediately after the exorcistic climax (9.42) and for the second time in this section (i.e., 9.1–50), Jesus stresses that he 'is about to be betrayed into human hands' (9.44b). For in this light, and unless Jesus should prove to be as unreliable as this section's narrator seems to be, responsibility for the divine mission will eventually fall to the disciples, even though their response to this very disclosure betrays an inauspicious combination of fear and lack of insight (9.45).[86] Viewed together, therefore, the story in 9.37–43a (esp. 9.40) and the passion prediction in 9.43b–45 put worrisome clouds of doubt over the sunny picture of the disciples provided back in 9.1–10a. And these reservations become even more salient in the immediately ensuing segments (9.46–50), where Jesus has to counter the disciples with increasing directness for the conventional assumptions they express about status (9.46–48) and group boundaries (9.49–50).

---

[83] Note, e.g., the referential link between τοὺς δώδεκα (9.1, 12) and τῶν μαθητῶν σου (9.40), the repetition of the δύναμις/δύναμαι word group (9.1, 40), and the synonymy of δαιμόνιον and πνεῦμα as they are used in these verses (9.1, 39, 42, 49). These features reinforce the argument developed below that, *contra* Nolland, *Luke*, I, p. xlii, Luke 9.1–50 has a unity and coherence that bear significantly on the interpretation of its constituent units; cf. Moessner, 'Luke 9:1–50', pp. 582–605; and R. F. O'Toole, 'Luke's Message in Luke 9:1–50', *CBQ* 49 (1987), pp. 74–5.

[84] Cf. J. B. Green, *Gospel of Luke*, p. 388.

[85] Cf. O'Toole, 'Luke's Message', p. 81; and Moessner, 'Luke 9:1–50', pp. 591–4.

[86] The juxtaposition of faithlessness (9.41) and fearfulness (9.45) as qualities of the disciples is consistent with the antonymous relationship between faith and fear at earlier points in the narrative (e.g., 8.50).

In the exchange about group boundaries (9.49–50), which is interpreted below as the closing part of an inclusio whose opening is 9.1–6, the words of the apostle John about the unfamiliar exorcist (9.49) are represented as a response ('Ἀποκριθεὶς δὲ 'Ιωάννης εἶπεν . . .) to the preceding dialogue about status (9.46–48). Consequently, although the shift in topic from 'whoever welcomes this child' (9.48) to 'someone casting out demons' (9.49) may seem abrupt, an implicit link between the two can be deduced which not only is warranted by the immediate co-text but also sheds additional light on the tension between 9.1–10 and 9.40.[87] To be more precise, both of these motifs are explicitly linked in this context to the idea of acting in the name of Jesus, a concept whose repetition in these verses has several noteworthy effects. First, by drawing attention not just to the matter of Jesus' name but also to the related motifs of welcoming children and casting out demons, it underscores the thematic correspondences between this pair of units and the preceding exorcism story, and thereby strengthens the ties between all three segments;[88] but just as important, it also serves to highlight a deficiency in the disciples' value system: namely, and at least at this stage in their training, they invest far greater value in acquiring advantages of honour for themselves – both over each other (9.46) and over those associated with similar missions (9.49) – than they do in honouring and welcoming others, particularly others from lower levels of the social hierarchy, such as the child whom Jesus places by his side precisely in order to correct this tendency (9.47).

Understood in this light, then, the two units in 9.46–50 help to clarify the sociocultural dynamics that lie behind the exorcistic fiasco reported in 9.40. More specifically, as the demoniac in this context is best understood as a child comparable to that received by Jesus in 9.47–48 and thus a figure of low status,[89] the social bond that would have been initiated with the boy through provision of healing could easily have been viewed by the disciples as a risk to their own honour, which, like that of virtually

---

[87] Cf. Kirschläger, *Jesu exorzistisches Wirken*, p. 205. In view of the linear aspects of co-text, questions about how Jesus' response to John in 9.49–50 relates to material positioned much later in Luke–Acts (e.g., Luke 11.23; Acts 19.13–20) are not discussed here but rather in the next chapter, on Acts 16.16–18.

[88] Most notably the lexemes δαιμόνιον, ἐκβάλλω, and the παῖς/παιδίον group, all of which co-occur in 9.37–43a, are likewise found together in 9.46–50.

[89] The similarity between the boy (παῖς, 9.42) in our story and the child in 9.46–48 is suggested by the references to the latter as a παιδίον (9.47–48), a term which overlaps substantially with παῖς in sense (LSJ, s.v. 'παιδιόθεν' and 'παῖς') and serves in this context to form a lexical string with it. On the devaluation of young children throughout the Roman world, see S. Dixon, *The Roman Family* (Baltimore, 1992), pp. 116–18; W. V. Harris, 'Towards a Study of the Roman Slave Trade', *MAAR* 36 (1980), p. 123; P. Garnsey and R. Saller, *The Roman Empire: Economy, Society and Culture* (London, 1987), pp. 138–9.

everyone else in the Graeco-Roman world, was a limited good that had to be protected.[90] Consequently, the non-specific and very ambiguous characterisation of the disciples in 9.40 as having been 'unable' to cast out the boy's demon can (and probably should) be read in a manner which makes our narrator's unreliability, in the end, only apparent rather than real: to be precise, the disciples' inability in this instance did not consist of a failure either to expel a demon they had wholeheartedly tried to expel or to heal a boy they had genuinely tried to heal; rather, it consisted of an unwillingness to welcome the boy for healing in the first place.

Thus, as in Luke 8.1–56 so also here in 9.1–50, the exorcism theme intersects a variety of other prominent concerns that find expression in the co-text.[91] The motifs of exorcism and the demonic in themselves, however, actually have a more explicit and prominent place in the present section than they do in chapter eight; for in addition to playing a central role in the narrative tension and climax of the present story of healing, they are also underscored by virtue of their presence at both the beginning and end of 9.1–50 (9.1–2, 49–50). Indeed, precisely since exorcism figures not only in the present episode but also at both the beginning and end of this larger complex, the internal design and potentially schematic structure of this section invites further attention; for if we can establish how exorcism and the demonic relate to other prominent interests in this part of the narrative, we might also be able to gauge what degree of prominence these themes have vis-à-vis other topics in Luke's larger narrative programme and thus to specify what kind of role they could have played in the whole composition's original situation.

Fortunately, much of the foundation for this pursuit has already been laid in observations made above. Most notably, by recalling the premium placed on exorcistic healing back in 9.1–2, the interchange regarding the unfamiliar exorcist in 9.49–50 helps to form the closing element of an inclusio and simultaneously gives exorcism a foregrounded position in this section as a whole.[92] This same instance of correspondence finds additional strength, moreover, in the repetition of the welcoming motif in

---

[90] Cf. Pilch, 'Sickness and Healing', p. 194; Malina, *New Testament World*, pp. 33, 89–90.

[91] In Luke 8.1–56, e.g., exorcism intersects Luke's interests in women, discipleship and money (8.1–3); the devil's opposition to the word of God (8.4–21); and impurity (8.26–56).

[92] Both Schürmann, *Das Lukasevangelium*, I, p. 579, and Bovon, *Luc (1, 1–9,50)*, p. 509, briefly note the correspondence between the beginning and end of 9.1–50 but overlook the potential chiasm (detailed below) to which it contributes. As the only occurrence of δαιμόνιον in 9.1–50 other than those in vv. 1 and 49 is that in 9.42, where the nominative singular is used to denote a single demonic participant, the occurrence of the accusative plural both in 9.1 and in 9.49 increases the schematising potential of the correspondence.

this part of the narrative,[93] with the disciples' obligation to welcome children (9.47–48) recalling instruction back in 9.5 about how the disciples should respond when they themselves are not welcomed.

The sense that a genuine inclusio is formed by 9.1–6 and 9.46–50 is powerfully confirmed by further examination of the postulated frame's internal structure. Directly preceding the inclusio's closing element, for instance, Jesus' prediction in 9.43b–45 of his impending betrayal corresponds on several levels to the unit that directly follows the commissioning (9.7–9), in which Jesus is forebodingly compared by Herod Antipas and others to John the Baptist (martyred but believed by some to have been raised).[94] Immediately after this latter unit, then, comes a short piece that includes both a report by the apostles of their initial post-commissioning achievements (9.10) and a summary of the kerygmatic and therapeutic successes experienced by Jesus himself directly afterwards (9.11) – a piece, therefore, whose particular pattern of themes and concepts anticipates that of the present exorcism narrative (9.37–43a).[95] Then, positioned just inside these two units, are, first, the story of miraculous feeding in 9.12–17, whose various biblical models include well-known stories involving Moses and Elijah,[96] and, second, the transfiguration account, where Moses and Elijah's appearance with Jesus on the mountain (9.30–34) develops their less explicit intertextual presence back in 9.12–17. And finally, occupying the central and potentially most prominent position in this whole complex structure are three short units of dialogue and teaching that move swiftly from the status and reputation of Jesus (9.18–21), to a prediction by Jesus of his own passion and resurrection (9.22), and thence to the implications of Jesus' status

[93] Each of this section's five occurrences of the verb δέχομαι without the prepositional prefix is found in either the opening or the closing element of the complex (i.e., 9.1–6 and 9.46–50). The inclusio is strengthened by the occurrence in vv. 2 and 48 of ἀποστέλλω, which is not used elsewhere in this section of Luke's narrative.

[94] This would scarcely be the first instance in Luke's Gospel of a macrostructural scheme being employed to define the relationship between Jesus and the Baptist. On the presence of similar strategies in Luke 1–2 and 3.1–20, see T. E. Klutz, 'The Value of Being Virginal: Mary and Anna in the Lukan Infancy Prologue', in G. J. Brooke (ed.), *The Birth of Jesus: Biblical and Theological Reflections* (Edinburgh, 2000), pp. 82–6; T. E. Klutz, 'A Redaction-Critical Study of Luke 3:1–20', MA thesis, Wheaton College Graduate School (1989), pp. 46, 116–19; and R. Laurentin, *Structure et Théologie de Luc I–II*, Ebib (Paris, 1957), pp. 26–33. The parallelism between 9.7–9 and 9.43b–45 includes both the correspondence between the perplexity of Herod (9.7) and the imperceptiveness of the disciples (9.45), and the similarity between the martyrdom of the Baptist and the fate of Jesus.

[95] Note in particular the similarity in lexical collocation and sense between 9.11 (οἱ ὄχλοι, τῆς βασιλείας τοῦ θεοῦ, and ἰᾶτο) and the exorcism story (ὄχλος, 9.37; τῇ μεγαλειότητι τοῦ θεοῦ, 9.43; and ἰάσατο, 9.42).

[96] See esp. Exod. 16.1–36 and 1 Kgs 17.1–16, but also 2 Kgs 4.42–44.

and fate for the present life and future prospects of the disciples (9.23–27).[97] The resultant chiastic structure of 9.1–50 can thus be summarised as follows:

> A. Exorcism, mission and (in)hospitality (9.1–6)
> B. Jesus and the fate of John the Baptist (9.7–9)
> C. Disciples' success and Jesus' ministry of healing (9.10–11)
> D. Supramundane provision that echoes the great prophets (9.12–17)
> E. Christological confession, passion prediction, and discipleship (9.18–27)
> D'. Supramundane manifestation with the great prophets (9.28–36)
> C'. Disciples' exorcistic failure and Jesus' success (9.37–43a)
> B'. The fate of Jesus himself (9.43b–45)
> A'. Exorcism, mission and hospitality (9.46–50)

This structure, which to my knowledge has not been discussed in previous Lucan scholarship, has several implications that are worth noting here. First of all, as the importance of receiving others hospitably and being willing to form dyadic contracts with strangers is highlighted not only by the parallelism of 9.1–6 (esp. 9.5) and 9.46–50 (esp. 9.48) but also in the description of Jesus' therapeutic successes in Bethsaida (i.e., element C, esp. 9.11), this same motif's complete absence from the latter description's parallel (i.e., the exorcism story) reinforces the conjecture offered above concerning the reasons for the disciples' failure, namely, they never received the boy and his father hospitably in the first place. As the outcome of a given exorcism in this milieu can therefore be significantly influenced by mundane social factors such as the relative statuses of the patient and the healer, the willingness of the healer(s) to enter into reciprocal contracts of exchange with strangers (including those of relatively lower status), and the degree of hospitality extended by the healer to the patient and possibly also their kin (and vice versa, 9.5), the whole performance is conditioned as much by mundane social norms and expectations as it is by demonological factors.

Furthermore, as the analysis above shows that a willingness to accept and enter into dyadic alliance with patients (regardless of their status) can make a decisive difference in regard to therapeutic outcomes, it indirectly confirms part of the cultural analysis offered in the last chapter, where the socially constructed process of becoming a demoniac was seen to

---

[97] These three units stand out together from the materials directly before and after them chiefly by virtue of the preponderance of verbal processes in their main narrative clauses. In brief, following the orientating relational process denoted by συνῆσαν in 9.18, every process mentioned by the narrator in this section is verbal/symbolic in nature.

involve the patient and their local community in an agonistic dialectic of mutual rejection. If this prior analysis is valid, then one might expect to find evidence elsewhere in the tradition that effective exorcistic reversal of the demonisation process would have among its essential features a gracious offer of human acceptance, group membership, and a new social identity. This is precisely what we find assumed and implied in the chiastic structure of Luke 9.1–50.

And finally, as the approaching death of Jesus is strongly emphasised in this section not only by its central and thus unparalleled position in the chiasm (9.22) but also by its presence in two other elements that correspond to one another in the same complex (i.e., 9.7–9 and 43b–45), this motif possesses even greater salience in this section than exorcism does; thus, while the exorcism theme cannot be accurately estimated as having anything less than a foregrounded position in this section, it is nevertheless subordinate in prominence to Luke's frontgrounded interest in Jesus' death. Here, then, more clearly than at any previous juncture in Luke's Gospel, we see signs that, while the implied author of Luke–Acts regards exorcism as important, he does have other communicative goals which for him possess greater importance and to which the exorcism traditions can be made subservient.

Cultural context

The contrast that emerges in the present story between the failure of the disciples and the success of Jesus distinguishes this episode from those in 4.33–37 and 8.26–39. In addition to fulfilling important ideological and rhetorical functions discussed earlier in this chapter (e.g., to attribute to Jesus a unique degree of honour and status), this same contrast also creates an excellent opportunity for comparative study; for as discussed below, several ancient narratives of exorcistic healing from the same broad cultural and historical context have features that shed light not only on aspects of Jesus' exorcistic method but also on the sorts of contexts in which narratives of contrast between therapeutic failure and success were most likely to have relevance.

However, before occupying ourselves with this latter issue and closely related matters, we would do well to note at least some of the main assumptions this episode shares with the stories analysed in the last two chapters. Jesus, the demoniac's father and the story's narrator, for instance, are united in taking for granted the existence of demonic spirits whose agency might be inferred in a particular situation of illness (9.39, 42). Furthermore, although the interface between demons and impurity is not given as much emphasis in the present story as it is back in 8.26–39, it is nevertheless presupposed in the narration of Jesus' rebuke of 'the unclean spirit' in 9.42. Like most folk healers, moreover, but in contrast to Apollonius of Tyana in *VA* 4.20 in particular, Jesus once again takes at face value the client's view (in this case, the father's) of the illness, its aetiology and symptoms, showing no more inclination here than in the two previous exorcisms to correct the prior folk diagnosis.[98]

With the demoniac boy's illness and impurity having adverse implications both for his father's family line and for everyone that had contact with him, the negative consequences of spirit-illness for the patient's family receive more explicit attention in the present narrative than they do in the previous two, though early audiences almost certainly would have inferred similar meanings from the other stories on the basis of their own culture-specific knowledge of these matters. The presence and force of these implications are strengthened, in fact, by another assumption which has already been discussed in relation to the story in 8.26–39: namely, that either the demoniac or their surrogate was morally responsible for the affliction, that the illness had befallen the victim because of sin.[99] This notion can be deduced from at least two different kinds of features in the present narrative. First, as Jesus' allusion to Deuteronomy 32.5, 20 has already been shown above (under 'intertextuality') to derive part of its force from the Deuteronomy passage's co-text, the emphasis throughout this part of Deuteronomy on the causal nexus between misfortune and religious infidelity[100] would probably have been heard by Luke himself as one of the strongest connotative echoes produced by this particular intertext. This impression is supported, in fact, not only by the more overt presence of the sin–misfortune nexus in a variety of other contemporaneous documents[101] but also by the conversational pragmatics

---

[98] Cf. Pilch, 'Sickness and Healing', p. 199.

[99] Cf. Mark 2.5 (par. Matt. 9.2; Luke 5.20); Mark 2.15–17 (par. Matt. 9.10–13; Luke 5.30–32); John 5.14; 9.1–2; Jas 5.14–16.

[100] See esp. Deut. 27.15–26; 28.15–68; 29.15–28; 31.16–21, 24–29; 32.15–26. The intertextual utility of LXX Deut. 27–32 for the present story is reinforced by its emphasis on how the behaviour of Israelite parents impacts the fortunes of their children (e.g., 28.4, 11, 18, 32, 41, 53–60) and by its use of the noun νόσος (i.e., the same term used in Luke 9.1 and several other NT passages (e.g., Matt. 10.1; Luke 4.40–41; 6.18–19) to signify illnesses caused by demons) to denote the maladies Israel would suffer as a consequence of her sins (LXX Deut. 28.59 (ms. A); 29.21). On illness as a sign of sin in ancient Jewish and early Christian aetiologies of illness, see Avalos, *Health Care and the Rise of Christianity*, pp. 37, 64–5.

[101] In addition to the sources discussed below, see *4QPrayer of Nabonidus ar* frags 1–3 line 4, where the exorcistic healing of the Babylonian king Nabonidus is facilitated in part by forgiveness of his sins.

of the exchange in 9.40–41; to be more precise, since Jesus' allusion to Deuteronomy 32 both directly follows an implicit challenge by the father to Jesus' honour in 9.40 and directly precedes Jesus' own highly direct command that the father bring his son into Jesus' immediate presence, the allusion looks very much like part of a counter-challenge that serves both to defend the collective honour of Jesus' group and to keep alive the possibility of a mutually beneficial relationship with the man. In view then of the availability of the sin–misfortune nexus as a semantic resource in Luke's milieu, and since an insinuation that the man's own religious shortcomings had played a key role in his son's illness would constitute an apt and typically cunning riposte by Jesus, religious infidelity of one kind or another should probably be understood as the cause of this particular instance of spirit-illness.

And finally, the assumption that authority over impure spirits was relevant not just to exorcism in the narrow sense but to all forms of healing is realised both in the present story and in its antecedent co-text. In the climax narrated in 9.42, for instance, it can be deduced from the parallelism between ἐπετίμησεν and ἰάσατο, which implicitly presents exorcism and healing as two facets of a single ritual process; and the same idea finds expression near the beginning of the chiasm in the relationship between the exorcistic 'power and authority' given to the disciples on the one hand (9.1) and both the purpose and initial results of their commissioning on the other hand (9.2, 6).[102]

Success and failure in the context of exorcistic culture

In contextualising this episode in relation to its immediate co-text (i.e., 9.1–50), the analysis above found that the contrast between the disciples' therapeutic failure and Jesus' victory plays a prominent role not only in the exorcism story itself but also in the larger chiastic structure of which it is a part. Surprisingly, though, while both the function of this contrast on a narrative level and the various parallels to its constituent motifs in the history of religions have received ample attention in previous scholarship,[103] the contrast between exorcistic success and failure as a whole has not been contextualised as effectively as it now can be in

---

[102] Cf. J. B. Green, *Gospel of Luke*, p. 358. Since demons are explicitly mentioned in relation to the gift of 'power and authority' in 9.1 but not in the ensuing clauses that signify the purpose and results of the commissioning (ἰᾶσθαι τοὺς ἀσθενεῖς, 9.2; θεραπεύοντες πανταχοῦ, 9.6), they should almost certainly be understood as implicitly present in the illnesses which these latter clauses mention. Cf. Luke 10.9–17.

[103] See, e.g., Twelftree, *Jesus the Exorcist*, pp. 93–6.

relation to culturally appropriate comparative materials. Three narrative texts in particular, one of which is from fourth- or third-century BCE Egypt and the other two from the Qumran corpus, are especially illuminating in this regard.

The Egyptian text, entitled *The Legend of the Possessed Princess* in J. B. Pritchard's *Ancient Near Eastern Texts*,[104] is a narrative inscription that was discovered near the Temple of Amon at Karnak. Much of its complicating action and interest revolve around the spirit-affliction and eventual healing of a certain Bint-resh, who is identified as the younger sister of Ramses II's non-Egyptian wife Nefru-Re.[105] As Nefru-Re moreover is said to have been given to Ramses II as part of an impressive tribute from her father, the Prince of Bekhten, who later undertakes the long (seventeen-month) journey from Bekhten to Thebes in order to persuade Ramses II to send one of Egypt's renowned wise men to heal his younger daughter, the story significantly parallels the Lucan account in regard to the interplay that takes place between exorcistic healing on the one hand and kinship dynamics and religio-political propaganda on the other. Indeed, as the Egyptian story may have been composed shortly before the demise of the Persian Empire in 332 BCE,[106] its historical fiction of a thirteenth-century eastern prince travelling all the way to Thebes in order to barter with the Egyptian king for urgently needed magico-medical assistance could have packed a very strong and historically relevant political punch.

But even more important for our present interests, in addition to presupposing that effective therapy for the princess could not be obtained either in the kingdom of Bekhten itself or in any of the Persian provinces between Bekhten and far-away Egypt – an assumption that already implies a failure of sorts (i.e., a region-wide shortage of effective health care) – the storyteller also narrates a more overt form of non-success: after Ramses II's royal scribe Thut-em-heb arrives in Bekhten in order to attend to the ill princess, he discovers her to be possessed by a spirit of illness that is too strong to be managed by his own therapeutic devices. The princess's father, however, remaining confident that the solution resides in Egypt, makes appeal to Ramses II yet again, this time requesting that one of Egypt's powerful *gods* be sent to deal with the demon. Finally, after the great Theban god 'Khonsu-in-Thebes-Nefer-hotep'

---

[104] The text is sometimes called the 'Bentresh Stela' due to the material on which it was written.

[105] For the text see Pritchard, *ANET*, pp. 29–31; and E. A. W. Budge, *Egyptian Magic* (London, 1899; repr., 1972), pp. 207–12.

[106] *ANET*, p. 29.

confers magico-medical power to one of his subordinate forms, namely 'Khonsu-the-Carrier-out-of-Plans', the latter travels with his priestly attendant to Bekhten where, by helping to arrange a ritual that allows the lesser spirit to leave without losing face, he facilitates a peaceful relocation of the demon to the place from which he originally came.[107]

A lengthy list of similarities and differences between this story and Luke 9.37–43a could easily be produced, but what has greatest relevance to our present interest is the juxtaposition, sequencing and content of the exorcistic failure and the subsequent success. Most importantly, as soon as the princess's illness is recognised by the royal scribe to be the work of a powerful demon, all parties involved in the matter take for granted that effective treatment will require the presence and direct application of divine power; the validity of this assumption, moreover, is fully confirmed by the exorcistic consequences of the Egyptian deity's subsequent arrival in Bekhten.[108] By contrast, and as already observed above, the Lucan story contains no hint that the presence or absence of divine power contributed to the difference between the disciples' and Jesus' performances; and yet, in regard to the more general assumption that exorcistic success requires the presence of divine authority, the Lucan account does indeed concur with the Egyptian text by implying that the divine energies essential for exorcistic victory were brought into play by the presence of Jesus himself. Precisely how the Lucan narrative implies this, however, can be best appreciated by means of a comparison with the *1QGenesis Apocryphon* and other ancient texts that include reference to the phenomenon of exorcistic rebuking, a process discussed in detail below.

In regard to our present concern, though, the most noteworthy characteristic of the *1QGenesis Apocryphon* is that it is one of two Qumranian examples of rewritten biblical narrative which, like the Bint-resh story, include either explicit or implicit contrast between exorcistic failure and success. As in the *Legend of the Possessed Princess*, in fact, so also in *1QGenesis Apocryphon* and *4QPrayer of Nabonidus*, the motif in question is part of a larger thematic pattern that sheds light on the aims of the Lucan episode. Most notably, in the Qumran narratives the contrast

---

[107] On exorcistic relocation of the demon, cf. Luke 8.31–33; and Tobit 8.3.

[108] The deity's presence and power are mediated by his statue, which is transported over land and water from Thebes to Bekhten. As discussed by W. Helck, '"Phönizische Dämonen" im frühen Griechenland', *Archäologischer Anzeiger* (1987), 445–7, and D. Harden, *The Phoenicians* (Harmondsworth, 1971), p. 82, carved images of the Egyptian deity Bes had been transported and used for similar purposes much earlier, from the fifteenth century BCE into the Iron Age.

between success and failure is collocated with (1) an insinuation that the affliction in question was due to sin;[109] (2) the verb כתש ('to afflict, shatter'), whose meaning in these contexts is very similar to that of συντρίβω in Luke 9.39;[110] (3) an emphatic difference of religion between the power that succeeds and that which fails;[111] and (4) a strong ideological bias in favour of the power that succeeds, which in both cases is politically subordinate to that which falters.[112]

As the flop of the disciples in Luke 9.37–43a is not only evaluated negatively itself in its immediate co-text but is also part of a larger section in which the image of the disciples gets worse and worse (9.1–50),[113] the third and fourth points are especially important for our purposes here. To be precise, although the contrast between the Lucan Jesus and his disciples is not the sort of ethnically orientated and holistic difference found in the Qumran contrasts, the generic similarities between these texts nevertheless confirm the highly negative implications of the Lucan contrast for the image of the disciples; yet, precisely because the disciples' identity is closely intertwined with that of Jesus whereas the identity of the failed powers in the Qumran texts is not interdependent at all with that of the Lord, the differences between these texts foreground a difficulty in Luke's strategy that is only faintly apparent at non-comparative levels of analysis: namely, the Lucan contrast cannot elevate the authority of Jesus himself without simultaneously undermining the collective honour of Jesus' group. The comparative perspective we now have on the contrast in Luke, therefore, puts a new frame around the questions asked earlier about what Luke could have expected this strategy to achieve.

Driven by this more encompassing perspective back into Luke's own narratives, we should notice at the outset that the only other passage in Luke–Acts where exorcistic failure and success are juxtaposed is Acts 19.11–20, where several authorial strategies work in concert to effect a strong sense of continuity between Jesus and Paul (see under 'Co-text' in next chapter, pp. 228–42). Furthermore, and as discussed at length in the

---

[109] *1QGenesis Apocryphon ar* xx 8–9, 15; *4QPrayer of Nabonidus ar* frags 1–3 line 4.
[110] *1QGenesis Apocryphon ar* xx 16, 20, 29; *4QPrayer of Nabonidus ar* frags 1–3 lines 1, 3.
[111] *1QGenesis Apocryphon ar* xx 18–29; *4QPrayer of Nabonidus ar* frags 1–3 lines 3–4, 7–8.
[112] *1QGenesis Apocryphon ar* xx 8–29; *4QPrayer of Nabonidus ar* frags 1–3 lines 4–8. Cf. *b. Meil.* 17b, where the emperor is represented as having relied on the exorcistic services of the second-century rabbi Simeon ben Yohai for the healing of his possessed daughter; for further comparative discussion of this tradition, see Geller, 'Jesus' Theurgic Powers', pp. 141–2.
[113] Cf. O'Toole, 'Luke's Message', p. 81; Moessner, 'Luke 9:1–50', pp. 591–4.

next chapter, the Jesus–Paul parallel that emerges in Acts 19.11–20 stems not only from features of that part of the Acts narrative itself (e.g., 19.15) but also from that material's macrostructural correspondences both to Luke 8.26–56 and to the present section (9.1–50). And finally, there is the shadowy (and therapeutically successful!) exorcist in Luke 9.49–50, whom Jesus defends against the disciples' criticism and who looks in several respects like a prefiguration of the Paul of Acts.[114] Thus, viewed within this wider set of cultural and co-textual frames, Luke's motives for utilising the contrast between Jesus and the disciples should probably be read as having less to do with the authority of Jesus than with the reputation of Paul, whose hotly contested status in Acts is discussed at greater length in the next chapter.

While a desire to enhance Jesus' authority was therefore most likely not Luke's primary motive for presenting the contrast as he presents it, the contrast does nonetheless have one facet which – especially when viewed from a comparative perspective – very much heightens the cosmic authority and power of Jesus. The feature in question is the reference in Luke 9.42 to Jesus rebuking the demon, a process whose implications are illuminated especially well by the exorcism narrated in *1QGenesis Apocryphon* but also by other ancient sources in which the lexis of exorcistic rebuke occurs.

The grammar of exorcistic rebuke in *1QGenesis Apocryphon*

In *1QGenesis Apocryphon*, whose exorcism episode is part of a novelistic rewriting[115] of Genesis 12.10–13.2 (i.e., the deception and affliction of Pharaoh in regard to Sarai's relationship with Abram),[116] the exorcistic process of rebuking (נער) is mentioned twice. In the first instance, the process is projected as an immediately desirable state of affairs when Pharaoh orders Abram to pray that the spirit[117] afflicting the ruler himself and all the males of his house 'may be commanded to depart' (ותתגער,

---

[114] On this parallel see the discussion in the next chapter under 'Macrostructural co-text and implied situation', pp. 229–31.

[115] On the genre of *1QGenesis Apocryphon* and its relationship, as rewritten Bible, to the Targumim and Midrashim in particular, see C. A. Evans, 'The Genesis Apocryphon and the Rewritten Bible', *RevQ* 13 (1988), pp. 164–5.

[116] As noted by N. Avigad and Y. Yadin, *A Genesis Apocryphon: A Scroll from the Wilderness of Judea* (Jerusalem, 1956), p. 6, the Qumran text appears to have been influenced by Gen. 20.1–18 as well, which is a doublet of the story in Gen. 12.10–13.2.

[117] Although רוח in this context has been interpreted by Avigad and Yadin, *Genesis Apocryphon*, pp. 25–6, 43–4, and M. Burrows, *More Light on the Dead Sea Scrolls* (New York, 1958), p. 389, as envisaging a gust of wind rather than an evil spirit, 'spirit' is the sense understood by most authorities, among whom are W. Kirschläger, 'Exorzismus

xx 28).[118] In the second instance, which is found in the very next line (xx 29), Abram as narrator recounts the subsequent rebuke which resulted in the spirit's actual removal. As the target of the rebuke in both instances is therefore the spirit of affliction, the basic sense of נער in these contexts ('rebuke, command to depart') is virtually identical to that of ἐπιτιμάω in Luke 9.42 (cf. Luke 4.35),[119] which is the term employed most often in the LXX to render נער into Greek.[120]

Understandably, then, with both Jesus and Abram being associated with processes of exorcistic rebuke, many scholars have been eager to stress the parallel,[121] whose significance is heightened by the similarity between Abram's therapeutic 'laying on of hands' (*1QGenesis Apocryphon* xx 29) and the Lucan Jesus' use of touch in Luke 13.10–17. Notwithstanding the similarities, however, careful examination of the whole transitivity structure of each key clause discloses several significant and largely unnoticed differences in regard to the action's participant structure. More specifically, when Pharaoh instructs Abram to pray that the 'evil spirit may be commanded to depart' from his royal house (ותתגער מנה רוחא דא באישתא, xx 28), he uses a *passive* stem (the ithpaal) of the verb נער, makes רוחא דא באישתא ('this evil spirit') the *subject* of the clause, and omits the agent who actually performs the action of rebuking. Furthermore, since Abram is not instructed to utter the command himself but only to pray that it might take place, the envisaged agent in this process is not Abram himself but rather the God to whom he prays.[122]

This conceptualisation of the action differs very significantly from that found in the key clause of Luke 9.42 (ἐπετίμησεν δὲ ὁ Ἰησοῦς τῷ πνεύματι τῷ ἀκαθάρτῳ). In contrast for instance to the passive forms of

---

in Qumran?', *Kairos* 18 (1976), p. 140; A. Dupont-Sommer, 'Exorcismes et guérisons dans les récits de Qoumrân', in G. W. Anderson et al. (eds), *VTSup* 7 (Leiden, 1960), pp. 249–50; A. E. Sekki, *The Meaning of Ruah at Qumran*, SBLDS 110 (Atlanta, 1989), p. 170; E. Osswald, 'Beobachtungen zur Erzählung von Abrahams Aufenthalt in Ägypten im "Genesis-Apokryphon" ', *ZAW* 72 (1960), p. 15; and J. A. Fitzmyer, *The Genesis Apocryphon of Cave One: A Commentary*, BibOr 18A, 2nd edn (Rome, 1971), pp. 65, 131, 138. In line with the latter view, it seems highly improbable that a gust of wind would have been understood to have afflicted only Pharaoh and his household.

[118] Unless indicated otherwise, citations from *1QGenesis Apocryphon* are from Fitzmyer, *Genesis Apocryphon*, pp. 62–6. On the sense of נער in these particular lines, see A. Caquot, 'נער', *TDOT*, III, p. 52; Fitzmyer, *Genesis Apocryphon*, p. 138.

[119] Cf. Caquot, 'נער', p. 52; Dupont-Sommer, 'Exorcismes et guérisons', p. 249 n. 3; and Kirschläger, 'Exorzismus in Qumran?', p. 142–3.

[120] See LXX Gen. 37.10; Ruth 2.16; Pss 9.6; 67.31; 105.9; 118.21; and Zech. 3.3.

[121] See, e.g., Twelftree, *Jesus the Exorcist*, p. 44; and Vermes, *Jesus the Jew*, p. 66.

[122] The structure of the rebuking process is represented essentially the same way in the ensuing narration of the demon's actual expulsion (ואתגערת מנה [רוחא באישתא], 'and the evil spirit was commanded to depart from him', xx 29).

נער in *1QGenesis Apocryphon* xx 28–29, an active form of ἐπιτιμάω is used in the Lucan story (cf. Luke 4.35); and whereas Abram prays that the exorcistic command will be given by God, the Lucan Jesus assumes authority to perform the rebuke himself, impacting the demon in his context far more directly than Abram does the one in his.[123] The functional role filled by Jesus in Luke's narrative, therefore, is essentially identical to that played in the Qumran story not by Abram but rather by God.

The impression just sketched, moreover, coheres with other assumptions and ideas attested in the most relevant comparative materials. For instance, in Zechariah 3.2 and several later texts either influenced by or similar to it, the process of rebuking Satan or other evil spirits is represented as having God as the agent of the action, a key assumption being that creatures near the top of the cosmic hierarchy cannot be appropriately rebuked by those closer to the bottom.[124] Furthermore, both the transitivity patterns and the implied cosmologies of these texts exemplify a closely related and more widely disseminated assumption, namely that real success against demonic powers requires access to divine resources. In this light, and since the Lucan Jesus shows no sign of being dependent on external sources of power and even dares to perform the exorcistic rebuke himself, the identification of his role with that of God himself is difficult to escape.

Shamanic ecstasy, exorcistic ritual and narrative transformation

In dealing above with the immediate and wider co-text of the Lucan episode, I have already commented on various types of cohesive strings and chains which tie this unit to that directly preceding it (i.e., the transfiguration story, 9.28–36). Here, however, I wish to propose that as soon as these two units are contextualised in relation to a shamanic culture like that of Jesus and the Gospels, an additional level of coherence and meaning becomes apparent in the two units' juxtaposition and sequencing.

---

[123] The contrast is overlooked by Kirschläger, 'Exorzismus in Qumran?', pp. 142–3, Vermes, *Jesus the Jew*, p. 66, and Twelftree, *Jesus the Exorcist*, p. 44, with the last two giving the erroneous impression that the exorcistic rebuke in the Qumranian text is pronounced by Abram rather than by God.

[124] See *1QWar Scroll* xiv 10 (par. *4QWar Scroll*ᵃ 8–10 i 7); Jude 9; *Tg.* Zech. 3.2; *ShR* 2.182; *AMB* amulet 1.5–6; 2.8–11; 9.2–4; 14.9; 15.24; *AMB* bowl 11.5–6; *AMB* genizah 4.3; *CAIB* 24.14; and *L.A.B.* 60.3. Certainly by the Late Antique era of the bowls and amulets but probably much earlier, both the divine rebuke of Satan and the biblical language employed to represent it had become formulaic. Cf. Caquot, 'נער', p. 52; K. J. Cathcart and R. P. Gordon (eds), *The Targum of the Minor Prophets: Translation, Introduction, Apparatus, and Notes*, vol. XIV of *The Aramaic Bible*, ed. Martin McNamara (Edinburgh, 1989), p. 190 n. 2.

In order to grasp this extra layer of significance, I should clarify what sort of figure I have in mind when referring to the 'shaman'. One influential and relatively restrictive definition that is useful for my purposes here sees the 'shaman' as someone who (a) demonstrates mastery over the spirits of fortune and misfortune; (b) has access to and makes use of powerful spirit allies; (c) attracts apprentices to whom he transmits the methods and paraphernalia of his role; (d) legitimates his practices and actions in terms of a recognised theoretical or cosmological perspective; and (e) acquires special status and recognition due to the services he provides to his clients and community.[125] Like several other recent discussions of shamanism, this same approach also assigns high import to the shaman's initiation crisis, an experience of uncontrolled spirit-possession and illness which, if healed, can function as an opportunity for psychological growth and development consonant with the profile of the 'wounded healer'.[126]

The potential utility of this image of the shaman for understanding the Lucan Jesus becomes apparent, I think, as soon as we remind ourselves of a few interrelated and relatively uncontroversial facts concerning the representation of Jesus in the present story and its narrative co-text. Perhaps the most obvious of these is that Jesus possesses a special measure of power and authority over the spirits of illness and impurity (e.g., Luke 4.36). Furthermore, and especially significant for the present discussion, just before Jesus heals the possessed boy in the present story both he and a small group of his followers have an experience which in each of the three Synoptic accounts looks very much like a visionary trance or altered state of consciousness.[127] Third, much earlier in the Gospel Jesus undergoes a rite which occasions the beginning of a unique relationship with the divine spirit (Luke 3.21–22). Shortly after this, moreover, and like many of the patients he is later described as healing, Jesus himself experiences a diabolic assault on his own person (Luke 4.1–13), going through a stage of intense conflict and trouble marked by ascetic exercise (fasting), agonistic communication with a spirit being (the devil), and proximity to death. Eventually, Jesus' special skills of healing become so firmly established that their transmission to his disciples and other types of admirers becomes a social reality.[128] Jesus also gives his healing activities something of a theoretical justification both by interpreting them as indications of the eschatological kingdom's imminence

---

[125] F. Bowie, *Anthropology of Religion*, p. 198.
[126] See, e.g., ibid., pp. 200, 205; Walsh, 'Psychological Health of Shamans', pp. 114–18; and Winkelman, *Shamanism*, pp. 79–81.
[127] Luke 9.28–36 (par. Matt. 17.1–8; Mark 9.2–8).
[128] See, e.g., Luke 9.1–9, 49–50; 10.1–20.

and by offering a generalised critique of contemporary modes of exorcistic health care.[129] And finally, several different voices in Luke's narrative bestow on Jesus uniquely high honour and status.[130]

Viewing at least part of Luke's portrait of Jesus as shaman-like, therefore, scarcely does violence to the complex integrity of Luke–Acts as a whole. Indeed, as hinted recently in separate studies by John Ashton and Stevan Davies, a proper awareness of the growing body of data regarding shamanism and spirit-possession might require a substantial rethinking of what sorts of happenings in the Synoptic tradition can be attributed a basis in real historical events.[131] For purposes of the present inquiry, though, a less far-reaching and more modest intervention is all that is needed.

In the last chapter, my discussion of cultural context touched briefly on the likelihood that the exorcism Jesus is assumed to have performed in Mark 3.22–30 took place while he was experiencing an altered state of consciousness, which was probably induced deliberately through a process of prolonged fasting and which Jesus himself interpreted as possession by the Holy Spirit (Mark 3.29). This particular combination and sequencing of religious experiences is far more similar to that narrated in Luke 9.28–43a – where Jesus' success in exorcistic healing directly follows (both in temporal point of view and in narrative sequencing) the visionary experiences narrated in the transfiguration story (9.28–36) – than a superficial comparison of the two narratives might suggest; for in both contexts exorcism is closely associated with one form or other of altered state of consciousness. But more importantly, while comparison of Luke's presentation of these materials with those of Matthew and Mark shows that redactional creativity has affected various features in each account, the more general combination and sequencing of religious experiences common to all three versions of these events undoubtedly has less to do with redactional activity or authorial intentions than with one increasingly recognised fact about visionary experience and folk healing: namely, the two occur very often together in the same context, with the former frequently preceding the latter and directly enhancing its effectiveness.

While the comparative evidence for this pattern cannot be discussed at length here, a few examples are worth mentioning from recent scholarship in this area. According to Fiona Bowie, for instance, one of the characteristic activities of shamanic practitioners among the Tungus of Eastern

---

[129] Eschatological significance: Luke 10.18; 11.20. Critique of contemporary practice: Luke 11.24–26.
[130] See, e.g., Luke 1.35, 43, 76; 2.11; 3.15–17; 4.34, 41; 9.20, 35.
[131] Ashton, *Religion of Paul*, pp. 62–72; and Davies, *Jesus the Healer*, pp. 15–21.

Siberia is that of entering into trance states which, by facilitating communication with the cosmologically appropriate spirit beings, enable the shaman to bring healing and protection to their client(s).[132] Similarly, in a summary of recent ethnographic work on shamanistic healing in traditional Korean society, Catherine Bell describes the exorcisms performed in that context not only as normally having a stage in which the shaman goes into a trance, which is construed by the participants as possession by one of the deities, but also as being preceded by a divinatory session in which trance is essential for the success of the performance.[133] And finally, in a powerful ethnography of exorcism ritual in Sri Lanka, Bruce Kapferer has found a direct relation between the trance states of the exorcists and those of the patient, the former playing a key role in the induction of the latter in more than half the performances observed by Kapferer himself.[134]

Not surprisingly, therefore, the existence of this same general pattern is repeatedly affirmed in recent cross-cultural studies of shamanic practice.[135] Furthermore, the pattern is realised in specific contexts that are directly relevant to the present inquiry: in addition to its probable occurrence in the present section of Luke and in Mark 3.20–35, it can also be observed in the Marcan juxtaposition and sequencing of Jesus' baptism and testing (Mark 1.9–13), where once again encounter with the demonic follows directly on the heels of visionary experience.[136] In this light, the pattern's potential contribution to our understanding of Luke 9.37–43a seems strong.

As for what this contribution might be, both synchronic and diachronic levels of the present analysis are powerfully affected. If for instance our definition of genre includes the idea of a staged sequence of goal-orientated activities whose basic purpose is recognised by members of a given culture,[137] then the pattern discussed above suggests that the episode in Luke 9.37–43a can be read not only as an example of a single microstructural genre (i.e., 'exorcism story') but also as merely the

---

[132] Bowie, *Anthropology of Religion*, p. 191.   [133] Bell, *Ritual*, p. 117.
[134] Kapferer, *Celebration of Demons*, p. 271.
[135] See, e.g., R. Noll, 'Mental Imagery Cultivation as a Cultural Phenomenon: The Role of Visions in Shamanism', *Current Anthropology* 26 (1985), pp. 445–6; Winkelman, *Shamanism*, pp. 85–92; and I. M. Lewis, 'Is There a Shamanic Cosmology?', in R. Mastromattei and A. Rigopoulos (eds), *Shamanic Cosmos: From India to the North Pole Star* (Venice, 1999), p. 120.
[136] See also Acts 13.1–12, where Paul and Barnabas' conflict with and victory over the diabolically inspired Elymas 'the magician' immediately follows a revelation by the Holy Spirit.
[137] Eggins, *Systemic Functional Linguistics*, pp. 26–33.

final part of a two-stage narrative complex of vision–healing. The same consideration also puts the disciples' exorcistic failure in a new light: perhaps their unwillingness to welcome the demoniac's father, for instance, was made more likely by their non-participation in the visionary séance that directly preceded and enhanced the performance of Jesus. Moreover, while the existence of this pattern in a wide range of comparative contexts scarcely proves the historicity of either the transfiguration or the exorcism in this section of the Synoptics, it does heighten the likelihood that events of this kind could have occurred and contributed to the formation of Luke 9.28–43a and its parallels.[138]

Awareness of the vision–healing sequence can contribute to the present reading in ways not yet discussed; but in order to exploit the full potential of this awareness, we must first consider select features of the Marcan parallel.

Although scepticism has been expressed at several points above about the value of simple versions of the two-source hypothesis, I have little doubt either that the Gospel of Mark was the first of the canonical Gospels to be produced or that a narrative Gospel source very much like it was employed in the making of the Gospel of Luke. Consonant with these convictions, the treatment of cultural context in the last chapter indicates several ways in which the Marcan parallel to the present story is a considerably more realistic representation of exorcism than Luke's account is. Indeed, one of the two main points I wish to make at this juncture is directly related to the observations offered earlier concerning exorcism's frequent recourse to violent and potentially dangerous methods. More specifically, by describing the exorcism's final stage in terms of death and resurrection (Mark 9.26–27),[139] the narrator of Mark's account not only provides realistic detail that coheres with the demon's pre-departure violence but also compares the final phase of the healing to experiences that strikingly fit the cross-cultural pattern of shamanic initiation illnesses.[140]

Although in theory this similarity could be entirely accidental and void of significance, a more meaningful type of relation is indicated by several factors. Both in the Gospel of Mark and in the sayings source shared by Matthew and Luke, for instance, Jesus himself undergoes a form of spirit-affliction that looks very much like a shamanic initiation crisis and which therefore would have given him an ideal basis of experience for enabling

---

[138] Cf. Ashton, *Religion of Paul*, p. 71.   [139] Cf. *Acts of Thomas* 75, 77, 81.
[140] See Walsh, 'Psychological Health of Shamans', p. 116; and Winkelman, *Shamanism*, pp. 81–3.

others with such afflictions to overcome their illness.[141] Furthermore, since Luke explicitly characterises the Jesus movement as including several former demoniacs (8.1–3) and as giving exorcism a prominent place in its activities (9.1–9; 10.1–20), we have good reasons to infer that many of the movement's members had either been healed themselves of spirit-affliction at some point or had been strongly impacted by the suffering and healing of kin with such illnesses.[142] As Jesus' own ability both to heal and to transmit therapeutic power to others depends therefore in great measure on his own prior shamanic experience of initiatory affliction, the similarity we find in Mark's account between the final stage of the boy's healing (Mark 9.26–27) and the death-and-rebirth pattern of shamanic initiation crises is scarcely surprising; for many of Jesus' patients must already have been en route to shamanic emergency – with all its dangers and possibilities – when Jesus first encountered them.

The difference between Mark and Luke on this matter therefore confirms that, as at numerous other points so also here, the Marcan account gives us a picture of Jesus' exorcistic performance which is more consonant with the images of shamanic healing in recent comparative studies of illness and folk health care. Before the implications of this judgement can be satisfactorily teased out for our understanding of Luke 9.37–43a, however, one further feature of the Marcan parallel needs to be considered.

Fasting, shamanic healing, and the text of Mark 9.29

As both the critical apparatus of the United Bible Societies' *Greek New Testament* and the marginal notes of recent translations (e.g., the NRSV) indicate, the manuscript tradition for Mark 9.29 is divided over whether the words καὶ νηστείᾳ should be included in the text. If included, the words would directly follow the noun προσευχῇ and thus form the very end of Jesus' response to the disciples' query about why they had been unable to drive out the demon. The Marcan Jesus' reply would therefore be suggesting, first, that the reason the disciples failed in this instance is that their exorcistic methods had not included both prayer and fasting, which were essential to success against this type of demon; and furthermore that

---

[141] Mark 1.12–13 (par. Matt. 4.1–11; Luke 4.1–13). On the relationship between the initiation crisis and the shaman's ability to heal others in the grip of spirit-affliction, see F. Bowie, *Anthropology of Religion*, pp. 205, 207; Winkelman, *Shamanism*, pp. 193, 267; and Lewis, *Religion in Context*, pp. 88, 91.

[142] See, e.g., Mark 7.24–30; Luke 4.38–39, 40; and the present story. Cf. Davies, *Jesus the Healer*, pp. 107–12; and Pilch, 'Sickness and Healing', pp. 187, 195.

both prayer and fasting were among the devices which Jesus himself used in this setting.

Increasingly, though, and often with a confidence befitting only the most straightforward kinds of decisions, influential commentators on Mark and authorities on the text of the NT are viewing καὶ νηστείᾳ as a doctrinally motivated scribal addition to a sentence that originally ended with προσευχῇ.[143] The precise motive for the addition, according to Bruce Metzger and others, was to legitimate later Christian and specifically monastic respect for fasting.[144] As for the mood of scholarly confidence, the editorial committee of the fourth edition of the UBS Greek NT categorises their own decision against καὶ νηστείᾳ as belonging to that class of judgements distinguished by the highest degree of text-critical certainty (i.e., level 'A'), which according to their own scales of confidence entails that they were in no doubt whatsoever about this decision;[145] when therefore in addition to all this a modern and widely respected commentary on Mark tells us that the words καὶ νηστείᾳ were often added to New Testament passages in which prayer by itself was mentioned,[146] we could scarcely be blamed if we simply joined the text-critical chorus and devoted our best energies to problems still in need of a solution.

Closer examination of the variants in question, however, as well as of the way they have been handled recently by leading critics, indicates that this difficulty is far less clear-cut than any of the short reading's chief proponents allow. For instance, in view of the established text-critical principle of beginning with the external evidence and using it as a check on the application of internal criteria,[147] the heavy reliance on fundamentally internal considerations by Metzger and the Alands – their arguments appeal more strongly to assumed differences in culture between the original author and subsequent scribes than to the date and character of the manuscript evidence[148] – is enough to arouse suspicion.

---

[143] See, e.g., M. D. Hooker, *The Gospel according to St Mark*, BNTC (London, 1991), p. 225; B. M. Metzger, *A Textual Commentary on the Greek New Testament* (Stuttgart, 1971), p. 101.

[144] Metzger, *Textual Commentary*, p. 101; B. Aland and K. Aland, *The Text of the New Testament*, trans. E. F. Rhodes (Grand Rapids and Leiden, 1987), p. 296.

[145] B. Aland et al. (eds), *The Greek New Testament*, 4th rev. edn (Stuttgart, 1993), pp. 3*, 155.

[146] See Hooker, *Mark*, p. 225, whose use of 'often' in this connection is misleading; for there are only two other instances in the NT (Acts 10.30; 1 Cor. 7.5) where 'fasting' might be a late addition to the text. Cf. B. M. Metzger, *The Text of the New Testament*, 2nd edn (Oxford, 1968), p. 203.

[147] Cf. Aland and Aland, *Text*, p. 275; Metzger, *Text of the New Testament*, p. 212.

[148] See Aland and Aland, *Text*, p. 296; Metzger, *Textual Commentary*, p. 101.

Where moreover they do comment on the manuscript tradition, they do so in a manner that only intensifies the doubts: the Alands, for instance, implicitly acknowledge that the agreement of ℵ*, B, 0274, k and Clement of Alexandria is not decisive but only 'quite adequate' support for the shorter reading,[149] while Metzger invokes support not from a particular manuscript but rather from shadowy text types whose ontological status has been seriously questioned by the Alands and others.[150]

Despite the impressive rhetoric of abstraction in appealing to 'the Alexandrian... the Western... and the Caesarean types of text',[151] Metzger's apparent confidence may stem from an inappropriate bias, criticised recently by J. K. Elliott because of its influence on the construction of the UBS and Nestle-Aland texts, in favour of readings attested in both ℵ and B regardless of the character of countervailing evidence.[152] The more modest confidence of the Alands, on the other hand, probably stems from an awareness of the strong external support for including καὶ νηστείᾳ, which is attested not only in the earliest witness pertinent to the problem – namely p45, rated by the Alands themselves as one of our three most important papyri[153] – but also in several important uncials (e.g., A, C, D, L, W, Δ, Θ and ψ), a secondary hand in ℵ, several minuscules distinguished by especially good readings in the Gospel of Mark (e.g., 33, 565, 892, 1342),[154] minuscule groups f1 and f13, and the manuscripts of the Byzantine Imperial text. Furthermore, while both the Alands and Metzger probably underestimate at least slightly the value of Codex Bezae (D^ea),[155] the Alands acknowledge that this manuscript's significance increases sharply when it agrees with other important witnesses (as it does here with p45).[156]

As p45's support for the longer reading plays an especially important role therefore in counter-balancing the combined weight of ℵ and B for the shorter text, any special tendencies this particular papyrus might have that

---

[149] Aland and Aland, *Text*, p. 296.
[150] Metzger, *Textual Commentary*, p. 101. On the difficulties of talking about 'text types', see, e.g., Aland and Aland, *Text*, p. 271.
[151] Metzger, *Textual Commentary*, p. 101.
[152] J. K. Elliott, 'The Relevance of Textual Criticism to the Synoptic Problem', in D. L. Dungan (ed.), *The Interrelations of the Gospels: A Symposium*, BETL 95 (Louvain, 1990), p. 348.
[153] Aland and Aland, *Text*, p. 240.
[154] On the quality of these particular minuscules, see Aland and Aland, *Text*, pp. 129, 131–2.
[155] On post-war textual criticism's bias against ms. D and distinctively 'Western' readings, see W. A. Strange, *The Problem of the Text of Acts*, SNTSMS 71 (Cambridge, 1992), pp. 23–4, 32–3.
[156] Aland and Aland, *Text*, p. 240.

could shed light on the present difficulty would surely be worth noting. In fact, there are two. First, as a careful study by E. C. Colwell has shown, the scribe of p45 'wielded a sharp axe';[157] indeed, as is conveniently illustrated in the Marcan passage's immediately preceding co-text (9.27), where the absence of καὶ ἀνέστη in p45 is undoubtedly secondary, this scribe had a far stronger tendency to omit words and phrases than to add them. Although the editor of p45 was, according to Colwell, seriously intent on producing a good copy, he freely exercised his editorial licence to shorten the text by omitting words whose presence is not required by clarity.[158] But just as important, his passion for conciseness extended so far that he was willing to omit the words καὶ τῆς πορνείας in the list of prohibitions in Acts 15.20, where the longer reading would clearly have served the interests of a truly ascetic scribe like that postulated by Metzger and Aland. In fact, at no point other than Mark 9.29 does p45 support a reading that could be characterised as evincing an ascetical bias.

Tenacious brevity and a willingness to background chastity are not what we should expect to find in a scribe who adds words that valorise control over the appetites of the body. And fortunately, the existence of such an improbable figure becomes unnecessary as soon as the various types of relevant internal evidence are considered carefully.

In the first place, although Metzger and Aland are demonstrably right to assume that asceticism in general and fasting in particular were much esteemed in Late Antique Christian devotion,[159] their tacit assumption that these later settings stood in significant discontinuity in this respect with the Jesus movement, its earliest successors, and its Second Temple Jewish matrix invites serious criticism. As noted in the last chapter, for instance, we should probably infer from Mark 3.20 that Jesus had been fasting in a specifically exorcistic context. Less ambiguous is the prolonged fast of Jesus in the Lucan and Matthaean versions of the temptation (Matt. 4.2; Luke 4.2), where once again the context involves conflict with the demonic. And, in addition to the lengthy list of ancient Jewish texts in which fasting is either favourably represented or

---

[157] E. C. Colwell, 'Scribal Habits in Early Papyri: A Study in the Corruption of the Text', in J. P. Hyatt (ed.), *The Bible in Modern Scholarship* (Nashville, 1965), p. 383.

[158] Ibid., pp. 378, 380, 383–5.

[159] See, e.g., P. Brown, *The Body and Society: Men, Women, and Sexual Renunciation in Early Christianity* (New York, 1988), pp. 218–24; G. Clark, 'Women and Asceticism in Late Antiquity: The Refusal of Status and Gender', in V. L. Wimbush and R. Valantasis (eds), *Asceticism* (Oxford, 1995), pp. 39–43; S. Rubenson, 'Christian Asceticism and the Emergence of the Monastic Tradition', in Wimbush and Valantasis (eds), *Asceticism*, pp. 49, 55.

directly commended,[160] the New Testament writings themselves include images of Anna the prophetess, John the Baptist and his followers, Paul and Barnabas, and the Pharisees all engaged in fasting in one sort of setting or another.[161] The argument from cultural environment, therefore, gives no more support to the shorter reading than it gives to the longer.

Probability begins to lean decisively in favour of καὶ νηστείᾳ, in fact, when the possibilities of harmonisation are taken into account. Most significant in this regard is a phenomenon akin to what Colwell discusses under the heading 'harmonisation to the immediate context',[162] which in principle includes the co-text of the entire Gospel in question. More specifically, if a scribe copying Mark 9.29 happened to recall the controversy about fasting in Mark 2.18–22,[163] where the Jesus movement is distinguished from the Pharisees and the Baptist circle by a disinclination to fast, he would have been far more likely to *omit* a commendation of fasting by Jesus than to add it.[164] To put this another way, by contributing to a logical inconsistency in the teaching of Jesus, the longer reading is clearly the more difficult; but since it also coheres with the portrayal of Jesus in Mark 3.20–35, the longer reading is not so difficult that only an accident in transmission could explain it.

Although this type of harmonising scenario is by no means unlikely, it is only one of a couple that can satisfactorily explain how καὶ νηστείᾳ could have been dropped from the original. Particularly in view of the frequent

---

[160] See, e.g., 2 Sam. 12.16–23; Neh. 9.1; 1 Esd. 8.50; Tobit 12.8; 1 Macc. 3.47; 2 Macc. 13.12; Judith 4.13; 8.6; Philo *Spec. II* 193–203. As noted by E. Isaac, 'The Significance of Food in Hebraic-African Thought and the Role of Fasting in the Ethiopian Church', in Wimbush and Valantasis (eds), *Asceticism*, pp. 336–7, the fasts in Jewish Scripture might be best considered non-ascetic; but for my present purposes neither the differences between ascetic and non-ascetic fasting nor the related difficulty of defining 'asceticism' is sufficiently important to merit discussion.

[161] See Matt. 9.14–15 (par. Mark 2.18–20; Luke 5.33–35); Luke 2.37; 18.12; Acts 13.2–3; 14.23. For additional references and discussion, see J. D. M. Derrett, 'Primitive Christianity as an Ascetic Movement', in Wimbush and Valantasis (eds), *Asceticism*, pp. 89, 93; and Böcher, *Dämonenfurcht und Dämonenabwehr*, pp. 29, 274.

[162] Colwell, 'Scribal Habits', pp. 377–8.

[163] As the controversy over fasting in Mark 2.18–22 not only belongs to the triple tradition but also has Jesus' rejection of fasting in a foregrounded position – the verb νηστεύω occurs six times in 2.18–20 – many scribes would have stood an excellent chance of remembering it. Strengthening the likelihood of this scenario is the monastic scribes' tendency to memorise extensive portions of the biblical text, on which see Metzger, *Text of the New Testament*, pp. 87, 197.

[164] The motive for omission in this case would be to remove an inconsistency from the text of the Gospel, a very common cause of textual corruption according to Aland and Aland, *Text*, p. 285.

occurrence of harmonistic corruption in the Synoptics,[165] the possibility of assimilation to the Matthaean or Lucan parallel (or both) deserves consideration. In the long form of Matthew's version (17.21), for instance, the words τοῦτο δὲ τὸ γένος οὐκ ἐκπορεύεται εἰ μὴ ἐν προσευχῇ καὶ νηστείᾳ, which lack strong support in the manuscript tradition and have a blatantly secondary character, are best explained in terms of assimilation to the longer reading of Mark 9.29.[166] Nevertheless, as Matthew's account is itself textually unstable on the matter, greater insight into the origins and history of the Marcan variants can be obtained by comparison with Luke's account, which has no manuscript support at all for the reference to fasting but does include mention of prayer in the first part of the vision–healing sequence (Luke 9.28–29). Consequently, and especially since Mark is known to have been more prone to harmonistic corruption by its Synoptic parallels than vice versa,[167] a scribe whose exemplar of Mark had the longer reading of 9.29 but who also knew the Lucan version of the story could easily have been tempted to revise the Marcan text by omitting the reference to fasting.

Whatever source-critical assumptions the interpreter might have, this solution of the difficulty in Mark 9.29 has important implications for a comparative reading of the Lucan episode. Most notably, since fasting is a widely attested method of effecting altered states of consciousness conducive to healing and other shamanic performances,[168] the Lucan portrayal of Jesus lacks the shamanic aspect of the Marcan account on this particular detail. Furthermore, although the Lucan emphasis on prayer in 9.28–29 is at least indirectly relevant to the exorcistic victory narrated immediately afterwards, the role of prayer in exorcism is far less explicit in Luke than it is in Mark, where the connection is asserted very directly (Mark 9.29). And finally, these last two points of divergence contribute

---

[165] See Elliott, 'Relevance of Textual Criticism', pp. 348–55; Aland and Aland, *Text*, pp. 285–6; Colwell, 'Scribal Habits', pp. 377–8.

[166] Aland and Aland, *Text*, p. 296.   [167] Ibid., p. 285.

[168] On fasting as a method of inducing religious ecstasy in antiquity, see W. C. Bushell, 'Psychophysiological and Comparative Analysis of Ascetico-Meditational Discipline: Toward a New Theory of Asceticism', in Wimbush and Valantasis (eds), *Asceticism*, pp. 553–7, 562; M. D. Swartz, '*Hêkālôt Rabbātî* §§ 297–306: A Ritual for the Cultivation of the Prince of the Torah', in V. L. Wimbush (ed.), *Ascetic Behavior in Greco-Roman Antiquity: A Sourcebook*, Studies in Antiquity & Christianity (Minneapolis, 1990), p. 229; E. R. Dodds, *The Greeks and the Irrational* (Berkeley, 1951), pp. 110, 140–1; G. Luck, *Arcana Mundi: Magic and the Occult in the Greek and Roman Worlds* (Baltimore, 1985), pp. 8, 11. For anthropological discussion of similar phenomena in more recent contexts, see F. D. Goodman, *How about Demons? Possession and Exorcism in the Modern World* (Bloomington, 1988), p. 11; Lewis, *Ecstatic Religion*, p. 34; 'Shamanic Cosmology', p. 120; Winkelman, *Shamanism*, pp. 149–50.

to a larger pattern of differences that involve the death-and-resurrection motif (Mark 9.26–27), the response of the bystanders (Luke 9.43a), and the timing of the demon's final assault on the boy. By comparison with Mark on these points, and notwithstanding the shamanic traits found in Luke's own portrayal of Jesus, the Lucan account has Jesus acting less like a shaman than like the highest source of exorcistic authority in the cosmos.

Conclusion

My application of sociostylistics to Luke 9.37–43a has facilitated noteworthy findings in three interrelated areas of interpretation. First of all, in regard to the passage's immediate co-text, it has helped to identify an instance of chiasm that indicates not only the most prominent concerns in Luke 9.1–50 as a whole – Jesus' messiahship, suffering, and example for his followers (9.18–27) – but also the relative prominence of exorcism within this larger structure. More specifically, although the exorcism theme in Luke 9.1–50 lacks some of the prominence given to the key motifs in 9.18–27, its presence at both the beginning and the end of this section (9.1–2, 6–7, 11, 37–43a, 49–50) causes it to stand out from the text's background and to possess at least an intermediate level of salience.

On the one hand, then, exorcism is far too prominent in this section to be dismissed as a minor or tangential concern; but on the other hand, it is also clearly subordinate to other interests that have a more direct relation to the life of discipleship. In my treatment below of Acts 16.16–18, where exorcism is found to contribute to an even larger and more encompassing literary macrostructure than that discovered in Luke 9.1–50, it occupies a very similar position in the implied author's hierarchy of interests, though the content of his chief concern emerges more clearly in that discussion than it has emerged here.

In regard to the linguistic style of the exorcism episode itself, the most striking phenomenon is found not on any single level of the text's structure but rather in a cluster of features that semantically reinforce each other across several different levels. The features in question – for instance the transitivity and parallelism of the three clauses in 9.42b (ἐπετίμησεν δὲ ὁ Ἰησοῦς τῷ πνεύματι τῷ ἀκαθάρτῳ καὶ ἰάσατο ... καὶ ἀπέδωκεν), and the implicature produced by the reference to 'the majesty of God' in 9.43a – cumulatively serve to frontground the authority and honour of Jesus, whose position in the narrative's assumed cosmic hierarchy is functionally equivalent to that of God. Indirectly, this emphasis also strengthens the defence of Paul in the Lucan writings' final exorcism story; for as discussed further in the next chapter the portrayal of Paul in Acts 16.16–40 derives much of its force from the Jesus–Paul parallels between that section and the stories in Luke 8.26–39 and 9.37–43a.

Finally, much of my analysis of the story's cultural context either agrees with or strongly reinforces the key findings of the stylistic analysis. Comparative study of several ancient sources in regard to the contrast between exorcistic success and failure, the phenomenon of exorcistic rebuke, and the power necessary for victory against demons confirms that the authority attributed to Jesus in this episode is of a divine character. Yet not all of the comparative evidence fits so neatly into this pattern. Most notably, although Jesus is more conspicuously divine and less shamanic in Luke 9.28–43a than he is in the Marcan parallel (9.2–8, 14–29), the vision–healing sequence in Luke 9.28–43a possesses a certain shamanic quality that probably goes back to Jesus himself and therefore gives at least a vague sense of this tradition's ideological trajectory over time. Precisely in giving this sense, however, and thus in preserving traces of an earlier and less supramundane image of Jesus, this same feature also stands in tension with some of the key emphases in Luke's own adaptation of the vision–healing tradition.

4

PAUL, JEWISH IDENTITY, AND THE EXORCISM IN ACTS 16.16–18

In chapter 3 my discovery of a chiastic pattern in Luke 9.1–50 was shown to have several important consequences for the interpretation of 9.37–43a in particular. That same discovery also has significant implications for my reading of the story in Acts 16.16–18. Most notably, the subordination of exorcism as a theme to Luke's interest in the death of Jesus and its implications for discipleship (Luke 9.18–27) creates an expectation that subsequent references to exorcism in Luke's volumes may likewise be part of some larger schematic structure whose primary emphasis falls on non-exorcistic concerns. But just as significant, when Luke 9.1–50 and its constituent units are read not only as part of the Lucan Gospel but also as integral components of the larger macrotextual unity of Luke–Acts, that section's concluding element – the interchange about the strange exorcist who is not associated with the twelve but none the less performs exorcisms in Jesus' name (9.49–50) – offers strong clues regarding the identity of the particular schematic structure that gives the Acts 16 story its specific rhetorical weight in Luke's argument. For reasons discussed fully below, that structure is best understood as consisting of the Jesus–Paul parallels, which, though increasingly recognised for their role in tying Luke's two volumes together into a single story, have specific features that are often overlooked.

In addition to forming a parallel with the exorcism material in Luke 9.1–50 (especially vv. 49–50), and as set forth in detail below, the story in Acts 16.16–18 also contributes to a parallel with the narrative in Luke 8.26–39, which subsequently helps to effect yet another Jesus–Paul scheme in Acts 19.11–20. As these correspondences cumulatively register a powerful impact on the macrostructural texture of Luke–Acts as a whole and therefore possess a high degree of aesthetic salience, they enable the present episode to exert a strong revisionary influence on the meanings of its antecedent co-text – including most especially the last two exorcism stories in the Gospel – and they therefore affect very strongly the cumulative force of the exorcism stories as a group. As in

Luke 9.1–50, moreover, so also in the more encompassing schemes that emerge in the present episode, exorcism itself should be seen neither as the main ideological interest – precisely what *that* might be is taken up briefly in the sections below on co-text and context of culture – nor as a merely peripheral concern shrinking into the background. Why exorcism ought to be viewed instead as possessing an intermediate level of prominence in Luke's volumes, what other concerns in the rhetorical programme of Luke–Acts take priority over it, and how it functions in relation to those concerns are the key questions addressed in the ensuing analysis, whose key text reads in Greek as follows:

> 16 Ἐγένετο δὲ πορευομένων ἡμῶν εἰς τὴν προσευχὴν παιδίσκην τινὰ ἔχουσαν πνεῦμα πύθωνα ὑπαντῆσαι ἡμῖν, ἥτις ἐργασίαν πολλὴν παρεῖχεν τοῖς κυρίοις αὐτῆς μαντευομένη. 17 αὕτη κατακολουθοῦσα τῷ Παύλῳ καὶ ἡμῖν ἔκραζεν λέγουσα· οὗτοι οἱ ἄνθρωποι δοῦλοι τοῦ θεοῦ τοῦ ὑψίστου εἰσίν οἵτινες καταγγέλλουσιν ὑμῖν ὁδὸν σωτηρίας. 18 τοῦτο δὲ ἐποίει ἐπὶ πολλὰς ἡμέρας. διαπονηθεὶς δὲ Παῦλος καὶ ἐπιστρέψας τῷ πνεύματι εἶπεν· παραγγέλλω σοι ἐν ὀνόματι Ἰησοῦ Χριστοῦ ἐξελθεῖν ἀπ' αὐτῆς· καὶ ἐξῆλθεν αὐτῇ τῇ ὥρᾳ.

Cohesion, boundaries and story structure

Much of this story's internal cohesion stems from lexical repetition and co-reference. For instance, after using the first person plural pronoun ἡμῶν in 16.16a ('as *we* were going to the synagogue'), the narrator employs the same pronoun on two other occasions before the end of the unit: first, in the immediately ensuing clause (παιδίσκην τινὰ ἔχουσαν πνεῦμα πύθωνα ὑπαντῆσαι ἡμῖν, 16.16), where ἡμῖν includes both Paul and his travelling companions; and again in 16.17, where Paul is not encompassed by ἡμῖν but is none the less associated closely with its referent. In addition to stringing together the clauses of verses 16 and 17 to form a larger supra-sentential piece of discourse, this repetition of the first person plural pronoun heightens the authority of the narrator's representation of the actions in question.

The cohesion of the unit is reinforced and extended by the occurrences of the noun πνεῦμα in verses 16 and 18. In 16.16, where the particular spirit in question is mentioned for the first time in Luke–Acts, the noun phrase that denotes it (i.e., πνεῦμα πύθωνα 'a pythian spirit'[1]) is

---
[1] The various difficulties presented by this phrase are discussed below under 'Lexis', pp. 214–15.

appropriately anarthrous; consequently, when πνεῦμα is used again in 16.18 to denote the same spirit, the anaphoric article that occurs with it encourages the reader to infer a reference chain between the term's two occurrences in verses 16 and 18.

Like the pythian spirit, the slave-girl has not participated in any of the action prior to 16.16, where she is introduced by the indefinite expression παιδίσκην τινά. Immediately thereafter she is denoted by the pronouns ἥτις and αὐτῆς in 16.16, αὕτη in 16.17, and αὐτῆς in 16.18. In a relatively short stretch of text, therefore, the girl is mentioned on five occasions by four different lexemes, with all four of the pronominal expressions pointing back to the referent signified by παιδίσκην τινά. By using a variety of co-referential expressions to refer repeatedly to this one participant, the narrator effects a strong sense of cohesion between these clauses.

Some of these same devices also help to indicate the location of this unit's boundaries. As noted above, neither the slave-girl nor the spirit plays any role in the larger narrative prior to 16.16, so that their introduction together at this point indicates the existence of a boundary between verses 15 and 16. Similarly, as the spirit exits the story at the end of 16.18 and the girl takes leave in the very next clause, the closing boundary of the same unit would seem to lie somewhere around the end of 16.18 and the beginning of 16.19.[2] In order to identify this latter seam more precisely, we merely need to observe that the climax of this episode is reached in the final clauses of 16.18, where Paul's expulsion of the spirit is narrated. Thus, although these verses have significant ties to their immediate co-text (i.e., 16.11–15, 19–40), they also constitute a fully formed story by themselves.[3]

As for the story's structure, the exorcistic resolution (16.18) has just been noted. In 16.16 a concise 'orientation' is given, indicating *who* was involved in the action: Paul and his companions, the girl, the spirit who inspires her speech, and the girl's masters; *when* it occurred: as Paul and his companions were travelling to the synagogue and after the girl had followed them for many days; and *where*: en route to the imagined house of prayer (cf. 16.13). The 'complicating action' comes in 16.17–18a,

---

[2] Cf. P. R. Trebilco, 'Paul and Silas – "Servants of the Most High God" (Acts 16:16–18)', *JSNT* 36 (1989), p. 58.

[3] Although the events of 16.19–24 arise very directly from those narrated in 16.16–18, the effort by M. Veillé ('Ecriture et prédication: Actes 16/16–24', *ETR* 54 (1979), 271–8) to read 16.16–24 as the basic unit of analysis is not convincing, chiefly because 16.19–24 contains nothing that can function as a denouement of the proposed unit. Views similar to Veillé's, with comparable liabilities, are commended by G. Schille, *Die Apostelgeschichte des Lukas*, THKNT 5 (Berlin, 1983), p. 346; and J. Roloff, *Die Apostelgeschichte*, NTD 5 (Göttingen, 1981), pp. 242–3.

where the girl's relentless pursuit and unsolicited endorsement of Paul's group are narrated. And finally, there is an especially significant instance of 'evaluation' in 16.16, where the narrator characterises the slave-girl as one 'who brought great gain to her masters by soothsaying' (trans. mine), a characterisation that deserves at least brief attention here.

In 16.16, by characterising the girl's oracular behaviour as a means of great income for her owners, the narrator insinuates that the owners were using her in a greedy and dishonourable way.[4] Furthermore, by labelling the same activity with a term whose usage in the LXX is normally associated with the illegitimate intermediary practices of Israel's enemies (μαντεύομαι), the narrator characterises the girl as a virtual symbol of paganism, an embodiment of conduct forbidden in Jewish Scripture, a walking and talking antonym of Judaism.[5] As a result the immediately ensuing events – most notably the expulsion of the pythian spirit (16.18) but also the consequent accusations brought against Paul and Silas (16.19–21) – ultimately convey an image of the narrator and his companions (especially Paul) as Torah-observant Jews, who not only stand firm against the forces of paganism but also subvert the most acquisitive and immoral elements of the same system. The Lucan Paul and his friends, therefore, incarnate an alternative blend of values that pious Jews, proselytes and God-fearers in Luke's audience could easily have found attractive.

Repetition and paronomasia

Several instances of repetition in 16.16–18 not only contribute to the story's cohesion but also shape its ideational and rhetorical effects. The two occurrences of the name Παῦλος in verses 17 and 18 form a notable

---

[4] Luke's criticism of the girl's masters should be read not as indicative of hostility to slavery per se but rather as a reflection of hostility towards the accumulation of capital (especially that obtained through deceptive oracles). On the accumulation of capital as 'greed' in the ancient Mediterranean world, see, e.g., Malina, *New Testament World*, pp. 97–9; on the generally unsympathetic attitude of upper-class Romans towards the circumstances of their slaves, and on early Christianity's implicit endorsement of the slavery system, see K. R. Bradley, *Slaves and Masters in the Roman Empire: A Study in Social Control* (Oxford, 1987), pp. 33–40, 114.

[5] In LXX Deut. 18.10; 1 Sam. 28.9(8); 2 Kgs 17.17; Jer. 34(27).9; Ezek. 12.24; 13.6, 23; 21.21(26); 21.23(28), 29(34); and 22.28, the activity denoted by the verb μαντεύομαι is either prohibited or represented in a very negative manner. Cf. B. Trémel, 'Voie du salut et religion populaire: Paul et Luc face au risque de paganisation', *LumVie* 30/153–4 (1981), p. 101; and S. H. Kanda, 'The Form and Function of the Petrine and Pauline Miracle Stories in the Acts of the Apostles (Part 1)', PhD dissertation, Claremont Graduate School (1974), p. 199.

example. More specifically, as the use of first person plural verbs and pronouns in the immediately preceding co-text is sufficient on its own to imply the participation of Paul in the action, the explicit mention of Paul's name in 16.17 in conjunction with the pronoun (τῷ Παύλῳ καὶ ἡμῖν) marks a significant deviation in usage: whereas earlier Paul was included in the pronoun's referent (e.g., 16.15, 16), here in verses 17 and 18 he is implicitly excluded from it. Why the shift? As it scarcely aids clarity, it must be attributed either to compositional infelicity (perhaps careless editing of a source) or to a desire to highlight the participation of Paul in particular at this point. The latter option is by far the better;[6] for as discussed further in several of the sections below, the storyteller was virtually required to foreground Paul at this point in order to achieve his most important rhetorical aim in this unit, namely to produce a strong sense of continuity and harmony between Paul and Jesus.

Another noteworthy instance of repetition involves the morpheme -αγγελλ, which is present in both καταγγέλλουσιν (16.17) and παραγγέλλω (16.18). The two words' linear and semantic proximity to one another is sufficient by itself to suggest the possibility of a deliberate paronomasia. Yet far more than proximity contributes to this impression. The combination of vowel sounds and consonants at the end of παραγγέλλω σοι ἐν (i.e., ω + σοι + ἐν), for instance, are phonetically very similar to those in the ending of καταγγέλλουσιν (i.e., -ουσιν), creating an instance of end-rhyme that reinforces the correspondence between the verb stems. Furthermore, and as discussed in greater detail below under 'Co-text', the storyteller's keen-witted use of ἐξέρχομαι in 16.18–19 to denote both the expulsion of the spirit and the consequent evaporation of the slave-owners' income displays the same capacity for play that I see in 16.17–18. The main function of the wordplay in 16.17–18 would probably be to underscore the difference between the religion of Paul and that of the girl. More specifically, whereas the girl's pythian spirit implicitly excludes itself from the missionaries' wide audience (οὗτοι οἱ ἄνθρωποι... καταγγέλλουσιν ὑμῖν), Paul explicitly addresses his highly direct and antagonistic response solely to the spirit (παραγγέλλω σοι ἐν ὀνόματι Ἰησοῦ Χριστοῦ); thereby, Paul emerges as a Jewish messianist who has no room for contaminating alignments with pagan manticism.

---

[6] Cf. S. E. Porter, 'The "We" Passages', in D. W. J. Gill and C. Gempf (eds), *The Book of Acts in Its Graeco-Roman Setting*, vol. II of *The Book of Acts in Its First Century Setting* (Grand Rapids and Carlisle, 1994), p. 563; and E. Haenchen, 'Das "Wir" in der Apostelgeschichte und das Itinerar', in *Gott und Mensch: Gesammelte Aufsätze* (Tübingen, 1965), I, p. 249.

Finally, we should not overlook the two occurrences of ἐξέρχομαι in 16.18, where the term is used both in Paul's exorcistic command (παραγγέλλω σοι ἐν ὀνόματι 'Ιησοῦ Χριστοῦ ἐξελθεῖν ἀπ' αὐτῆς) and in the narrator's description of the spirit's response (καὶ ἐξῆλθεν αὐτῇ τῇ ὥρᾳ). To be sure, the use of ἐξέρχομαι to denote both the exorcistic word of Paul and the actual departure of the spirit is almost predictable in this context, for the same verb functions in both of these ways in the Lucan Gospel's first two exorcism narratives (Luke 4.35; 8.29, 33); yet here in Acts 16.18 the two occurrences are so close to one another – they are separated by only three words (ἀπ' αὐτῆς· καὶ) – that the concord between command and response has special salience.[7] As the same connection is underscored even further by the intensive pronoun αὐτῇ (with τῇ ὥρᾳ directly after ἐξῆλθεν), which stresses the command's immediate success,[8] the authority of Paul as a legitimate representative of Jesus Christ stands out as an especially prominent motif in this episode.

Lexis

While some terms in this story merit special attention because they make a distinctive contribution to the text's illocutionary force, others deserve comment chiefly because they present interpretative difficulties. The last word in the clause πορευομένων ἡμῶν εἰς τὴν προσευχήν (16.16), on the other hand, needs analysis for both of these reasons. Whereas the normal function of προσευχή in New Testament usage is to denote 'prayer',[9] here in 16.16 it is clearly referring to something else. A well-established alternative usage is the metonymic sense 'house of prayer', which, as discussed further below, overlaps one of the most common meanings of συναγωγή (i.e., the local Jewish assembly, not necessarily including a building).[10] Nevertheless, the occurrence of προσευχή in the present story has been interpreted by many commentators as referring neither to a prayer-house nor to a local Jewish assembly but rather to 'an informal

---

[7] To adapt the words of Tannehill, *Narrative Unity*, II, p. 198: when the evil spirit 'went out', the owners' profits 'went out'; cf. M. Lods, 'Argent et magie dans le livre des Actes', *PLu* 28/4 (1980), p. 289.

[8] Cf. J. Jeremias, ''Εν ἐκείνῃ τῇ ὥρᾳ, (ἐν) αὐτῇ τῇ ὥρᾳ', *ZNW* 42 (1949), pp. 215–16; and BAGD, s.v. 'ὥρα'.

[9] See, e.g., Luke 6.12; Acts 1.14; 10.4; Rom. 1.10; Eph. 1.16; Col. 4.12; 1 Pet. 3.7; Rev. 5.8; 8.3.

[10] BAGD, s.v. 'συναγωγή'; and Cohen, *From the Maccabees to the Mishnah*, pp. 111–12. See also the thorough treatment of the inscriptional evidence by I. Levinskaya, *The Book of Acts in Its Diaspora Setting*, vol. V of *The Book of Acts in Its First Century Setting* (Grand Rapids and Carlisle, 1996), pp. 213–25.

meeting place, perhaps in the open air'.[11] The justification normally given for this reading is that the place envisaged in 16.16 is represented in the preceding co-text (16.13) as occupied solely by women, the quorum of ten men necessary for the assembly having thus not been present.[12]

This latter interpretation, however, finds no support either in the usage of προσευχή in other texts from this period or in a careful reading of Acts 16.13–16 itself. For instance, whenever Philo and Josephus use προσευχή to refer to something other than prayer, they envisage a meeting house or an enclosed structure of some sort;[13] not once do they hint that a place in the open air might be in view. Furthermore, as the narrator describes the place in 16.13 as one he and his companions merely '*supposed*' (ἐνομίζομεν) was the site of a προσευχή, what he subsequently says they actually found in this location – namely, a group of women by the river – should not be identified as the denotatum of our noun. Indeed, as the προσευχή in 16.13 is not presented as a reality but only as an erroneous supposition,[14] there is no reason to interpret the word as having anything other than its usual sense.[15] Read this way, moreover, the term serves in verses 13 and 16 to reinforce one of the narrator's favourite

[11] BAGD, s.v. 'προσευχή'; cf. R. A. Culpepper, 'Paul's Mission to the Gentile World: Acts 13–19', *RevExp* 71/4 (1974), p. 494; Fitzmyer, *Acts*, p. 585.

[12] Cf. W. Stegemann, *Zwischen Synagoge und Obrigkeit: Zur historischen Situation der lukanischen Christen*, FRLANT 152 (Göttingen, 1991), p. 212 n. 88; F. F. Bruce, *The Acts of the Apostles: The Greek Text with Introduction and Commentary* (Grand Rapids and Leicester, 1983), p. 358.

[13] See, e.g., Philo *Flacc.* 41.7; 45.2; 48.1; 49.4; 53.2; 122.3; *Leg.* 132.6; 134.3; 137.3; 138.3; 148.3; 152.2; 156.2; 157.3; 165.1; 191.1; 346.3; 371.3; Josephus *Vita* 277.2; 280.5; 293.6. As προσευχή in many of these contexts denotes a structure that has either been burnt with fire or demolished in some other fashion, a physical building of some kind must be in view. On προσευχή in Philo in particular, see Goodenough, *Jewish Symbols*, II, pp. 85–6. On the relevant inscriptional evidence, see Levinskaya, *Diaspora Setting*, pp. 213–25; Schürer, *History of the Jewish People*, II, pp. 425–6 n. 5; 439–41.

[14] In several other ancient Greek texts but especially elsewhere in Luke–Acts, the grammatical complement of νομίζω is a thought or belief implied to be erroneous; see, e.g., Plato *Ap.* 24b; 1 Tim. 6.5; Luke 2.44; 3.23; Acts 7.25; 8.20; 14.19; 16.27. Neither Barrett, *Acts*, II, p. 781, nor Fitzmyer, *Acts*, p. 585, both of whom decide against the presence of a building, explores the potential relationship between the meaning of ἐνομίζομεν in 16.13 and προσευχήν in vv. 13 and 16.

[15] *Contra* Stegemann, *Synagoge und Obrigkeit*, p. 212 n. 88. On the relationship between νομίζω in 16.13 and the meaning of προσευχή in vv. 13 and 16, see C. Zettner, *Amt, Gemeinde, und kirchliche Einheit in der Apostelgeschichte des Lukas*, Europäische Hochschulschriften 23/423 (Frankfurt, 1991), p. 306 n. 1. On the stance defended above, see also Klauck, *Magie und Heidentum*, p. 78; M. Hengel, 'Proseuche und Synagoge: Jüdische Gemeinde, Gotteshaus und Gottesdienst in der Diaspora und in Palästina', in G. Jeremias et al. (eds), *Tradition und Glaube: Das frühe Christentum in seiner Umwelt* (Göttingen, 1971), p. 171; and Schürer, *History of the Jewish People*, II, pp. 439–40.

images, namely that of Paul as a loyal Jew who remains committed to his ancestral traditions; for in addition to continuing to observe the sabbath (16.13), he seeks out a Jewish house of prayer in each city he visits, even in those which happen not to have one (16.13, 16).[16]

Comparable difficulty surrounds the use of πύθων in 16.16, where the problem is compounded by uncertainties about the identity of the text. Although the genitive form πύθωνος is supported by many manuscripts (e.g., p45 and the Majority text), the accusative πύθωνα has weightier support among early witnesses and represents the more difficult reading.[17] What makes the accusative more difficult, it should be noted, is the ambiguity of its relationship with the word πνεῦμα, which immediately precedes it in the relative clause τινὰ ἔχουσαν πνεῦμα πύθωνα. As for the possibilities, πύθωνα in that context could be either (1) appositional to πνεῦμα ('a spirit – that is, *a python*'),[18] or (2) appositional to παιδίσκην τινὰ ἔχουσαν πνεῦμα as a whole ('a spirit-possessed slave-girl – that is, *a ventriloquist*'),[19] or (3) adjectival, qualifying πνεῦμα ('a *pythian* spirit', i.e., a spirit subordinate to the deity Apollo and responsible for inspiring the oracular revelations of diviners[20]).

On strictly lexical grounds the first of these options should probably be dismissed; for the use of πύθων as a substantive to denote a spirit that inspires the utterances of a soothsayer is not attested prior to its occurrence in the *Pseudo-Clementine Homilies* 9.6.13,[21] which is probably no earlier than the first half of the third century. Indeed, apart from its many occurrences as a proper name, πύθων normally serves in earlier and contemporaneous references to denote either the dragon slain by Apollo or any of a number of ventriloquists.[22]

---

[16] Cf. Zettner, *Amt*, pp. 305–6.   [17] Cf. Metzger, *Textual Commentary*, p. 448.

[18] Cf. T. Hopfner, *Griechisch-Ägyptischer Offenbarungszauber*, Studien zur Palaeographie und Papyruskunde 21 (Leipzig, 1924; repr., Amsterdam 1983), II/2, p. 133 (par. 276); E. Langton, *Essentials of Demonology* (London, 1949), pp. 177–8; I. H. Marshall, *The Acts of the Apostles*, TNTC (Leicester and Grand Rapids, 1980), p. 268; Roloff, *Apostelgeschichte*, p. 245.

[19] See, e.g., Plutarch *De Def. Or.* 414.e; and Hesychius *Lexicon* (A–O) ε.123, who identifies πύθων as a synonym of ἐγγαστρίμυθος, ἐγγαστρίμαντις, and στερνόμαντις. Although πύθων itself is unattested in the LXX, ἐγγαστρίμυθος occurs there fifteen times, each of which has negative connotations.

[20] Cf. W. Foerster, 'πύθων', in *TDNT* VI, p. 920; I. R. Reimer, *Women in the Acts of the Apostles: A Feminist Liberation Perspective*, trans. L. M. Maloney (Minneapolis, 1995), pp. 154–6; BDF, p. 126.

[21] Cf. Foerster, 'πύθων', pp. 918–19.

[22] The monster slain by Apollo: Strabo 9.3.12; Plutarch *Aetia Romana et Graeca* 293.c; 294.f; *De fac.* 945.a–b; *De Is. et Os.* 360.e; Lucian *Salt.* 38; Pausanius 2.7.7; and 2.30.3. Ventriloquists: see n. 20 above.

If the choice between the remaining options had to be made strictly on the basis of usage in texts from around Luke's time or earlier, the preferred option would be to take πύθωνα as appositional to παιδίσκην τινὰ ἔχουσαν πνεῦμα as a whole, the resultant sense being 'a spirit-possessed slave-girl – that is, a ventriloquist'. Yet this option too is plagued by serious liabilities, the most notable of which is collocational in nature. More specifically, by having πύθωνα refer back to παιδίσκην, and with πνεῦμα thus being left unmodified, this option requires the narrator to deviate from a pattern present in every other New Testament passage in which πνεῦμα is used with ἔχω to signify demon-possession: namely, πνεῦμα is always accompanied in these cases by a modifier indicating what kind of spirit was 'had'.[23] In this light πύθωνα should almost certainly be interpreted as functioning adjectivally to qualify πνεῦμα, their combined sense being 'a pythian spirit'.[24]

Unlike the demonic beings in Luke's Gospel, therefore, who make their victims impure and ill,[25] the spirit in the present story is characterised chiefly by its routine inspiration of oracular pronouncements. This sort of spirit would have been understood by most pagans in Luke's milieu as either beneficial or neutral;[26] but ultimately, from the perspective of the narrator of Acts, it is just as noxious as any of the impure spirits expelled earlier by Jesus. And one of the ways this latter evaluation is communicated is through the word used in 16.16 to denote the girl's oracular practice.

The term employed in that context is μαντεύομαι, which has a wide range of potential meanings in texts from around Luke's time. Occasionally, for instance, either this verb or one of its compound forms (e.g., διαμαντεύομαι) is used to convey the idea of consulting an oracle.[27] In other contexts one term or other from the same group (e.g., προμαντεύομαι) signifies the process of having a vague premonition, as opposed to a clear vision or confident expectation, concerning an event in the future.[28] In

---

[23] See Mark 3.30; 7.25; 9.17; Luke 4.33; 13.11; Acts 8.7; and 19.13.

[24] Cf. Schille, *Apostelgeschichte*, pp. 343–5; I. R. Reimer, *Women*, pp. 154–6. On the adjectival use of substantives, see BDF, p. 126, which cites πνεῦμα πύθωνα in particular as an example. Luke is especially fond of this kind of construction, other examples being Luke 24.19; Acts 1.16; 3.14; 10.28; and 22.3.

[25] E.g., Luke 4.31–37; 8.26–39; 9.37–43.

[26] Cf. I. R. Reimer, *Women*, pp. 166–7; and see below, pp. 243–5.

[27] See, e.g., Josephus *Ap.* 1.306; Plutarch *Thes.* 36.1; *De Pyth. or.* 403.b, d; *Aetia Romana et Graeca* 294.e; 302.d.

[28] See esp. Philo *Conf.* 118.6, where the vague perception associated with μαντεύομαι is contrasted with the clear foresight associated with προοράω; cf. Philo *Jos.* 106.4; 182.4; *Cher.* 27.2; and Josephus *J.W.* 1.610.

still other settings it envisages a more specific prediction without external inspiration.[29] And finally, it sometimes denotes oracular activity inspired by an intermediary spirit.[30]

Particularly as the girl in Acts 16 is said to have been possessed by 'a pythian spirit', whose *raison d'être* would have been precisely to inspire oracular speech, the sense that best fits Acts 16.16 is that mentioned last. At the same time, though, and especially in a polyphonic context like Luke's, μαντευομένη could easily have conveyed ideological nuances beyond the basic sense just established. In order to determine what these extra meanings might have been, we need to consider above all its usage in the LXX, not only because a distinctively septuagintal register has already been effected for the story in 16.16 ('Εγένετο δέ[31]) but also because the connotations of μαντεύομαι in the LXX fit very well in the context of the present episode.

Significantly, every occurrence of μαντεύομαι in the LXX serves to designate a process of divination.[32] As an intermediary agent of inspiration is explicitly mentioned in two of these contexts (Deut. 18.10; 1 Sam. 28.8), moreover, and should probably be understood as implicitly present in the others, the term's basic sense in the LXX is very similar to that established above for its use in Acts 16.16. But more importantly, in all of its septuagintal occurrences μαντεύομαι carries pejorative connotations. In Deuteronomy 18.10, for example, μαντεύομαι designates intermediary behaviour prohibited by the Lord himself. In 2 Kings 17.17 it denotes one of several abominable activities that provoke the Lord to punish Israel by means of the Assyrians. And in 1 Samuel 28.9(8) it refers to the necromantic (and thus illegal) process which the medium of Endor – a peripheral and thus unholy intermediary – is requested to perform for King Saul. In summary, in the LXX μαντεύομαι invariably designates oracular practices that are evaluated negatively by the authors of Jewish Scripture.

In this light, and with the spirit that inspires the girl's mantic activities eventually being cast out 'in the name of Jesus Christ' (16.18), μαντεύομαι

---

[29] See, e.g., Philo *Spec.* 3.18, where the predictions used by kings to justify fratricide are neither assumed nor implied to be divinely inspired.

[30] See, e.g., Plutarch *De Alex. fort.* 331.d; Josephus *Ant.* 6.330; *J.W.* 3.405.

[31] On Luke's use of the LXX to effect a contextually appropriate 'biblical' style, see, e.g., Barrett, *Acts*, II, pp. xlv–xlvi. Surprisingly, though, neither Barrett, *Acts*, II, pp. 784–5, nor Fitzmyer, *Acts*, p. 586, comments on the septuagintal usage of μαντεύομαι, whose connotations in the present context affect how the anarthrous character of ὁδὸν σωτηρίας should be understood (16.17, discussed below).

[32] See LXX Deut. 18.10; 1 Sam. 28.8; 2 Kgs 17.17; Mic. 3.11; Jer. 34.9; Ezek. 12.24; 13.6, 23; 21.21, 23, 29; 22.28.

probably had the same sort of pejorative overtones for the author and first readers of Acts 16.16 that it had for the translators of the LXX.[33] Had the author wished to present the girl's activity in a more positive fashion, he could easily have labelled it προφητεύουσα instead of μαντευομένη.[34] And finally, as the word's derogatory overtones in 16.16 echo the Jewish biblical point of view concerning illegitimate intermediaries,[35] they help to characterise Paul and his companions as keepers of Torah, guardians of Jewish distinctiveness, and opponents of accommodation.

In terms of this story's contribution to the structure and force of Luke–Acts as a whole, however, the narrator's representation of the girl in 16.16 is less weighty than the girl's repeated assertion about Paul and his companions, namely οὗτοι οἱ ἄνθρωποι δοῦλοι τοῦ θεοῦ τοῦ ὑψίστου εἰσίν, οἵτινες καταγγέλλουσιν ὑμῖν ὁδὸν σωτηρίας (16.17). As the phrase τοῦ θεοῦ τοῦ ὑψίστου is used in exactly the same form back in Luke 8.28, and with both utterances being embedded in exorcism stories, its occurrence here in 16.17 raises the possibility that the present episode and that in Luke 8.26–39 ought to be read as parallel to one another.[36] Similar to Jesus, for instance, who is described by the Gerasene demoniac as υἱὲ τοῦ θεοῦ τοῦ ὑψίστου, Paul and his friends are characterised by the slave-girl as δοῦλοι τοῦ θεοῦ τοῦ ὑψίστου (16.17). In both instances, moreover, the occurrence of ὕψιστος on the lips of a demoniac recalls the use of the same word by non-Israelite characters depicted in the LXX.[37]

---

[33] Cf. Twelftree, *Christ Triumphant*, p. 112.

[34] There are many occurrences of προφητεύω in the LXX, and most of these refer to prophecy inspired by the Lord. See, e.g., Num. 11.25–27; 1 Sam. 10.5-6, 10–11, 13; 1 Kgs 22.18; 2 Chron. 20.37; Ezra 5.1; 1 Esd. 6.1; Sir. 46.20; Jer. 33(26).12, 20; 35(28).8; 36(29).27; Ezek. 4.7; 6.2; 11.4, 13; 21.2(7), 9(14), 14(19), 28(33); Joel 2.28 (3.1); and Amos 2.12; 3.8. προφητεύω conveys comparably positive overtones in Luke 1.67; 2.17, 18; 19.6; 21.9; 1 Cor. 14.1–5, 24, 31, 39; 1 Pet. 1.10; Jude 14; and Rev. 10.11; 11.3.

[35] The immediate co-text of the best-known septuagintal passage in which μαντεύομαι occurs, namely Deut. 18.10, is explicitly cited in both Acts 3.22 and 7.37, indicating that at least the implied author of our story could have appreciated the word's septuagintal overtones.

[36] Cf. Roloff, *Apostelgeschichte*, p. 245; and W. Neil, *The Acts of the Apostles*, NCB (London and Grand Rapids, 1973), p. 182.

[37] See Gen. 14.19, 20; Num. 24.16; Isa. 14.14; Dan. 3.26; and 1 Esd. 6.31; 8.19, 21. For further discussion of how ὕψιστος is used in the LXX and other Jewish texts from the Second Temple period, see Trebilco, 'Paul and Silas', pp. 53–7; Levinskaya, *Diaspora Setting*, pp. 95–7. Unlike τοῦ θεοῦ τοῦ ὑψίστου in Luke 8.28, the parallel expression in Acts 16.17 has potential to generate multiple and even discordant meanings on different levels of discourse; for although on the level of discourse between implied author and reader it sounds very much like an echo of Luke 8.28, in the embedded discourse between the girl and her presumably pagan auditors in Philippi it could be associated with any deity one might imagine at the top of the cosmic hierarchy (cf. Barrett, *Acts*, II, p. 786). On the denotative promiscuity of both ὕψιστος and θεός ὕψιστος in pagan texts and inscriptions

The slave-girl's characterisation of Paul's group as proclaiming 'a way of salvation' (ὁδὸν σωτηρίας, 16.17) increases the contact between the stories still further: while the noun σωτηρία does not occur in Luke 8.26–39, the cognate verb σώζω does (Luke 8.36), appearing on the lips of the herdsmen who announce 'how the one who had been demonised was saved [ἐσώθη]';[38] and similarly, although the verb σώζω is not used in Acts 16.16–18, a form of it is utilised immediately afterwards in the account of what happened at the Philippian jail (16.19–40), where in reply to the jailer's query, τί με δεῖ ποιεῖν ἵνα σωθῶ (16.30), Paul and Silas proclaim, πίστευσον ἐπὶ τὸν κύριον 'Ιησοῦν καὶ σωθήσῃ σὺ καὶ ὁ οἶκός σου (16.31).[39]

The prominence of the salvation motif is heightened not only by the recurrence of the term σώζω in 16.30–31 but also by the sense of culture-clash and irony produced by the different meanings of the σώζω/σωτηρία word group in this section of the narrative (i.e., 16.16–40). More specifically, with the jailer having just been tempted to end his own life (16.27), what he means by σώζω in 16.30 cannot be the same thing Paul and Silas mean by it in 16.31. But just as significant, the reason this latter conversation even takes place in these circumstances – at a prison in Philippi, with a jailer as interlocutor – is that the slave-girl has just used this same terminology in a way that misrepresents Paul's gospel as merely one of several paths to salvation ('a way of salvation', 16.17),[40] provoking him to perform an exorcism (16.18) that leads in turn to his own imprisonment (16.19–24).

---

from the Imperial period, see Trebilco, 'Paul and Silas', pp. 51–2, 58–65; and B. Rapske, *The Book of Acts and Paul in Roman Custody*, vol. III of *The Book of Acts in Its First Century Setting* (Grand Rapids and Carlisle, 1994), pp. 116–17. In regard to the relevance of the inscriptions for interpreting Acts 16.17, Levinskaya (*Diaspora Setting*, pp. 84–95, 98–100) persuasively argues that the phrase's potential for pagan connotations has been exaggerated (e.g., by Trebilco) but, in pressing for a specifically Jewish reference, ignores key aspects of the Acts passage's co-text and setting (e.g., the ambiguity of Apolline oracle, the implications of anarthrous ὁδόν, and the associations of μαντεύομαι with religious falsehood).

[38] As the term σώζω is absent from both Synoptic parallels, and as σωτηρία and σωτήριον never appear in Matthew or Mark but occur a total of six times in Luke's Gospel (1.69, 71, 77; 2.30; 3.6; and 19.9) and seven times in Acts (4.12; 7.25; 13.26, 47; 16.17; 27.34; and 28.28), salvation has to be considered a major theme not only in this particular parallel but throughout Luke–Acts as a whole. Cf. I. H. Marshall, '"Israel" and the Story of Salvation: One Theme in Two Parts', in Moessner (ed.), *Jesus and the Heritage of Israel*, pp. 342, 353–7; Marshall, *Historian and Theologian*, pp. 92–102.

[39] Thus, in addition to contributing to the parallel with Luke 8.26–39, σωτηρίας in 16.17 also previews the salvation experienced by the Philippian jailer in the ensuing co-text; cf. Tannehill, *Narrative Unity*, II, p. 197.

[40] On the interpretation of ὁδὸν σωτηρίας (16.17) see below under 'Intertextuality', pp. 224–6.

In addition to heightening the sense of irony in the story, the narration of Paul's expulsion of the spirit in 16.18 also reinforces the lexical strings which tie this episode to that in Luke 8.26–39. In this regard the noun ὄνομα, used by Paul in the formula ἐν ὀνόματι 'Ιησοῦ Χριστοῦ (16.18), is particularly significant. As the same noun is used back in Luke 8.30, where Jesus requests his demonic opponent's name, its occurrence here in Acts 16.18 strengthens the macrostructural parallelism created by the links noted above.[41] On the other hand, lest the resultant continuity between Paul and Jesus be misconstrued as an assertion of cosmic equality, the particular use to which 'the name' is put here in 16.18 signifies an important difference between the two figures: whereas Jesus never invokes the name of any source of authority outside himself, Paul explicitly relies in this context on 'the name of Jesus Christ',[42] with ὄνομα fulfilling its common function as a metonym for power.[43]

Transitivity

As in the exorcism stories in Luke's Gospel so in Acts 16.16–18, patterns and shifts in transitivity play an important role both in the characterisation of participants in the action and in the realisation of story structure. This contribution can be seen most clearly when the participation profile of each major character is considered in the text's own discursive sequence. The possessed girl, for example, fills the role of 'actor' in a surprisingly large share of the story's material processes. She meets (ὑπαντῆσαι, 16.16) the narrator and his companions; brings great gain (ἐργασίαν πολλὴν παρεῖχεν, 16.16) to her masters; follows (κατακολουθοῦσα, 16.17) Paul and his companions; prolongs her dogged

---

[41] Cf. Tannehill, *Narrative Unity*, II, p. 197; and Schmithals, *Apostelgeschichte*, p. 150. Surprisingly, although the parallel is strengthened further by (1) the verb ὑπαντάω, two of whose four occurrences in Luke–Acts are in Acts 16.16 and Luke 8.27, and (2) the public hostility which both of the exorcisms arouse (Luke 8.37; Acts 16.19–24), it is ignored by Radl, *Paulus und Jesus*.

[42] For further discussion of the contrast, see Kahl, *Miracle Stories*, p. 83. As the name of Jesus also plays a prominent role in the Lucan Peter's ministry (Acts 2.21, 38; 3.6, 16; 4.7, 10, 12, 17, 18; 5.28, 40), its occurrence here in 16.18 on the lips of Paul has potential to effect a *Paul–Peter* parallel as well, which could have been designed to counter damaging rumours known from other sources (e.g., Gal. 2.11–21) about the two figures' conflicts.

[43] See, e.g., Matt. 7.22; Mark 9.38 (par. Luke 9.49); 16.17; Luke 10.17; Acts 3.6; 4.7, 10, 12, 30; and 19.13; LXX 1 Sam. 17.45; 1 Kgs 18.24; 2 Kgs 2.24; Pss 19.8; 43.6; 53.3; 88.25; 117.10–12; and Isa. 50.10. For further discussion of the relationship between name and power, see J. A. Ziesler, 'The Name of Jesus in the Acts of the Apostles', *JSNT* 4 (1979), pp. 33–5; Grundmann, *Kraft*, p. 98; and below under 'The name of the exorcist', pp. 251–5.

pursuit of Paul's group for many days (τοῦτο δὲ ἐποίει ἐπὶ πολλὰς ἡμέρας, 16.18); and, as the deleted agent in διαπονηθείς (16.18), eventually causes Paul to become greatly annoyed. As Paul and his companions, on the other hand, serve as actor only once (in πορευομένων, 16.16) in this same part of the story, and with the girl furthermore functioning as sayer in ἔκραζεν λέγουσα (16.17), a striking contrast gradually unfolds between these participants in terms of their influence on their surroundings: for the first two thirds of the story, the possessed girl is plainly the more dynamic participant.

The impact of this pattern on the force of the story as a whole can be gauged only when other key participants in the action have been analysed in a similar fashion. Significantly, Paul and his fellow travellers function passively as the goal in three of the five material processes performed by the girl (i.e., ὑπαντῆσαι in 16.16, κατακολουθοῦσα in 16.17, and διαπονηθείς in 16.18). Although the Paul group plays other roles in the story – for example as the 'carrier' in the relational process εἰσίν and as the 'sayer' in καταγγέλλουσιν, 16.17 – prior to the denouement they do not affect their environment in any way. This picture is not substantially altered, moreover, by the two processes that immediately follow the reference to Paul's annoyance in 16.18: while Paul's roles as 'behaver' in ἐπιστρέψας and 'sayer' in εἶπεν anticipate the forthcoming climax, in themselves they do not represent him as influencing any other participant in his environment.

Immediately thereafter, with the quotation of Paul's speech to the spirit (16.18b), the climax of the episode begins. And not surprisingly, its beginning is signalled by a shift in transitivity: in παραγγέλλω σοι ἐν ὀνόματι Ἰησοῦ Χριστοῦ Paul represents himself not only as performing an action which, though verbal, has strongly material overtones but also as impacting another participant in the story, with the spirit (i.e., σοι) functioning as the 'target' of Paul's verbal action.[44] As the possessed slave-girl had dominated the encounter up to this point, this shift produces a powerful sense of reversal, which along with the irony and wordplay discussed above gives the story a high degree of entertainment value.

Several of the processes in this story are also linked to ideologically significant indicators of circumstance, two of which – εἰς τὴν προσευχήν (16.16) and ἐν ὀνόματι Ἰησοῦ Χριστοῦ – have already been discussed in connection with lexis. Others that merit comment are ἐπὶ πολλὰς ἡμέρας

---

[44] In terms of process type and participant structure, therefore, παραγγέλλω σοι is comparable to ἐπετίμησεν δέ ὁ Ἰησοῦς τῷ πνεύματι τῷ ἀκαθάρτῳ back in Luke 9.42.

(16.18a), αὐτῇ τῇ ὥρᾳ (following καὶ ἐξῆλθεν in 16.18c), and τοῖς κυρίοις αὐτῆς ('for her masters', 16.16).

ἐπὶ πολλὰς ἡμέρας (16.18a), as an indicator of indefinite temporal extent, serves to disclose in general terms how long the slave-girl did (ἐποίει) what she is portrayed doing in 16.17. Simultaneously, though, the same phrase also indirectly encourages the audience to sympathise with Paul in his annoyance at her behaviour: despite the danger which association with this girl posed to Paul's already vulnerable claim on the heritage of Israel, he was scarcely short-tempered with her but patiently endured her pronouncements 'for many days'. Thus, while the ensuing exorcism leaves no room for doubt about the great distance between Paul's Jesus and the girl's pythian spirit, ἐπὶ πολλὰς ἡμέρας implicitly attributes to Paul virtues of patience and self-control that would have been admired by the widest possible audience.

Directly following Paul's exorcistic command, the narrator places the process of the spirit's departure in a precise temporal setting, namely as having occurred 'that same hour' (αὐτῇ τῇ ὥρᾳ, 16.18c). Attributive αὐτῇ here strongly encourages the reader to infer that the spirit's departure did not merely follow Paul's command but was actually caused by it. With the command having been issued moreover 'in the name of Jesus Christ', and in view of the foregrounded correspondence between Paul's command and the spirit's departure, the phrase ultimately serves to highlight the divine authority and power that are now accessible in the ascended Jesus. However, as discussed below in the discussion of co-text, the question of who has rights of access to this power is an issue Luke was unable to ignore; and the way he addresses it, particularly in Acts 19.11–20, offers valuable clues to the kind of situation that originally constrained the production of Luke–Acts as a whole.

Finally, the circumstance of advantage signified by τοῖς κυρίοις αὐτῆς ('for her masters', 16.16) implies what is conveyed more explicitly in 16.19: the slave-girl was being used dishonourably by her owners. To be sure, in the Imperial age slaves were expected to be entirely at the disposal of their masters and were employed in a wide range of money-making enterprises;[45] but from Luke's perspective, this particular slave was producing income by giving oracles that were false and religiously misleading. Accordingly, as at several other points in Luke–Acts so also here, the opponents of the author's heroes are characterised as greedy and dishonourable.[46]

---

[45] Bradley, *Slaves and Masters*, pp. 15–16, 115–16.
[46] See, e.g., Luke 16.14; 22.3–6; Acts 5.1–11; 16.19; 19.19, 24–25; 24.26.

Verbal aspect

Eighteen words in this story have tense-form inflections, with the present tense being used eight times, the aorist seven times, and the imperfect three. None of the present and aorist forms deviates from expected usage; but the imperfects, by occuring where the aorist would have served equally well and might even have been expected, invite special attention.

In the aside concerning the slave-girl's value to her masters (ἥτις ἐργασίαν πολλὴν παρεῖχεν τοῖς κυρίοις αὐτῆς μαντευομένη, 16.16), the imperfect tense verb παρεῖχεν depicts her production of financial gain as a past action still in progress at the time Paul and his friends first encountered her ('who was providing great gain for her masters'). The imperfect has potential which the aorist παρέσχεν would have lacked to represent both the progressive character of the girl's productivity and its relative time. However, especially as the aorist would have been just as appropriate in this context, more than representational concerns appear to have motivated this particular selection of the imperfect; indeed, as the same clause not only has ἐργασίαν with the exaggerative quantifier πολλήν in front of the verb – and thus in a marked position – but is also followed by the ideologically loaded adverbial μαντευομένη, the imperfect is almost certainly part of a larger effort to highlight the link between the great profits and the false prophecy.[47] With the cash connection therefore having been underscored in several different ways, the story's audience can hardly disapprove when they learn that Paul exorcised the spirit and put an end to this polluted enterprise (16.18–19).

The other occurrences of the imperfect – ἔκραζεν in 16.17 ('she kept crying out') and ἐποίει in 16.18 ('she kept on doing this') – are associated with a single phenomenon which both verbs represent as happening repeatedly in the past. In light of their co-referentiality, and as ἐποίει in particular is not only intensified by the occurrence of ἐπὶ πολλὰς ἡμέρας in the same clause but also followed directly by three aorist forms in succession (διαπονηθείς, ἐπιστρέψας, εἶπεν),[48] the two imperfects foreground what a nuisance the girl was making of herself to Paul and his associates. Paul's eventual annoyance (διαπονηθείς, 16.18) is therefore no ill-tempered outburst but rather an expression of righteous indignation.

---

[47] On the capacity of the imperfect to highlight action which the aorist would put in the background, see Fanning, *Verbal Aspect*, pp. 243, 248–9; and Porter, *Verbal Aspect*, pp. 198–207.

[48] As the narrator would have no reason to emphasise Paul's annoyance, διαπονηθείς exemplifies the aorist's common function as the narrative background tense, helping the imperfect ἐποίει to stand out by contrast. On the significance of an imperfect occurring with a series of aorists, see Fanning, *Verbal Aspect*, pp. 248–9.

Presuppositions and implicatures

The reference at the beginning of this story to 'the prayer-house' (τὴν προσευχήν) involves an assumption which, though seldom noted, sheds light on the Lucan writings' original context of production; namely, by referring to the prayer-house without indicating the distinguishing features of this entity, the narrator appears to presuppose a general familiarity with such places on the part of his audience. In theory, of course, the narrator might do this because he himself has already defined or otherwise clarified this concept earlier in the larger story; but in the present case the assumed knowledge can be found neither in the immediately preceding co-text, where another unexplained reference to the prayer-house can be found (16.13), nor in any of the occurrences of the semantically related term συναγωγή in earlier segments of Luke–Acts.[49] The occurrences of προσευχή in this context become even more significant as soon as we recognise that the meaning defended for it above, under 'Lexis', is far better attested in Jewish sources than in pagan ones.[50] The implied audience of this story therefore consists of people who possess at least basic knowledge of this distinctively Jewish phenomenon.

In addition to knowing what a προσευχή involves, this same audience is expected to be familiar with pythian spirits and pagan modes of divination, both of which are introduced in 16.16 without explanation or definition. Significantly, neither πύθων nor μαντεύομαι is used elsewhere in the NT, and the former is also absent from several major corpora of ancient Jewish writings in Greek (e.g., the LXX, Philo, Josephus). None the less, the author of the present episode takes the reality of such things for granted and apparently expects his audience to do the same. In the cultural context of Luke–Acts, therefore, people who know about a distinctively Jewish phenomenon such as the προσευχή can be expected to believe simultaneously in the reality of pythian spirits and pagan divination, and thus to have knowledge of a wider range of religious experiences and fields of meaning.[51]

---

[49] Most notably, the first occurrence of συναγωγή in Luke–Acts (i.e., Luke 4.15) is, like προσευχή, in the present context, completely unexplained.

[50] As noted in BAGD, s.v. 'προσευχή', the word does sometimes serve in pagan sources to denote a place of prayer, but in these instances the place in question is a pagan place of worship rather than a synagogue. On the usage of προσευχή in Jewish sources to denote a prayer-house, see Levinskaya, *Diaspora Setting*, pp. 213–25; Klauck, *Magie und Heidentum*, p. 78.

[51] By overlooking the presupposed knowledge in Acts 16.16, Tyson, *Images of Judaism*, p. 34, exaggerates at least slightly when he speaks of the implied reader's 'paucity of information about Gentile religious life'.

As nearly all of this story's key implicatures have already been discussed above in connection with other kinds of stylistic devices, only a couple remain that merit our attention here. First, in the speech attributed to Paul in 16.18, the use of παραγγέλλω in the first person singular suggests that Paul sees himself as possessing authority over the spirit. Although this impression can be inferred from the word's connotations in this context alone, it is also amply confirmed by the usage of παραγγέλλω elsewhere in Luke–Acts and in many other ancient Greek writings, where those who give orders are normally implied to have authority to do so.[52] Furthermore, although the clause in question attributes this confidence to Paul himself rather than to the narrator, there is nothing in the context to suggest that the narrator viewed this confidence as misplaced; indeed, he implicitly validates it when, in the very next clause, he reports the immediate success of Paul's command (καὶ ἐξῆλθεν αὐτῇ τῇ ὥρᾳ, 16.18c).

Similarly, in 16.18 the phrase ἐν ὀνόματι Ἰησοῦ Χριστοῦ conveys meanings beyond its basic semantic sense. For instance, as the overt goal of Paul's whole utterance in this context is to expel the spirit from the girl, his use of ἐν ὀνόματι Ἰησοῦ Χριστοῦ in the same breath implies the belief that invoking Jesus' name would somehow enable him to achieve his aim. But just as important, when the audience of this story discovers in the same verse that the spirit immediately responded in the desired manner (i.e., καὶ ἐξῆλθεν αὐτῇ τῇ ὥρᾳ, 16.18c), they are led to infer that Paul's conviction about Jesus' name was in fact very well founded.

Intertextuality

The anarthrous noun phrase ὁδὸν σωτηρίας, placed at the end of the slave-girl's speech in 16.17, is only treated cursorily in a wide range of critical commentaries, as if its function in this context were utterly unambiguous.[53] As rightly stressed by P. Trebilco, however, the absence of the article creates uncertainty as to whether the phrase should be assigned an individualising sense (i.e., 'the way of salvation') or a qualitative nuance (i.e., 'a way of salvation').[54] If moreover the qualitative reading is adopted, the girl would be representing the message of the missionaries

---

[52] See, e.g., Aeschylus *Pers.* 469; Herodotus 3.25, 147; 7.147; 8.70; Plato *Resp.* 415b; Thucydides 7.43; Luke 5.14; 8.29, 56; 9.21; Acts 1.4; 4.18; 5.28, 40; 10.42; 15.5; 16.23; 23.22, 30; 1 Cor. 7.10; 1 Thess. 4.11; 2 Thess. 3.4, 6, 10, 12; 1 Tim. 1.3; 4.11; 5.7; 6.13, 17. Cf. LSJ, s.v. 'παραγγέλλω'.

[53] See, e.g., Barrett, *Acts*, II, p. 787; and Fitzmyer, *Acts*, p. 586.

[54] Trebilco, 'Paul and Silas', pp. 64–5.

in a manner very different from how they themselves understood it; more specifically, she would be implying that their message was merely one of several alternative paths to 'salvation'.[55]

As Trebilco observes, ὁδός is normally accompanied by the article where its referent is the particular 'way' of life approved by the author of Acts.[56] This factor by itself constitutes almost decisive support for the non-particular reading of ὁδὸν σωτηρίας in 16.17. However, as this interpretation affects so much else in the story (e.g., Paul's motive for expelling the spirit), and with scholarly exegesis having largely overlooked it,[57] additional evidence in its favour ought to be mentioned.

Above, in my treatment of lexis, both 'Εγένετο δέ and μαντευομένη (16.16) were interpreted as deriving much of their force from distinctively septuagintal patterns of usage, with the verb μαντεύομαι in particular and its cognates having negative associations in nearly all their biblical contexts. The negative overtones of the μαντεύομαι group can, however, be defined with greater specificity; to be precise, they consist at least partly of the impression that the mantic activities in question cannot be trusted to provide reliable information. Connotations of deceptiveness and unreliability cling to μαντεύομαι, for instance, in eleven of its twelve occurrences in the LXX;[58] one of these eleven, moreover, is Deuteronomy 18.10, which the author of Luke–Acts not only knew but was conspicuously fond of.[59] In this light, associations with falsehood should almost certainly be inferred from μαντεύομαι in Acts 16.16 as well, so that anything the slave-girl says in this context ought to be suspected of deceitful intent. Thus, when she is cited directly afterwards as

---

[55] Cf. ibid., p. 65; Klauck, *Magie und Heidentum*, pp. 82–3; Rapske, *Roman Custody*, p. 117 n. 13.

[56] Trebilco, 'Paul and Silas', p. 64. Of the eleven occurrences of ὁδός in Acts where the approved 'way' is either clearly or potentially intended (2.28; 9.2; 13.10; 16.17; 18.25, 26; 19.9, 23; 22.4; 24.14, 22), nine are articular, the two exceptions being 2.28 and the present passage.

[57] See, e.g., Barrett, *Acts*, II, pp. 786–7; F. Martin, 'Le geôlier et la marchande de pourpre: Actes des Apôtres 16, 6–40 (Première partie)', *Sémiotique et Bible* 59 (1990), p. 25; Fitzmyer, *Acts*, p. 586; G. Schneider, *Die Apostelgeschichte*, HTKNT 5 (Freiburg, 1982), II, p. 215; H. Conzelmann, *Acts of the Apostles*, trans. J. Limburg, A. T. Kraabel and D. H. Juel, Hermeneia (Philadelphia, 1987), p. 131; G. Krodel, *Acts*, ACNT (Minneapolis, 1986), p. 308; Schmithals, *Apostelgeschichte*, p. 176; Marshall, *Acts*, pp. 268–9; Schille, *Apostelgeschichte*, p. 345; Bruce, *Book of the Acts*, pp. 312–13; Neil, *Acts*, p. 182; E. Haenchen, *The Acts of the Apostles: A Commentary*, trans. B. Noble and G. Shinn (Oxford, 1971), p. 495; Roloff, *Apostelgeschichte*, p. 245.

[58] LXX Deut. 18.10; 2 Kgs 17.17; Mic. 3.11; Jer. 34(27).9; and Ezek. 12.24; 13.6, 23; 21.21(26), 23(28), 29(34); 22.28. The single exception is 1 Sam. 28.9(8).

[59] One verse or another of Deuteronomy 18 is widely recognised to have influenced Luke 7.39; 9.35; 24.25; and Acts 3.22; 19.19. On the role of Deuteronomy 18 in Luke–Acts see Evans and Sanders (eds), *Luke and Scripture*, pp. 71, 190–1.

describing the missionaries as heralds, not of τὴν ὁδὸν τῆς σωτηρίας but of ὁδὸν σωτηρίας, her meaning is most probably 'a way of salvation', the implications of which flatly contradict the position of the narrator and heroes of Luke–Acts.[60] Indeed, as the implications of this phrase stand at odds not only with the soteriology of the implied author but also with Jewish monotheism, Paul's annoyance at the girl can be seen from a Jewish perspective as not merely excusable but exemplary.

Immediate co-text

The present episode has strong links to the material that immediately surrounds it. The article τήν, for example, attached to προσευχήν (16.16), presupposes the reference back in 16.13 to the same Jewish prayer-house. Moreover, the process of travelling to this location (πορευομένων... προσευχήν, 16.16) should probably be identified with the journey mentioned back in 16.13a, where the narrator and his companions are said to have gone to a place they *'supposed'* was the site of a prayer-house. To be sure, the temporal relation between verses 13 and 16 is not altogether clear;[61] but without construing some kind of link between them, the reader is doomed to disorientation, both temporal and spatial.

In addition to creating a lexical string between verses 13 and 16, the occurrences of προσευχή also contribute to a theme that is present both within the exorcism story itself and in the materials surrounding it, namely the emphasis on the faithfulness of Paul and his co-workers to Jewish custom. More specifically, between verses 11 and 40 of this same chapter Paul and his friends are depicted not only as observing the sabbath and searching for a Jewish prayer-house (16.13, 16) but also as receiving hospitality from a Gentile worshipper of the God of Israel

---

[60] See, e.g., Acts 4.12.

[61] As the temporal orientation of the narrator in 16.13–15 differs from that in 16.16–18, the sequence of 'real world' events in the story does not correspond to their order of presentation in the text. The former is best understood as follows: (1) the narrator and his companions travel to a location just outside the city which they erroneously believed to be the site of a Jewish prayer-house (16.13); (2) en route they encounter the slave-girl, who begins to prophesy in a fashion that will eventually become unbearable to Paul (16.16–17); (3) the missionaries meet Lydia, who accepts their message and extends hospitality to them (16.14–15), and (4) during their stay with Lydia, the missionaries continue their evangelistic work around Philippi but find themselves hampered by the girl until Paul expels the spirit from her (16.18). Cf. Schille, *Apostelgeschichte*, p. 345; for further discussion of the problem, see also C.-J. Thornton, *Der Zeuge des Zeugen: Lukas als Historiker der Paulusreisen*, WUNT 56 (Tübingen, 1991), p. 279; Tannehill, *Narrative Unity*, II, p. 197; B.A. Cullom, 'Acts 16:6–40: A Redactional and Socio-Historical Analysis', PhD dissertation, University of Notre Dame (1985), p. 85.

(16.14–15, 40),[62] experiencing hardship in Philippi at least partly because they are Jewish (16.20–40), and combating pagan intermediary practices that are prohibited by Jewish law (16.18). As discussed in greater detail below, this same set of images corresponds to motifs found elsewhere in the Paul section of Acts and therefore offers valuable clues to the kind of situation Luke–Acts as a whole may have been composed in.

Our story also has significant links to what immediately follows it. In the first sentence of 16.19 (i.e., ἰδόντες δὲ <u>οἱ κύριοι αὐτῆς</u> ὅτι <u>ἐξῆλθεν</u> ἡ ἐλπὶς τῆς <u>ἐργασίας</u> αὐτῶν), for instance, the words οἱ κύριοι αὐτῆς, ἐξῆλθεν and ἐργασίας all pick up motifs that have just been encountered in 16.16–18. As ἐργασίαν is already highlighted in 16.16 both by its position in the clause and by its connection with πολλήν, its re-occurrence in 16.19 causes it to stand out as one of the most prominent features of the whole Philippi narrative (16.11–40). As for what precisely it emphasises, the link in 16.19 between the loss of revenue and the charges pressed by the girl's masters reveals all: contrary to their own self-presentation as guardians of the imperial order, the owners have far less interest in Roman law than in their own profitable scam.[63]

This same point is developed further through the use of ἐξέρχομαι in 16.19 shortly after its two occurrences in the preceding verse. With the verb itself being repeated but its grammatical subject being changed in 16.19, the exorcism is seen from two very different perspectives: whereas the narrator views the event chiefly as the departure of a noxious spirit (16.18), the slave-owners view it as the destruction of a lucrative business (16.19).[64]

And finally, the various ties just noted are part of a larger network of devices that give 16.11–40 as a whole its own schematic structure and identity. At both the beginning and the end of this section, for instance, references to the city of Philippi (16.12, 39) distinguish the setting of the interjacent action from that of the events in the surrounding narrative, while simultaneously forming a frame around the exorcism and prison episodes.[65] This framing effect, moreover, is reinforced by the narration of Paul and Silas' return to the home of Lydia, with whom the mission in Philippi both begins and ends (16.13–15, 40). As these features clearly impact the structure and meaning of 16.11–40 as a whole, they unavoidably

---

[62] On σεβομένη τὸν θεόν (16.14) as denoting a Gentile sympathiser with Judaism, see Fitzmyer, *Acts*, pp. 449–50, 520, 586.

[63] Cf. Haenchen, 'Das "Wir"', p. 249.

[64] Cf. Tannehill, *Narrative Unity*, II, p. 198; Lods, 'Argent et magie', p. 289.

[65] Cf. C. H. Talbert, *Reading Acts: A Literary and Theological Commentary on the Acts of the Apostles* (New York, 1997), p. 148.

affect the interpretation of the exorcism in 16.16–18, in ways that are explored in some detail below.

Macrostructural co-text and implied situation

While my discussion of the parallel between the present story and Luke 8.26–39 included several observations on the stories' respective co-texts, my primary interest was the connections between the stories themselves. However, as that discussion demonstrated that the exorcism by Paul stands inside a frame marking off 16.11–40 as a whole, the relationship between this latter section and the co-text of Luke 8.26–39 deserves to be examined more closely.

Expanding the co-textual frame

Several factors suggest that this parallel has even greater salience than was appreciated above. For instance, although the motif of nakedness in Luke 8.27, 35 has no parallel in Acts 16.16–18, it does have one in 16.22 of the same chapter, where Paul and Silas have their clothes torn off before being beaten with rods.[66] Similarly, while the physical constraints that are used to control the Gerasene demoniac (Luke 8.29) possess no analogue in the portrayal of the inspired slave-girl, they do correspond to devices that are used against Paul and Silas in the Philippian jail (Acts 16.24).[67] And, although neither of the exorcism stories includes any reference to meteorological phenomena or disturbances in the realm of nature, both of them are tightly linked to narratives that do mention such happenings, with the earthquake in Acts 16.26 recalling the storm in Luke 8.23–25.

The parallelism of these two larger sections is expanded by several other shared motifs, the most notable of which are (1) the request by local residents that God's agent depart from their geographical area (Luke 8.37; Acts 16.39);[68] (2) the role of 'fear' in inspiring the request that God's

---

[66] The occurrence of the nakedness motif in both sections is noteworthy to the extent that it is not commonplace in Luke's writings, his only other references to it being those in Luke 10.30 and Acts 19.16.

[67] The Greek noun δεσμοφύλαξ, which denotes the jailer in Acts 16 (vv. 23, 27, 36) and occurs in no other section of Luke's writings, is morphologically related to the verbs δεσμεύω and φυλάσσω, which in Luke–Acts are found together only in Luke 8.29 and Acts 22.4.

[68] With both requests exemplifying a syntagmatic pattern found nowhere else in the NT – namely, ἐρωτάω + an infinitive of ἀπέρχομαι + a circumstance of spatial separation signified by ἀπό with the genitive – this particular correspondence is perhaps more indicative of deliberate design than any of the others.

agent(s) depart (Luke 8.37; Acts 16.38–39); (3) the actual departure of God's agent(s) in accordance with the request (Luke 8.37; Acts 16.40); (4) the interconnected motifs of faith and salvation (Luke 8.25, 36, 48–50; Acts 16.30–31, 34); (5) the physical trembling and submissive prostration of a recipient of salvation (Luke 8.47; Acts 16.29);[69] (6) sleep interrupted by disturbance in the natural environment (Luke 8.23, 52; Acts 16.27);[70] (7) close brushes with death for key participants in the action (Luke 8.24, 52; Acts 16.27); and (8) the οἶκος/οἰκία as a place closely associated with salvation (Luke 8.27, 39; Acts 16.15, 31–32). While none of these links on its own is particularly noteworthy, their cumulative weight is difficult to ignore. Viewed collectively, they reinforce the parallel established on other grounds between Luke 8.26–39 and Acts 16.16–18. As a result continuity between the activities of Paul and those of Jesus is highlighted even further, yet without compromising the sense that real progress in the realisation of the divine plan (cf. Acts 1.8) is being achieved.

Neither this parallel, however, nor any of the others between Jesus and Paul in Luke–Acts, should be understood to imply that Paul is equal to Jesus in honour and authority. In the parallel just considered, for instance, Jesus is able to achieve exorcistic success without relying on any source of authority outside himself, whereas Paul is explicitly dependent on the name of Jesus. Furthermore, although the role of the Holy Spirit in shaping the missionary work of Paul's circle (16.6–7) recalls the role of the Spirit in the life of Jesus (Luke 3.22; 4.1, 14, 18), Paul and his associates are subordinate to the Spirit in a manner that, according to Luke's first volume, Jesus is not; indeed, in Acts 16.6–7 the Spirit to whom Paul's circle submits is tacitly identified precisely as τὸ πνεῦμα 'Ιησοῦ. Thus, in the sole context where a fully developed story is devoted to an exorcism performed by the Lucan Paul, his relationship with Jesus is chiefly that of a legitimate and very loyal follower.

Jesus' affirmation of Paul

With this same issue of legitimate discipleship having already been raised in conjunction with the motif of exorcism in the name of Jesus back in

---

[69] Like some of the other components of this parallelism, the vocabulary for 'trembling' in particular is far from commonplace either in Luke–Acts or in other parts of the NT. Within Luke–Acts the only other occurrence of the noun ἔντρομος (Acts 16.29) is that found in Acts 7.32, while the only context in which Luke employs the cognate verb τρέμω is Luke 8.47.

[70] The adjective ἔξυπνος ('awake', Acts 16.27) is morphologically related to the verb ἀφυπνόω ('to fall asleep', Luke 8.23) and, like the latter, is an NT hapaxlegomenon.

Luke 9.49–50, the possibility that the present episode might parallel not only Luke 8.22–56 but also the Gospel's third exorcism story (Luke 9.37–43a) and its ensuing co-text (9.43b–50) deserves serious consideration. Although Lucan scholarship has shown virtually no interest in this suggestion,[71] much can be said in its favour. First, as the noun used for the girl in Acts 16.16, παιδίσκη, has only four occurrences in Luke–Acts and probably refers here to one who was still a child, it has high potential to recall the boy (παῖς, Luke 9.42) healed by Jesus and the child (παιδίον) featured in the related teaching that immediately follows (9.47–48). Furthermore, the story in Luke 9.37–43a, unlike its Synoptic parallels (Matt. 17.14–21; Mark 9.14–29), begins with a set of lexicogrammatical features that anticipates the beginning of the present unit.[72] Third, in the dialogue about the unfamiliar exorcist (Luke 9.49–50), the figure whom the apostles 'hinder' represents a socioreligious type to which the Lucan Paul corresponds in several notable ways: he expels demons in the name of Jesus (Luke 9.49; Acts 16.18), stands outside the circle of the twelve apostles, encounters opposition from the latter (Acts 9.26), and yet is embraced by Jesus as an ally; Paul, moreover, is the only figure in Luke–Acts who matches this category in all the particulars just mentioned.[73] And finally, since one effect of this parallel would be to ground the legitimacy of Paul's ministry not only in Jesus' exorcistic pattern but also in his explicit and authoritative teaching on group boundaries, it would cohere almost perfectly with much of what Luke has to say about Paul elsewhere in Acts.

In addition then to foregrounding the authority of Jesus over the demonic realm, the Lucan stories of exorcism participate in macrostructural schemes that cut across the two volumes of Luke–Acts and help to tie the whole narrative complex together. Yet much more than cohesion is realised by these schemes. By also forming a layer of discursive structure on top of that found in any one of the stories on its own, these correspondences foreground the extra meanings they create, which in turn shed light on the situation in which they were first produced.[74] Indeed, precisely because these meanings emerge primarily from a reading of

[71] Tannehill, e.g., who is more alert than most to the existence of intratextual parallels, says nothing about a link between the present narrative and Luke 9.37–50 in his treatment of Acts 15.36–16.40 (see *Narrative Unity*, II, pp. 194–205).

[72] The sequence in both cases is the septuagintism Ἐγένετο δέ + a temporal participle of motion + a main verb from the συναντάω/ ὑπαντάω group.

[73] The seventy-two (Luke 10.1, 17–20), e.g., are never described as encountering resistance from the twelve; and the seven sons of Scaeva fail to expel the demon (Acts 19.13–16).

[74] Cf. R. Fowler on 'extra structure and extra meanings' in *Linguistic Criticism*, pp. 69–73.

Luke–Acts as a whole, they constitute the best evidence we have for the type of situation that inspired Luke's whole two-volume composition;[75] and clearly this situation had much to do with questions about the legitimacy of Paul. However, for the same theoretical reasons that make these schemes foundational to situational reconstruction, a variety of other textual and ideational features which the exorcism stories intersect need to be considered before the task of reconstruction can be undertaken in earnest.

Paul among the greedy and the Judeophobic

As already noted above, the significance of the exorcism in Acts 16.16–18 is greatly enriched by its relations to other parts of 16.11–40. Indirectly, in fact, by being embedded in this particular co-text, the story in 16.16–18 contributes not only to the parallel with the exorcism in Luke 8.26–39 but also to thematic patterns and emphases that involve far more than exorcism and demons, and which almost certainly reveal more about Luke's original situation than his exorcism stories on their own do.[76] In the account of the political and economic consequences of Paul's exorcism, for instance, the accusation levelled by the slave-girl's owners – namely, that Paul and his friends advocate customs which are illegal and anti-Roman (16.20–21) – corresponds to so many other hostile charges cited in the Lucan volumes that it must have had special relevance to the situation Luke understood himself to be addressing;[77] indeed, in several instances the correspondence involves not only the content of the accusation itself but also the point of view from which the narrator treats it and the combination of motifs that occur with it. To cite a single example, just as Paul and Silas are hauled before the governing authorities because of their opponents' greed (16.19) but are eventually set free by Roman officials as innocent men (16.35–40), so Jesus is betrayed for the sake of money (Luke 22.3–6) but subsequently declared innocent by Roman officials (Luke 23.1–25, 47). As with the Jesus–Paul schemes treated above, moreover, so too with this one, the involvement of not just one but both Lucan volumes in the parallel gives its content special importance for any attempt to recover Luke's original situation; and especially since the

---

[75] The methodological principle is expressed aptly by Halliday, *Language as Social Semiotic*, p. 150: 'We shall not find the entire context of situation of a text neatly laid out before us by a single sentence. It is only by considering the text as a whole that we can see how it springs from its environment and is determined by the specific features of that environment.'

[76] Cf. Tannehill, *Narrative Unity*, II, p. 197.

[77] Luke 23.2, 13–15, 22, 41, 47; Acts 17.6–7; 18.13; 23.29; 25.8, 18–19; 28.18.

innocence theme is not only prominent in the Paul narratives of Acts but also far more pronounced in Luke's Gospel than it is in either Matthew or Mark,[78] it reinforces the impression that the reputation of Paul was central to the ideological contest that shaped the composition of Luke–Acts as a whole.[79]

While the episode in which Jesus is betrayed by Judas for money is clearly not an exorcism story, it does include a distinctively Lucan note about Judas' ploy having been influenced by Satan (Luke 22.3); and significantly, this adds another string to the cord of motifs that tie Luke 22–23 to Acts 16.16–40. The combination of ideas which therefore co-occur in each of these contexts – the political innocence of Luke's heroes, their enemies' shameful greed, and the diabolical power associated with the human opposition – is in fact one of Luke's favourite rhetorical recipes. Several variations of this mixture will be considered below; but one in particular has special importance for interpreting the Jesus–Paul parallels.

The piece in question is Acts 19.11–20, where the extraordinary power of God in the healing ministry of Paul (19.11–12) is contrasted sharply with the exorcistic impotence of certain Jewish competitors (19.13–16). This part of Luke's narrative, it should be noted, contains his first reference to a demonic spirit following the story in Acts 16.16–18; and as the larger section in which this piece is embedded focuses on developments in Ephesus (18.24–20.1), which is the final stage of Paul's second missionary journey (16.6–20.1), it forms the conclusion of a still larger complex of material to which the ministry in Philippi is the beginning.[80] These observations by themselves suggest at least the possibility of a significant relationship between the Philippian and Ephesian sections of this section of Acts.

The degree to which Acts 19.11–20 complements Luke's whole exorcism theme, including the story set in Philippi, has on the whole been underestimated in scholarly exegesis.[81] Especially when read in conjunction with its immediate co-text (19.21–20.1), this unit contains a cluster of motifs that closely parallels those collocated in Acts 16.16–40: once again, interest in the demonic (19.12–16) co-occurs with images of deviant religiosity (19.13–19, 23–27), economic self-interest (19.17–19, 23–27),

---

[78] Cf. Esler, *Community and Gospel*, pp. 202–5.

[79] Cf. J. Jervell, *The Theology of the Acts of the Apostles*, New Testament Theology (Cambridge, 1996), pp. 11–17; Jervell, *People of God*, pp. 146–7, 163–5, 173–5.

[80] Talbert, *Reading Acts*, pp. 146–7, 172.

[81] Barrett, *Acts*, II, pp. 900–14, e.g., says nothing about the episode's thematic connections to either Acts 16.16–18 or the exorcisms in Luke's Gospel.

and political challenge and response (19.28–20.1).[82] Furthermore, just as the possessed girl in chapter 16 is evaluated negatively despite her positive challenge to the missionaries' honour ('servants of the Most High God'), so the sons of Scaeva are portrayed unfavourably even though they acknowledge the high cosmic status of 'the Jesus whom Paul proclaims'. And just as the hostility in Philippi is explained in terms of greed (16.16, 19), misunderstanding (16.35–39), and Judeophobia (16.20–21), so in Ephesus the antipathy of the artisans and their sympathisers is represented as stemming from economic self-interest, public confusion, and anti-Jewish prejudice (19.32–34).

In both of these sections, then, and at least partly through the embedded discourses of the pagan opponents themselves, Luke identifies Paul (and indirectly himself) with an idealised Judaism that puts him firmly at odds with the values of paganism, which is portrayed in these and several other sections of Acts in the worst possible light.[83] But just as important, the repetition of this whole compositional pattern presupposes a particular type of context, namely one in which Paul's honour needed defence and his mission needed to be represented as posing no threat to the public good of Roman order.

Paul: ally of Jesus and foe of magicians

In view of the parallels just noted between the Philippi and Ephesus narratives of Acts, we might expect the latter section – and especially the exorcism materials in 19.11–20 – to pick up and develop the correspondences of the former to the exorcism stories in Luke's first volume. Although this possibility has been virtually ignored by Lucan scholarship, it has numerous strengths that deserve consideration.[84]

Especially once the parallel between Acts 16.16–18 and Luke 8.26–39 has been recognised, the form and content of the demon's speech in Acts 19.15 cries out for special attention;[85] for one of this speech's

---

[82] Tannehill, *Narrative Unity*, II, p. 198, notes the economics parallel but overlooks the other motifs that contribute to the correspondence.

[83] Cf. Acts 14.11, 15; 17.16, 22, on which see Jervell, 'The Church of Jews and Godfearers', pp. 17–18.

[84] Tannehill, *Narrative Unity*, II, p. 237, rightly points out links to Luke 6.18–19 and Acts 5.12, 15–16, where the motif of therapeutic touch in particular is present, but says nothing about connections to Luke 8.26–56.

[85] Much of my discussion here of Acts 19.11–20 is adapted from T. E. Klutz, '"Naked and Wounded": Foregrounding, Relevance, and Situation in Acts 19.13–20', in S. E. Porter and J. T. Reed (eds), *Discourse Analysis of the New Testament: Essays in Theory and Practice* (Sheffield, 1999), pp. 261–2.

most remarkable effects is its indirect assertion of continuity between Jesus and Paul. τὸν [μὲν] ᾽Ιησοῦν γινώσκω, replies the demon to the itinerants, καὶ τὸν Παῦλον ἐπίσταμαι, ὑμεῖς δὲ τίνες ἐστέ? The sense of deep and fundamental harmony here between Luke's two main heroes is foregrounded by several different stylistic devices working in concert. For instance, the first two lines stand in synonymous parallelism to one another, highlighting correspondences not only between γινώσκω and ἐπίσταμαι but also between ᾽Ιησοῦν and Παῦλον.[86] Second, the propositional agreement between these same lines is strengthened by their phonaesthetic and metrical properties: the repetition of the masculine article τόν, the phonemic correspondence between the masculine accusative singular endings of ᾽Ιησοῦν and Παῦλον, and the conformity of each line to an eight-syllable measure powerfully reinforce the impression of unity and continuity.[87] And finally, while the third line diverges from the first two both metrically (it has seven syllables rather than eight) and grammatically (it is a question rather than a declaration), it still ought to be taken with the other two as part of a unified tristich; for the divergence just noted does not represent a merely ordinary or arbitrary difference, but materially reinforces a semantic opposition between the third line and the previous two.

To put this latter point another way, as the demon's discourse implies not only a profound unity between Paul and Jesus (lines one and two) but also a stark contrast between the Jesus–Paul solidarity and the itinerants (line three), and as this same combination of similarity and difference is not produced by the mere propositional sense of any single line but rather by the whole pattern of agreements and disagreements between all three, the speech of the demon ought to be read as a single tristichic unit.[88] To a degree then that has been largely ignored by commentators, the utterance by the demon replicates on a microdiscursive level precisely what the parallel between Luke 8.26–39 and Acts 16.16–18 accomplishes at the level of macrostructure: in addition to highlighting continuity between

---

[86] On the basic synonymy of the two verbs in this context, see Barrett, *Acts*, II, p. 910.

[87] On the role of metre (i.e., syllabic measure) in producing rhythm in Greek poetry, see W. W. Goodwin, *A Greek Grammar*, new edn. (London, 1894), pp. 348–9. Note that the iota at the beginning of ᾽Ιησοῦν would not have been pronounced like consonantal 'y' but rather as a distinct vowel; cf. G. Zuntz, *Greek: A Course in Classical and Post-Classical Greek Grammar from Original Texts*, Biblical Languages: Greek 4 (Sheffield, 1994), II, pp. 28, 34.

[88] This impression of identification and opposition is strengthened still further when the sorts of processes represented by the verbs in these three lines are taken into consideration: while both of the verbs in the first two lines represent processes of the mental variety, the verb in the third line represents a relational process.

Jesus and Paul, it also sketches boundaries that set this harmonious pair apart from the types of mediators Luke considers inadequate.[89]

Several other features of the narrative in Acts 19.11–20 sound like echoes of the story in Luke 8 and its immediate co-text (i.e., 8.26–56), reinforcing the effects just noted of the demon's speech. For instance, whereas Jesus transforms the demoniac of Gerasa from a state of nakedness to one of wearing clothes (8.27, 35), the Jewish itinerants suffer the dishonour of being stripped naked themselves (19.16), with neither their own reputation nor that of the 'magic' in which they traffick faring any better than their apparel (19.17–19). Similarly, whereas Jesus in effect cleanses the demoniac of his multiple impurities, the itinerants are physically degraded to a state out of keeping with priestly standards of purity.[90] Third, whereas in Luke 8.39 Jesus enables the man to leave the tombs and return to his home, the itinerants in Acts 19.16 are themselves forced to vacate a home. Furthermore, whereas the exorcism in Luke 8.26–39 involves an entire 'legion' of demons being vanquished by a solitary exorcist, the event in Acts 19.13–20 involves a whole group of seven exorcists being humiliated by a single demon. Fifth, whereas the 'fear' inspired by the action of Jesus (8.35, 37) stems at least partly from the drowning of impure animals (i.e., the swine) and ultimately leads to a hostile reaction, the 'fear' aroused by the public humiliation of Scaeva's sons results in the burning of profane books (19.19) and ultimately brings honour to 'the name of the Lord Jesus' (19.17). And finally, just as the immediate co-text of Luke 8.26–39 has Jesus conveying therapeutic power merely through contact with his clothing (8.44), so the immediate co-text of Acts 19.13–20 has Paul mediating divine aid merely through the touch of his handkerchiefs and aprons (19.11–12).

This last correspondence, by forming another parallel between Jesus and Paul, anticipates the first two lines uttered by the demon in 19.15, giving the unity of Luke's two main protagonists an even higher degree of salience than was appreciated above. But just as significant, all the other

---

[89] On the macrostructural parallels between the heroes of Luke–Acts, see esp. Radl, *Paulus und Jesus*, p. 44; Tannehill, *Narrative Unity*, II, pp. 49–50, 74–7, 162, 237; and D. P. Moessner, ' "The Christ Must Suffer": New Light on the Jesus – Peter, Stephen, Paul Parallels in Luke–Acts', *NovT* 28 (1986), pp. 221–7.

[90] In view of the itinerants' priestly lineage (19.14), Luke's description of them in 19.16 as γυμνοὺς καὶ τετραυματισμένους is rich in dramatic irony; for one of the requisites of legitimate priestly functioning is the wearing of special sacerdotal garments, an important function of which is to cover the shame of the priest's nakedness (Exod. 28.40–43), and the injuries denoted by τετραυματισμένους would almost certainly be among the 'blemishes' that disqualify their owners from priestly service (cf. LXX Lev. 21.16–24). On blemishes and priestly functioning: Philo *Spec*.1.103; *m. Ḥul*. 1.6; and *m. Bek*. 7.1–7. On the importance of priestly garments: Lev. 16.4, 24, 32; *m. Zebaḥ*. 2.1.

links just listed serve to foreground the contrast between Jesus and the itinerants, with the humiliation of the latter being underscored at every point. As the itinerants are in fact subjected to the most carnivalesque lampooning suffered by any character in the whole book of Acts, we would do well to ponder at least briefly what it is about these figures – or at least the socioreligious type they symbolise – that makes them so blameworthy in Luke's eyes. After all, in their dealings with the demonised, do they not appeal to the name of Jesus, just as both Paul and the figure approved by Jesus himself in Luke 9.49–50 do?

One valuable but widely overlooked clue can be detected in the content of the incantatory formula used by the itinerants themselves. To be precise, when the sons of Scaeva try to master the demon by invoking 'the name of the Lord Jesus' (19.13), their brief definition of the latter as the one 'whom *Paul* preaches' does more than simply attempt to exploit Jesus' cosmic authority, for it also implies that the itinerants themselves, unlike Paul, do not actually proclaim Jesus; rather, they only want to use him as a source of supramundane power.

Not surprisingly, therefore, the contrast between the itinerants and Jesus is accompanied by a sharp differentiation between the itinerants and Paul. Indeed, in the segments of the Ephesus narrative leading up to and directly following the story in 19.13–20, almost everything Paul and his co-workers do contributes to this contrast on one level or another. As this same material furthermore corresponds at several points not only to Luke 8.26–56 but also to Luke 9.37–50 and its co-text, reading it in light of the Jesus–Paul parallels may give additional insight into the architecture of Luke–Acts as a whole and its contextual implications.

Paul and Jesus in the architecture of Luke–Acts

The episode in Acts 19.13–20 and the Ephesus material that directly precedes it (18.24–19.12) are tied together by so many lexicogrammatical and thematic strings that the contrast between Paul and the sons of Scaeva is almost impossible to miss. For instance, just before using the verb ἐπιχειρέω in 19.13 to denote the itinerants' miscarried bid to oust 'the evil spirit' (τὸ πνεῦμα τὸ πονηρόν, 19.15–16), the narrator twice employs the etymologically related noun χείρ in connection with the far more effectual actions performed by Paul, whose mighty 'hands' mediate both divine healing (19.11–12) and authentic experience of 'the Holy Spirit' (τὸ πνεῦμα τὸ ἅγιον, 19.6). Similarly, the phrase translated 'the word of the Lord' occurs both in the summary of Paul's ministry of proclamation (τὸν λόγον τοῦ κυρίου, 19.10) and – with a striking inversion of the construction's internal order – at the end of the story about Scaeva's sons (τοῦ κυρίου ὁ λόγος, 19.20), with both the public argumentation of Paul (19.8–10) and the instance of phrasal inversion (19.20) causing the counterpoised absence of 'the word' in the mission of the itinerants (cf. 19.13–14) to stand out more prominently. Third, the phrase τὸ ὄνομα τοῦ κυρίου Ἰησοῦ, in addition to occurring twice in the story about Scaeva's sons (19.13, 17) and once back in 19.5, ought to be understood as present in sense, despite its formal absence, at the end of 19.12 as well;[91] for the use of adjunctive καί in the first clause of 19.13 ('Now some of the itinerant Jewish exorcists *also* tried to name the name . . .') implies that Paul too had been routinely invoking Jesus' name for exorcistic purposes.[92] And finally, the repetition of the verb πιστεύω in this section (18.27; 19.2, 4, 18) reinforces the cohesion effected by the strings just noted and thereby heightens the salience of the key contrast.

In terms of structural and contextual significance, however, the correspondences just surveyed are probably less weighty than those between the story in 19.13–20 and the short transitional piece that directly follows it (19.21–22).[93] In itself the link between these latter segments is uncomplicated. The temporal clause 'Ὡς δὲ ἐπληρώθη ταῦτα (19.21), for instance, at the transition's beginning, clearly refers back to the events just narrated, with 'these things' in particular probably encompassing everything recounted to that point in the Ephesus section of Acts (i.e., 18.24–19.8). And in view of the rich correspondence between 19.13–20 and the second exorcism story in Luke's Gospel (8.26–39), where Jesus' reversal of the demoniac's misfortunes is presented as a fulfilment of Isaiah 58.6–7, the verb ἐπληρώθη should probably be understood to imply not simply that these events took place but rather that they fulfilled part of the divine plan made known in Jewish Scripture.[94] Consequently, in the immediately ensuing clauses of the transition, the representation of Paul's plans for the next stage of his travels (19.21–22) – he will return to Macedonia and Achaia, and from there go on to Jerusalem and then

---

[91] The complete sense of the clause would therefore be τὰ τε πνεύματα τὰ πονηρὰ ἐκπορεύεσθαι ἐν τῷ ὀνόματι τοῦ κυρίου Ἰησοῦ; for roughly similar syntax and transitivity in the same discursive field, cf. Luke 10.17: καὶ τὰ δαιμόνια ὑποτάσσεται ἡμῖν ἐν τῷ ὀνόματί σου.

[92] Cf. Barrett, *Acts*, II, p. 907; and note Paul's explicit use of ἐν ὀνόματι Ἰησοῦ Χριστοῦ in Acts 16.18, which strengthens the case for the name's implicit presence here in 19.12.

[93] Tannehill, *Narrative Unity*, II, pp. 239–40, briefly notes the link between Acts 19.21 and Luke 9.51 but, perhaps because he overlooks the larger set of ties between the two passages' antecedent co-texts, underestimates its significance.

[94] Cf. J. T. Squires, *The Plan of God in Luke–Acts*, SNTSMS 76 (Cambridge, 1993), p. 2 n. 8; and p. 121 n. 1.

Rome – is tightly chained, both referentially and thematically, to the exorcism materials in 19.11–20.

What we have in Acts 19.11–22, therefore, is first of all a combination of materials that deal with exorcistic failure, success, and the factors that determine legitimacy in this domain (19.11–20), followed by a brief but structurally important transition (19.21–22) that anticipates the climax of the volume. This sequence should not sound unfamiliar; for it is a pattern Luke's readers have already encountered back in the Gospel's third exorcism story and its co-text (Luke 9.1–56), where the same interests in exorcistic failure, success, and legitimacy[95] all co-occur and directly precede a major transition (9.51–56) that anticipates the denouement of the volume.

Since a major correspondence between these larger blocks of co-text would affect our understanding not only of Acts 19.11–20 but also of the Lucan stories it parallels (i.e., Acts 16.16–18; Luke 8.26–39; 9.37–43a), additional evidence in its favour ought to be noted, especially since it is widely overlooked in scholarly commentary. Each of the transitional units (i.e., Luke 9.51–56; Acts 19.21–22), for instance, includes the lexis of fulfilment (συμπληροῦσθαι in Luke 9.51; ἐπληρώθη in Acts 19.21), the syntagm πορεύεσθαι εἰς Ἱεροσόλυμα, a specification of the geographical area(s) to be visited by the main protagonist before he reaches his final destination, a preparatory sending of assistants to the next area to be visited, and disclosure of two of the assistants' names. None of this pattern's constituent features, moreover, is shared by the Gospel transition's parallels in Matthew 19.1–2 and Mark 10.1. Accordingly, its presence in both Luke 9.51–56 and Acts 19.21–22 strengthens the impression that the two pieces instantiate a potentially significant correspondence.

Furthermore, as each of these transitions is directly preceded not only by material involving exorcism (i.e., Luke 9.49–50; Acts 19.11–20) but also by units exemplifying other interests (i.e., Luke 9.1–48; Acts 18.24–19.10), the possibility that these other interests contribute to the same correspondence deserves consideration. In Luke 9.1–11, for instance, where first the twelve and then Jesus are portrayed as engaged in preaching and healing, the ministry of healing is closely associated with 'the kingdom of God', just as it is in the Acts account of Paul's ministry in Ephesus (19.8–12). Second, although the hostility which Jesus prepares the twelve to encounter in their mission (9.5) is never actually experienced by them in Luke 9.1–50, it is encountered by Paul in Ephesus

---

[95] Exorcistic failure: Luke 9.40–41; success: Luke 9.1–11, 42–43a; and the relevance of group boundaries to exorcistic legitimacy: Luke 9.49–50.

(19.9), where he responds to it in a fashion that conforms to the spirit of Jesus' teaching. Furthermore, in Luke 9.7–20 two instances of misunderstanding are reported concerning Jesus' relation to John the Baptist, highlighting an issue that likewise surfaces twice in the Ephesus section of Acts (18.24–26; 19.1–4). Fourth, while the Baptist is never slandered in either Luke 9.1–50 or Acts 18.24–19.20, in each section he is firmly subordinated to Jesus, whose superior status is articulated in both contexts by the application of τὸν Χριστόν and comparably honorific titles to his person.[96] Fifth, in both sections disciples and discipleship have a prominent place, with characters deficient in understanding (i.e., Peter and Apollos) being given the necessary instruction to improve their faith. In Luke 9.28–36, moreover, as in Acts 19.1–7, the programme of instruction for at least some of these disciples includes an experiential element involving altered states of consciousness. And finally, since half of the twelve occurrences of the number δώδεκα in Luke's Gospel are clustered together in chapters eight and nine, and with several of these functioning in a conspicuously symbolic way (Luke 8.43; 9.17), the quantification of the 'disciples' in Acts 19.7 – the number of men who, having received the spirit, 'spoke in tongues and prophesied' was ὡσεὶ δώδεκα – fits very neatly into this same scheme of parallels.[97]

The correspondence noted earlier between Luke 8.26–39 and Acts 16.16–18 is matched, therefore, by the relationship between Luke 9.1–56 and Acts 18.24–19.22. By arching across much of Luke–Acts, these parallels help to tie the two volumes together and highlight continuity between Jesus and Paul. But just as important, the general sense of cohesion and continuity in all this depends on the particular thematic strings that collectively realise the correspondence. As the content, volume and overall lyric of these strings furthermore would have been chosen by Luke to suit his situation, an attempt to outline them should make it possible to draw some inferences about that situation's key features and contours.

Prominence, relevance and situation

My analysis of the Lucan exorcism stories and their related co-textual schemes suggests that the most prominent emphases in these passages are as follows:

1. The exorcistic work of Paul stands in direct continuity with that of Jesus.

---

[96] See Luke 9.19–20; Acts 18.25, 28; 19.3–5.
[97] After Acts 7.8, δώδεκα occurs only here and in 24.11.

2. Although the continuity between Jesus and Paul does not entail equality of function or of status, it does underscore very strongly Paul's legitimacy as a disciple.

3. In contrast to the performances of Jesus and Paul, both of whom are successful at exorcism without exception, attempts by certain other exorcists end in failure, which is attributed in one instance to the exorcists' unwelcoming response to the demoniac (Luke 9.37–50) but in another to ideological error (Acts 19.8–20);[98] however, as processes of extending welcome (especially to persons of very low status) and receiving it are essential features of the kingdom Jesus has inaugurated, the causes of failure in these cases ought to be seen as two sides of the same eschatological coin.

4. Both in his own exorcisms and in those achieved through Paul, Jesus is characterised as having authority comparable to that ascribed in Jewish Scripture to the God of Israel.

5. The sense of legitimacy and truth in Jesus' and Paul's exorcisms is powerfully enhanced by their rich correspondence to Jewish biblical prophecy and narrative pattern.

6. Although the general phenomenon of healing is represented favourably in several passages of Jewish Scripture,[99] exorcism in the narrow sense is not even mentioned; consequently, Luke's tacit but uniquely clear conceptualisation of his protagonists' exorcisms as a form of healing serves indirectly to enhance the coherence of his biblical intertextual rhetoric.

7. Luke defines Paul in particular not only by associating him with Jesus and Jewish ancestral tradition but also by portraying him as unambiguously antagonistic to any sort of accommodation to paganism.

8. Opposition to Jesus' and Paul's exorcisms is closely linked to dishonourable interests, especially economic ones, which are often inspired by diabolic power.

And (9) while hostility to Paul's exorcistic and related activities leads to various accusations against his person (e.g., that he is an enemy of Roman order), public officials in the Roman cities of Philippi and Ephesus judge him to be innocent of these charges, echoing for Luke's audience the emphatic declaration by Pilate of the innocence of Jesus (Luke 23.1–25).

To be sure, by itself this combination of emphases does not tell us everything we need to know in order to infer the type of situation that shaped the composition of Luke–Acts as a whole. However, if Suzanne Eggins is right to claim that a text's linguistic patterns allow us to deduce 'aspects

---

[98] I.e., as noted above, the itinerants do not proclaim 'the kingdom of God' heralded by Jesus (e.g., Luke 9.11) and Paul (e.g., Acts 19.8).

[99] Gen. 20.17; Exod. 15.26; Deut. 32.39; Pss 60.2; 107.20; 147.3; Isa. 19.22; 30.26; 57.18–19; 61.1; Hos. 6.1; Tobit 12.3.

of the context in which it was produced and ... within which it would be considered appropriate',[100] then this same combination should enable us to make at least a few interesting inferences about the Lucan writings' original context. For instance, Luke's emphasis on Paul's continuity with Jesus would have had optimal relevance to an audience that viewed Paul as highly significant for its own identity but which was also prone, for that very reason, to being unsettled by challenges to his honour. In this regard Luke's foregrounded identification of Paul with Jesus suggests that the status of the latter was probably more secure than that of Paul; still, unless most or even all of Luke's first volume was utterly irrelevant to its original context of production, the honour of Jesus himself must also have been under threat – due chiefly, perhaps, to the rumours surrounding his most controversial missionary. Similarly, Luke's representation of Paul as a Torah-observant Jew who firmly resisted accommodation to paganism looks very much like a response to Jewish accusations that Paul was now an apostate, whose advocacy of table-fellowship between Jew and non-Jew in the churches of the diaspora was compromising Jewish distinctiveness and identity;[101] in this connection, it should also be noted that Jewish communities which viewed Paul as deviant and knew about his teratological powers could easily have labelled him a 'magician' – even worse, a magician who promoted the honour of someone executed by the Romans on charges of treason – and represented him in this light to local magistrates.[102]

These types of rumours about Paul would almost certainly have impacted public opinion about Jesus as well, whose reputation was inextricably bound up with Paul's in many churches of the diaspora (cf. Acts 19.13). Consequently, the same agonistic milieu sketched thus far helps to explain two other frontgrounded features in the exorcism stories, namely Jesus' participation in the authority of the God of Israel and his multi-faceted identification with Jewish ancestral tradition; for indirectly, and especially when viewed as part of Luke's rhetoric of Jesus–Paul continuity, these emphases give Paul purchase on some of the highest authority in the cosmos, while simultaneously answering challenges to his churches' claim on the Jewish biblical heritage.

Luke's emphasis on Paul's legitimacy as a disciple, moreover, presupposes debates of a specifically intra-Christian character, for the quality of Paul's commitment to Jesus in particular is unlikely to have been a concern among those outside the churches. Thus, while Luke normally characterises opposition to Paul as coming from unbelieving outsiders

---

[100] Eggins, *Systemic Functional Linguistics*, p. 7.
[101] See, e.g., Gal. 2.11–14.   [102] Cf. Bovon, *Luc (1–9,)*; p. 25.

(often Jewish but sometimes pagan), he clearly acknowledges in at least a few instances that there were also insiders – especially Jewish ones – who had doubts about Paul's legitimacy. In reality, of course, the doubts inside must have been shaped in various ways by the opposition outside; and to his credit, Luke hints in a few places at how the gossip networks in these different domains may have intersected.[103]

Due chiefly, however, to his need to highlight unity and harmony within the Jesus movement, Luke puts most of the blame for Paul's difficulties on the shoulders of outsiders; and consonant with this tendency, two of the themes summarised above serve primarily to define and underscore the boundaries between those outside and those inside. First, whereas Jesus' and Paul's exorcisms are firmly associated with 'the kingdom of God' (Luke 9.1–11; Acts 19.8–12), the exorcistic efforts of the competition are marked by a comparative lack of eschatological urgency and power;[104] in Luke's own immediate situation, therefore, this emphasis would have constituted a counter-challenge to the external opposition among the Jews in particular, asserting in effect that the latter lacked the eschatological experience and status facilitated by faith in the Pauline Jesus. And finally, by repeatedly describing the opposition as inspired by Satan and greed, Luke not only sharpens the boundaries between in-group and out-group but also provides further evidence that much of his material on demons and exorcism has been strongly conditioned by ideological struggles of the sort outlined here; for unless Luke's negative portrayals of figures such as the sons of Scaeva and Elymas the magician (Acts 13.4–12) were fashioned at least partly as responses to slander levelled against his own heroes,[105] these images would have been at best pointless. Indeed, had Luke misread his situation badly, this aspect of his narrative could easily have caused offence to his earliest audiences, who therefore would have been unlikely to value his text in a manner conducive to its subsequent success.

Context of culture

Comparison of the story in Acts 16.16–18 with a range of other ancient Mediterranean texts on similar topics can deepen and complicate our

---

[103] See, e.g., Acts 21.17–26, especially vv. 21 and 24, where law-observant Jewish members of the Jerusalem church are portrayed as having been told by other unspecified Jews (probably out-group) that Paul teaches Jews in the diaspora to forsake Moses.

[104] See, e.g., Luke 11.24–26; Acts 19.13–16.

[105] On continuity in the magic accusations levelled by outsiders from the time of Jesus to the mid-second century, see M. Q. Smith, *Jesus the Magician*, pp. 53–6.

understanding of how this episode might have functioned for its author and earliest audiences. Luke's characterisation of the pythian spirit, for instance, when read alongside other ancient sources on divination and oracles, can tell us a great deal both about ideological aspects of demon-possession in antiquity and about the Acts episode's own cultural rhetoric. The relationship between 'the name of Jesus Christ', moreover, and those of powerful deities on the one hand and of other mighty exorcists (e.g., Kings David and Solomon) on the other hand, can be richly illuminated by comparison with the Solomon tradition and various ancient incantatory formulas. And by enabling us to see how little the implied author of this story is concerned about the post-exorcism fate of the slave-girl, the same broadly comparative approach sheds further light on what this author was primarily concerned about and thereby facilitates a cross-check on some of the inferences drawn above about his situation.

Prophecy, polyphony and the social construction of demon-possession

Perhaps because the word πύθωνα in 16.16 requires exegetes to wrestle with so difficult a combination of lexicogrammatical and text-critical puzzles, the implications of the word's contextualisation in the present story for understanding the social aspects of demon-possession have received surprisingly little attention. The matter must be discussed, however, if we want to read this episode in relation to the social and cultural tensions of its earliest context of reception.

As noted above in my treatment of 'lexis', the phrase πνεῦμα πύθωνα denotes a type of spirit which most of Luke's pagan contemporaries would have associated with a completely legitimate and beneficial form of religious activity, namely the provision of oracles. The associations of the noun πύθων and its cognates with the well-known myth and ritual of the Delphic oracle in particular serve to connect this spirit to Pythian Apollo, the great god of manticism, the link being strengthened both by the occurrence of μαντεύομαι in the same verse and by the typically Apolline ambiguity of the girl's utterance.[106] Although the nature of the relationship between the girl's pythian spirit and Apollo himself is unspecified in the present episode, a conceptualisation like that of Plutarch's, with

---

[106] On the collocation of πύθων and μαντεύομαι, cf. Reimer, *Women*, p. 155. On Apollo's fame for ambiguity, cf. H. W. Parke, *Greek Oracles* (London, 1967), pp. 143–4; and R. Flaceliere, *Greek Oracles*, trans. D. Garman, 2nd edn. (London, 1976), pp. 53–4. The ambiguity of oracles more generally is criticised in Lucian *Alex*. 10.

the oracles being inspired not directly by Phoebus himself but rather by intermediary daimons subordinate to him,[107] cannot be far from the mark.

Furthermore, although Delphi and other old oracular-centres were in a phase of declining prestige and popularity in the era that concerns us here, Apolline oracles in other parts of the Greek world continued to be active and prosperous, especially in Asia Minor but also in Macedonia.[108] As the ascendancy of Rome after the Second Punic War led to a decrease in Apollo's importance for purposes of official consultation by embassies,[109] inquirers closer to Luke's era came with questions of less public gravity: in Plutarch's characterisation, '"Is one to marry?" "Is one to go on a voyage?" "Is one to give a loan?"'[110] A Plutarch, of course, can sneer that such concerns are 'trivial and vulgar' (*De Pyth. or.* 408.b); but in a time of relative peace, these are the kinds of questions that have central importance to most people, and the socio-political conditions that helped to make them so in Luke's milieu also helped to create a market for individual prophet-diviners and charlatan types such as Alexander of Abonuteichos, whose portrayal by Lucian of Samosata is broadly comparable to the representation of the oracle business in Acts 16.16–19.[111] In this light, moreover, both the emphasis in 16.16 on the great profits which the girl's gift enabled her to earn and the local crowd's post-exorcism alliance with the owners against Paul and Silas achieve high marks on realism.

In discourse between pagans in the early Imperial period, therefore, a phrase like πνεῦμα πύθωνα would normally have had the sort of positive charge that is associated with divinatory practice as a whole in the speech of Q. Lucilius Balbus, the spokesman for Stoic philosophy in Cicero's *On the Nature of the Gods*, whose argument for the existence of the gods includes weighty appeal to the prestige of manticism: 'Magna augurum auctoritas; quid, haruspicum ars nonne divina' (2.12).[112] As Balbus' understanding of the *modus operandi* of soothsaying and similar types of manticism was probably comparable to that of his fellow Stoic Lucan, who assumed that these activities involved states of ecstasy and possession by one divine power or other,[113] he would have found the idea of

---

[107] See Plutarch *De def. or.* 414.e.   [108] Parke, *Oracles*, pp. 133–40.
[109] Ibid., p. 132.
[110] Plutarch *De Pyth. or.* 408.b, cited in and discussed by Parke, *Oracles*, pp. 135–6.
[111] See Lucian *Alex.* 7–8, 10, 19, where commerce in oracles is criticised for exploiting human fears, hopes and gullibility.
[112] As noted however by C. Lévy, 'De Chrysippe à Posidonius: variations stoïciennes sur le thème de la divination', in J.-G. Heintz (ed.), *Oracles et prophéties dans l'antiquité* (Paris, 1997), p. 328, Balbus does not speak for all Stoic thinkers on this matter, some of whom (e.g., Cicero himself) evaluated divination in a more ambivalent fashion.
[113] Lucan *Pharsalia* 5.86–224.

exorcising such a spirit extraordinarily odd. Similarly, since neither the slave-girl in our story nor her owners show any sign of doubting her pythian spirit's essential goodness, they too would have thought exorcism completely irrelevant in this context: from their point of view, as the agent of possession that inspired the girl's utterances was neither evil nor impure, it scarcely needed to be expelled. Many pagan philosophers and most members of the Empire's uneducated classes would have agreed,[114] whatever judgements they might have formed about the economic facets of the case.

The implied situation of Acts 16.16–18, however, is manifestly far from being completely pagan. Indeed, although Luke assumes that his audience needs no explanation of the pythian spirit, he also expects them to evaluate this phenomenon in terms of the intertextual and narrative frame that he himself has put around this reference. For instance, as noted earlier in this chapter, the narrator begins this episode in a style that evokes the religious world and values of the LXX; he furthermore describes the girl's activities not only as being part of an exploitative scheme by her owners but also as a form of occult practice condemned by Jewish Scripture (Deut. 18.11); and, although the initial reference to the pythian spirit does evoke, as Reimer has well observed, different connotations from those elicited by references elsewhere in the narrative to demonic beings,[115] the reference's own syntax and collocational pattern – grammatically, πνεῦμα πύθωνα fills the same slot which at several earlier points in the narrative has been filled by πνεῦμα ἀκάθαρτον or πνεῦμα πονηρόν – simultaneously hint at the sort of demonisation which this spirit will undergo in the ensuing action. The story's denouement, with the spirit being expelled like an ordinary demon, coheres perfectly with this reading.[116]

The conflict between the two cosmic powers in this story therefore instantiates a much wider struggle between the massive weight of pagan traditions of revelation on the one hand and the rhetorically ambitious but still tiny and fragile cult of Christ on the other hand. What Bakhtin calls '*raznorečie*'[117] is therefore on full display in this context, with the term πύθων in particular being stretched and torn between its long history

---

[114] For discussion of the evidence, see, e.g., F. G. Downing, 'Magic and Scepticism in and around the First Christian Century', in Klutz (ed.), *Magic*, p. 90; J. Dillon, *The Middle Platonists: A Study of Platonism 80 B.C. to A.D. 220*, rev. edn. (London, 1996), pp. 89–90; and A. S. Pease and J. H. Croon, 'Divination', in *OCD*, p. 357.

[115] Reimer, *Women*, p. 160.

[116] Cf. D. Marguerat, 'Miracle and Magic in Acts', in Klutz (ed.), *Magic*, p. 111; and Klauck, *Magie und Heidentum*, p. 80.

[117] I.e., heteroglossia; or, as explained by M. Holquist ('Introduction', in *The Dialogic Imagination: Four Essays by M. M. Bakhtin*, trans. C. Emerson and M. Holquist (Austin,

of positive meaning in pagan divinatory practice and its negative contextualisation in the present narrative. Yet we should not overlook this tension's potential to illuminate a certain diachronic aspect of the story as well. More specifically, and whatever our judgement on this episode's historicity, both the conflict just noted and the point of view from which it is narrated illustrate beautifully the socially constructed and ideological nature of demon-possession in Luke's ancient Mediterranean context; for despite Luke's heavy demonisation of the pythian spirit, the number of people in the Roman colony of Philippi who would have shared his point of view on this matter must be reckoned exceedingly small. Indeed, precisely because demon-possession presupposes a collective process whereby the victim is stigmatised by a number of significant and influential others in their particular locale, the present story's heavily pagan context of reference weighs at least lightly against its historicity; still, credible ways of reconstructing a historical event behind this episode can be imagined, and one of these will be considered below.

The demonisation of the pythian spirit, moreover, exemplifies a rhetorical phenomenon that is richly attested in the history of ancient religious conflict. In 1 Corinthians 10.14–22, for instance, the deities that were honoured in the traditional pagan ceremonies of ancient Corinth are redescribed by the apostle Paul as demonic beings.[118] Centuries earlier several authors of the Hebrew Bible applied the demon label to deities honoured by Israel's neighbours and by the assimilationists in her own population,[119] while the translators who produced the LXX employ δαιμόνιον twice to render references to foreign 'idols' in their Hebrew exemplars.[120] The same process can be observed in sources as diverse in date and content as the *Gathas* (c. sixth century BCE), in which the leading deities of Persia's pre-Zarathustrian pantheon (i.e., the daevas) are

---

1981), p. xix), the propensity of individual utterances to instantiate multiple registers and socio-ideological varieties of language.

[118] Cf. 2 Cor. 6.14–16; Gal. 4.8–11 and Col. 2.18–20; Rev. 9.20.

[119] See, e.g., Deut. 32.17; Ps. 106.37. The identification of 'Beelzebul' with 'Satan' in the Beelzebul Controversy (Matt. 12.24–26; Mark 3.22–23; Luke 11.15–18) reflects a very similar process, whereby the Syro-Palestinian deity Baal Zebul (i.e., Baal the Prince) was demonised in Israelite propaganda into the arch-demonic opponent of Yhwh; cf. W. Herrmann, 'Baal Zebub בעל זבוב', *DDD*, cols 293–4. On the related tendency of ancient religions in general to demonise each other's deities, see J. Z. Smith, 'Demonic Powers', p. 433; E. Dhorme, 'La démonologie biblique', in *Maqqél shâqédh: Hommage à Wilhelm Vischer* (Montpellier, 1960), p. 48.

[120] E.g., LXX Isa. 65.11; Ps. 95.5; see also Baruch 4.7, though it is impossible to be certain about the Hebrew original of Baruch at this point. On the LXX translators' more general tendency to engage in demonising interpretation of the Hebrew Bible, see Annen, *Heil für die Heiden*, pp. 140–1.

demonised as the wicked 'seed of the Bad Thought ... and of the Lie and of Arrogance' (*Y.* 32.3–5);[121] and the various Nag Hammadi tractates that include one form or another of the biblical-demiurgical myth, according to which the creator-god of Jewish Scripture is a demonic creature full of ignorance and envy.[122] Thus, wherever inter-religious conflict erupted in this milieu – indeed, even where the conflict was *intra*-religious – accusations of demon-worship had opportunity to fly, with the preferred deity of the opponent being castigated as an inferior spirit of evil.

Manumission, damaged property and the politics of Jewish identity

According to the narrator of Acts 16, the slave-girl began to follow the missionaries when they were en route to the local Jewish prayer-house (16.16), and she kept up her pursuit 'for many days' (16.18). Although the narrator shows no interest in the details of the missionaries' interactions with the Jewish community of Philippi during this time, Paul and his friends almost certainly would have used the local synagogue as part of a larger and more complex social network for facilitating the spread of their message.[123] Whatever the nature of their intentions towards the slave-girl, they therefore would have given her a point of contact with the city's Jewish community, much of which would probably have shared Paul and the narrator's perspective on her pythian spirit.

As the potential significance of this scenario has been fully explained by Richter Reimer,[124] my aim here is chiefly to summarise and adapt the main points of her work. Like a number of non-Jewish temples around this time, Jewish synagogues sometimes offered asylum for mistreated slaves and even created opportunities for them to acquire freedom through a process of sacral manumission, which entailed an obligation by the former slave to attach themselves to the Jewish community and practise Judaism.[125] Indeed, as the Jewish προσευχή was well known for its role in these arrangements, the girl may even have hoped that by following

---

[121] R. C. Zaehner, *The Dawn and Twilight of Zoroastrianism* (London, 1961), pp. 37–9; I. Gershevitch, *The Avestan Hymn to Mithra: With an Introduction, Translation, and Commentary* (Cambridge, 1959), pp. 51, 63. On the pre-Zarathustrian status of the daevas, see also *Y.* 44.20.

[122] See, e.g., *Orig. World* 100.1–101.4; *Hyp. Arch.* 86.27–91.10; *Ap. John* 9.25–24.32.

[123] Cf. A. J. Malherbe, *Social Aspects of Early Christianity*, 2nd edn. (Philadelphia, 1983), pp. 64, 68–9.

[124] See Reimer, *Women*, pp. 180–2, which offers a valuable summary and interpretation of the key manumission inscriptions and other relevant evidence.

[125] Ibid., pp. 181–2.

the Jewish missionaries and using them to access the local Jewish place, she might eventually be released from her present owners.[126] Furthermore, since most of the local Jews and God-fearers would probably have shared Paul and Silas' negative judgement on the girl's particular variety of manticism, the synagogue would have provided an effective plausibility structure for a demonising redescription of her pythian spirit and created a promising environment for exorcistic success. A sacral manumission in the synagogue therefore constitutes a historically plausible setting for the exorcism narrated in Acts 16, notwithstanding the heavily pagan religious context of Philippi as a whole.

On the other hand, a number of historically plausible settings could be imagined without any of them being satisfactorily commensurable with our narrative; and the scenario just envisaged fails to fit the story in Acts 16 in a couple of noteworthy ways. In the first place, the closest the narrator of this episode comes to describing anything like a sacral manumission is his reference to the προσευχή in 16.16, where initial contact between the missionaries and the prayer-house remains to be narrated. But just as important, in a synagogal setting of manumission we might have expected something other than annoyance on the part of Paul (16.18), whose expulsion of the girl's spirit is motivated less by a commitment to securing her freedom than by a desire to terminate her potentially misleading advertisements.

Whatever one's disposition concerning the sacral manumission thesis, Paul's expulsion of the pythian spirit has weighty implications for contextualising the story in relation to its material culture. Most notably, since an effective exorcism in this setting would have ruined the girl's special profit-making skill and thus constituted damage to her masters' property, the one who caused the destruction (i.e., Paul as exorcist) would have been liable according to Roman property law to compensate the owners with payment equivalent to the girl's redemption price;[127] as Reimer points out, payment of the compensation in this case would have been tantamount to an act of purchase or redemption.[128] However, while the owners are clearly represented by the narrator as concerned about their economic loss (16.19), they represent themselves, in the speech attributed to them in 16.20–21, not as seeking compensation for damages but rather as guardians of civic concord and Roman ancestral custom, both of which, they allege, are under threat from the missionaries. Thus, although the political, religious and economic threads in this part of Luke's narrative fabric are too tightly interwoven to be effectively separated out, a shift

---

[126] Ibid., p. 181.   [127] Ibid., p. 182.   [128] Ibid., pp. 177, 182.

of emphasis in this section from the economic (16.19) to the religious and the political (16.20–21) is none the less to be observed. Brief but careful reflection on the sociocultural conditions for this shift may shed further light on the rhetorical motivations and implied situation of Luke's narrative.

In the first place, in addition to having damaged the property of local elites, whose high level of social status and prosperity is entailed by their appeal to legal redress,[129] Paul belongs to a group of outsiders whose alien presence in the city has been publicly advertised for many days by the girl. As Jews, moreover, Paul and Silas represent a minority group which, though quantitatively small in Philippi, was probably subject to the same combination of hatred and respect, revulsion and attraction, that Jews experienced in many parts of the Empire at this time.[130] Furthermore, both the content of the girl's speech and its contribution to Paul's economically destructive intervention imply a public rather than a private setting for the exorcistic performance, which therefore should probably be imagined as having had witnesses. And finally, since Paul's mode of exorcism consists of a command 'in the name of Jesus Christ', his action would have looked to pagan observers like a destructive incantation which invoked the power of a new and distinctly un-Roman divinity;[131] indeed, by achieving Paul's aim so impressively, this alien cosmic power would have seemed a serious threat to the existing socioreligious structures of the city.

Jews, outsiders, new and alien divinities, incantations that damage the property of established locals – here we have ideal conditions for a magic accusation.[132] The last of these elements on its own would have sufficed to bring down charges of *malum carmen*, according to F. Graf's fine treatment of the history of Roman law on this matter;[133] and, since in the ensuing co-text Paul and Silas differ from real 'magicians' by refusing to

---

[129] On the bias of Roman law in favour of the elite and wealthy, see N. Purcell, 'The Arts of Government', in J. Boardman, J. Griffin and O. Murray (eds), *The Roman World* (Oxford, 1988), p. 172; Rapske, *Roman Custody*, pp. 119–20, 129.

[130] On the size of the Jewish community in Philippi, see P. Oakes, *Philippians: From People to Letter*, SNTSMS 110 (Cambridge, 2001), pp. 58–9, 87. On ambivalence towards Jews in the early Imperial age, see P. Schäfer, *Judeophobia: Attitudes towards the Jews in the Ancient World* (Cambridge, MA, 1997), pp. 192–5.

[131] Cf. Poupon, 'L'Accusation de magie', pp. 73–5, who includes the use of Jesus' name among the various factors that encouraged pagans to accuse early Christians of magical practice.

[132] Cf. C. S. de Vos, 'Finding a Charge that Fits: The Accusation against Paul and Silas at Philippi (Acts 16.19–21)', *JSNT* 74 (1999), 51–63; Graf, *La magie dans l'antiquité gréco-romaine*, p. 79.

[133] See Graf, *La magie dans l'antiquité gréco-romaine*, pp. 52–73.

escape from prison even when they had opportunity to do so,[134] an indirect response to this type of accusation may be part of Luke's motivation in this section (16.25–40). Yet, in a setting where either explicit accusations of 'magic' practice or charges of ritual damage to property might have been predicted from the antecedent stages of the contest, the very tacitness of these concerns in the discourse of the girl's owners causes the more explicit aspects of their utterance to take on special salience: in brief, the missionaries are nothing but stereotypical Jews ('Ιουδαῖοι ὑπάρχοντες, 16.20),[135] promoting as usual their ghastly un-Roman customs and causing the predictable riot and discord.

Significantly, distinctions like that attested in Ignatius of Antioch, between 'Judaism' and 'Christianity' (*Magn.* 8.1–10.3), have no place here in the accusations presented by the owners. As far as the latter are concerned, the missionaries of Christ are simply part of the larger Jewish virus, whose widely alleged misanthropy and un-Roman (and un-Greek) exclusivism would have been confirmed afresh here by Paul's unwillingness to accommodate the pagan diviner and by his destruction of property. Not for the last time in antique sources, the tar used in pagan slander against the cult of Christ comes from the same bucket employed against the Jews.[136] Both the hostile stereotyping of the Jews as a whole and the stark contrast between them and 'us...Romans' (ἡμῖν...'Ρωμαίοις οὖσιν, 16.21) have cultural antecedents in sources ranging from Cicero's speech *Pro Flacco*, whose defence of the former governor of Roman Asia, Lucius Valerius Flaccus, against charges of corruption in regard to the annual collection for the Jerusalem temple, defines the influential 'crowd of the Jews' as antithetical to the public interest of all Rome;[137] to the *Additions to Esther*, in which the political leaders of Persia (i.e., Artaxerxes and Haman) are represented as Greek-style anti-semites who paint the Jews as hostile, unassimilable, ungovernable, contrary to imperial unity, and worthy of complete extermination (13.1–7).

---

[134] On the role of escaping from prison in early Christian and Late Antique stereotyping of magicians, see A. Reimer, 'Prison Breaks', pp. 191–2.

[135] As noted by W. Elliger, *Paulus in Griechenland: Philippi, Thessaloniki, Athen, Korinth*, SBS 92/93 (Stuttgart, 1978), pp. 55–6, the structure of the slave-owners' speech serves to accentuate the contrast between 'Ιουδαῖοι and 'Ρωμαίοις, but since 'Ιουδαῖοι ὑπάρχοντες stands not only at the centre of their speech but also between lines that are broadly parallel to one another (ἐκταράσσουσιν ἡμῶν τὴν πόλιν... καταγγέλλουσιν ἔθη ἃ οὐκ ἔξεστιν), the contrast is perhaps less prominent than the emphatic Jewishness of the missionaries and the anti-Judaism of their antagonists. On the latter point, cf. Rapske, *Roman Custody*, pp. 120, 133.

[136] On pagan application of existing anti-Jewish motifs to the Christ cult, see Schäfer, *Judeophobia*, pp. 190–2.

[137] Cicero *Pro Flacco* 67.

Furthermore, by portraying the slave-girl's owners as justifiably smug in their assumption that the magistrates would be receptive to such anti-Judaic pleas (16.20b–24), Luke implicitly puts the municipal authorities in a shockingly bad light;[138] and against any hermeneutical suspicion that this facet of the narrative is all Lucan fabrication, the owners' presumption closely resembles that of Cicero in the speech just mentioned, whose audience is expected to share at least some of the speaker's prejudices against the Jews.[139] To be sure, on the level of communication between implied author and implied audience, the content of the owners' slander also contributes indirectly to the Lucan narratives' wider claim on the Jewish-biblical heritage of Israel, reinforcing Luke's own image of the cult of Christ and its leading missionary as the ideal embodiment of Judaism.[140] According to the values promoted by this larger metanarrative, if Paul and Silas suffer for the sake of Jewish difference, they do so in honour of the Holy One of Israel, who has promised to protect and rescue those who love him (Ps. 91.14–16). In line therefore with observations made above at other levels of analysis, the ethnic aspects of this narrative's rhetoric presuppose an audience that would be able to feel both sympathy for any Jews in these kinds of circumstances and disapproval towards any Roman officials of Judeophobic disposition.

The name of the exorcist

As already noted above, the use of Jesus' name in the present episode contributes to the macrostructural parallels between this passage and the exorcism materials in Luke 8.26–39 and 9.49–50. In these latter two contexts, however, the types of beings whose names are envisaged differ, with the concern in Luke 8.30 being the name of the demon but that in 9.49 being the name of Jesus. Considered collectively, therefore, and regardless of the precise significance of the formula in Acts 16.18 in particular, these passages illustrate an important religious assumption whose presence in Luke's wider context of culture merits attention, namely that knowledge

---

[138] Bad, that is, from a point of view sympathetic to Judaism. On the other hand, and probably due in part to the earthquake (Acts 16.26), whose effect on the prison could easily have been interpreted as a sign of disapproval from the missionaries' god, the magistrates not only release Paul and Silas the very next day (16.35–36) but also apologise to them (16.37–39), proving that the missionaries' message and activities were viewed by the civic officials as ultimately not so subversive after all; cf. L. Portefaix, *Sisters Rejoice: Paul's Letter to the Philippians and Luke–Acts as Seen by First-Century Philippian Women*, ConBNT 20 (Stockholm, 1988), pp. 170, 172.

[139] Schäfer, *Judeophobia*, pp. 182, 280 n. 15.

[140] Rapske, *Roman Custody*, pp. 133–4, recognises the emphasis on Paul's Jewishness and creatively uses it to explain the delay in Paul's disclosure of his citizenship but overlooks its contribution to the larger narrative construction of Paul's Jewish identity.

and invocation of various types of names were capable of either enhancing or ensuring success at exorcism.

The names that might be invoked to acquire ritual power in exorcistic and similar settings, both in the ancient Near East and in the Graeco-Roman world, ranged from those of deities and angelic beings to those of demons and legendary exorcists. Although exorcistic and apotropaic formulas have been preserved in which no name of power occurs,[141] one sort of epithet or other is invoked in most cases; and due to the relative positions of deities, demonic beings and humans in most ancient cosmologies, the names most frequently called upon belong to divine beings.[142] In *AEMT* 25, for instance, which is one of our earliest extant texts exemplifying this strategy (*c.* 2100 BCE), incantatory power is marshalled by appealing not merely to one but to several deities – Re', Horus, Osiris, Shu, Geb, Heka, Nun – in order to ensure exorcistic success against a single demon.[143] Similarly, in several texts representing diverse genres and widely divergent settings, authority over demons and mythic powers is sought through appeal to the ancient Syro-Palestinian deity Baal:[144] (1) in a Ugaritic incantation against various types of maleficent spirits and illegitimate intermediaries (e.g., 'sorcerers', 'binders', and 'youth soothsayers'), the spirits are expelled in the name of Baal and the intermediaries in the name of Horon;[145] (2) in the Ugaritic myth of *Baal and Yam*, in which Yam (i.e., 'Sea') represents the demonic powers of chaos,[146] Baal is addressed by his consort Athtart as 'the Name' (2.iv.28)

---

[141] Cf. Thraede, 'Exorzismus', col. 47; and J. P. Sørensen, 'The Argument in Ancient Egyptian Magical Formulae', *AcOr* 45 (1984), p. 12. Neither Apollonius in Philostratus *VA* 4.20, e.g., nor the Syrian exorcist described in Lucian *Philops.* 16 is described as using *nomina sacra* in their performance; see also Tobit 8.2–3, where the ritual used to drive away Asmodeus includes no incantatory formula.

[142] Cf. Twelftree, *Jesus the Exorcist*, p. 41.

[143] See also *AEMT* 23; *The Hymn of a Thousand Strophes* 3.18–22 (*NERTOT*, p. 24); and *The Hymn of Mer-Sekhmet* 8.3 (*NERTOT*, pp. 26–7).

[144] See also *KTU* I, p. 82, lines 1 and 3, where the narrator enjoins Baal to 'seize the serpents' and 'stop the arrows of Rashpu' (i.e., afflictions caused by a spirit of pestilence); for translation and discussion of this text, see J. C. de Moor and K. Spronk, 'More on Demons in Ugarit (*KTU* 1.82)', *UF* 16 (1984), 237–50. On Baal's reputation in ancient Canaanite religion as the prince of healers and exorcists, see Herrmann, 'Baal Zebub', cols 293, 295.

[145] Lines 1–2, 8–10 of *Ras Ibn Hani* 78/20, translated and discussed in Avishur, 'Ghost-Expelling Incantation', pp. 15–16; for further discussion of the same text, see de Moor, 'Incantation'. Although the shaming of Baal and his prophets in 1 Kgs 18.20–29 is manifestly Yahwist polemic, the references to his prophets calling on the deity's 'name' and attempting to embody his presence through ritually induced states of ecstasy probably captures an authentic dimension of exorcistic rituals performed in his name; cf. Herrmann, 'Baal Zebub', col. 261.

[146] Stolz, 'Sea', cols 1395–6.

just before being urged to 'scatter' and destroy his opponent completely; and (3) much later, in a second- or third-century CE recipe preserved in the Greek magical papyri (*PGM* 21.1–29), Baal and several other powerful names are invoked in order to guarantee that 'no spirit, no visitation, no daimon, no evil being will oppose' the recipe's user.

Comparison of these texts with the Lucan Paul's utterance in Acts 16.18 helps to contextualise the latter in a couple of noteworthy ways. On the one hand, as in Acts 16 so in these texts, the discourse of invoking powerful names instantiates a seldom-noticed theory of language – we might think of it as a magico-religious variety of essentialism – according to which the mention of a name is able to make available in the context of utterance the reputation and influence of the one named;[147] in all of these contexts, moreover, the attempt to access the desired power takes for granted the widely attested conviction that a person's honour or reputation is essentially encapsulated by their name.[148] But just as important, the exorcistic command cited in Acts also diverges from those just summarised, either through its appeal to the name of a single cosmic power or through the immediacy of its impact;[149] in this light, and especially as the expulsion of the pythian spirit constitutes an indirect assault on a still higher power (i.e., Apollo), the authority implicitly attributed to the name of Jesus Christ in Acts 16 compares very favourably with that ascribed to the divine names in these other documents. Indeed, since the invocation of Jesus' name directly follows the ambiguous discourse of the slave-girl, it has potential to be construed not only as a formula of incantatory power but also as an attempt by the Lucan Paul to disambiguate the girl's slippery references to 'the Most High God'.

Although most of the extrabiblical materials just canvassed derive from settings distant from that of Luke–Acts, they none the less make a valuable contribution to comparative study, not least by enabling us to appreciate the continuities which stand alongside the changes in the history of ancient Near Eastern and Mediterranean incantatory practice.[150] The utterance in

---

[147] Invocation of names in this milieu assumes a theory of language broadly similar to that assumed in ancient use of historiolas, i.e., stories which D. Frankfurter ('Narrating Power: The Theory and Practice of the Magical *Historiola* in Ritual Spells', in Meyer and Mirecki (eds), *Ancient Magic*, pp. 463–4) helpfully describes as making present 'a distinctly separate event from the mythic past'.

[148] Cf. Malina, *New Testament World*, pp. 100–2.

[149] Baal's victory over Yam, e.g., does not occur instantaneously but results from a staged and protracted process of conflict (*Baal and Yam* 2.iv.1–40).

[150] On the continuities between ancient Near Eastern and much later incantatory materials, see esp. P.-E. Dion, 'Raphaël l'Exorciste', *Biblica* 57 (1976), pp. 403–4; and Penney and Wise, 'By the Power of Beelzebub', pp. 629–30, 649–50; A. Green, 'Beneficent Spirits',

Acts 16, however, can certainly be illuminated further by comparison with sources closer to it in provenance or religious point of view. In this regard Psalm 91, *11QApocryphal Psalms*, and Josephus' portrayal of Solomon in *Ant.* 8.42–9 deserve special consideration.

In Psalm 91, which is echoed at least three times in the Gospel of Luke,[151] those who know the 'name' of the Lord are given assurance of the deity's protection and salvific presence (91.14–16). Several of the dangers against which this name serves as a prophylactic – for instance 'the terror of the night', 'the pestilence that stalks in darkness', and 'the destruction that ravages at midday' (91.5–6) – were probably understood as demonic entities by the author of the psalm's Hebrew text;[152] and the translator(s) who rendered these phrases into the Greek of the LXX made their demonological overtones more explicit by translating the last of these items, מקטב ישוד צהרים, as ἀπὸ συμπτώματος καὶ δαιμονίου μεσημβρινοῦ (91.6b). Furthermore, as Yhwh's reference in the psalm to 'those who know my name' is clarified through parallelism with 'those who love me' (91.14), the knowledge essential for receiving the promised protection should not be reduced to a matter of impersonal or amoral cognition; on the contrary, and especially when viewed in relation to the co-text of the psalm as a whole (especially 91.1–2, 9–10), this knowledge must be seen as embedded in a context of interpersonal trust and covenantal fidelity.[153] As in a number of incantatory texts from around this time and much later, therefore, so also in this psalm effectual knowledge of a divine name for apotropaic or related aims presupposes the existence of a contractual arrangement between the name's user and the designated deity, with the usual sorts of obligations being in force for the human client(s);[154] indeed, the difference between the exorcistic success of Paul, as seen both in the

---

p. 80; G. Wilhelm, 'Ein neues Lamaštu-Amulett', *ZA* 69 (1979), 34–40; Twelftree, *Jesus the Exorcist*, p. 15; Naveh and Shaked, *Amulets and Magic Bowls*, p. 13.

[151] See Luke 4.10–11, where Satan cites Ps. 91.11; Luke 10.17–20, which echoes Ps. 91.13; and Luke 13.34, where Jesus alludes to Ps. 91.4; cf. Garrett, *Demise of the Devil*, pp. 55–6, 107, 138 n. 66, 139 nn. 70–1.

[152] C. Stuhlmueller, 'Psalms', in *HBC*, p. 476.

[153] See esp. vv. 1–2 and 9–10, where the desired protection is promised only to those 'who dwell [ישב] in the shelter of the Most High', who already trust in Yhwh and have made him their refuge.

[154] The larger of the two Phoenician amulets from Arslan Tash (c. seventh century BCE), published in *ANESTP*, p. 222, and *NERTOT*, pp. 248–9, offers an especially interesting parallel: the amulet's incantatory inscription refers to itself twice as a 'covenant' (lines 1 and 9), which includes a promise from the deity Horon to guard the women of his harem (i.e., the female users of the amulet) against demonic attack. For further discussion of the amulet and its text, see D. S. Sperling, 'An Arslan Tash Incantation: Interpretations and Implications', *HUCA* 53 (1982), pp. 9–10; and A. Caquot, 'Observations sur la première tablette magique d'Arslan Tash', *JANESCU* 5 (1973), 46–9. On the presence of similar

present episode and in Acts 19.11–12, and the failure of the seven sons of Scaeva (19.13–20) can be partly explained by reference to the presence or absence of precisely this sort of arrangement.

Although Psalm 91 has no overtly exorcistic or apotropaic function in its Masoretic and Septuagintal manifestations, it came to be used for these purposes in Second Temple and Late Antique times.[155] In *11QApocryphal Psalms*, for instance, a relatively free rendering of Psalm 91 follows three highly fragmentary apocryphal psalms of exorcism,[156] one of which includes both a reference to the reliability of Yhwh's name and a historiola stressing his role in the paradigmatic separation of cosmogonic light from darkness (ii 8–12). As the whole collection furthermore has sources of cohesion that allow it to be read as a single unified composition,[157] the emphasis just noted on the reliability and power of Yhwh's name is able to acquire additional force in col. v lines 4–7, where, in a prescribed 'incantation in the name of Yhwh', the demonic opponent is not only represented as 'darkness' rather than 'light' – forming a lexical string with the same terms back in col. ii line 12 – but is also directly taunted: 'Who are you, O offspring of man and of the seed of the holy ones? Your face is the face of delusion, and your horns are horns of illusion' (v 6–7a). Thus, in addition to actualising the paradigmatic potential of the Jewish biblical myth of creation in order to overcome a present spirit of darkness (v 5), these portions of *11QApocryphal Psalms* confirm that the outcome of exorcistic battle in this milieu was understood to depend almost entirely on the names of the ritual's cosmic participants, their respective reputations and lineages, and the presence or absence of contractual bonds between exorcist and deity.

To this extent, moreover, these same passages shed light not only on the cosmic power attributed to the name of Jesus in Acts 16.18 but also on the rhetorical question which the sons of Scaeva are asked by the demon

---

contractual arrangements in Late Antique spells and incantations, see Meyer and Smith, 'Introduction', in *Ancient Christian Magic*, p. 5.

[155] In the Matthaean and Lucan versions of the temptation story, e.g., the devil employs a variation of this interpretation against Jesus (Ps. 91.11–12 in Matt. 4.6; Luke 4.10–11); and Jesus himself reads the psalm (91.13) this way in Luke 10.19. See also *AMB* bowl 11 (fourth to fifth century CE), lines 6–7, where exorcistic healing is sought by citing Ps. 91.1 and Deut. 6.4.

[156] On the exorcistic content and function of *11QApocryphal Psalms*, see P. S. Alexander, '"Wrestling against Wickedness in High Places": Magic in the Worldview of the Qumran Community', in S. E. Porter and C. A. Evans (eds), *The Scrolls and the Scriptures: Qumran Fifty Years After*, JSPSup 26 (Sheffield, 1997), p. 326; E. Puech, 'Un rituel d'exorcismes, essai de reconstruction', *RQ* 55 (1990), pp. 396–7; P. A. Torijano, *Solomon the Esoteric King: From King to Magus, Development of a Tradition*, JSJSup 73 (Leiden, 2002), pp. 45–7.

[157] On the unity of *11QApocryphal Psalms*, see Torijano, *Solomon*, p. 51 n. 17.

in Acts 19.15: 'Jesus I know, and Paul I know; but who are you?' As the question 'Who are you?' in settings of exorcism normally had the demon(s) in the role of addressee rather than that of sayer,[158] the unconventional participant structure of the question in Acts 19.15 intensifies the lampooning of the Jewish itinerants in their failure to master their demonic opponent; and since this same feature also suggests that, at least at this point in Luke's narrative, the implied author was less interested in the authority of Jesus over the demon(s) than in the inferiority of the itinerants to Paul, it supports the thesis put forward earlier in this chapter regarding the function and relative prominence of the exorcism theme in Luke–Acts as a whole: namely, although exorcism lies closer to the foreground than to the background in Luke's volumes, it is nevertheless best interpreted as subservient to wider questions revolving around the reputation of Paul.

By contributing to the correspondence between the present episode and the exchange about the strange exorcist in Luke 9.49–50, the use of Jesus' name in Acts 16.18 also implicitly positions Paul within a healthcare tradition. The text's implied audience, for instance, knows that the name of Jesus Christ has been used in therapeutic settings before, not only after his crucifixion (Acts 3.6) but even during his own lifetime (Luke 9.49); and since Jesus' own exorcistic healings have already been represented by the Lucan Peter as corresponding to the ministry of David to King Saul,[159] the audience of Acts 16 possesses everything they need in order to construct an honourable chain of tradition in which to place the exorcism performed by Paul, who thereby is given purchase on the commodity of all commodities in his tradition-orientated society, namely the prestige of antiquity and ancestral custom.

None of this is odd by the standards of Luke's cultural context. Although his interest in embedding Paul in a noble exorcistic heritage is undoubtedly constrained by specific situational factors discussed earlier in this chapter, Luke's efforts in this connection were underwritten by ideational and rhetorical resources whose wider availability is confirmed by consideration of contemporaneous sources on the same topic. One of the most problematic features of *11QApocryphal Psalms*, for instance,

---

[158] In addition to *11QApocryphal Psalms* v 6–7a, see *T. Sol.* 2.1; 3.6; 4.3; 5.2; 7.3; 8.1 et al. On the formulaic use of 'Who are you?' in settings of exorcism, see Torijano, *Solomon*, pp. 51–68.

[159] LXX 1 Sam. 16.13–14 in Acts 10.38. The echo is often overlooked by commentators (e.g., Fitzmyer, *Acts*, pp. 464–5) but is strongly supported by the volume of lexical and thematic correspondence (e.g., the collocation of χρίω, πνεύματι ἁγίῳ, δύναμις, spirit affliction and healing in both texts).

is the reference in its second column to Solomon (ii 2), whose mention in a text that highlights demons is certainly appropriate (for reasons discussed below) and may even reflect an attempt by the text's composer to identify himself and the text's users with Solomon's fame for incantatory and exorcistic wisdom. On the other hand, as the name of Solomon in this context is preceded by lacunae that make the reference's original function virtually unintelligible, it allows no confident inferences to be drawn about the construction of exorcistic chains of tradition at Qumran.

Fortunately, both in the same document and in *11QPsalms^a*, the origins of exorcistic wisdom are traced in a much less enigmatic manner back to Solomon's father David, whose praiseworthy achievements are summarised in the latter text as including the composition of four prophetically inspired 'songs to perform over those stricken [by evil spirits]' (xxvii 9–10). Since David is furthermore characterised in *11QApocryphal Psalms* as the author both of the rewritten version of Psalm 91 and of the 'incantation in the name of Yhwh',[160] his contribution of ancestral authority to the exorcistic practices commended in these texts is at least broadly comparable to that evoked in Acts 10.38 and 16.18. But just as important, at no point in either *11QApocryphal Psalms* or *11QPsalms^a* is the name of either Solomon or David used specifically in the invocational formula 'in the name of x'; the only figure who can fill this slot, at least in the Qumran text, is Yhwh,[161] whose functional equivalent in Acts 16.18 is therefore Jesus Christ.

As implied above, although the role of David in these texts is far clearer than Solomon's is, the presence of Solomon's name in *11QApocryphal Psalms* is scarcely surprising when this text's interests in demonology and exorcism are recognised; for Solomon is closely associated with demonological, apotropaic and exorcistic wisdom in a variety of documents and traditions from the Second Temple and Late Antique periods.[162] Indeed, one of the most convincing arguments for a relatively early origin (first or second century BCE) for the link between Solomon and the demons is the highly allusive and indirect character of the linkage between these interests in Luke 11.14–32 (par. Matt. 12.22–42), where the collocation of Solomon, exorcism and association with Beelzebul not only anticipates

---

[160] See *11QApocryphal Psalms* v 4 and vi 3.
[161] The same comparative point can be made from *4QExorcism ar* 1 i 4 if Penney and Wise, 'By the Power of Beelzebub', pp. 631–2, are justified in reading אנה מומה לכן בשם יהוה ('I adjure you by the name of Yhwh').
[162] E.g., Wisd. 7.20; Luke 11.14–32 (par. Matt. 12.22–42); Josephus *Ant.* 8.42–9; *L.A.B.* 60.3; *Apoc. Adam* 78.30–79.12; *Testim. Truth* 70.5–29; *Orig. World* 106.27–107.3. For discussion and bibliography, see D. C. Duling, 'Solomon, Testament of', *ABD* VI, pp. 118–19; Torijano, *Solomon*, pp. 317–30.

the more highly developed elaboration of these motifs in *T. Sol.* 3.1–6 and 6.1–11 but also presupposes an audience to which this whole complex of ideas was already familiar.[163] Furthermore, in order to function effectively as a claim to honour by Jesus, the comparison of Jesus to Solomon in Luke 11.31 (par. Matt. 12.42) must be interpreted as assuming that, in regard to things demonological and exorcistic, Solomon was indeed widely recognised and honoured. Yet, in regard to the prestige and power associated with the name of Solomon, no source has greater potential to enrich the present analysis than Josephus' representation of the king in *Ant.* 8.42–9.

Like its immediate co-text, *Ant.* 8.42–9 is devoted to portraying Solomon as the ideal ruler. Although Josephus makes no reference to demons or exorcism in the first section of this unit (8.42–4), he does highlight the universal range and comparative excellence of Solomon's wisdom in a fashion that closely resembles the eulogy to David in *11QPsalms*^{a} xxvii 1–11. In both cases, for instance, the idealised figure is first portrayed as having acquired a unique grant of general knowledge and wisdom from God, with the remainder of the encomium emphasising the quantity and topical range of the figure's literary output. In regard to the latter emphasis, moreover, the two texts resemble one another not only in style and sequencing but even in their numerical estimates of the compositions produced: the Qumranian David's output is explicitly reckoned to be 4,050 songs, while all the Solomonic writings quantified by Josephus add up to 4,005. And finally, although Josephus differs from *11QPsalms*^{a} by giving no quantitative summary of his subject's specifically exorcistic compositions, the two texts do share an interest in compositions of this register. In all of this, it is worth adding, *11QPsalms*^{a} and *Ant.* 8.42–9 stand much closer to one another than either of them does to Acts 16 or, for that matter, any other part of Luke's writings.

However, in contrast to the final lines of the Qumran text, where the exorcistic compositions of David are summarised in the briefest possible manner (col. xxvii lines 9–10), the second part of the Josephan passage (8.45–9) constitutes an outline of the whole history of the Solomonic tradition, locating its origins in Solomon's own exorcistic learning (8.45a), then representing it as a transmitted body of knowledge which continues to benefit humanity in Josephus' own day (8.45b–46), and concluding with an idealised example of its effective application in recent magico-medical

---

[163] I.e., a presupposition which, in order to be appropriate and intelligible for the relatively wide audience envisaged by Luke, must have been in circulation for several decades at minimum; cf. Torijano, *Solomon*, pp. 111–17; D. C. Duling, 'Solomon, Exorcism, and the Son of David', *HTR* 68 (1975), 235–52; and M. Q. Smith, *Jesus the Magician*, p. 80.

praxis (8.47–9). The concluding example, moreover, which highlights the ritual and incantatory actions performed by a Jewish contemporary of Josephus' named Eleazar, is especially relevant to the present study, partly because it enriches our understanding of how exorcistic chains of tradition in this context can function; more specifically, whereas the invocation of 'the name of Jesus Christ' in Acts 16.18 not only brings honour to Jesus but also contributes a much-needed layer of legitimacy to the image of Paul, Eleazar's successful employment of Solomonic ritual and incantatory formulas in *Ant.* 8.47–9 brings fame and recognition almost solely to Solomon.[164] But just as important, in this same part of the narrative, Josephus describes Eleazar's exorcistic technique as including mention of Solomon's name: after drawing out the demon through the patient's nostrils, Eleazar 'adjured the demon never to come back into him, speaking Solomon's name and reciting the incantations which he had composed' (8.47). Should we therefore imagine that the name of Solomon was being called on by Eleazar (and perhaps others) just as 'the name of Jesus Christ' was being called on by the Lucan Paul, in a formula of exorcistic invocation?

Clearly, as this part of Josephus' description is tightly conjoined with a reference to Eleazar's use of Solomonic incantations, it contributes both to the image of a chain of tradition and to the passage's emphasis on the greatness of Solomon. Furthermore, in this same sentence Josephus also describes Eleazar as employing a formula of adjuration, where a powerful name would certainly be at home. Yet, since the name of Solomon is not actually embedded in the adjuration formula summarised by Josephus, and since the mention of Solomon by Eleazar is implicitly represented as something separate from the incantation proper,[165] an invocation 'in the name of Solomon' is probably not what we should imagine here. More likely is a claim to prestigious (i.e., Solomonic) authorship for the incantation that immediately followed. As the envisaged demon would have been expected to know the reputation of Solomon just as demons in other ancient settings were expected to know the reputations of Paul (Acts 19.15) and Hanina ben Dosa (*b. Pes.* 112b), Eleazar's attribution of the incantations to Solomon would have served to heighten their authority and power in the eyes of the demons.

---

[164] Note esp. *Ant.* 8.49: 'When this [i.e., the visible confirmation of the demon's departure] was done, the understanding and wisdom of Solomon were clearly revealed... in order that all men may know the greatness of his nature and how God favoured him.'

[165] *Contra* Twelftree, *Jesus the Exorcist*, p. 52, who interprets *Ant.* 8.46–9 as implying that Solomon's name was used in the incantation proper.

Indeed, since the sequence of the two key circumstantial clauses in the Josephan narrative (Σολόμωνός τε μεμνημένος καὶ τὰς ἐπῳδὰς ἃς συνέθηκεν ἐκεῖνος ἐπιλέγων, 8.47) probably corresponds to the order of the actions they represent,[166] the relationship in this context between the name of Solomon and the incantations he composed closely resembles that between the name of David and the incantation in *11QApocryphal Psalms* v 4–14, where the references to David precede the incantation proper and function much the way superscriptions do in the canonical Psalms. Thus, comparative analysis of Josephus *Ant.* 8.42–9 reinforces the impression formulated above that the name of Jesus Christ in Acts 16.18 is functionally less analogous to the names of glorious exorcists from the past than to the name of Yhwh.[167]

Of genre and gender: why Luke is silent about the fate of the slave-girl

As Josephus' main goal in *Ant.* 8.42–9 is to emphasise the wisdom and virtue of Solomon, he gives almost no attention to either the background or the future direction of the healed demoniac. Yet, precisely in emphasising the Solomon legacy's power, Josephus does provide a couple of clues regarding these matters for anyone interested in them: namely, when Solomon's exorcistic prescriptions are applied to the afflicted, the expelled demons never return to their former victim (8.45); and this same positive outcome is the express aim of the adjuration attributed to Eleazar in particular (8.47). Since Josephus' narrative furthermore makes it easy to read the second feature in light of the first,[168] it indirectly encourages its audience to infer that the demon expelled by Eleazar never bothered the man again.

Concerning the post-exorcism fate of demoniacs in general, Josephus' account well exemplifies the tendency of most ancient narratives that deal with these sorts of matters. Most, in fact, put about the same degree of emphasis on the demoniac's future that Josephus does; a few give it more attention; and still others even less.[169] But nearly all afford at least a hint of how life changed for the former demoniac – if only in the short term.

---

[166] I.e., first the mention of Solomon, then the recitation of the incantations.

[167] Again, *contra* Twelftree, *Jesus the Exorcist*, p. 52, who as noted above obscures the differences between Eleazar's mention of Solomon's name and early Christian invocation of Jesus' name. For a view similar to that taken here, see Davies, *Jesus the Healer*, pp. 91–2.

[168] The two features are tied together by a strong lexical string, with μηκέτ'... ἐπανήξειν in 8.47 corresponding to μηκετ' ἐπανελθεῖν in 8.45.

[169] *About the same*: 1 Sam. 16.23; *1QGenesis Apocryphon* xx 29–30; Luke 9.42; *L.A.B.* 60.3; Josephus *Ant.* 6.168, 211; *Acts of Thomas* 8.81. *More*: Tobit 8–14; Mark 9.26–27;

In this regard the narrative in Acts 16 evinces a conspicuous deviation: neither the narrator nor the other voices in the narrative say anything about the expelled spirit's potential return to the girl, and at no point in the complications and dialogue that ensue in 16.19–40 is the girl even mentioned. This silence speaks even louder, moreover, when we recall from the treatment of transitivity earlier in this chapter that the girl is by far the most dynamic participant in the story prior to Paul's speech act of exorcistic command in 16.18. As the ultimate effect of all this is a complete vacuum of information about the girl's life after exorcism,[170] the idea that Luke represents the event as a 'liberation' – a thesis over which recent feminist interpreters are surprisingly divided[171] – has no discernible support either in the narrative itself or in its various levels of context.[172]

The question most worthy of our attention here, then, is why Luke's narrative deviates from the generic norm as it does on this matter. What factors of context might have constrained the formulation of this feature in particular? Three possible explanations, which need not be seen as mutually exclusive, merit our consideration. First, and especially since the only other demoniac in comparable narratives whose post-exorcism fate receives no attention whatsoever is the female victim in the Bint-resh Stela (lines 22–26), the silence might be due to matters of gender; however, while this consideration may help to explain the feature in question, it cannot account for it fully since elsewhere Luke shows a distinctively strong interest in the roles of formerly possessed women in the Jesus movement (Luke 8.1–3). Second, unless the slave-girl became attached after the exorcism either to the προσευχή or to the household of Lydia and found a way of making herself valuable in one of those settings – a possibility which, notwithstanding the richly informed imagination of Reimer,[173] finds no support in Luke's narrative – she would have lacked the requisite social status and economic worth for serving as an exemplary convert; against this explanation, however, stands the overt interest of Luke in the post-exorcism fate of the Gerasene demoniac (Luke 8.35–39), whose destitution is no less severe than that of the slave-girl.

And third, since the topical shift in 16.19–21 to Paul and Silas' religious and political status occurs precisely where information concerning

---

Luke 8.35–39 (par. Mark 5.15–20); Philostratus *VA* 4.20; 6.43; *4QPrayer of Nabonidus* frags 1–3 lines 1–8; *Acts of Thomas* 5.49. *Less*: Matt. 8.32–33; 17.18; Mark 1.26; 7.30; Luke 4.35.

[170] Cf. Klauck, *Magie und Heidentum*, p. 87; I. R. Reimer, *Women*, pp. 157, 176.

[171] Liberation is surprisingly taken for granted by Seim, *Double Message*, p. 174, but rejected after careful consideration by Reimer, *Women*, pp. 180–4.

[172] Cf. Klauck, *Magie und Heidentum*, p. 87. [173] See Reimer, *Women*, pp. 180–4.

the girl's future might have been expected, the narrative's silence regarding the latter might be chiefly a reflection of the high importance and contextual relevance of the concerns that *are* addressed in these verses. And in fact, although both of the considerations noted above may have encouraged the silence in question, this third factor is far more likely to have played the key role. For instance, in addition to occupying the position that might have been filled by information about the girl, the material in 16.19–21 enables Luke to address two issues whose direct relevance to his implied situation could have led to the girl's narrative disappearance, namely the missionaries' claim on the heritage of Israel (16.20) and their opponents' accusations regarding their un-Roman practices (16.20–21). Furthermore, and as already discussed above, the comparatively lengthy section to which these verses belong (16.19–40) exemplifies a strong attempt to address these same issues – with the missionaries' release from prison, public acquittal and return to the home of the God-fearing Lydia reinforcing the desired image of pious Jews who pose no threat to Rome. And finally, this same image coheres with the implied author's ideological point of view and key emphases in several other sections of the Lucan narratives.[174]

Thus, by integrating analysis of genre with the implied situation sketched earlier in this chapter, the present reading helps not only to define the problem of the slave-girl's sudden disappearance from the narrative but also to interpret this feature in relation to the story's cultural and rhetorical contexts. To be precise, due chiefly to the influence of anti-Paul slander in Luke's own situation but also in part to an honour-orientated culture that Luke himself unavoidably internalised, his interest in defending the reputation of Paul was so much stronger than his interest in the fate of the girl that he was willing to sacrifice the latter on the altar of the former.

Conclusion

My analysis of Acts 16.16–18 in its various levels of context has produced two sets of interpretative results which, on reflection, can be seen to complement one another. On one axis, for instance, lies a set of features that work in concert so as to construct an idealised Jewish identity for Paul and his co-workers, whose distinctive values and attitudes are identified

---

[174] On the claim to Israel's inheritance, see, e.g., Luke 2.46–55; 4.16–21; 7.18–23; 24.25–27, 32; Acts 2.16–21; 8.26–35; 15.12–21; 26.22–23. On the threat to Roman order, see, e.g., Luke 23.1–6, 13–22, 40–41, 47; Acts 17.1–7, 16–21; 18.12–17; 19.23–41; 23.26–30; 25.1–26.32.

with those of the storyteller by means of the text's first person plural narration. Examples of this emphasis include (1) the septuagintal narrative style of 16.16; (2) the missionaries' search in Philippi for the Jewish prayer-house, whose prominence is enhanced by its correspondence to the synagogue in which Jesus heals the man in Luke 4.33–37; (3) the multiple instances of macrostructural correspondence between the exorcistic deed of Paul and those attributed in Luke's first volume to Jesus, who in that context is emphatically identified with the Jewish biblical heritage; (4) the distinctively Jewish associations and identity of the cosmic power by whose authority Paul commands the spirit, and who has already been implicitly characterised in the exorcism stories of Luke's first volume as a functional embodiment of the God of Israel; (5) the anti-Judaic accusations by the slave-girl's owners, whose stereotypical castigation of Paul and Silas as Jews indirectly reinforces the implied author's own characterisation of the missionaries; and (6) Paul's willingness to suffer as a Jew (16.20–24) and wait on providence for deliverance (16.25–36) before disclosing that he is also a Roman citizen (16.37–38).

The other set of meanings coheres around a sense of antipathy to everything pagan in the context of reference. Examples of this tendency include (1) the stylistic effect of πύθωνα being placed in a grammatical slot whose parallels elsewhere in Luke–Acts are filled by ἀκάθαρτον; (2) the negative connotations of μαντευομένη, which in this context should probably be read as involving religious falsehood in particular; (3) the emphasis on the oracular enterprise's great economic profitability, which, though it might be defensible in itself on grounds of contemporary slave–master relations, is shameful in this instance because of the spirit's apparent unreliability; (4) the non-particular (and thus non-exclusivistic) force of anarthrous ὁδόν, whose religious content is misleading from the implied author's point of view; (5) the Apolline oracle's reputation for ambiguity in the wider context of culture; (6) the referential vagueness of τοῦ θεοῦ τοῦ ὑψίστου, especially on the lips of a Gentile in a context where Jews constitute only a tiny proportion of the city's population; and (7) the ritual-symbolic act of exorcism itself, which in this context implicitly represents Paul and his friends as the religious antithesis of everything the girl, her pythian spirit, and her masters stand for.

From the standpoint of many participants in ancient discourse between Jews and pagans, being both an ideal Jew and an embodiment of anti-paganism must have seemed like two sides of the same coin, whatever size the common ground between ancient Judaism and paganism was in reality. As both of these aspects furthermore possess very high prominence in the present episode, their combined weight constitutes a strikingly high degree of self-consciousness about the identity, historical antecedents and public image of the implied author's religious ideology and heroes. So energetic an effort of self-definition, moreover, implies a particular type of extratextual situation, which, even if it cannot be conceptualised as peculiar to a specific locale or community, can and should none the less be sketched as an aid to interpretation. Although the analysis above has not dealt with this matter in a comprehensive way, it has been able to infer at least one hermeneutically important facet of the four Lucan narratives' situational context; namely, their composition was powerfully constrained by controversies over the reputation of Paul, the quality of his Jewish credentials, and the status of his mission in the eyes of Roman authority.

CONCLUSION

In order to derive maximum insight from the method described in chapter 1, each of the analyses above has approached its particular story in a deliberately schematising fashion, breaking the text down into several different levels of style (e.g., transitivity and intertextuality) and context (e.g., co-text and culture). In chapter 4, however, my treatments of co-text, implied situation, and context of culture began to pull together the main discoveries from the various levels of analysis and lay out the contours of an interpretative synthesis. My aim here is to finish what I began to do there.

In the interest of producing a synthesis, the relationship between my genre-critical inquiry into the Acts 16 narrative's silence about the fate of the slave-girl and my prior sketch of the four stories' implied situation has special importance. More specifically, by demonstrating how that particular instance of silence helps to foreground an image of Paul as an ideal Jew who embodies the antithesis of paganism and nobly endures the Judeophobic machinations of greedy charlatans and gullible magistrates, my cultural analysis of Acts 16.16–18 and its immediate co-text confirms a central thesis in my prior reconstruction of the exorcism stories' context of situation: namely, as the implied audience of these episodes needed reassurance that both Paul and the Jesus he preached were loyal to Jewish ancestral custom and legitimate heirs to the heritage of Israel, that audience itself must have been either partly Jewish, or partly composed of the sorts of Gentiles represented by Lydia in Acts 16 (i.e., those who to one degree or another had sympathised with Judaism before joining the Christ cult), or constituted chiefly by a combination of those two socioreligious types.

Although this sort of scenario is increasingly gaining scholarly support as the best way to understand the original situation of Luke–Acts as a whole,[1] it has not until now been argued to have strong backing from a

---

[1] See e.g. the comments by Moessner and Tiede, 'Conclusion: "And some were persuaded..."', p. 363.

close reading of the exorcism stories in particular. Furthermore, when W. Kirschläger published in 1981 the only scholarly study comparable both in topic and in scope to this one, the idea that the author of Luke–Acts was a Gentile from a pagan background addressing an audience of Gentiles much like himself was so widely endorsed amongst New Testament scholars that Kirschläger apparently sensed no need to discuss alternatives such as that adopted here.[2] Thus, by creating a conversation between my own discourse analysis of the exorcism stories and modern scholarship on the Lucan writings' context of production, the present study both reinforces the emerging scholarly consensus on the Lucan writings' original context and sharply diverges from previous scholarship's best attempt to imagine how the exorcism stories functioned in their original milieu.

As noted in the last chapter, however, the rhetorical problem confronting the author of Luke–Acts involved not only the legitimacy of Jesus' and Paul's claim on the heritage of Israel but also doubts about the quality of Paul's connection with Jesus. Hence the aesthetically salient schema of Jesus–Paul parallels (e.g., Luke 8.26–39 and Acts 16.16–18) which, in defining Paul by strongly identifying him with Jesus, confirm that direct challenges to the honour of Jesus were doing far less damage in Luke's situation to the faith of believers than those levelled at the reputation of Paul. By responding to these challenges with the rhetoric of the Jesus–Paul parallels, the ancient author was able to take for granted that a substantial part of his audience had already identified themselves through faith with the Jesus of the Christ-cult and was continuing to honour Jesus despite the challenges being posed to the reputation of his controversial missionary.

With Luke therefore defining Paul in good measure by reference to the image of Jesus constructed in his first volume, the various microdiscursive features of that prior image acquire pronounced relevance to the definitive contests of the Lucan writings' original context of situation. For instance, the Jesus through whom Paul is partly defined by Luke is himself characterised in all three exorcism stories of the Gospel as fulfilling Jewish biblical prophecy (e.g., Isa. 58.6–7; 61.1–2; 65.3–4) and playing roles reminiscent of the most noble heroes in the sacred traditions of biblical Israel (e.g., Deut 32.5, 20; 1 Kgs 17.18; 2 Kgs 4.8–37). A few of these intertextual linkages, moreover, are made more rhetorically noteworthy either by their absence from one or two Synoptic parallels, or by the Lucan version's comparatively higher volume of correspondence to its biblical intertext. Furthermore, as the demonic power that

---

[2] See Kirschläger, *Jesu exorzistisches Wirken*, pp. 9–10 n. 4.

Jesus expels is described in each of the Gospel stories as one spirit or more of 'impurity', the image of Jesus that cumulatively emerges from these accounts is most emphatically that of a guardian of Jewish holiness and the special codes by which Jewish identity is constructed. And the Jewish-biblical aura surrounding Jesus is made still more prominent by the high frequency of Septuagintisms that occur in the exorcism stories and their respective co-texts.

In several interrelated ways, though, a degree of authority even higher than that constructed by the strategies just described is attributed to Jesus in these episodes and their immediate co-texts. For example, in light of the allusions to LXX Psalm 105.7–12 in Luke 8.26–39 and the immediately preceding story in Luke 8.22–25, the correspondence between the god who 'rebuked the Red Sea' and destroyed the enemies of his people in the waters of 'the deep' on the one hand, and the figure who in Luke 8.22–39 'rebuked . . . the raging waves' and dispatched the legion of demons into the lake on the other hand, implicitly compares Jesus not to some merely human deliverer but rather to 'the Most High', the Lord God of Israel himself. My comparative study of Jewish extrabiblical references to the rebuking of demonic beings strongly confirms that this particular facet of the Gospel stories has Jesus playing a functional role normally filled in other texts by God alone.

The Christological implications of these points are powerfully reinforced by several other aspects of my comparative analysis. For instance, when the contrast between exorcistic failure and success in Luke 9 is read in relation to similar contrasts found in other ancient narratives of exorcism (e.g., *The Legend of the Possessed Princess*), the difference can be understood at least partly as a matter of whether divine power is made present in the setting of therapy. Similarly, the invocation of Jesus' name as a source of exorcistic power and authority both in the Acts 16 episode and in the ensuing co-text of the story in Luke 9 (vv. 49–50) has Jesus filling a role usually filled in ancient exorcistic invocational formulas by one high-ranking deity or another. And finally, especially in comparison with the parallel episodes in Mark, the exorcism stories in Luke's Gospel feature an exorcist-healer who in several respects looks less like a shaman than like the ultimate source of therapeutic power in the entire cosmos.

In the exorcism stories, therefore, the Jesus through whom the Lucan Paul is partly defined stands not only on a horizontal axis that directly connects him with the ideal figures and prophetic expectations of Israel's sacred traditions but also at the top of a cosmic hierarchy, over whose unclean spirits and divinatory daimons he enjoys unqualified authority. This same capstone of the cosmic pyramid, moreover, legitimates Paul not only by establishing patterns of action to which Paul conspicuously conforms in Luke's second volume but also by having approved – long before Paul steps onto the stage of Luke's narrative – the very type of mission which Paul fulfils in the Acts 16 episode (cf. Luke 9.49–50). Furthermore, in that latter episode, the authenticity of Paul's link to the head of the Christ cult is strikingly demonstrated both by his method of exorcism and by its effect: Paul's exorcistic command is uttered not with the presumption that he himself has power to remove the spirit but rather 'in the name of Jesus Christ' (Acts 16.18); and the effect of this name being used for this purpose by this missionary could not be more dramatic than it is, with the spirit vacating the girl (and wrecking her owners' dubious business) 'that very hour' (Acts 16.18).

Although much of this interpretation derives most directly from the comparative levels of my analysis, it is no less dependent on my prior treatments of literary and linguistic detail, on which the cultural aspects of my interpretation are substantially based. But in addition to informing my cultural analyses in this general way, the more strictly linguistic aspects of the analysis have shown that several different types of stylistic features in our four stories reinforce in a more immediate fashion the emphasis just noted on the divine quality of Jesus' exorcistic authority. Indeed, at least one type of feature or another in each story gives rise to an image of Jesus as someone who uniquely bears in his own person the power of God. This impression is created in Luke 4.33–37, for instance, by the lexis and transitivity associated with Jesus' symbolic process of exorcistic rebuke (4.35), whose absence from the story about Paul in Acts 16 underscores the unique position in this regard of Jesus. A very similar effect is achieved in Luke 8.26–39 by the schematic pattern of repetition which is completed in the climax following that story's second cycle of complicating action, with ὁ θεός and ὁ Ἰησοῦς standing in conspicuous parallelism with one another (8.39). In Luke 9.37–43a, the same type of meaning is conveyed by means of presupposition, with 'the majesty of God' (9.43a) being assumed present by the bystanders in a setting where God has not been explicitly mentioned. And finally, nearly the same idea is communicated via implicature in Acts 16.18, where Paul's successful use of 'the name of Jesus Christ' implies the superior status and authority of that name over the pythian spirit and the great pagan god of manticism to whom it was subordinate, Pythian Apollo.

Thus, within the cosmic hierarchy assumed and constructed by Luke's own two-volume narrative discourse, Paul could not have been associated with a higher source of authority and status than that with which Luke identifies him. Furthermore, as this facet of Luke's defence of Paul has been inferred above not chiefly from the design of Luke–Acts as a whole but more specifically from the cumulative force and schematic interrelations of the exorcism stories, a nuanced assessment of the relative prominence these stories possess in the Lucan writings can be put forward here as a conjecture for scholarly evaluation and debate: on the one hand, these four stories are subordinate to the Lucan volumes' more pervasive interests in defending the honour of Paul and identifying both Paul and Jesus with the highest sources of authority in the assumed context of culture; on the other hand, by playing an integral role in Luke's macrostructural development of those same interests, the exorcism narratives are sufficiently prominent to give us insight into the general type of situation Luke–Acts as a whole was designed to address.

BIBLIOGRAPHY

Achtemeier, P. J., 'The Lukan Perspective on the Miracles of Jesus: A Preliminary Sketch', in C. H. Talbert (ed.), *Perspectives on Luke–Acts* (Edinburgh, 1978), pp. 153–67.
Aichinger, H., 'Zur Traditionsgeschichte der Epileptiker-Perikope Mk 9,14–29 par Mt 17,14–21 par Lk 9,37–43a', in A. Fuchs (ed.), *Probleme der Forschung*, SNTU 3 (Vienna, 1978), pp. 114–43.
Aland, B. and Aland, K., *The Text of the New Testament*, trans. E. F. Rhodes (Grand Rapids and Leiden, 1987).
Aland, B. et al. (eds), *The Greek New Testament*, 4th rev. edn (Stuttgart, 1993).
Alexander, L. C. A., *The Preface to Luke's Gospel: Literary Convention and Social Context in Luke 1.1-4 and Acts 1.1*, SNTSMS 78 (Cambridge, 1993).
 Review of *A Critical and Exegetical Commentary on the Acts of the Apostles*, by C. K. Barrett; and of *The Acts of the Apostles: A Socio-Rhetorical Commentary*, by B. Witherington, III, *JTS* 52/2 (2001), 691–703.
Alexander, P. S., 'Incantations and Books of Magic', in E. Schürer, *The History of the Jewish People in the Age of Jesus Christ*, ed. G. Vermes et al. (Edinburgh, 1973–87), III.1, pp. 342–79.
 '"Wrestling against Wickedness in High Places": Magic in the Worldview of the Qumran Community', in S. E. Porter and C. A. Evans (eds), *The Scrolls and the Scriptures: Qumran Fifty Years After*, JSPSup 26 (Sheffield, 1997), pp. 318–37.
Alföldy, G., *The Social History of Rome*, trans. D. Braund and F. Pollock, rev. edn (London, 1988).
Allison, D. C., *Jesus of Nazareth: Millenarian Prophet* (Minneapolis, 1998).
Annen, F., *Heil für die Heiden: Zur Bedeutung und Geschichte der Tradition vom besessenen Gerasener (Mk 5,1–20 parr.)*, FTS 20 (Frankfurt, 1976).
Ashton, J., *The Religion of Paul the Apostle* (New Haven, 2000).
Audollent, A. (ed.), *Defixionum Tabellae* (Paris, 1904).
Aune, D. E., 'Magic in Early Christianity', in *ANRW* II.23.2, pp. 1507–57.
 'Exorcism', in *ISBE* II, pp. 242–5.
Avalos, H., *Illness and Health Care in the Ancient Near East: The Role of the Temple in Greece, Mesopotamia, and Israel*, HSM 54 (Atlanta, 1995).
 Health Care and the Rise of Christianity (Peabody, 1999).
Avigad, N. and Yadin, Y., *A Genesis Apocryphon: A Scroll from the Wilderness of Judea* (Jerusalem, 1956).
Avishur, Y., 'The Second Amulet Incantation from Arslan Tash', *UF* 10 (1978), 29–36.

'The Ghost-Expelling Incantation from Ugarit (Ras Ibn Hani 78/20)', *UF* 13 (1981), 13–25.

Baarda, T., 'Gadarenes, Gerasenes, Gergesenes and the "Diatessaron" Traditions', in E. E. Ellis and M. Wilcox (eds), *Neotestamentica et Semitica: Studies in Honour of Matthew Black* (Edinburgh, 1969), pp. 181–97.

Babbitt, F. C., et al. (eds), *Plutarch's Moralia*, LCL, 11 vols (Cambridge, MA, 1927–65).

Baillet, M., *Qumrân Grotte 4 III (4Q482–4Q520)*, DJD VII (Oxford, 1982).

Bar-Efrat, S., *Narrative Art in the Bible*, trans. D. Shefer-Vanson, JSOTSup 70 (Sheffield, 1989).

Barrett, C. K., *A Critical and Exegetical Commentary on the Acts of the Apostles*, ICC, 2 vols (Edinburgh, 1994, 1998).

Bauernfeind, O., *Die Worte der Dämonen im Markusevangelium* (Stuttgart, 1927).

Bell, C., *Ritual: Perspectives and Dimensions* (Oxford, 1997).

Berger, P. L. and Luckmann, T., *The Social Construction of Reality: A Treatise in the Sociology of Knowledge* (Harmondsworth, 1967).

Betz, H. D. (ed.), *The Greek Magical Papyri in Translation Including the Demotic Spells* (Chicago, 1986).

Betz, O., 'δύναμις', *NIDNTT* II, pp. 601–6.

Beyerlin, W. (ed.), *Near Eastern Religious Texts Relating to the Old Testament*, trans. J. Bowden (London, 1978).

Bilde, P., *Flavius Josephus between Jerusalem and Rome: His Life, His Works, and Their Importance*, JSPSup 2 (Sheffield, 1988).

Birch, D., *Language, Literature, and Critical Practice*, Interface Series (London, 1989).

Blount, B. K., *Cultural Interpretation: Reorienting New Testament Criticism* (Minneapolis, 1995).

Boas, F., *The Mind of Primitive Man*, rev. edn (New York, 1938; repr., 1965).

Böcher, O., *Dämonenfurcht und Dämonenabwehr: Ein Beitrag zur Vorgeschichte der christlichen Taufe*, BWANT 90 (Stuttgart, 1970).

Das Neue Testament und die dämonischen Mächte, SBS 58 (Stuttgart, 1972).

Bock, D. L., *Proclamation from Prophecy and Pattern: Lucan Old Testament Christology*, JSNTSup 12 (Sheffield, 1987).

Bonz, M. P., *The Past as Legacy: Luke–Acts and Ancient Epic* (Minneapolis, 2000).

Booth, R. P., *Jesus and the Laws of Purity: Tradition History and Legal History in Mark 7*, JSNTSup 13 (Sheffield, 1986).

Borghouts, J. F. (ed.), *Ancient Egyptian Magical Texts*, Religious Texts Translation Series, Nisaba 9 (Leiden, 1978).

Bovon, F., *L'Evangile selon saint Luc (1,1–9,50)*, CNT 3A (Geneva, 1991).

Bowersock, G. W., 'Introduction', in *Philostratus: Life of Apollonius* (Harmondsworth, 1970), pp. 9–22.

Bowie, E. L., 'Apollonius of Tyana: Tradition and Reality', in *ANRW* II.16.2, pp. 1652–99.

Bowie, F., *The Anthropology of Religion: An Introduction* (Oxford, 2000).

Bradley, K. R., *Slaves and Masters in the Roman Empire: A Study in Social Control* (Oxford, 1987).

Braude, W. G. and Kapstein, I. J., *Pesikta de-Rab Kahana: Rabbi Kahana's Compilation of Discourses for Sabbaths and Festal Days* (Philadelphia, 1985).

Brawley, R. L., *Luke–Acts and the Jews: Conflict, Apology, and Conciliation*, SBLMS 33 (Atlanta, 1987).
— *Text to Text Pours Forth Speech: Voices of Scripture in Luke–Acts*, Indiana Studies in Biblical Literature (Bloomington, 1995).
Brenk, F. E., 'In the Light of the Moon: Demonology in the Early Imperial Period', in *ANRW* II.16.3, pp. 2068–145.
Brown, G. and Yule, G., *Discourse Analysis*, Cambridge Textbooks in Linguistics (Cambridge, 1983).
Brown, P., *The Body and Society: Men, Women, and Sexual Renunciation in Early Christianity* (New York, 1988).
Bruce, F. F., *The Acts of the Apostles: The Greek Text with Introduction and Commentary* (Grand Rapids and Leicester, 1983).
— *The Book of the Acts*, NICNT, rev. edn (Grand Rapids, 1988).
Budge, E. A. W., *Egyptian Magic* (London, 1899; repr., 1972).
Burridge, R. A., *What Are the Gospels?*, SNTSMS 70 (Cambridge, 1992).
— 'About People, by People, for People: Gospel Genre and Audiences', in R. J. Bauckham (ed.), *The Gospels for All Christians: Rethinking the Gospel Audiences* (Grand Rapids, 1998).
Burrows, M., *More Light on the Dead Sea Scrolls* (New York, 1958).
Bushell, W. C., 'Psychophysiological and Comparative Analysis of Ascetico-Meditational Discipline: Toward a New Theory of Asceticism', in V. Wimbush and R. Valantasis (eds), *Asceticism* (Oxford, 1995), pp. 549–65.
Busse, U., *Die Wunder des Propheten Jesus: Die Rezeption, Komposition und Interpretation der Wundertradition im Evangelium des Lukas*, FB 24 (Stuttgart, 1979).
Butler, C. S., 'Systemic Linguistics, Semantics, and Pragmatics', in E. H. Steiner and R. Veltman (eds), *Pragmatics, Discourse and Text: Some Systemically-inspired Approaches* (London, 1988), pp. 13–27.
Buzy, D., 'Le premier séjour de Jésus à Capharnaüm', in *Mélanges bibliques: Rédiges en l'honneur de André Robert*, Travaux de l'Institut Catholique de Paris 4 (Paris, 1957), pp. 411–19.
Byrne, B., *Romans*, Sacra Pagina 6 (Collegeville, 1996).
Caquot, A., 'Sur quelques démons de l'Ancien Testament (Reshep, Qeteb, Deber)', *Sem* 6 (1956), 53–68.
— 'Observations sur la première tablette magique d'Arslan Tash', *JANESCU* 5 (1973), 45–52.
— 'נער', *TDOT*, III, pp. 49–53.
Carter, R., 'Introduction', in J. Sinclair (ed.), *Language and Literature: An Introductory Reader in Stylistics*, Aspects of English (London, 1982), pp. 1–13.
Castelli, E. A. et al. (eds), *The Postmodern Bible* (New Haven, 1995).
Cathcart, K. J. and Gordon, R. P. (eds), *The Targum of the Minor Prophets: Translation, Introduction, Apparatus, and Notes*, vol. xiv of *The Aramaic Bible*, ed. Martin McNamara (Edinburgh, 1989).
Chadwick, J. and Mann, W. N. (eds), *The Medical Works of Hippocrates* (Oxford, 1950).
Charlesworth, J. H. (ed.), *The Old Testament Pseudepigrapha*, 2 vols (Garden City, 1983–5).
Chomsky, N., *Language and Mind* (New York, 1972).

Clark, G., 'Women and Asceticism in Late Antiquity: The Refusal of Status and Gender', in V. L. Wimbush and R. Valantasis (eds), *Asceticism* (Oxford, 1995), pp. 33–48.
Cluysenaar, A., *Introduction to Literary Stylistics: A Discussion of the Dominant Structures in Verse and Prose* (London, 1976).
Cohen, S. J. D., *From the Maccabees to the Mishnah*, Library of Early Christianity (Philadelphia, 1987).
Colson, F. H. and Whitaker, G. H. (eds), *Philo*, LCL, 10 vols (Cambridge, MA, 1929–62).
Colwell, E. C., 'Scribal Habits in Early Papyri: A Study in the Corruption of the Text', in J. P. Hyatt (ed.), *The Bible in Modern Scholarship* (Nashville, 1965), pp. 370–89.
Conybeare, F. C. (ed.), *Philostratus: The Life of Apollonius*, LCL, 2 vols (Cambridge, MA, 1948).
Conzelmann, H., *Acts of the Apostles*, trans. J. Limburg, A. T. Kraabel and D. H. Juel, Hermeneia (Philadelphia, 1987).
Cotterell, P. and Turner, M., *Linguistics and Biblical Interpretation* (Downers Grove, IL, 1989).
Crystal, D., *Linguistics*, 2nd edn (London, 1985).
—*The Cambridge Encyclopedia of Language* (Cambridge, 1987).
Crystal, D. and Davy, D., *Investigating English Style*, English Language Series 1 (Harlow, 1969).
Culler, J., *Structuralist Poetics: Structuralism, Linguistics, and the Study of Literature* (London, 1975).
—*Framing the Sign: Criticism and Its Institutions* (Oxford, 1988).
Cullom, B. A., 'Acts 16:6–40: A Redactional and Socio-Historical Analysis', PhD dissertation, University of Notre Dame (1985).
Culpepper, R. A., 'Paul's Mission to the Gentile World: Acts 13–19', *RevExp* 71/4 (1974), 487–97.
Danby, H. (ed.), *The Mishnah* (Oxford, 1933).
Danker, F. W., *Benefactor: Epigraphic Study of a Graeco-Roman and New Testament Semantic Field* (St. Louis, 1982).
—*Jesus and the New Age*, rev. edn (Philadelphia, 1988).
Davidson, D., 'Thought and Talk', in *Inquiries into Truth and Interpretation* (Oxford, 1984), pp. 155–70.
Davies, S. L., *Jesus the Healer: Possession, Trance, and the Origins of Christianity* (London, 1995).
Delling, G., 'Josephus und das Wunderbare', *NovT* 2 (1957–8), 291–309.
de Moor, J. C., 'An Incantation against Evil Spirits (Ras Ibn Hani 78/20)', *UF* 12 (1980), 429–32.
de Moor, J. C. and Spronk, K., 'More on Demons in Ugarit (*KTU* 1.82)', *UF* 16 (1984), 237–50.
Derrett, J. D. M., 'Spirit-possession and the Gerasene Demoniac: An Inquest into History and Liturgical Projection', *Man* 14/2 (1979), 286–93.
—'Contributions to the Study of the Gerasene Demoniac', *JSNT* 3 (1979), 2–17.
—'Legend and Event: The Gerasene Demoniac: An Inquest into History and Liturgical Projection', in E. A. Livingstone (ed.), *Studia biblica 1978: Sixth International Congress on Biblical Studies, Oxford 3–7 April 1978*, JSNTSup 2 (Sheffield, 1980), pp. 61–74.

'Primitive Christianity as an Ascetic Movement', in V. L. Wimbush and R. Valantasis (eds), *Asceticism* (Oxford, 1995), pp. 88–107.

Deselaers, P., *Das Buch Tobit* (Göttingen, 1982).

de Vos, C. S., 'Finding a Charge that Fits: The Accusation against Paul and Silas at Philippi (Acts 16.19–21)', *JSNT* 74 (1999), 51–63.

Dhorme, E., 'La démonologie biblique', in *Maqqél shâqédh: Hommage à Wilhelm Vischer* (Montpellier, 1960), pp. 46–64.

Dillon, J., *The Middle Platonists: A Study of Platonism 80 B.C. to A.D. 220*, rev. edn (London, 1996).

Dion, P. E., 'Raphaël l'exorciste', *Biblica* 57 (1976), 399–417.

Dixon, S., *The Roman Family* (Baltimore, 1992).

Dodds, E. R., *The Greeks and the Irrational* (Berkeley, 1951).

Douglas, M., *Natural Symbols: An Exploration in Cosmology* (New York, 1973).

Downing, F. G., 'Magic and Scepticism in and around the First Christian Century', in T. E. Klutz (ed.), *Magic in the Biblical World: From the Rod of Aaron to the Ring of Solomon*, JSNTSup 245 (London, 2003), pp. 86–99.

Duling, D. C., 'Solomon, Exorcism, and the Son of David', *HTR* 68 (1975), 235–52.

—'Solomon, Testament of', in *ABD* VI, pp. 117–19.

Dunn, J. D. G. and Twelftree, G. H., 'Demon-Possession and Exorcism in the New Testament', *Churchman* 94/3 (1980), 210–25.

Dupont-Sommer, A., 'Exorcismes et guérisons dans les récits de Qoumrân', in G. W. Anderson et al. (eds), *VTSup* 7 (Leiden, 1960).

Durant, A. and Fabb, N., 'Introduction', in D. Attridge et al. (eds), *The Linguistics of Writing: Arguments Between Language and Literature* (Manchester, 1987), pp. 1–15.

Eagleton, T., *Literary Theory: An Introduction* (Oxford, 1983).

—*The Ideology of the Aesthetic* (Oxford, 1990).

Eberlein, H., 'Zur Frage der Dämonischen im Neuen Testament', *NKZ* 42 (1931), 499–509, 562–72.

Eco, U., *Semiotics and the Philosophy of Language* (London, 1984).

Eggins, S., *An Introduction to Systemic Functional Linguistics* (London, 1994).

Eisenman, R. and Wise, M. (eds), *The Dead Sea Scrolls Uncovered: The First Complete Translation and Interpretation of 50 Key Documents Withheld for Over 35 Years* (Shaftesbury, 1992).

Eliade, M., *Shamanism: Archaic Techniques of Ecstasy*, trans. W. R. Trask (Princeton, 1964).

Elliger, W., *Paulus in Griechenland: Philippi, Thessaloniki, Athen, Korinth*, SBS 92/93 (Stuttgart, 1978).

Elliott, J. K., 'The Relevance of Textual Criticism to the Synoptic Problem', in D. L. Dungan (ed.), *The Interrelations of the Gospels: A Symposium*, BETL 95 (Louvain, 1990), pp. 348–59.

Empson, W., *The Structure of Complex Words* (London, 1951; repr., 1985).

Enkvist, N., 'Stylistics and Textlinguistics', in W. Dressler (ed.), *Current Trends in Textlinguistics* (Berlin, 1978), pp. 174–90.

—'What Ever Happened to Stylistics?', in U. Fries (ed.), *The Structure of Texts*, Swiss Papers in Language and Literature 3 (Tübingen, 1987), pp. 11–28.

Epstein, I. (ed.), *Hebrew-English Edition of the Babylonian Talmud*, trans. H. Friedman, 35 vols. (London, 1962–88).

Esler, P. F., *Community and Gospel in Luke–Acts: The Social and Political Motivations of Lucan Theology*, SNTSMS 57 (Cambridge, 1987).
Evans, C. A., 'The Genesis Apocryphon and the Rewritten Bible', *RevQ* 13 (1988), 153–66.
— 'Prophecy and Polemic: Jews in Luke's Scriptural Apologetic', in C. A. Evans and J. A. Sanders (eds), *Luke and Scripture: The Function of Sacred Tradition in Luke–Acts* (Minneapolis, 1993), pp. 171–211.
— 'Apollonius of Tyana', in C. A. Evans and S. E. Porter (eds), *Dictionary of New Testament Background: A Compendium of Contemporary Biblical Scholarship* (Downers Grove, IL, 2000), pp. 80–1.
Evans, C. F., *Saint Luke*, TPINTC (London and Philadelphia, 1990).
Fairclough, N., *Critical Discourse Analysis: The Critical Study of Language*, Language in Social Life Series (London, 1995).
Fanning, B. M., *Verbal Aspect in New Testament Greek*, Oxford Theological Monographs (Oxford, 1990).
Fearghail, F. O., *The Introduction to Luke–Acts: A Study of the Role of Luke 1,1-4,44 in the Composition of Luke's Two Volume Work*, AnBib 126 (Rome, 1991).
Feldman, L. H., 'Josephus's Portrait of Hezekiah', *JBL* 111 (1992), 608–10.
Fenasse, J.-M., 'Le Christ "Saint de Dieu"', *MScRel* 22 (1965), 26–32.
Ferguson, E., *Demonology of the Early Christian World*, Symposium Series 12 (Lewiston, 1984).
Fiebig, P., *Jüdische Wundergeschichten des neutestamentlichen Zeitalters* (Tübingen, 1911).
Fine, J., 'Cognitive Processes in Context: A Systemic Approach to Problems in Oral Language Use', in E. H. Steiner and R. Veltman (eds), *Pragmatics, Discourse, and Text: Some Systemically-Inspired Approaches* (London, 1988), pp. 171–80.
Fish, S. E., *Is There a Text in This Class? The Authority of Interpretative Communities* (Cambridge, MA, 1980).
Fitzmyer, J. A., *The Genesis Apocryphon of Cave One: A Commentary*, BibOr 18A, 2nd edn (Rome, 1971).
— 'The Composition of Luke, Chapter 9', in C. H. Talbert (ed.), *Perspectives on Luke–Acts* (Edinburgh, 1978), pp. 139–52.
— *The Gospel according to Luke (I–IX): Introduction, Translation, and Notes*, AB 28 (New York, 1981).
— 'Satan and Demons in Luke–Acts', in *Luke the Theologian: Aspects of His Teaching* (London, 1989), pp. 146–74.
— *The Acts of the Apostles: A New Translation with Introduction and Commentary*, AB 31 (New York, 1998).
Flaceliere, R., *Greek Oracles*, trans. D. Garman, 2nd edn (London, 1976).
Foerster, W., 'πύθων', in *TDNT* VI, pp. 917–20.
Fowler, R., *Linguistics and the Novel*, New Accents (London, 1977).
— *Literature as Social Discourse: The Practice of Linguistic Criticism* (London, 1981).
— *Linguistic Criticism* (Oxford, 1986).
Frankfurter, D., 'Narrating Power: The Theory and Practice of the Magical *Historiola* in Ritual Spells', in M. Meyer and P. Mirecki (eds), *Ancient Magic and Ritual Power* (Leiden, 1995), pp. 457–75.

Fredriksen, P., 'Did Jesus Oppose the Purity Laws?', *BibRev* II (June 1995), 18–25, 42–6.
Freedman, H. and Simon, M. (eds), *Midrash Rabbah*, 10 vols (London, 1939).
Freeman, M., *Rewriting the Self: History, Memory, Narrative* (London, 1993).
Fridrichsen, A., *The Problem of Miracle in Primitive Christianity*, trans. R. A. Harrisville and J. S. Hanson (Minneapolis, 1972).
— 'Jesu Kampf gegen die unreinen Geister', in A. Suhl (ed.), *Der Wunderbegriff im Neuen Testament*, trans. D. Fehling (Darmstadt, 1980), pp. 245–59.
Gager, J. G., 'Jews, Gentiles, and Synagogues in the Book of Acts', *HTR* 79/1–3 (1986), 91–9.
— *Curse Tablets and Binding Spells from the Ancient World* (Oxford, 1992).
García Martínez, F. and Tigchelaar, E. J. C., *The Dead Sea Scrolls Study Edition*, 2 vols (Leiden and Grand Rapids, 2000).
Garnsey, P. and Saller, R., *The Roman Empire: Economy, Society and Culture* (London, 1987).
Garrett, S. R., *The Demise of the Devil: Magic and the Demonic in Luke's Writings* (Minneapolis, 1989).
Gasque, W. W., *A History of the Interpretation of the Acts of the Apostles*, 2nd edn (Peabody, 1989).
Geertz, C., *Available Light: Anthropological Reflections on Philosophical Topics* (Princeton, 2000).
Geller, M. J., 'Jesus' Theurgic Powers: Parallels in Talmud and Incantation Bowls', *JJS* 28 (1978), 141–55.
— *Forerunners to Udug-hul: Sumerian Exorcistic Incantations*, Freiburger Altorientalische Studien 12 (Stuttgart, 1985).
George, A., 'Le miracle dans l'oeuvre de Luc', in X. Léon-Dufour (ed.), *Les miracles de Jésus selon le Nouveau Testament* (Paris, 1977), pp. 249–68.
Gershevitch, I., *The Avestan Hymn to Mithra: With an Introduction, Translation, and Commentary* (Cambridge, 1959).
Gibson, J. C. L. (ed.), *Canaanite Myths and Legends*, 2nd edn (Edinburgh, 1977).
Girard, R., *The Scapegoat*, trans. Y. Freccero (Baltimore, 1986).
Goldin, J., 'The Magic of Magic and Superstition', in E. S. Fiorenza (ed.), *Aspects of Religious Propaganda in Judaism and Early Christianity* (South Bend, 1976), pp. 115–48.
Goodenough, E. R., *Jewish Symbols in the Greco-Roman Period*, II, *The Archaeological Evidence from the Diaspora* (New York, 1953).
Goodman, F. D., *How about Demons? Possession and Exorcism in the Modern World* (Bloomington, 1988).
Goodwin, W. W., *A Greek Grammar*, new edn (London, 1894).
Goulder, M. D., *Luke: A New Paradigm*, JSNTSup 20, 2 vols (Sheffield, 1989).
Grabbe, L., 'Leviticus', in J. Barton and J. Muddiman (eds), *The Oxford Bible Commentary* (Oxford, 2001), pp. 91–109.
Graf, F., *La magie dans l'antiquité gréco-romaine: Idéologie et pratique* (Paris, 1994).
Grayston, K., 'Exorcism in the New Testament', *EpR* 2 (1975), 90–4.
Green, A., 'Beneficent Spirits and Malevolent Demons: The Iconography of Good and Evil in Ancient Assyria and Babylonia', *Visible Religion* 3 (1984), 80–105.
Green, J. B., '"The Message of Salvation" in Luke–Acts', *ExAud* 5 (1989), 21–34.

The Gospel of Luke, NICNT (Grand Rapids, 1997).
Gregory, M. and Carroll, S., *Language and Situation*, Language and Society Series (London, 1978).
Grelot, P., 'Sur l'Apocryphe de la Genèse (col. XX, ligne 26)', *RevQ* 2 (1958), 273–6.
Gruenthaner, M. J., 'The Demonology of the Old Testament', *CBQ* 6 (1944), 6–27.
Grundmann, W., *Der Begriff der Kraft in der neutestamentlichen Gedankenwelt* (Stuttgart, 1932).
Das Evangelium nach Lukas, 2nd edn, THKNT 3 (Berlin, 1961).
'δύναμαι', *TDNT* II, pp. 284–317.
Haenchen, E., 'Das "Wir" in der Apostelgeschichte und das Itinerar', in *Gott und Mensch: Gesammelte Aufsätze*, I (Tübingen, 1965), pp. 243–71.
The Acts of the Apostles: A Commentary, trans. B. Noble and G. Shinn (Oxford, 1971).
Halliday, M. A. K., *Language as Social Semiotic: The Social Interpretation of Language and Meaning* (London, 1978).
An Introduction to Functional Grammar (London, 1985).
Halliday, M. A. K. and Hasan, R., *Language, Context, and Text: Aspects of Language in a Social-Semiotic Perspective*, Language Education, 2nd edn (Oxford, 1989).
Harden, D., *The Phoenicians* (Harmondsworth, 1971).
Harmer, J. R. and Lightfoot, J. B. (eds), *The Apostolic Fathers: Revised Greek Texts with Introductions and English Translations* (London, 1891; repr., Grand Rapids, 1988).
Harmon, A. M., Kilburn, K. and Macleod, M. D. (eds), *Lucian*, LCL, 8 vols (Cambridge, MA, 1913–67).
Harrington, H. K., *The Impurity Systems of Qumran and the Rabbis: Biblical Foundations*, SBLDS 143 (Atlanta, 1993).
Harris, W. V., 'Towards a Study of the Roman Slave Trade', *MAAR* 36 (1980), 117–40.
Harvey, A. E., *Jesus and the Constraints of History* (London, 1982).
Hays, R. B., *Echoes of Scripture in the Letters of Paul* (New Haven, 1989).
Helck, W., '"Phönizische Dämonen" im frühen Griechenland', *Archäologischer Anzeiger* (1987), 445–7.
Hemer, C., *The Book of Acts in the Setting of Hellenistic History*, ed. C. H. Gempf (Tübingen, 1989; repr., Winona Lake, IN, 1990).
Hendrickx, H., *The Miracle Stories of the Synoptic Gospels* (San Francisco, 1987).
Hengel, M., 'Proseuche und Synagoge: Jüdische Gemeinde, Gotteshaus und Gottesdienst in der Diaspora und in Palästina', in G. Jeremias et al. (eds), *Tradition und Glaube: Das frühe Christentum in seiner Umwelt* (Göttingen, 1971), pp. 157–84.
Hennecke, E., *New Testament Apocrypha*, trans. R. McL. Wilson et al., 2 vols (Philadelphia, 1963–5).
Herrmann, W., 'Baal Zebub בעל זבוב', in *DDD*, cols 293–6.
Hilgert, E., 'Symbolismus and Heilsgeschichte in den Evangelien: Ein Beitrag zu den Seesturm- und Gerasenerzählungen', in F. Christ (ed.), *Oikonomia: Heilsgeschichte als Thema der Theologie* (Hamburg, 1967), pp. 51–6.

Hobsbawm, E., 'Introduction: Inventing Traditions', in E. Hobsbawm and T. Ranger (eds), *The Invention of Tradition* (Cambridge, 1992), pp. 1–17.
Hodges, J. C. and Whitten, M. E., *Harbrace College Handbook*, 7th edn (New York, 1972).
Hollenbach, P., 'Jesus, Demoniacs, and Public Authorities', *JAAR* 44 (1981), 567–88.
— 'Help for Interpreting Jesus' Exorcisms', in E. H. Lovering (ed.), *SBLSP* 32 (1993), 119–28.
Holquist, M., 'Introduction', in *The Dialogic Imagination: Four Essays by M. M. Bakhtin*, trans. C. Emerson and M. Holquist (Austin, 1981), pp. xv–xxxiv.
Hooker, M. D., *The Gospel according to St Mark*, BNTC (London, 1991).
Hopfner, T., *Griechisch-Ägyptische Offenbarungszauber*, Studien zur Palaeographie und Papyruskunde 21, 2 vols (Leipzig, 1921–4; repr., Amsterdam, 1974–83).
Horsley, R. A., *Archaeology, History, and Society in Galilee: The Social Context of Jesus and the Rabbis* (Valley Forge, 1996).
Howard, J. K., *Disease and Healing in the New Testament: An Analysis and Interpretation* (Lanham, MD, 2001).
Hull, J. M., *Hellenistic Magic and the Synoptic Tradition*, SBT 2/28 (London, 1974).
Isaac, E., 'The Significance of Food in Hebraic-African Thought and the Role of Fasting in the Ethiopian Church', in V. L. Wimbush and R. Valantasis (eds), *Asceticism* (Oxford, 1995), pp. 329–42.
Isbell, C. D., *Corpus of the Aramaic Incantation Bowls*, SBLDS 17 (Missoula, 1975).
Jacobsen, T., *The Treasures of Darkness: a History of Mesopotamian Religion* (New Haven, 1976).
Janowitz, N., *Magic in the Roman World: Pagans, Jews and Christians*, Religion in the First Christian Centuries (London, 2001).
Janowski, B., 'Azazel עזאזל', in *DDD*, cols 240–8.
Jeremias, J., ' Ἐν ἐκείνῃ τῇ ὥρᾳ, (ἐν) αὐτῇ τῇ ὥρᾳ', *ZNW* 42 (1949), 214–17.
Jervell, J., *Luke and the People of God: A New Look at Luke–Acts* (Minneapolis, 1972).
— 'The Church of Jews and Godfearers', in J. B. Tyson (ed.), *Luke–Acts and the Jewish People: Eight Critical Perspectives* (Minneapolis, 1988), pp. 11–20.
— *The Theology of the Acts of the Apostles*, New Testament Theology (Cambridge, 1996).
Jirku, A., *Die Dämonen und Ihre Abwehr im Alten Testament* (Leipzig, 1912).
Kahl, W., *The New Testament Miracle Stories in Their Religious-Historical Setting: A Religionsgeschichtliche Comparison from a Structural Perspective* (Göttingen, 1994).
Kanda, S. H., 'The Form and Function of the Petrine and Pauline Miracle Stories in the Acts of the Apostles (Part 1)', PhD dissertation, Claremont Graduate School (1974).
Kapferer, B., *A Celebration of Demons: Exorcism and the Aesthetics of Healing in Sri Lanka*, 2nd edn (Oxford and Washington, 1991).
Kaufmann, Y., *The Religion of Israel: From Its Beginnings to the Babylonian Exile*, translated and abridged by M. Greenberg (London, 1960).

Kee, H. C., 'The Terminology of Mark's Exorcism Stories', *NTS* 14 (1968), 232–46.
— *Miracle in the Early Christian World: A Study in Sociohistorical Method* (New Haven, 1983).
— *Medicine, Miracle, and Magic in New Testament Times*, SNTSMS 55 (Cambridge, 1986).
Kirschläger, W., 'Exorzismus in Qumran?', *Kairos* 18 (1976), 135–53.
— *Jesu exorzistisches Wirken aus der Sicht des Lukas: Ein Beitrag zur lukanischen Redaktion*, ÖBS 3 (Klosterneuburg, 1981).
Klauck, H.-J., *Magie und Heidentum in der Apostelgeschichte des Lukas*, SBS 167 (Stuttgart, 1996).
Kleist, J. A., 'The Gadarene Demoniacs', *CBQ* 9 (1947), 101–5.
Klostermann, E., *Das Lukasevangelium*, HNT 5, 3rd edn (Tübingen, 1975).
Klutz, T. E., 'A Redaction-Critical Study of Luke 3:1-20', MA thesis, Wheaton College Graduate School (1989).
— 'With Authority and Power: A Sociostylistic Investigation of Exorcism in Luke–Acts', PhD thesis, University of Sheffield (1996).
— '"Naked and Wounded": Foregrounding, Relevance, and Situation in Acts 19.13–20', in S. E. Porter and J. T. Reed (eds), *Discourse Analysis of the New Testament: Essays in Theory and Practice* (Sheffield, 1999), pp. 258–79.
— 'The Grammar of Exorcism in the Ancient Mediterranean World: Some Cosmological, Semantic, and Pragmatic Reflections on How Exorcistic Prowess Contributed to the Worship of Jesus', in C. C. Newman, J. R. Davila and G. S. Lewis (eds), *The Jewish Roots of Christological Monotheism: Papers from the St. Andrews Conference on the Historical Origins of the Worship of Jesus* (Leiden, 1999), pp. 156–65.
— 'The Value of Being Virginal: Mary and Anna in the Lukan Infancy Prologue', in G. J. Brooke (ed.), *The Birth of Jesus: Biblical and Theological Reflections* (Edinburgh, 2000), pp. 71–87.
— 'Reinterpreting Magic in the World of Jewish and Christian Scripture: An Introduction', in T. E. Klutz (ed.), *Magic in the Biblical World: From the Rod of Aaron to the Ring of Solomon*, JSNTSup 245 (London, 2003), pp. 1–9.
Kollmann, B., *Jesus und die Christen als Wundertäter: Studien zu Magie, Medizin und Schamanismus in Antike und Christentum*, FRLANT 170 (Göttingen, 1996).
Kotansky, R., 'Greek Exorcistic Amulets', in M. Meyer and P. Mirecki (eds), *Ancient Magic and Ritual Power*, Religions in the Graeco-Roman World 129 (Leiden, 1995), pp. 243–77.
Kraeling, C. H., *Gerasa: City of the Decapolis* (New Haven, 1938).
Kress, G., 'Textual Matters: The Social Effectiveness of Style', in D. Birch and L. M. O'Toole (eds), *Functions of Style* (London, 1988), pp. 126–41.
Krodel, G., *Acts*, ACNT (Minneapolis, 1986).
Kurz, W. S., 'Promise and Fulfillment in Hellenistic Jewish Narratives and in Luke and Acts', in D. Moessner (ed.), *Jesus and the Heritage of Israel* (Harrisburg, 1999), pp. 147–70.
Labov, W., *Language in the Inner City* (Philadelphia, 1972).
Lamarche, P., 'Le Possédé de Gérasa (Mt 8, 28–34; Mc 5, 1–20; Lc 8, 26–39)', *NRT* 90 (1968), 581–97.

Langton, E., *Essentials of Demonology* (London, 1949).
Laurentin, R., *Structure et Théologie de Luc I–II*, Ebib (Paris, 1957).
Leech, G. N., *Semantics* (Harmondsworth, 1974).
— *The Principles of Pragmatics*, Longman Linguistics Library (London, 1983).
— 'Stylistics and Functionalism', in D. Attridge et al. (eds), *The Linguistics of Writing: Arguments Between Language and Literature* (Manchester, 1987), pp. 76–88.
Leech, G. N. and Short, M. H., *Style in Fiction: A Linguistic Introduction to English Fictional Prose*, English Language Series 13 (London, 1981).
Leenhardt, F.-J., 'An Exegetical Essay: Mark 5:1–20', in R. Barthes et al. (eds), *Structural Analysis and Biblical Exegesis*, trans. A. M. Johnson (Pittsburgh, 1974), pp. 85–115.
Leivestad, R., *Christ the Conqueror: Ideas of Conflict and Victory in the New Testament* (London, 1954).
Lemke, J. L., 'Text Structure and Text Semantics', in E. H. Steiner and R. Veltman (eds), *Pragmatics, Discourse, and Text: Some Systemically-inspired Approaches* (London, 1988), pp. 158–70.
Léon-Dufour, X., 'L'épisode de l'enfant épileptique', in *Etudes d'Evangile* (Paris, 1965), pp. 183–227.
Levine, B. A., *In the Presence of the Lord: A Study of Cult and Some Cultic Terms in Ancient Israel*, SJLA 5 (Leiden, 1974).
Levinskaya, I., *The Book of Acts in Its First Century Setting*, V, *The Book of Acts in Its Diaspora Setting* (Grand Rapids and Carlisle, 1996).
Levinsohn, S. H., *Textual Connections in Acts*, SBLMS 31 (Atlanta, 1987).
Levinson, S. C., *Pragmatics*, Cambridge Textbooks in Linguistics (Cambridge, 1983).
Lévy, C., 'De Chrysippe à Posidonius: variations stoïciennes sur le thème de la divination', in J.-G. Heintz (ed.), *Oracles et prophéties dans l'antiquité* (Paris, 1997), pp. 321–43.
Lewis, I. M., *Religion in Context: Cults and Charisma* (Cambridge, 1986).
— *Ecstatic Religion: A Study of Shamanism and Spirit Possession*, 2nd edn (London, 1989).
— 'Is There a Shamanic Cosmology?', in R. Mastromattei and A. Rigopoulos (eds), *Shamanic Cosmos: From India to the North Pole Star* (Venice, 1999), pp. 117–27.
Lods, M., 'Argent et magie dans le livre des Actes', *PLu* 28/4 (1980), 287–93.
Loisy, A., *L'Evangile selon Luc* (Paris, 1924).
Louw, J. P. and Nida, E. A., *Lexical Semantics of the Greek New Testament*, SBLRBS 25 (Atlanta, 1992).
Luck, G., *Arcana Mundi: Magic and the Occult in the Greek and Roman Worlds* (Baltimore, 1985).
Lyons, J., *Chomsky*, Modern Masters (London, 1970).
— *Language, Meaning and Context*, Fontana Linguistics (London, 1981).
Lyons, W. J. and Reimer, A. M., 'The Demonic Virus and Qumran Studies: Some Preventative Measures', *DSD* 5/1 (1998), 16–32.
Mack, B., *A Myth of Innocence: Mark and Christian Origins* (Philadelphia, 1988).
MacMullen, R., *Enemies of the Roman Order: Treason, Unrest, and Alienation in the Empire*, paperback edn (London, 1992).

MacRae, G. W., 'Miracles in the *Antiquities* of Josephus', in C. F. D. Moule (ed.), *Miracles: Cambridge Studies in Their Philosophy and History* (London, 1965), pp. 129–47.
Malherbe, A. J., *Social Aspects of Early Christianity*, 2nd edn (Philadelphia, 1983).
Malina, B. J., *The New Testament World: Insights from Cultural Anthropology*, 3rd edn (Louisville, 2001).
Malina, B. J. and Neyrey, J., 'Jesus the Witch: Witchcraft Accusations in Mt. 12', in *Calling Jesus Names: The Social Value of Labels in Matthew* (Sonoma, CA, 1988).
Malina, B. J. and Rohrbaugh, R. L., *Social-Science Commentary on the Synoptic Gospels* (Minneapolis, 1992).
Marcus, R. (ed.), *Philo Supplements*, LCL, 2 vols (Cambridge, MA, 1953).
Marguerat, D., 'Miracle and Magic in Acts', in T. E. Klutz (ed.), *Magic in the Biblical World: From the Rod of Aaron to the Ring of Solomon*, JSNTSup 245 (London, 2003), pp. 100–24.
Marshall, I. H., *Luke: Historian and Theologian* (Grand Rapids, 1970).
The Gospel of Luke: A Commentary on the Greek Text, NIGTC (Exeter, 1978).
The Acts of the Apostles, TNTC (Leicester and Grand Rapids, 1980).
'"Israel" and the Story of Salvation: One Theme in Two Parts', in D. P. Moessner (ed.), *Jesus and the Heritage of Israel: Luke's Narrative Claim upon Israel's Legacy* (Harrisburg, PA, 1999), pp. 340–57.
Martin, D. B., *The Corinthian Body* (New Haven, 1995).
Martin, F., 'Le geôlier et la marchande de pourpre: Actes des Apôtres 16, 6–40 (Première Partie)', *Sémiotique et Bible* 59 (1990), 9–29.
Mason, S., *Josephus and the New Testament* (Peabody, 1992).
Masson, C., 'Le démoniaque de Gérasa: Marc 5:1–20 (Matthieu 8:28–34; Luc 8:26–39)', in *Vers les sources d'eau vive: Etudes d'exégèse et de théologie du Nouveau Testament*, Publications de la Faculté de Théologie, Université de Lausanne (Lausanne, 1961), pp. 20–37.
Mattill, A. J., 'The Jesus–Paul Parallels and the Purpose of Luke–Acts: H. H. Evans Reconsidered', *NovT* 17 (1975), 15–46.
McCarter, P. K., '1 Kings', in *HBC*, pp. 305–22.
McCasland, S. V., *By the Finger of God: Demon Possession and Exorcism in Early Christianity in the Light of Modern Views of Mental Illness* (New York, 1951).
McCown, C. C. (ed.), *The Testament of Solomon* (Leipzig, 1922).
McRay, J. R., *Archaeology and the New Testament* (Grand Rapids, 1991).
Meier, J. P., *A Marginal Jew: Rethinking the Historical Jesus*, II, *Mentor, Message, and Miracles* (New York, 1994).
Menzies, R. P., *The Development of Early Christian Pneumatology with Special Reference to Luke–Acts*, JSNTSup 54 (Sheffield, 1991).
Metzger, B. M., *The Text of the New Testament*, 2nd edn (Oxford, 1968).
A Textual Commentary on the Greek New Testament (Stuttgart, 1971).
Meyer, M. and Smith, R. (eds), *Ancient Christian Magic: Coptic Texts of Ritual Power* (San Francisco, 1994).
Michalowski, P., 'Carminative Magic: Towards an Understanding of Sumerian Poetics', *ZA* 71 (1981), 1–18.
'On Some Early Sumerian Magical Texts' *Or* 54 (1985), 216–25.

Milik, J. T., '"Prière de Nabonide" et autres écrits d'un cycle de Daniel', *RB* 63 (1956), 407–15.
Miller, M. H., 'The Character of Miracles in Luke–Acts', PhD dissertation, Graduate Theological Union (1971).
Mills, M. E., *Human Agents of Cosmic Power in Hellenistic Judaism and the Synoptic Tradition*, JSNTSup 41 (Sheffield, 1990).
Minear, P. S., 'Luke's Use of the Birth Stories', in L. E. Keck and J. L. Martyn (eds), *Studies in Luke–Acts* (Nashville, 1966), pp. 111–30.
Moessner, D. P., 'Luke 9:1–50: Luke's Preview of the Journey of the Prophet like Moses of Deuteronomy', *JBL* 102 (1983), 575–605.
'"The Christ Must Suffer": New Light on the Jesus – Peter, Stephen, Paul Parallels in Luke–Acts', *NovT* 28 (1986), 220–56.
Moessner, D. P. and Tiede, D. L., 'Conclusion: "And some were persuaded..."', in D. P. Moessner (ed.), *Jesus and the Heritage of Israel: Luke's Narrative Claim upon Israel's Legacy* (Harrisburg, 1999), pp. 358–68.
Morgan, M. A. (ed.), *Sepher ha-Razim: The Book of the Mysteries*, SBLTT 25 (Chico, 1983).
Morgenthaler, R., *Statistik des neutestamentlichen Wortschatzes* (Zurich, 1958).
Mowinckel, S., *Religion und Kultus* (Göttingen, 1953).
The Psalms in Israel's Worship, trans. D. R. Ap-Thomas (Oxford, 1962).
Mussner, F., *Die Wunder Jesu: Eine Hinführung* (Munich, 1967).
Myers, C., *Binding the Strong Man: A Political Reading of Mark's Story of Jesus* (Maryknoll, 1988).
Naveh, J. and Shaked, S., *Amulets and Magic Bowls: Aramaic Incantations of Late Antiquity*, 2nd edn (Jerusalem, 1987).
Neil, W., *The Acts of the Apostles*, NCBc (London and Grand Rapids, 1973).
Neusner, J., *The Wonder-Working Lawyers of Talmudic Babylonia: The Theory and Practice of Judaism in Its Formative Age* (New York, 1987).
Nielsen, H. K., *Heilung und Verkündigung: Das Verständnis der Heilung und ihrers Verhältnisses zur Verkündigung bei Jesus und in der ältesten Kirche*, trans. D. Harbsmeier, ATDan 22 (Leiden, 1987).
Nietzsche, F., *Beyond Good and Evil: Prelude to a Philosophy of the Future*, trans. R. J. Hollingdale (repr., Harmondsworth, 1990).
Noll, R., 'Mental Imagery Cultivation as a Cultural Phenomenon: The Role of Visions in Shamanism', *Current Anthropology* 26 (1985), 443–51.
Nolland, J., *Luke*, WBC 35, 3 vols (Dallas, 1989–93).
Nützel, J. M., 'Elija- und Elischa- Traditionen im Neuen Testament', *BK* 41/4 (1986), 160–71.
Oakes, P., *Philippians: From People to Letter*, SNTSMS 110 (Cambridge, 2001).
Osswald, E., 'Beobachtungen zur Erzählung von Abrahams Aufenthalt in Ägypten im "Genesis-Apocryphon"', *ZAW* 72 (1960), 7–25.
O'Toole, R. F., 'Luke's Message in Lk 9:1–50', *CBQ* 49 (1987), 74–89.
Palmer, F., *Semantics*, 2nd edn (Cambridge, 1981).
Parke, H. W., *Greek Oracles* (London, 1967).
Pease, A. S. and Croon, J. H., 'Divination' in *OCD*, pp. 356–7.
Penney, D. L. and Wise, M. O., 'By the Power of Beelzebub: An Aramaic Incantation Formula from Qumran (4Q560)', *JBL* 113 (1994), 627–50.
Perkins, P., 'Gerasa', *HBD*, p. 340.

Pervo, R. I., *Profit with Delight: The Literary Genre of the Acts of the Apostles* (Philadelphia, 1987).
Pesch, R., 'Ein Tag vollmächtigen Wirkens Jesu in Kapharnaum (Mk 1:21-34. 35-39)', *BibLeb* 9/2 (1968), 114–28.
Der Besessene von Gerasa: Entstehung und Überlieferung einer Wundergeschichte, SBS 56 (Stuttgart, 1972).
Petzke, G., *Die Traditionen über Apollonius von Tyana und das Neue Testament*, SCHNT 1 (Leiden, 1970).
'Die historische Frage nach den Wundertaten Jesu: Dargestellt am Beispiel des Exorzismus Markus IX.14–29 par.', *NTS* 22/2 (1976), 180–204.
Pilch, J. J., 'Sickness and Healing in Luke–Acts', in J. H. Neyrey (ed.), *The Social World of Luke–Acts: Models for Interpretation* (Peabody, 1991), pp. 181–210.
'Insights and Models for Understanding the Healing Activity of the Historical Jesus', in E. H. Lovering (ed.), *SBLSP* 32 (1993), pp. 154–77.
Healing in the New Testament: Insights from Medical and Mediterranean Anthropology (Minneapolis, 2000).
Pinker, S., *The Language Instinct: The New Science of Language and Mind* (London, 1995).
Piper, R., *Wisdom in the Q-Tradition*, SNTSMS 61 (Cambridge, 1989).
Portefaix, L., *Sisters Rejoice: Paul's Letter to the Philippians and Luke–Acts as Seen by First-Century Philippian Women*, ConBNT 20 (Stockholm, 1988).
Porter, S. E., *Verbal Aspect in the Greek of the New Testament, with Reference to Tense and Mood*, Studies in Biblical Greek 1 (New York, 1989).
Idioms of the Greek New Testament, Biblical Languages: Greek 2 (Sheffield, 1992).
'The "We" Passages', in D. W. J. Gill and C. Gempf (eds), *The Book of Acts in Its Graeco-Roman Setting*, vol. II of *The Book of Acts in Its First Century Setting* (Grand Rapids and Carlisle, 1994), pp. 545–74.
Poupon, G., 'L'accusation de magie dans les Actes apocryphes', in F. Bovon (ed.), *Les Actes apocryphes des apôtres* (Geneva, 1981), pp. 71–85.
Pratt, M. L. and Traugott, E. C., *Linguistics for Students of Literature* (New York, 1980).
Preisendanz, K. and Heinrichs, A. (eds), *Papyri Graecae Magicae: Die griechischen Zauberpapyri*, rev. 2nd edn, 3 vols (Leipzig, 1973–4).
Prince, G., *Narratology: The Form and Function of Narrative*, Janua Linguarum, Series Maior 108 (The Hague and Berlin, 1982).
Pritchard, J. B. (ed.), *Ancient Near Eastern Texts Relating to the Old Testament*, 3rd edn (Princeton, 1969).
Puech, E., 'Un rituel d'exorcismes, essai de reconstruction', *RQ* 55 (1990), 377–408.
Purcell, N., 'The Arts of Government', in J. Boardman, J. Griffin and O. Murray (eds), *The Roman World* (Oxford, 1988), pp. 150–81.
Radl, W., *Paulus und Jesus im lukanischen Doppelwerk: Untersuchungen zu Parallelmotiven im Lukasevangelium und in der Apostelgeschichte*, Europäische Hochschulschriften 23/49 (Berne, 1975).
Das Lukas-Evangelium, ErFor 261 (Darmstadt, 1988).
Rahlfs, A. (ed.), *Septuaginta*, 2 vols (Stuttgart, 1935).

Rapske, B., *The Book of Acts and Paul in Roman Custody*, vol. III of *The Book of Acts in Its First Century Setting* (Grand Rapids and Carlisle, 1994).
Ravens, D. A., 'Luke 9:7-62 and the Prophetic Role of Jesus', *NTS* 36 (1990), 119-29.
Reimer, A., 'Virtual Prison Breaks: Non-Escape Narratives and the Definition of "Magic" ', in T. E. Klutz (ed.), *Magic in the Biblical World: From the Rod of Aaron to the Ring of Solomon*, JSNTSup 245 (London, 2003), pp. 125-39.
Reimer, I. R., *Women in the Acts of the Apostles: A Feminist Liberation Perspective*, trans. L. M. Maloney (Minneapolis, 1995).
Reitzenstein, R. (ed.), *Hellenistische Wundererzählungen* (Leipzig, 1906).
Ribichini, S., 'Gad גד', in *DDD*, cols 642-6.
Rice, G. E., 'Luke 4:31-44: Release for the Captives', *AUSS* 20 (Spring 1982), 23-8.
Rimmon-Kenan, S., *Narrative Fiction: Contemporary Poetics*, New Accents (London, 1983).
Robbins, V. K., 'Social-Scientific Criticism and Literary Studies: Prospects for Cooperation in Biblical Interpretation', in P. F. Esler (ed.), *Modelling Early Christianity: Social-Scientific Studies of the New Testament in Its Context* (London, 1995), pp. 274-89.
— *Exploring the Texture of Texts: A Guide to Socio-Rhetorical Interpretation* (Valley Forge, 1996).
Robinson, J. M. (ed.), *The Nag Hammadi Library in English*, 3rd rev. edn (San Francisco, 1990).
Rockwell, J., 'A Theory of Literature and Society', in J. Routh and J. Wolff (eds), *The Sociology of Literature: Theoretical Approaches*, Sociological Review Monograph 25 (Keele, 1977), pp. 32-41.
Roloff, J., *Die Apostelgeschichte*, NTD 5 (Göttingen, 1981).
Rubenson, S., 'Christian Asceticism and the Emergence of the Monastic Tradition', in V. L. Wimbush and R. Valantasis (eds), *Asceticism* (Oxford, 1995), pp. 49-57.
Sabourin, L., *L'Evangile de Luc: Introduction et commentaire* (Rome, 1985).
Saggs, H. W. F., *The Encounter with the Divine in Mesopotamia and Israel* (London, 1978).
Salmon, M., 'Insider or Outsider? Luke's Relationship with Judaism', in J. B. Tyson (ed.), *Luke–Acts and the Jewish People: Eight Critical Perspectives* (Minneapolis, 1988), pp. 76-82.
Sanders, E. P., *Jewish Law from Jesus to the Mishnah: Five Studies* (London and Philadelphia, 1990).
Sanders, J. A., 'From Isaiah 61 to Luke 4', in C. A. Evans and J. A. Sanders (eds), *Luke and Scripture: The Function of Sacred Tradition in Luke–Acts* (Minneapolis, 1993), pp. 26-45.
Saville-Troike, M., *The Ethnography of Communication: An Introduction*, 2nd edn, Language in Society 3 (Oxford, 1989).
Schäfer, P., *Judeophobia: Attitudes towards the Jews in the Ancient World* (Cambridge, MA, 1997).
Schiffman, L. H. and Swartz, M. D. (eds), *Hebrew and Aramaic Incantation Texts from the Cairo Genizah: Selected Texts from Taylor-Schechter Box K1*, Semitic Texts and Studies 1 (Sheffield, 1992).

Schille, G., *Die Apostelgeschichte des Lukas*, THKNT 5 (Berlin, 1983).
Schmid, J., *Das Evangelium nach Lukas*, 4th edn, RNT 3 (Regensburg, 1960).
Schmidt, D. D., 'Rhetorical Influences and Genre: Luke's Preface and the Rhetoric of Hellenistic Historiography', in D. Moessner (ed.), *Jesus and the Heritage of Israel* (Harrisburg, 1999), pp. 27–60.
Schmithals, W., *Die Apostelgeschichte des Lukas*, Zürcher Bibelkommentare (Zurich, 1982).
Schneider, G., *Das Evangelium nach Lukas*, ÖTKNT 3, 2 vols (Gütersloh, 1977). *Die Apostelgeschichte*, HTKNT 5, 2 vols (Freiburg, 1980–2).
Schürer, E., *The History of the Jewish People in the Age of Jesus Christ (175 B.C.–A.D. 135)*, ed. G. Vermes et al., 3 vols (Edinburgh, 1973–87).
Schürmann, H., *Das Lukasevangelium: Erster Teil: Kommentar zu Kap. 1,1-9,50*, HKNT 3/1 (Freiburg, 1969).
Seccombe, D., 'Luke and Isaiah', *NTS* 27/2(1981), 252–9.
Segal, A. F., 'Hellenistic Magic: Some Questions of Definition', in R. van den Broek and M. J. Vermaseren (eds), *Studies in Gnosticism and Hellenistic Religions*, EPRO 91 (Leiden, 1981), pp. 349–75.
Seim, T. K., *The Double Message: Patterns of Gender in Luke–Acts*, Studies of the New Testament and Its World (Edinburgh, 1994).
Sekki, A. E., *The Meaning of Ruaḥ at Qumran*, SBLDS 110 (Atlanta, 1989).
Sharp, L. A., *The Possessed and the Dispossessed: Spirits, Identity, and Power in a Madagascar Migrant Town*, Comparative Studies of Health Systems and Medical Care (Berkeley, 1993).
Smith, J. Z., 'Good News Is No News: Aretalogy and Gospel', in J. Neusner (ed.), *Christianity, Judaism, and Other Greco-Roman Cults*, Part I, *New Testament* (Leiden, 1975), pp. 21–38.
'Towards Interpreting the Demonic Powers in Hellenistic and Roman Antiquity', in *ANRW* II.16.1, pp. 425–39.
'Trading Places', in M. Meyer and P. Mirecki (eds), *Ancient Magic and Ritual Power*, Religions in the Graeco-Roman World 129 (Leiden, 1995), pp. 13–27.
Smith, M. Q., 'Prolegomena to a Discussion of Aretalogies, Divine Man, the Gospels and Jesus', *JBL* 90 (1971), 174–99.
Jesus the Magician (London, 1978).
'Jewish Religious Life in the Persian Period', in W. D. Davies and L. Finkelstein (eds), *The Cambridge History of Judaism*, I, *Introduction; The Persian Period* (Cambridge, 1984), pp. 253–88.
Smith, M. Q. and Smith, E. W., '*De Superstitione* (*Moralia* 164E–171F)', in H. D. Betz (ed.), *Plutarch's Theological Writings and Early Christian Literature* (Leiden, 1975), pp. 22–35.
Sørensen, J. P., 'The Argument in Ancient Egyptian Magical Formulae', *AcOr* 45 (1984), 5–19.
Sperber, D. and Wilson, D., *Relevance: Communication and Cognition*, 2nd edn (Oxford, 1995).
Sperling, D. S., 'An Arslan Tash Incantation: Interpretations and Implications', *HUCA* 53 (1982), 1–10.
Spielmann, R., 'Collateral Information in Narrative Discourse', *Journal of Literary Semantics* 16 (1987), 200–26.
Squires, J. T., *The Plan of God in Luke–Acts*, SNTSMS 76 (Cambridge, 1993).

Stark, R., *The Rise of Christianity: A Sociologist Reconsiders History* (Princeton, 1995).
Starobinski, J., 'The Gerasene Demoniac: A Literary Analysis of Mark 5:1–20', in R. Barthes et al. (eds), *Structural Analysis and Biblical Exegesis*, trans. A. M. Johnson (Pittsburgh, 1974), pp. 57–84.
Stegemann, E. W. and Stegemann, W., *The Jesus Movement: A Social History of Its First Century*, trans. O. C. Dean (Minneapolis, 1999).
Stegemann, W., *Zwischen Synagoge und Obrigkeit: Zur historischen Situation der lukanischen Christen*, FRLANT 152 (Göttingen, 1991).
Steiner, E. H. and Veltman, R., 'Introduction', in *Pragmatics, Discourse, and Text: Some Systemically-Inspired Approaches* (London, 1988), pp. 1–13.
Sterling, G. E., '"Opening the Scriptures": The Legitimation of the Jewish Diaspora and the Early Christian Mission', in D. Moessner (ed.), *Jesus and the Heritage of Israel* (Harrisburg, 1999), pp. 199–225.
Stolz, F., 'Sea, םי', in *DDD*, cols 1390–402.
Strange, W. A., *The Problem of the Text of Acts*, SNTSMS 71 (Cambridge, 1992).
Stuhlmueller, C., 'Psalms', in *HBC*, pp. 433–94.
Swartz, M. D., '*Hêkôlôt Rabbātî* §§ 297–306: A Ritual for the Cultivation of the Prince of the Torah', in V. L. Wimbush (ed.), *Ascetic Behavior in Greco-Roman Antiquity: A Sourcebook*, Studies in Antiquity & Christianity (Minneapolis, 1990), pp. 227–34.
Szabò, Z., 'Text and Style: An Outline of the Methodological Bases of Stylistic Analysis', *Revue Romaine des Linguistiques* 30 (1985), 485–8.
Talbert, C. H., *Reading Acts: A Literary and Theological Commentary on the Acts of the Apostles* (New York, 1997).
Tan, P. K. W., 'Falling from Grice: The Ideological Trap of Pragmatic Stylistics', *Edinburgh Working Papers in Applied Linguistics* 1/1 (1990), 1–11.
Tannehill, R. C., *The Narrative Unity of Luke–Acts*, II, *The Acts of the Apostles* (Minneapolis, 1990).
  'The Story of Israel within the Lukan Narrative', in D. P. Moessner (ed.), *Jesus and the Heritage of Israel* (Harrisburg, 1999), pp. 325–39.
Tassin, C., 'Jésus, exorciste et guérisseur', *Spiritus* 120 (1990), 285–303.
Thackeray, H. St. J., et al. (eds), *Josephus*, LCL, 10 vols (Cambridge, MA, 1926–65).
Theissen, G., *The Miracle Stories of the Early Christian Tradition*, trans. F. McDonagh (Edinburgh, 1983).
  The Gospels in Context: Social and Political History in the Synoptic Tradition, trans. L. M. Maloney (Minneapolis, 1991).
Thompson, R. C. (ed.), *The Devils and Evil Spirits of Babylonia*, Luzac's Semitic Texts and Translation Series 14 (London, 1903–4).
Thornton, C.-J., *Der Zeuge des Zeugen: Lukas als Historiker der Paulusreisen*, WUNT 56 (Tübingen, 1991).
Thraede, K., 'Exorzismus', in *RAC*, VII, cols 44–117.
Throckmorton, B. H., 'Σώζειν, σωτηρία in Luke–Acts', *SE* 6 (1973), 515–26.
Tiede, D. L., *Prophecy and History in Luke–Acts* (Philadelphia, 1980).
Toolan, M., *Narrative: A Critical Linguistic Introduction*, Interface Series (London, 1988).
Torijano, P. A., *Solomon the Esoteric King: From King to Magus, Development of a Tradition*, JSJSup 73 (Leiden, 2002).

Trebilco, P. R., 'Paul and Silas – "Servants of the Most High God" (Acts 16:16–18)', *JSNT* 36 (1989), 51–73.

Trémel, B., 'Voie de salut et religion populaire: Paul et Luc face au risque de paganisation', *LumVie* 30/153–4 (1981), 87–108.

Trites, A. A., 'The Transfiguration in the Theology of Luke: Some Redactional Links', in L. D. Hurst and N. T. Wright (eds), *The Glory of Christ in the New Testament: Studies in Christology in Memory of George Bradford Caird* (Oxford, 1987), pp. 71–81.

Trudgill, P., *Sociolinguistics: An Introduction to Language and Society*, rev. edn (London, 1983).

Tuckett, C. M., 'Mark', in J. Barton and J. Muddiman (eds), *The Oxford Bible Commentary* (Oxford, 2001), pp. 886–922.

Turner, G. W., *Stylistics* (Harmondsworth, 1973).

Turner, M., 'The Spirit and the Power of Jesus' Miracles in the Lucan Conception', *NovT* 33 (1991), 124–52.

Twelftree, G. H., *Christ Triumphant: Exorcism Then and Now* (London, 1985).

— *Jesus the Exorcist: A Contribution to the Study of the Historical Jesus*, WUNT 54 (Tübingen, 1993).

— *Jesus the Miracle Worker: A Historical and Theological Study* (Downers Grove, IL, 1999).

Tyson, J. B., *The Death of Jesus in Luke–Acts* (Columbia, 1986).

— *Images of Judaism in Luke–Acts* (Columbia, 1992).

Vaganay, L., 'Les accords négatifs de Matthieu-Luc contre Marc: L'épisode de l'enfant épileptique (Mt. 17,14–21; Mc. 9,14–29; Lc. 9,37–43a)', in *Le problème synoptique: Une hypothèse de travail*, Bibliothèque de théologie 3/1 (Tournai, 1954), pp. 405–25.

Van der Loos, H., *The Miracles of Jesus*, NovTSup 11 (Leiden, 1965).

van Dijk, T. A., *Text and Context: Explorations in the Semantics and Pragmatics of Discourse*, Longman Linguistics Library 21 (London, 1977).

— *Studies in the Pragmatics of Discourse*, Janua Linguarum, Series Maior 101 (The Hague, 1981).

van Unnik, W. C., 'L'usage de σώζειν "sauver" et des dérivés dans les évangiles synoptiques', in *Sparsa Collecta, The Collected Essays of W. C. van Unnik, Part One: Evangelia, Paulina, Acta*, NovTSup 29 (Leiden, 1973) pp. 16–34.

Veeser, H. A., 'The New Historicism', in *The New Historicism Reader* (London, 1994), pp. 1–32.

Veillé, M., 'Ecriture et prédication: Actes 16/16–24', *ETR* 54 (1979), 271–8.

Vencovsky, J., 'Der gadarenische Exorzismus: Matt. 8, 28–34 und Parallelen', *CV* 14/1 (1971), 13–29.

Vermes, G., *Jesus the Jew: A Historian's Reading of the Gospels* (London, 1973).

— *The Religion of Jesus the Jew* (London, 1993).

Wales, K., *A Dictionary of Stylistics*, Studies in Language and Linguistics (London, 1989).

Walsh, R. N., *The Spirit of Shamanism* (New York, 1990).

— 'The Psychological Health of Shamans: A Reevaluation', *JAAR* 65/1 (1997), 101–24.

Waltke, B. K. and O'Connor, M., *An Introduction to Biblical Hebrew Syntax* (Winona Lake, IN, 1990).

Wells, L., *The Greek Language of Healing from Homer to New Testament Times*, BZNW 83 (Berlin, 1998).
Wenham, J., 'The Identification of Luke', *EvQ* 63/1 (1991), 3–44.
Wesselius, J. W., 'Notes on Aramaic Magical Texts', *BO* 39 (1982), 249–51.
Whitely, D. E. H., *The Theology of St. Paul* (Oxford, 1964).
Wienold, G., 'Textlinguistic Approaches to Written Works of Art', in W. Dressler (ed.), *Current Trends in Textlinguistics*, Research in Text Theory (Berlin, 1978), pp. 133–54.
Wilhelm, G., 'Ein neues Lamaštu-Amulett', *ZA* 69 (1979), 34–40.
Wilkinson, J., *The Bible and Healing: A Medical and Theological Commentary* (Grand Rapids, 1998).
Wilson, R., 'Child, Children', in *HBD*, pp. 161–2.
Wimsatt, W. K. and Beardsley, M., *The Verbal Icon* (Lexington, 1954).
Wink, W., *Unmasking the Powers: The Invisible Forces That Determine Human Existence* (Philadelphia, 1986).
Winkelman, M., *Shamanism: The Neural Ecology of Consciousness and Healing* (Westport, 2000).
Wise, M., Abegg, M. and Cook, E., *The Dead Sea Scrolls: A New Translation* (San Francisco, 1996).
Witherington, B., 'Editor's Addendum', in *History, Literature, and Society in the Book of Acts* (Cambridge, 1996), pp. 23–32.
Wojcik, J., *The Road to Emmaus: Reading Luke's Gospel* (West Lafayette, IN, 1989).
Yamauchi, E. M. (ed.), *Mandaic Incantation Texts*, AOS 49 (New Haven, 1967).
Zaehner, R. C., *The Dawn and Twilight of Zoroastrianism* (London, 1961).
Zettner, C., *Amt, Gemeinde, und kirchliche Einheit in der Apostelgeschichte des Lukas*, Europäische Hochschulschriften 23/423 (Frankfurt, 1991).
Ziesler, J. A., 'The Name of Jesus in the Acts of the Apostles', *JSNT* 4 (1979), 28–41.
Zuntz, G., *Greek: A Course in Classical and Post-Classical Greek Grammar from Original Texts*, Biblical Languages: Greek 4, 2 vols (Sheffield, 1994).

INDEX OF SOURCES DISCUSSED

Old Testament

Genesis
3   136
12.10–13.2   192
Exodus
LXX 4.24   164
10.7   46
LXX 24.9–25.9   174
28.40–43   235
32.1–35   174
Leviticus
5.2–3   117
6.14–18   117
6.24–30   117
11–15   145
15.19–30   145
15.32–33   145
16.1–34   144
16.3–4   146
16.4   100
16.4–32   100
16.10   145, 146
16.14–18   117
16.15–22   146
16.20–22   145
16.21–22   146
16.23–24   146
16.24–30   117
16.29–34   146
Numbers
19.1–10   134
Deuteronomy
6.4   255
18   225
LXX 18.10   216, 217, 225
18.11   245
18.15   174
27–32   187
LXX 32.5   156, 172, 173, 187

LXX 32.17   173
LXX 32.20   173, 187
33.52–55   46
1 Samuel
5–31   63
16–19   61, 63, 65, 66
16.1–23   61–62
16.8–12   61
16.13   61
LXX 16.13–14   256
16.15–23   62
16.16   62
16.23   61, 62, 260
18.10   62
19.4–5   63
19.9   62
LXX 28.8   216
1 Kings
17   112
17.1   57
17.1–18.1   60
17.9   57, 109
17.17   56
LXX 17.17–18   56
17.17–24   109
LXX 17.18   56, 60, 61, 78, 109
17.19–22   56
17.24   57
18.20–29   252
22.19–23   62
2 Kings
4.8–37   174–175
4.14–17   174
4.18–24   174
4.22–25   174
4.25   174
4.26   174
4.29–31   175
4.32–35   175

2 Kings (*cont.*)
4.36–37 175
5.14 61
LXX 17.17 216
2 Chronicles
18.18–22 62
24.20 100
Esther
4.1 100
LXX 5.1 100
Job
1.6–2.7 62
Psalms
91 254
LXX 90.1–16 110
91.1 255
91.1–2 254
91.5–6 254
91.6b 254
91.9–10 254
91.11–12 255
91.13 255
91.14 254
91.14–16 251, 254
LXX 95.5 135
LXX 105.7–12 99, 110–111, 115, 149, 267
LXX 105.8–10 102
106.37–39 115
Isaiah
40.3–5 102
46.4 156
58.3–5 111
58.6 58, 112
LXX 58.6–7 93, 94, 111–112, 118, 237
LXX 58.7 94
61.1 58, 61, 118
65.1–7 113
LXX 65.1–14 175–176
LXX 65.3 176
LXX 65.3–4 98, 110, 176
LXX 65.8–14 175
LXX 65.11 175
LXX 65.14 175
LXX 65.15 176
Daniel
LXX 7.27 166
LXX 8.7 165
Zechariah
3.1–2 62
3.2 194
13.2 127

Apocrypha

1 Esdras
1.4 166
4.40 166
Tobit
8–14 260
8.1–3 145
8.2–3 252
8.3 190
Judith
9.1 101
10.3 101
Additions to Esther
13.1–7 250
Wisdom of Solomon
2.23–24 136
Baruch
4.20 101
3 Macc.
4.6 165

New Testament

Matthew
4.2 202
4.6 255
4.23 51
8.28–34 89, 111
8.32–33 261
10.1 136
10.8 136
11.17–19 139
11.18 129, 139
12.22–42 113, 257
12.24–26 246
12.42 258
12.43–45 131
13.19 120
13.53–58 57
17.14–21 230
17.15 158, 177
17.18 161
17.18–21 171
17.21 204
19.1–2 238
Mark
1.9–13 197
1.21 51
1.21–22 31
1.21–28 31

Index of sources discussed 291

1.23   38, 44–45, 46
1.25–26   34
1.26   74, 261
1.27   128
2.18–20   203
3.20   129, 202
3.20–35   129, 203
3.21   129
3.21–22   129
3.22   129, 130, 138
3.22–23   246
3.22–30   196
3.28–29   129
3.29   196
3.30   129, 130
4.15   120
5.1–20   89, 111
5.13   92
5.15   93
5.15–20   260
5.16–17   91
5.18   103
5.19   94
6.1–6   57
7.1–23   128
7.1–30   127
7.19   128
7.25   128
7.30   261
9.2–8   206
9.14–29   136, 206, 230
9.17–18   160
9.19   160
9.20   165
9.25–26   165
9.25–27   157
9.25–29   171
9.26   74, 165
9.26–27   136, 198–199, 205, 260
9.27   202
9.29   199–205
10.1   238
Luke
1.1   60–61
1.1–4.32   44–51
1.35   47
1.68–72   111
3.6   102
3.21–22   195
3.22   229
4.1   229
4.1–13   60, 195
4.1–30   58–59
4.2   202

4.5–6   60
4.10–11   254, 255
4.14   229
4.15   38, 51
4.15–30   38
4.16   38, 51
4.16–30   59
4.18   58–59, 112, 229
4.18–19   59, 60, 118
4.20   38, 51
4.21   59
4.23–30   38
4.24   57
4.25–26   57, 60
4.25–30   91
4.26   109
4.27   45–51, 73, 116
4.28   34, 38, 51
4.28–29   38
4.29   34
4.31   32, 58
4.31–32   31, 32–33, 57–58, 80
4.31–37   30–31
4.31–43   58–59
4.31–44   61, 77, 80
4.32   31, 32, 57
4.33   29, 30, 38, 41, 42, 44–46, 51–52,
    62, 73, 103
4.33–34   30
4.33–37   14, 29, 32, 33, 58, 60, 86, 99,
    109, 116, 118, 125, 263
4.33–39   76
4.33–43   58
4.33–44   32–33
4.34   30, 42, 45, 46, 47, 53–54, 56–57,
    60, 64, 66, 78, 109
4.35   30, 35, 41, 42, 43, 46, 54, 62, 66,
    69–71, 74–75, 193, 194, 261, 268
4.35–36   31, 34
4.36   30, 34, 35, 39, 43, 46, 48–50,
    54–55, 60, 64, 66, 73, 109, 161, 180,
    195
4.37   43
4.38   91
4.38–39   58, 75–78, 80, 118
4.39   59, 75
4.40–41   58
4.41   59, 118
4.42–44   58, 59
4.43   58
4.43–44   59
6.17–19   116
6.18   116–117
6.18–19   233

Luke (*cont.*)
6.19 117
6.20 118
7.6–8 48
7.12 158
7.18–23 112, 117
7.21 117–118
7.24–35 139
7.28–35 118
7.33 119, 129, 139
7.36–50 119
8.1–3 119–120, 144, 199, 261
8.1–56 183
8.2 119
8.2–3 119
8.4–15 120
8.4–56 120
8.5 119, 120
8.12 119, 120
8.14 120
8.22–25 84, 110, 115, 120, 148–149, 267
8.22–39 111, 115, 267
8.22–56 115–116, 120, 230
8.23 229
8.23–25 228
8.24 229
8.25 115, 120, 229
8.26 84, 88–89, 107
8.26–27 85
8.26–39 12, 45, 46, 81, 83–84, 155, 206, 207, 217–218, 219, 229, 233, 235, 237, 238, 239, 267
8.26–48 117
8.26–56 137, 179, 192, 235, 236
8.27 82, 84, 85, 87, 92–93, 95, 100–101, 103, 106–112, 113, 133, 137, 146, 228, 229, 235
8.28 101, 103, 104, 109, 113, 114, 217
8.28–32 86
8.29 86, 87–88, 94, 95, 103, 104, 106–116, 228
8.30 82, 101, 219, 251
8.30–32 104
8.30–33 82
8.31 92, 98, 102, 105, 106, 108, 113, 114, 115
8.31–32 92, 104, 105
8.31–33 145
8.32 114
8.32–33 146
8.32–34 85
8.33 86, 95, 106

8.33–37 120
8.34 84, 89, 90
8.34–35 108
8.34–36 87
8.34–39 86
8.35 89, 90, 91, 92–93, 101, 108, 115, 141–142, 146, 228, 235
8.35–37 91, 120
8.35–38 108
8.35–39 90, 146, 260, 261
8.36 102, 103, 120, 218, 229
8.36–37 91
8.37 84, 89, 90–91, 95–96, 115, 228, 229, 235
8.37–39 90
8.38 103, 108, 114–115
8.39 84, 85, 87, 93, 94–95, 103, 229, 235, 268
8.40–56 84, 148
8.41 115
8.42 158
8.43 239
8.43–44 116
8.43–48 137
8.44 235
8.47 120, 229
8.48–50 229
8.49 116
8.49–55 137
8.50 120
8.52 229
8.53 116
9.1 180, 181, 188
9.1–2 156, 175, 179, 183
9.1–6 179, 182, 184
9.1–9 199
9.1–10 180, 181, 182
9.1–11 238, 242
9.1–40 181
9.1–50 13, 183, 186, 205, 207, 239
9.1–56 238, 239
9.2 188
9.5 184, 238
9.6 156, 180, 188
9.6–9 180
9.7–9 184, 186
9.7–20 239
9.10 156, 180, 184
9.11 184
9.12–17 184
9.17 239
9.18–21 184
9.18–22 179
9.18–27 205, 207

9.22   184, 186
9.23–27   185
9.28   168
9.28–29   204
9.28–36   154, 169, 178–179, 196, 239
9.28–43a   196, 198, 206
9.30–31   174
9.30–34   184
9.30–36   179
9.35   174
9.37   154, 157, 159, 162–164, 168, 171, 173, 175, 178
9.37–38   154, 155
9.37–39   178
9.37–42   178
9.37–43a   2, 12, 13, 54, 206, 230, 238
9.37–50   236, 240
9.38   154, 158, 160, 169, 170, 173, 174, 177–178
9.38–39   173
9.38–40   154, 174, 180
9.39   158, 159, 165, 170, 172, 191
9.40   155, 160, 167–168, 169, 175, 177, 181, 182, 183
9.40–41   188
9.41   154, 156, 159, 160, 169, 172, 173–174
9.41–42   174
9.42   118, 154, 156–157, 160–161, 165, 169, 170–171, 172, 174, 175, 176, 188, 192, 193–194, 205, 230, 260
9.43   154, 155, 157, 165–167, 168, 172, 178, 179, 205, 268
9.43b–45   155, 179, 181, 184, 186
9.43b–50   230
9.44   181
9.45   181
9.46–48   182
9.46–50   181, 182, 184
9.47   182
9.47–48   182, 184, 230
9.49   182, 230, 256
9.49–50   182, 183, 192, 207, 230, 236, 251, 256
9.51   238
9.51–56   238
10.1–20   199
10.17–19   66
10.17–20   60, 254
10.19   48, 255
11.14   126
11.14–22   66
11.14–32   257
11.15   48
11.15–18   246
11.19   132–133
11.20   46, 132
11.24   131
11.24–26   128, 131–133, 143, 144
11.26   131
11.31   258
13.10–17   193
13.11   126
13.34   254
22–23   232
22.3   232
22.3–6   231
22.47   168
23.1–25   231, 240
23.47   231
John
4.9   140
7.20   139
8.48–52   139
10.20   139
Acts
3.1–10   38
3.23   217
5.12   233
5.15–16   233
5.16   127
7.37   217
8.7   127
8.9   7
8.11   7
9.26   230
10.38   62, 76, 256, 257
10.38–39   61
13.1–12   197
13.4–12   242
13.6   7, 47
13.8   7
13.10   47
15.20   202
16.6–7   229
16.6–20.1   232
16.11–40   227
16.12   227
16.13   213–214, 226
16.13–15   226, 227
16.14–15   226, 227
16.15   211, 229
16.16   208, 209, 210, 211, 212–217, 221, 222, 223, 225, 226, 227, 230, 233, 243–247, 248, 263
16.16–17   226
16.16–18   13, 14, 92, 140, 141, 205, 226, 228, 229, 238, 239

Acts (*cont.*)
16.16–19   244
16.16–24   209
16.16–40   206, 218, 232
16.17   208, 211, 217–218, 222, 224–226
16.17–18   209, 211
16.18   209, 210, 212, 218–219, 220, 221, 222, 224, 226, 227, 230, 237, 248, 253, 256, 257, 259, 260, 268
16.18–19   211, 222
16.19   221, 227, 231, 233, 248
16.19–21   210, 261–262
16.19–24   209, 218
16.19–40   218, 262
16.20   250, 262
16.20–21   233, 248
16.20–24   263
16.20b–24   251
16.20–40   227
16.21   250
16.22   228
16.24   228
16.25–36   263
16.26   228, 251
16.27   229
16.29   229
16.30   218
16.30–31   229
16.31   218
16.31–32   229
16.34   229
16.35–36   251
16.35–39   233
16.35–40   231
16.37–38   263
16.37–39   251
16.38–39   229
16.39   227, 228
16.40   227, 229
18.24–26   239
18.24–19.8   237
18.24–19.12   236
18.24–19.20   239
18.24–19.22   239
18.24–20.1   232
18.27   237
19.1–4   239
19.1–7   239
19.2   237
19.4   237
19.5   237
19.6   236
19.7   239
19.8–10   237
19.8–12   238, 242
19.8–20   240
19.9   239
19.10   236
19.11   99
19.11–12   232, 235, 236, 255
19.11–20   7, 13–239
19.11–22   238
19.12   237
19.12–16   232
19.13   236, 237
19.13–14   72
19.13–16   232
19.13–19   99, 232
19.13–20   235, 236, 237, 255
19.15   233, 235, 256
19.16   127, 235
19.17   235
19.17–19   232, 235
19.18   237
19.19   235
19.20   237
19.21   237, 238
19.21–22   237–239
19.23–27   232, 233
19.32–34   233
21.17–26   242
Romans
5.12–21   136
1 Corinthians
10.14–22   246
15.26   136
Galatians
2.11–21   219
2 Peter
1.16   166
Revelation
9.20   246
Pseudepigrapha
L.A.B.
60.1   65
60.1–3   62, 64, 66, 67
60.3   65, 260
Testament of Solomon
3.1–6   258
6.1–11   258
7.5   149
22–2   149
22.9–15   149
23.2   149
25.5–7   149
Qumran
1QGenesis Apocryphon   190
xix–xx   140

xx 28   193
xx 28–29   194
xx 29   193
xx 29–30   260
4QDamascus Document[a]
6 i 6–13   126
4QExorcism ar   80, 137
1 i 4   76, 137, 257
1 i 5   137
1 ii 5–6   76
4QPrayer of Nabonidus ar   190
frags 1–3 lines 1–8   140, 261
frags 1–3 line 4   187
11QApocryphal Psalms
ii 2   257
ii 8–12   255
ii 12   255
v 4–7   255
v 5   255
v 6–7a   255
11QMelchizedek
ii 3–16   59
11QPsalms[a]
xxvii 1–11   258
xxvii 9–10   257, 258
Rabbinic Texts
b. Meil. 17b   123
b. Pes. 112a–b   72
b. Pes. 112b   259
b. Shab. 61a–61b   72
Philo
Conf.
118.6   215
Spec.
3.18   216
Flavius Josephus
Ant.
1.24   166
6   63
6.166   63
6.166–9   63
6.166–211   62, 63, 68
6.168   63, 260
6.209–11   63, 64
6.211   63
8.42–9   68, 258–260
8.45   72, 258, 260
8.45–6   258
8.45–9   258
8.47   75, 259, 260
8.47–9   259
8.49   259
Ap.
2.168   166

J.W.
2.480   89
Other Jewish Writings
AMB
bowl 11
6–7   255
Pesiq. Rb. Kah.
4.7   135
Christian Writings
Acts of Andrew
A.10.11–30   7, 13
Acts of John
43   7
Acts of Peter
6.17   7
9.31   7
Acts of Thomas
5.49   261
8.81   260
Ignatius
Magn.
8.1–10.3   250
Pseudo-Clementine Homilies
4.4   7
7.3   7
9.6.13   214
Other Ancient Sources
AEMT
25   252
Arslan Tash Amulet
1   254
9   254
Baal and Yam
2.iv.1–40   253
2.iv.28   252
Gathas
Y. 32.3–5   247
KTU
1.82 line 1   252
1.82 line 3   252
The Legend of the Possessed Princess
189
22–6   261
Ras Ibn Hani 78/20
1–2   252
8–10   252
Cicero
On the Nature of the Gods
2.12   244
Pro Flacco
67   250
Diodorus Siculus
Bibliotheca historica (lib. 1–20)
14.75   163

Galen
De sanitate tuenda libri vi
6.392.6   159
Hesychius
Lexicon (A–O)
ε.123   214
Hippocrates
Morb. Sacr.
1.52–100   72
1.65   72–73
1.81–90   72
7.1–25   72
12.6   72
12.6–8   72
Lucan
Pharsalia
5.86–224   244
Lucian
Alex.
7–8   244
10   243, 244
19   244
Philops.
16   69–71, 73, 252
31   73
PGM
4.1227   98
4.1227–64   98–99, 167
4.1239   98
4.1243   98
4.1245   98
4.1245–8   98
4.1246   98
4.1254   98
4.1262   98
4.3007–86   98
4.3065–81   98
4.3092   98
5.304–34   98
5.304–69   98
5.459–89   98
13.293–7   98
21.1–29   253
Philostratus
Vita Apollonii
1.2–3   125
3.38   68, 122
3.56   121
4.20   121, 122–125, 140, 141, 187, 252, 260
6.43   260
Plutarch
De liberis educandis
2.D.3   159
De Pyth. or.
408.b   244
Sull.
2.4.2   163
Strabo
9.3.12   214
Xenophon
An.
1.8.15.3   163
7.2.5.1   163

INDEX OF NAMES AND SUBJECTS

abstract 31
Aland, K. 201
Annen, F. 97
Apollo 214, 243–244, 253, 263
Apollonius of Tyana 68, 69, 75, 187, 252
asceticism 119, 138–139, 195, 202–203 *see also* fasting
Ashton, J. 56
audience 265–266
Avalos, H. 57
Azazel 145, 146

Bakhtin, M. M. 79, 245
Barrett, C. K. 213, 232
behavioural processes 40
Bell, C. 144, 130, 197
Bint-resh 189, 261
Böcher, O. 46
Bovon, F. 42, 149, 183
Bowie, F. 196
Burridge, R. 123–124
Busse, U. 110

chiasm 205, 207
children 158, 174, 177, 182–183
Chomsky, N. 22, 23
clothes 87, 92, 93, 100–101, 108, 112, 145, 146, 228, 235
coda 32
cohesion 29–30
Colwell, E. C. 202, 203
communicative presumption 53
complicating action 31
conversion 142–143, 261
corpse defilement 116, 126, 133–137
co-text 28, 57
Culler, J. 23

David (King) 61–62, 131, 256, 257, 258

death 229
  demonisation of 136, 137
  initiation crisis 195, 198–199, 205
  Jesus' 124, 207
demoniac(s)
  background of 87–88, 140–141, 142–143
  gender of 261
  post-exorcism future of 90, 94, 103–104, 260–262
  poverty of 118, 261
  status of 182, 261
  unconventionality of 137–139
demonisation 34, 118–119, 134, 138–141, 167, 185, 245–247 *see also* death
deviance 138–141, 148, 151
devil 60, 120, 136, 195
dialogism 80
discipleship 141–142, 185, 205, 207, 229, 239
divination 215–217, 223, 243–246
Douglas, M. 138
dyadic contract 119, 185

ecstasy 130, 144, 195, 196
Eggins, S. 240
Eleazar (the exorcist) 72, 131, 259
Elijah 45, 56–57, 60, 109, 112, 150, 184
Elisha 61, 73, 81, 97, 116
Empson, W. 126
Enkvist, N. 15
epilepsy 61, 62, 165
evaluation 31
Evans, C. A. 122
existential processes 40
exorcism
  failure of 156, 175, 180–181, 185, 188–192, 198, 238, 240, 255

297

exorcism (*cont.*)
    methods of   62, 65, 74–75, 82–123, 144–147, 170, 192–194, 219, 224, 229, 236, 249, 251–260
    ritual aspects   74–75, 130, 134, 144–148
    stories of   69–70
    traditions of   256–260
    violence of   54, 74–75, 124, 127, 198, 249

Fairclough, N.   66
fasting   139, 196, 199, 202–203
fever   75–77
Fish, S.   17
Fitzmyer, J. A.   23, 88, 213, 216
foregrounding   33
Fowler, R.   17–19, 33

genre potential   27
Gerasa   88–89
greed   222, 231–232
Green, J. B   132, 149

Halliday, M. A. K.   22, 23, 24, 25, 26, 36, 37, 40, 55, 161, 231
healing   62, 72–75, 112, 116–118, 123, 161, 182, 188, 189–190, 195–197, 204–205, 240
Hobsbawm, E.   67

iconicity   35
illness   62, 67–68, 132–136, 143–144, 158, 165, 172, 176, 186–188, 195, 198–199
illocutionary goal   53
implicature   52–53
implied situation   28
impurity   45, 58, 82, 96–97, 115–117, 118–125, 132, 148, 186, 235, 267
    see also corpse defilement
incantations   62, 66–67, 70–74, 98–99, 130, 137, 148, 249, 252–255, 257, 259–260
information structure   36–38
intertextuality   55–56
invented tradition   67

Janowski, B.   145
Jesus–Paul parallels   92, 192, 206, 207, 219, 228–236, 238–239, 240, 266
John the Baptist   118–119, 139, 140, 203, 239
Josephus   164

Kapferer, B.   197
Kee, H. C.   46
kingdom of God   195, 238, 240, 242
Kirschläger, W.   23, 25, 31, 32, 59, 74, 76, 174, 266
Kollmann, B.   74

Levinskaya, I.   218
Lewis, I. M.   142
linearisation problem   36–38

Mack, B.   128
magic   47, 82, 134, 241, 249, 253–263
Martin, D.   67–68
material processes   40
mental processes   40
Metzger, B. M.   200, 201, 202

Nolland, J.   34, 180
nominalisation   42

orientation   31

p45   201–202
paganism   45, 69–70, 72–73, 140, 151, 210, 215, 223, 227, 233, 240, 241, 243–246
participants   40–41
Paul
    annoyance of   221, 222, 226, 248
    Jewish loyalties of   210, 211, 214, 217, 226–227, 233, 240, 250, 251, 262, 263, 265
    reputation of   57, 191, 205, 230, 231, 232, 240, 241–242, 256, 261–262, 264, 269
Penney, D.   137
Philippi   246, 249
Philostratus   68
Pilch, J. J.   12–13, 120, 162, 165, 183, 187, 199
presupposition   50–51
process types   40

Reimer, I. R.   245, 247–248, 261
relational processes   40
repetition   33–34
resolution   31

Scaeva, sons of   234–237, 242, 255
septuagintism(s)   159–160, 164, 173, 216, 230, 263, 267
shamanism   31, 74–75, 129, 144, 194–199, 204, 206

Sharp, L. 142
slavery 210
Smith, J. Z. 122, 145
Solomon 72, 130, 131, 149, 257–260
soteriology 218, 226
Spielmann, R. 87
Stark, R. 125, 142
Starobinski, J. 97
story structure 31–32

Tannehill, R. 230, 233, 237
Theissen, G. 75
thematic organisation 36–38

Toolan, M. 19, 31–32
transitivity 39–41
Twelftree, G. H. 15, 17, 38, 86, 122, 129, 133, 147, 165, 255, 259

verbal aspect 49

Wells, L. 142
Wise, M. 137

Yohanan ben Zakkai 134–135
Yom Kippur 100, 144–148